P9-ARH-484

TOWARD A STEADY-STATE ECONOMY

CONTRIBUTORS

Barry Bluestone, Department of Economics, Boston University

Kenneth E. Boulding, Department of Economics, University of Colorado

Preston Cloud, Department of Geological Sciences, University of California, Santa Barbara

John Cobb, School of Theology at Claremont, California

Herman E. Daly, Department of Economics, Louisiana State University

Paul R. Ehrlich, Department of Biological Sciences, Stanford University

Richard England, Department of Economics, University of Massachusetts

Nicholas Georgescu-Roegen, Department of Economics, Vanderbilt University

Garrett Hardin, Department of Biology, University of California, Santa Barbara

John P. Holdren, Environmental Quality Laboratory, California Institute of Technology

Warren A. Johnson, Department of Geography, San Diego State College

Leon R. Kass, National Research Council, Washington, D.C.

C. S. Lewis (1898-1963), at the time of his death Professor of Medieval and Renaissance Literature at Cambridge University

Donella Meadows, Department of Demography, Dartmouth College

William Ophuls, Department of Political Science, Yale University

Jørgen Randers, Systems Dynamics Group, Sloan School of Management, Massachusetts Institute of Technology

E. F. Schumacher, Economist, Surrey, England

Walter A. Weisskopf, Department of Economics, Roosevelt University

TOWARD A STEADY-STATE ECONOMY

Edited by *Herman E. Daly*
Louisiana State University

W. H. FREEMAN AND COMPANY
San Francisco

Library of Congress Cataloging in Publication Data

Daly, Herman E comp.
Toward a steady-state economy.

Includes bibliographical references.
1. Economic development—Addresses, essays, lectures. 2. Economic history—1945- — Addresses, essays, lectures. 3. Statics and dynamics (Social sciences)—Addresses, essays, lectures. I. Title.
HD82.D3142 338'.09 72-5710
ISBN 0-7167-0799-3
ISBN 0-7167-0793-4 (pbk)

Printed in the United States of America

International Standard Book Number: paper, 0-7167-0793-4
cloth, 0-7167-0799-3

1 2 3 4 5 6 7 8 9 10

To my parents

PREFACE

Rather than attempting to set forth all points of view on all the issues of "environmental economics" or offering an empirical salad of case studies, this book seeks to present a single, coherent point of view—that of a steady-state economy—which is based on both physical and ethical first principles. This particular theoretical viewpoint seems to me (and to many other people) to be the one that is fundamentally correct and therefore most likely to yield useful insights and policies. The reader, of course, must judge this for himself. Other people have written or edited other books that present other viewpoints, but there is not as of this writing a collection presenting the case for a steady-state economy.

As students often realize more quickly than their professors, we absolutely must revise our economic thinking so that it will be more in conformity with the finite energy and resource limits of the earth, and with the finite limits of man's stomach. This revision will not be accomplished by a single mind, or even by a single volume containing the thoughts of many minds. The development of a steady-state economy will be the product of an unpredictable but conscious social evolution in which many ideas will be tried out. However, just as an auctioneer must begin by calling out some specific price, so it seems we must begin by calling out some specific notions about a steady-state economy, even though we know that they are no more likely to be the final solution than the auctioneer's initial price is likely to be the equilibrium price. Yet both initial actions provide starting points for a feedback process of approximation, by trial and error, to something better. That is sufficient justification for this book.

As editor of *Toward a Steady-State Economy*, I have provided a relatively long introduction to the general subject and relatively short introductions to each of the three main groups of readings. The major disciplinary thrust is political economy (Part II), but this is firmly set within the context of biophysical and moral constraints (Parts I and III, respectively).

Toward a Steady-State Economy will provide supplementary reading for introductory economics courses, as well as for a variety of courses in the social sciences and environmental studies. However, I expect its usefulness will by no means be limited only to these subjects.

Herman E. Daly

Baton Rouge
October 1972

CONTENTS

TOWARD A STEADY-STATE ECONOMY

INTRODUCTION

Herman E. Daly

PARADIGMS IN POLITICAL ECONOMY

This book is a part of an emerging paradigm shift in political economy. The terms "paradigm" and "paradigm shift" come from Thomas Kuhn's insightful book, *The Structure of Scientific Revolutions*,[1] in which Kuhn explores the ways in which entire patterns of thought—a kind of gestalt for which he uses the word paradigm—are established and changed. Kuhn contends that paradigm shifts, occasional discontinuous, revolutionary changes in tacitly shared points of view and preconceptions of science, are an integral part of scientific thought. They form the necessary complement to "normal science," which is what Kuhn calls the day to day cumulative building on the past, the puzzle solving, and the refining of models that fit within the paradigm shared by all the scientists of a field. Indeed, their preparation for scientific endeavors teaches science

1. Notes and references for the introduction will be found on pages 27–29.

Part of the introduction was originally published in *The Patient Earth*, John Harte and Robert H. Socolow, eds. Holt, Rinehart and Winston, 1971. Reprinted by permission of the publisher.

students to accept the prevailing paradigm so their work will adhere to the same designs, rules, and standards, thus assuring the *cumulative* building of knowledge.

Just as we are unconscious of the lenses in our own eyeglasses until we have trouble seeing clearly, so we are unconscious of paradigms until the clarity of scientific thought becomes blurred by anomaly. Even under the stress of facts that don't seem to fit, paradigms are not easily abandoned. If they were, the cohesion and coherence necessary to form a scientific *community* would be lacking: most anomalies, after all, do become resolved within the paradigm because they must if the paradigm is to command the loyalty of scientists. To abandon one paradigm in favor of another is to change the entire basis of intellectual community among the scientists within a discipline, which is why Kuhn calls such changes scientific "revolutions." Discontinuous with the preceding paradigm, a new paradigm at first must rely on its own criteria for justification, for many of the questions that can be asked and many of the answers that can be found are likely to be absent from the previous paradigm. Indeed, even logical debate between adherents to different paradigms is often very limited, for proponents of two paradigms may not agree on what is a problem and what is a solution.

The history of science contains numerous examples of anomalies that brought crisis to old paradigms and were answered with new ones. Shall we take the earth or the sun as the center of our cosmos? Does a stone swinging on a string represent constrained fall or pendulum motion? Are species fixed or slowly evolving? And problems arise in political economy that may require more than normal puzzle solving. Shall we conceive of economic growth as a permanent normal process of a healthy economy, or as a temporary passage from one steady state to another? Shall we take the flow of income or the stock of wealth as the magnitude most directly responsible for the satisfaction of human wants? Shall we conceive of land, labor, and capital as each being productive, and think in terms of three sources of value, or shall we conceive of labor as the only productive factor, the only source of value, recognizing that land and capital enhance the productivity of labor?

In a way, it all depends on how you want to look at it. And yet there is far more to it than that. Which point of view is simpler or more appealing aesthetically? Which removes the intellectually or socially most vexing anomalies? Which is likely to suggest the most interesting and fruitful problems for future research? These kinds of criteria are not reducible to logical or factual differences. They involve a gestalt, an element of faith, personal commitment, and values.

That revolutionary paradigm shifts, both large ones and small ones, are historically and logically descriptive of the physical sciences has been admirably shown by Kuhn in his book, and by Arthur Koestler, in *The Sleepwalkers*.[2] Michael Polanyi takes a related viewpoint in his admirable book, *Personal Knowledge*.[3] The focus of all three writers is physical science, and Koestler focuses especially on astronomy. But scientific revolutions characterize all of science, including political economy. Since values are a larger part of social science and also influence the acceptance or rejection of paradigms, such shifts may be even more characteristic of the social sciences.

The history of economic thought brings several such shifts to mind. In the mercantilist paradigm of the period of the Renaissance, wealth meant precious metal, treasure easily convertible into armies and national power. The way to attain wealth was from mines, or from a favorable balance of international trade. The implication of this paradigm was that the way to riches was to devote a nation's manpower to digging up metal that had no other use than as coinage, or to making goods to be given to foreigners in exchange for such minimally useful metal. Moreover, maintaining a surplus balance of trade required low prices on goods exported for sale in competitive markets, which meant low wages to home workers, inasmuch as labor was the major cost of production. Making sure that the supply of laborers was large was one means of keeping wages low. The anomalous outcome was that for a mercantilist nation to be "wealthy" it needed a large number of poor laborers.

The physiocrats of mid-eighteenth-century France—the first economic theorists—tried to explain economics in accordance with natural law, and saw agriculture and Mother Earth as the source of all net value. Reproduction of plants and animals provided the paradigm by which all other increase in wealth was understood. Money was sterile. The concept that it "reproduced" through interest was rejected because it did not fit the paradigm. But the anomaly of interest did not disappear, and the process of tracing all net value back to land became very complex.

The classical economists, witnesses to the problems of mercantilism as well as the beginnings of the Industrial Revolution, saw labor as the source of wealth, and division of labor and improvement in the "state of the arts" as the source of productivity. Their main concern was how the product of labor got distributed among the social classes that cooperated to produce it. Adam Smith believed that an "invisible hand"—competition—would control the economy and that a certain natural order would keep atomistic individuals from exploiting each other, harnessing individual self-interest to the social good. Classical economists thought that over the long run, population growth and diminishing returns would unavoidably channel the entire economic surplus into rent, thus reducing profit to zero and terminating economic growth. What was anomalous about classical economics was not its long run implications, however, but the then existing misery of the working class, misery which gave the lie to the belief that the "invisible hand" could effectively prevent exploitation.

To the extent he saw labor as the source of net economic product, Karl Marx was largely a classical economist. But in place of atomistic individuals acting in natural harmony and short-run cooperation among three classes—landlords, laborers, and capitalists—Marx saw two classes in direct day to day conflict, the owners of the means of production versus nonowners. The owners kept the net product of labor, paying the worker only what his replacement would cost. Atomistic competition would continue to exist *within* each class; but the essential idea of Marxist economics is the exploitative relation *between* classes, which Marx believed would lead to revolution. The earlier classical economists recognized the likelihood of long run class conflicts, but Marx emphasized this as a central economic factor, an emphasis constituting a paradigm shift.

The neoclassical economists shifted the paradigm back to atomism, though adding an analysis of imperfect competition as they did so. Their big change, however, was to conceive of net value as the result of psychic want satisfaction rather than the product of labor. The origin of value was subjective, not objective. The focus was not on distribution among classes, but on efficiency of allocation—how could a society get the maximum amount of want satisfaction from scarce resources, *given* a certain distribution of wealth and income among individuals and social classes? Pure competition provided the optimal allocation.

John Maynard Keynes, observing the economic problems of the 1930s, could not accept the anomaly presented by the wide disuse of resources that were supposed to be optimally allocated. He was less concerned that resources be "optimally" allocated in some refined sense than that they should not lie unused. Classical and neoclassical economics, with Say's Law among their premises, required that unemployment be viewed as an aberration. Social reality insisted that unemployment was central. Keynes changed the theoretical viewpoint accordingly.

The present day Keynesian-neoclassical synthesis seeks full macroeconomic employment and optimal microeconomic allocation of resources. The *summum bonum* to be maximized is no longer psychic want satisfaction, which is unmeasurable, but annual aggregate real output, GNP—Gross National Product—a value *index* of the *quantity* flow of annual production. Distribution recedes into the background, the goal being to make the total pie bigger, thereby enabling everyone to get absolutely more without changing the relative size of parts. Both full employment and efficient allocation serve to increase the growth of real GNP. Conversely, and perhaps more importantly, growth of GNP is necessary to maintain full employment. In one of the first important contributions to growth theory, Evesy Domar stated the issue very well,

> ... The economy finds itself in a serious dilemma: if sufficient investment is not forthcoming today, unemployment will be here today. But if enough is invested today, still more will be needed tomorrow.
>
> It is a remarkable characteristic of a capitalistic economy that while, on the whole, unemployment is a function of the difference between its actual income and its productive capacity, most of the measures (i.e., investment) directed toward raising national income also enlarge productive capacity. It is very likely that the increase in national income will be greater than that of capacity, but the whole problem is that the increase in income is temporary and presently peters out (the usual multiplier effect), while capacity has been increased for good. So far as unemployment is concerned, investment is at the same time a cure for the disease and the cause of even greater ills in the future.[4]

Thus continual growth in both capacity (stock) and income (flow) is a central part of the neoclassical growth paradigm. But in a finite world continual growth is impossible.[5] Given finite stomachs, finite lifetimes, and the kind of man who does not live by bread alone, growth becomes undesirable long before it becomes impossible. But the tacit, and sometimes explicit assumption of the Keynesian-neoclassical growthmania synthesis is that aggregate wants are infinite and should be served by trying to make aggregate production infinite, and that technology is an omnipotent *deux ex machina* who will get us out of any growth-induced problems.

To call the ideas and resultant changes hastily sketched above "paradigm shifts" is to use Kuhn's term with a bit of poetic license. In the physical sciences, to which Kuhn applied the term, reality does not change except on an evolutionary time scale. The *same* things are perceived in different ways. But social reality changes more rapidly. This, however, can be viewed as an additional reason for the periodic necessity of regrinding our lenses to a new prescription in the social sciences.

Ideology, ethical apology, and ethical criticism are also sources of paradigm shifts in the social sciences. As Marx said, the goal is not just to interpret the world but to change it. And he was right. Even if we wish to be neutral or "value-free" we cannot, because the paradigm by which people try to understand their society is itself one of the key determining features of the social system. No one denies that the distinction between "is" and "ought" is an elementary rule of clear thinking. To say "is" when we should say "ought" is wishful thinking. To say "ought" when we should say "is" (or never to say "ought" at all) is apology for the status quo. But these distinctions belong in the mind of the individual thinker. They are not proper lines for division of labor between individuals, much less between professions. Attempts to divide thought in this way contribute heavily to the schizophrenia of the modern age.

Kuhn notes that paradigm shifts are usually brought about by the young, or by people new to a discipline, those therefore relatively free of the established preconceptions. In accordance, we find that thought on a steady-state economy has been more eagerly received by physical scientists and biologists than economists, and by the relatively young among economists. The interest of the physical and life sciences in the issue of growth versus steady state is evident from the program of the American Association for the Advancement of Science (AAAS) 1971 meetings. Consider the following report:

> Another way of interpreting the content of the AAAS meeting is to describe major themes that keep recurring. . . . Three topics appear this year in a variety of forms and contexts. They seek answers to:
>
> How to live on a *finite* earth?
>
> How to live a *good life* on a finite earth?
>
> How to live a good life on a finite earth *at peace and without destructive mismatches*?[6]

The many sessions in which these themes appear are then listed, including the presidential address.

Simultaneously with the AAAS meetings in Philadelphia the American Economic Association (AEA) held meetings in New Orleans, where, judging from the detailed program, not one of these questions was even on the agenda. Yet one would think that the question "How to live a *good* life on a *finite* earth?" would be of more direct concern to economists than to physicists and biologists. Why this striking discrepancy? Do economists have more important questions on their minds? I think not. It is simply that economists must undergo a revolutionary paradigm shift and sacrifice large intellectual (and material?) vested interests in the perpetual growth theories and policies of the last thirty years before they can really come to grips with these questions. The advantage of the physical scientists is that, unlike economists, they are viscerally convinced that the world is a finite, open system at balance in a steady state, and they have not all invested time and energy in economic growth models. As Kuhn points out,

> Scientific revolutions . . . need seem revolutionary only to those whose paradigms are affected by them . . . astronomers, for example, could accept X-rays as a mere addition to knowledge, for their paradigms were unaffected by the existence of the new radiation. But for men like Kelvin, Crookes, and

> Roentgen, whose research dealt with radiation theory or with cathode ray tubes, the emergence of X-rays necessarily violated one paradigm as it created another. That is why these rays could be discovered only by something's first going wrong with normal research.[7]

A steady-state economy fits easily into the paradigm of physical science and biology—the earth is a steady-state open system, as are organisms. Why not our economy also, at least in its physical dimensions of bodies and artifacts? The economist forgot about physical dimensions long ago and centered his attention on value. But the fact that wealth is measured in value units does not annihilate its physical dimensions. Economists may continue to maximize value, and value could conceivably grow forever, but the physical mass in which value inheres must conform to a steady state, and the constraints of physical constancy on value growth will be severe and must be respected.

Perhaps this explains why many of the essays in this volume on political economy were written by physicists and biologists. But lest I be unfair to my own profession I must observe that some leading economists, particularly Kenneth Boulding and Nicholas Georgescu-Roegen, have made enormous contributions toward reorienting economic thought along lines more congruent with a finite physical world. It is time for the profession to follow their lead.[8]

It is hoped that anyone who wishes to follow that lead, or at least contemplates doing so, will find the present volume of help. The basic issue is the conflict between finitude and unlimited growth. The conflict of economic growth with biophysical constraints is considered in Part I. Part II focuses on the social constraints and the problems of design for, and transition to, a steady-state economy. In Part III the ethical problems and presuppositions of the steady state are considered. Thus the readings are grouped in a progression beginning with the purely physical, then the biological, then the social, and finally the ethical. While this ordering is convenient it must be remembered that it has been rather arbitrarily imposed by the editor after the fact. No such arrangement was in the minds of the authors as they wrote their articles. Consequently one generally finds that each article contains thoughts ranging from the physical to the theological. The classificatory arrangement is by emphasis only. Each article can be read independently of the others. Nor is there always agreement among the writers.

The organization of these essays might be further elucidated by reference to a kind of Aristotelian ordering.

The *ultimate end* is that with reference to which intermediate ends are directed. It is that which is good in itself and does not derive its goodness from any instrumental relation to any other end. Our perception of the ultimate is always cloudy, but necessary nonetheless, for

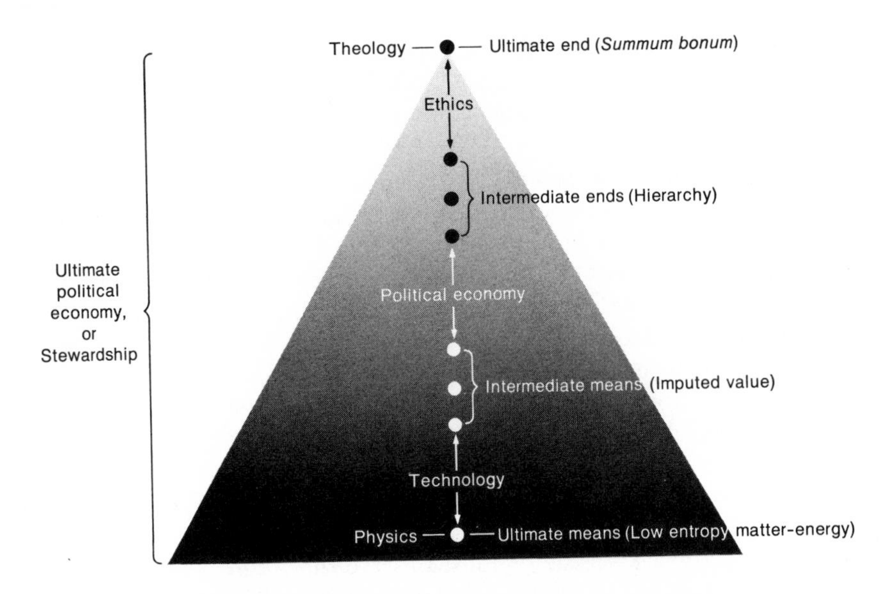

without a perception of the ultimate it would be impossible to order intermediate ends and to speak of priorities.

The *intermediate ends* are instrumental in designating, to varying degrees, the conditions necessary for approaching the ultimate. Examples of intermediate ends are wealth, income, health, knowledge, leisure, etc. Ethics relates the ultimate end and intermediate ends, and ranks the intermediate ends according to their ability to contribute to the ultimate.

The *intermediate means* are necessary for the attainment of one or more of the intermediate ends. Examples of intermediate means are capital equipment of all kinds, labor, conventional natural resources, and the natural services provided by the ecosystem. Value is (or in the case of natural services, should be) imputed to intermediate means according to how well they serve the hierarchy of intermediate ends at the margin determined by scarcity. What is political economy? The problem of organizing and valuing intermediate means in the way that best serves the hierarchy of intermediate ends (also, thus, the ultimate end if the intermediate ends are properly ranked).

The *ultimate means* are the fundamental useful stuff of the universe, i.e., low entropy matter-energy. Low entropy is a necessary but not sufficient condition for value. The nature of the ultimate means is studied by physics. The conversion of ultimate means into intermediate means is technology in the broadest sense. In this we include the natural technology of the ecosystem that provides the natural services of regeneration of renewable and life-cycle resources, the absorption of waste products, and so forth—indeed, the entire maintenance of our basic life support system. We also include human technology, which seeks to appropriate ultimate means effectively and to convert them into intermediate means—particularly into those intermediate means of highest imputed value.

The overall problem is how to use ultimate means to serve best the ultimate end. We might call this ultimate political economy, or stewardship. To state the problem in this way is to emphasize at once both its wholeness and the necessity of breaking it into more manageable subproblems, for the overall problem must be tackled one step at a time. Yet one step is valueless without the others, and one correct step is worse than valueless if the steps it takes for granted were false steps. If our concept of the ultimate is evil rather than good, then an inverted ethics is better for us than a consistent ethics. If our ethical priorities are upside down then an inverted or incorrect imputation of value to intermediate means is better than a correct imputation. If our intermediate means are incorrectly valued, then a technology that efficiently and powerfully converts ultimate means into the most valuable intermediate means is worse than a weak technology. And an erroneous physics that will cause technology to stumble rather than advance an evil end efficiently is better than a correct physics.

The parts of the total economic problem are not only related from the top down, but also from the bottom up. Our customary ethical ordering of intermediate ends conditions our perception of the ultimate. We tend to take our conventional priorities as given and then deduce the nature of the ultimate as that which legitimates the conventional priorities. We tend also to order our intermediate ends in such a way that we can effectively serve them with the existing valuation of intermediate means. Further, there is a tendency to value the intermediate means according to the technical and physical possibilities for producing them. If it is possible we must do it.

I do not mean to say that working only in one direction is always proper and the other always improper. The point is that the parts of the problem are highly interrelated and cannot be dealt with in isolation, and even though ideally our starting point should be the ultimate end, we can only see that end dimly and may find clues to its nature in our experience with ethical, economic, and even technical problems encountered on the way.

The total problem of relating the five subproblems—theology, ethics, political economy, technology, physics—is more delicate than any of the subproblems themselves, but not for that reason any less imperative. Surely everyone must have a vision of the total problem, otherwise he does not understand what his specialty is for. It is hoped that the collection of articles in this book will help to fill out such a total vision.

Clearly each stage can be dealt with only in a partial and incomplete manner. But the premise on which this volume rests is that it is better to deal incompletely with the whole than to deal wholly with the incomplete.

Let us now turn to an overview of the particular paradigm this collection seeks to develop, one that will lead to a steady-state economy. The terms "steady state" and "stationary state" are used synonymously. The former is common in physical sciences, the latter common in economics and demography.

THE STEADY-STATE ECONOMY

Any discussion of the relative merits of the steady, stationary, or no-growth economy, and its opposite, the economy in which wealth and population are growing, must recognize some important quantitative and qualitative differences between rich and poor countries, and between rich and poor classes within countries. To see why this is so consider the familiar ratio of Gross National Product (GNP) to total population (P). This ratio, per capita annual product (GNP/P), is the measure usually employed to distinguish rich from poor countries, and in spite of its many shortcomings, it does have the virtue of reflecting in one ratio the two fundamental life processes of production and reproduction. Let us ask two questions of both numerator and denominator for both rich and poor countries—namely, what is its quantitative rate of growth; and qualitatively, exactly what is it that is growing?

1. The rate of growth in the denominator, P, is much higher in poor countries than in rich countries. Although mortality is tending to equality at low levels throughout the world, fertility[9] in poor nations remains roughly *twice* that of rich nations. The average Gross Reproduction Rate (GRR)[10] for rich countries is around 1.5, and that for poor countries is around 3.0 (that is, on the assumption that all survive to the end of reproductive life, each mother would be replaced by 1.5 daughters in rich countries and 3 in poor countries). Moreover, all poor countries have a GRR greater than 2.0, and all rich countries have a GRR less than 2.0, with practically no countries falling in the area of the 2.0 dividing point. No other social or economic index divides the world so clearly and consistently into "developed" and "underdeveloped" as does fertility.[11]

2. Qualitatively the incremental population in poor countries consists largely of hungry illiterates; in rich countries it consists largely of well-fed members of the middle class. The incremental person in poor countries contributes negligibly to production, but makes few demands

on world resources—although from the point of view of his poor country these few demands of many new people can easily dissipate any surplus that might otherwise have been used to raise productivity.[12] The incremental person in the rich country contributes to his country's GNP, and to feed his high standard of living contributes greatly to depletion of the world's resources and pollution of its spaces.

3. The numerator, GNP, is growing at roughly the same rate in rich and poor countries, around four or five percent annually, with the poor countries probably growing slightly faster. Nevertheless, because of their more rapid population growth, the per capita income of poor countries is growing more slowly than that of rich countries. Consequently the gap between rich and poor is widening.[13]

4. The incremental GNP of rich and poor nations has an altogether different qualitative significance. This follows from the two most basic laws of economics: (a) the law of diminishing marginal utility, which really says nothing more than that people satisfy their most pressing wants *first*—thus each additional dollar of income or unit of resource is used to satisfy a less pressing want than the previous dollar or unit; (b) the law of increasing marginal cost, which says that producers *first* use the best qualities of factors (most fertile land, most experienced worker, and so on) and the best combination of factors known to them. They use the less efficient (more costly) qualities and combinations only when they run out of the better ones, or when one factor, such as land, becomes fixed (nonaugmentable). Also, in a world of scarcity, as more resources are devoted to one use, fewer are available for other uses. The least important alternative uses are sacrificed first, so that as more of any good is produced, progressively more important alternatives must be sacrificed—that is, a progressively higher price (opportunity cost) must be paid. Applied to GNP the first law means that the marginal (incremental) benefits from equal increments of output are decreasing, and the second law means that the marginal cost of equal increments in output is increasing. At some point, perhaps already passed in the United States, an extra unit of GNP costs more than it is worth. Technological advances can put off this point, but not forever. Indeed it may bring it to pass sooner because more powerful technologies tend to provoke more powerful ecological backlashes and to be more disruptive of habits and emotions. To put things more concretely, growth in GNP in poor countries means more food, clothing, shelter, basic education, and security, whereas for the rich country it means more electric toothbrushes, yet another brand of cigarettes, more tension and insecurity, and more force-feeding through more advertising. In sum, extra GNP in a poor country, assuming it does not go mainly to the richest class of that country, represents satisfaction of relatively basic

wants, whereas extra GNP in a rich country, assuming it does not go mainly to the poorest class of that country, represents satisfaction of relatively trivial wants.

For our purposes the upshot of these differences is that for the poor, growth in GNP is still a good thing, but for the rich it is probably a bad thing. Growth in population, however, is a bad thing for both: for the rich, population growth is bad because it makes growth in GNP (a bad thing) less avoidable; for the poor, population growth is bad because it makes growth in GNP, and especially in per capita GNP (a good thing), more difficult to attain. In what follows we shall be concerned exclusively with a rich, affluent-effluent economy such as that of the United States. Our purposes will be to define more clearly the concept of steady state, to see why it is necessary, to consider its economic and social implications, and finally to comment on an emergency political economy of finite wants and nongrowth.

THE NATURE AND NECESSITY OF THE STATIONARY STATE

The term *stationary state* (steady state) is used here in its classical sense.[14] Over a century ago John Stuart Mill, the great synthesizer of classical economics, spoke of the stationary state in words that could hardly be more relevant today, and will serve as the starting point in our discussion.

> But in contemplating any progressive movement, not in its nature unlimited, the mind is not satisfied with merely tracing the laws of its movement; it cannot but ask the further question, to what goal? . . .
>
> It must always have been seen, more or less distinctly, by political economists, that the increase in wealth is not boundless: that at the end of what they term the progressive state lies the stationary state, that all progress in wealth is but a postponement of this, and that each step in advance is an approach to it . . . if we have not reached it long ago, it is because the goal itself flies before us [as a result of technical progress].
>
> I cannot . . . regard the stationary state of capital and wealth with the unaffected aversion so generally manifested towards it by political economists of the old school. I am inclined to believe that it would be, on the whole, a very considerable improvement on our present condition. I confess I am not charmed with the ideal of life held out by those who think that the normal state of human beings is that of struggling to get on; that the trampling, crushing, elbowing, and treading on each other's heels which form the existing type of social life, are the most desirable lot of human kind, or anything but the disagreeable symptoms of one of the phases of industrial progress. The northern and middle states of America are a specimen of this stage of civilization in very favorable circumstances; . . . and all that these advantages

seem to have yet done for them (notwithstanding some incipient signs of a better tendency) is that the life of the whole of one sex is devoted to dollar-hunting, and of the other to breeding dollar-hunters.

. . . Those who do not accept the present very early stage of human improvement as its ultimate type may be excused for being comparatively indifferent to the kind of economical progress which excites the congratulations of ordinary politicians; the mere increase of production and accumulation. . . . I know not why it should be a matter of congratulation that persons who are already richer than anyone needs to be, should have doubled their means of consuming things which give little or no pleasure except as representative of wealth. . . . It is only in the backward countries of the world that increased production is still an important object: in those most advanced, what is economically needed is a better distribution, of which one indispensable means is a stricter restraint on population.

There is room in the world, no doubt, and even in old countries, for a great increase in population, supposing the arts of life to go on improving, and capital to increase. But even if innocuous, I confess I see very little reason for desiring it. The density of population necessary to enable mankind to obtain, in the greatest degree, all the advantages both of cooperation and of social intercourse, has, in all the most populous countries, been attained. A population may be too crowded, though all be amply supplied with food and raiment. It is not good for a man to be kept perforce at all times in the presence of his species. . . . Nor is there much satisfaction in contemplating the world with nothing left to the spontaneous activity of nature; with every rood of land brought into cultivation, which is capable of growing food for human beings; every flowery waste or natural pasture plowed up, all quadrupeds or birds which are not domesticated for man's use exterminated as his rivals for food, every hedgerow or superfluous tree rooted out, and scarcely a place left where a wild shrub or flower could grow without being eradicated as a weed in the name of improved agriculture. If the earth must lose that great portion of its pleasantness which it owes to things that the unlimited increase of wealth and population would extirpate from it, for the mere purpose of enabling it to support a larger, but not a happier or a better population, I sincerely hope, for the sake of posterity, that they will be content to be stationary, long before necessity compels them to it.

It is scarcely necessary to remark that a stationary condition of capital and population implies no stationary state of human improvement. There would be as much scope as ever for all kinds of mental culture, and moral and social progress; as much room for improving the Art of Living and much more likelihood of its being improved, when minds cease to be engrossed by the art of getting on. Even the industrial arts might be as earnestly and as successfully cultivated, with this sole difference, that instead of serving no purpose but the increase of wealth, industrial improvements would produce their legitimate effect, that of abridging labor.[15]

The direction in which political economy has evolved in the last hundred years is not along the path suggested in the quotation. In fact, most economists are hostile to the classical notion of stationary state and dismiss Mill's discussion as "strongly colored by his social views"[16] (as if the neoclassical theories were not so colored!), and "nothing so much as a prolegomenon to Galbraith's *Affluent Society*" (which also received a hostile reception from the economics professions). While giving full credit to Mill for his many other contributions to economics, most economists consider his discussion of the stationary state as something of a personal aberration. Also his "relentless insistence that every conceivable policy measure must be judged in terms of its effects on the birth rate" is dismisssed as "hopelessly dated." The truth, however, is that Mill is even more relevant today than in his own time.

Enough of historical background and setting. Let us now analyze the steady state with a view toward clarifying what Mill somewhat mistakenly thought "must have always been seen more or less distinctly by political economists," namely "that wealth and population are not boundless."

By "steady state" is meant a constant stock of *physical* wealth (capital), and a constant stock of people (population).[17] Naturally these stocks do not remain constant by themselves. People die, and wealth is physically consumed—that is, worn out, depreciated. Therefore the stocks must be maintained by a rate of inflow (birth, production) equal to the rate of outflow (death, consumption). But this equality may obtain, and stocks remain constant, with a high rate of throughput (equal to both the rate of inflow and the rate of outflow), or with a low rate. Our definition of steady state is not complete until we specify the rates of throughput by which the constant stocks are maintained. For a number of reasons we specify that the rate of throughput should be "as low as possible." For an equilibrium stock the average age at "death" of its members is the reciprocal of the rate of throughput. The faster the water flows through the tank, the less time an average drop spends in the tank. For the population a low rate of throughput (a low birth rate and an equally low death rate) means a high life expectancy, and is desirable for that reason alone—at least within limits. For the stock of wealth a low rate of throughput (low production and equally low consumption) means greater life expectancy or durability of goods and less time sacrificed to production. This means more "leisure" or nonjob time to be divided into consumption time, personal and household maintenance time, culture time, and idleness.[18] This too seems socially desirable, at least within limits.

To these reasons for the desirability of a low rate of throughput, we must add some reasons for the impracticability of high rates. Since matter and energy cannot be created, production inputs must be taken from the environment, which leads to depletion. Since matter and energy cannot be destroyed, an equal amount of matter and energy in the form of waste must be returned to the environment, leading to pollution. Hence lower rates of throughput lead to less depletion and pollution, higher rates to more. The limits regarding what rates of depletion and pollution are tolerable must be supplied by ecology. A definite limit to the size of maintenance flows of matter and energy is set by ecological thresholds which, if exceeded, cause a breakdown of the system. To keep flows below these limits we can operate on two variables: the *size* of the stocks and the *durability* of the stocks. As long as we are well below these thresholds, economic cost-benefit calculations of depletion and pollution can be relied on as a guide. But as these thresholds are approached, "marginal cost" and "marginal benefit" become meaningless, and Alfred Marshall's erroneous motto that "nature does not make jumps" and most of neoclassical marginalist economics become inapplicable. The "marginal" cost of one more step may be to fall over the precipice.

Of the two variables, size of stocks and durability of stocks, only the second requires further clarification. "Durability" means more than just how long a particular commodity lasts. It also includes the efficiency with which the after-use "corpse" of a commodity can be recycled as an input to be born again as the same or as a different commodity. Within certain limits, to be discussed below, durability of stocks ought to be maximized in order that depletion of resources be minimized.

One might suppose that the best use of resources would imitate the model that nature has furnished: a closed-loop system of material cycles powered by the sun (what A. J. Lotka called the "mill wheel of life" or the "world engine").[19] In such an "economy" durability is maximized, and the resources on earth could presumably last as long as the sun continues to radiate the energy to turn the closed material cycles.

Now man can set up an economy in imitation of nature in which all waste products are recycled. Instead of the sun, however, man chooses to use other sources of energy, because of the scale of his industrial activity. Even modern agriculture depends as much on geologic capital (to make fertilizers, machines, and pesticides) as on solar income. This capital (fossil fuels and fission materials), from which we now borrow, may not last more than a couple of centuries, but there is another possible energy source, controlled thermonuclear fusion, which may someday provide a practically inexhaustible supply of energy with little radioactive waste, thereby alleviating problems of resource depletion and radioactive contamination.

Nevertheless, the serious problem of waste heat remains. The second law of thermodynamics tells us that it is impossible to recycle energy, and that eventually all energy will be converted into waste heat. Eventually all life will cease as entropy or chaos approaches its maximum. But even before this very long-run universal thermodynamic-heat-death occurs, the second law of thermodynamics implies that we will be plagued by thermal pollution, for whenever we use energy we must produce unusable waste heat. When a localized energy process causes a part of the environment to heat up, we call this thermal pollution, and it can have serious effects on ecosystems, since life processes and climatic phenomena are regulated by temperature.

We have already argued that, given the size of stocks, the throughput should be minimized, since it is really a cost. But the throughput is in two forms, matter and energy, and the ecological cost will vary, depending on how the throughput is apportioned between them. The amount of energy throughput will depend on the rate of material recycling. If we recycle none of our used material goods, then we must expend energy to replace those goods from raw materials and this energy expenditure is in many instances greater than the energy needed to recycle the product. For example, the estimated energy needed to produce a ton of steel plate from iron ore is 2700 kilowatt-hours, whereas merely 700 kilowatt-hours is needed to produce the same ton by recycling scrap steel.[20] However, this is not the whole story. The mere expenditure of energy is not sufficient to close material cycles, since energy must work through the agency of material implements. To recycle aluminum cans requires more trucks to collect the cans as well as more energy to run the trucks. More trucks require more steel, glass, rubber, and so forth, which require more iron ore and coal, which require still more trucks. This is the familiar web of interindustry interdependence reflected in an input-output table.[21] All of these extra intermediate activities required to recycle the aluminum cans involve some inevitable pollution as well. If we think of each industry as adding recycling to its production process, then this will generate a whole chain of direct and indirect demands on matter and energy resources which must be taken away from final demand uses and devoted to the intermediate activities of recycling. It will take more intermediate products and activities to support the same level of final output.

As we attempt to recycle more and more of our produced goods, we will reach the point of diminishing returns; the energy expenditure alone will give rise to a ruinous amount of waste heat or thermal pollution. On the other hand, if we recycle too small a fraction of our produced goods, then nonthermal pollution and resource depletion become a severe problem.

The introduction of material recycling permits a trade-off—that is, it allows us to choose that combination of material and energy depletion and pollution which is least costly in the light of specific local conditions. "Cost" here means total ecological cost, not just pecuniary costs, and is extremely difficult to measure.

In addition to the trade-offs involved in minimizing the ecological cost of the throughput for a given stock, we must recognize that the "total stock" (consisting of wealth and people) is variable both in total size and in composition. Since there is a direct relationship between the size of the stock and the size of the throughput necessary to maintain the stock, we have a trade-off between size of total stock (viewed as benefit) and size of the flow of throughput (viewed as a cost)—that is, an increase in benefit implies an increase in cost. Furthermore, a given throughput can maintain a constant total stock consisting of a large substock of wealth and a small substock of people, or a large substock of people and a small substock of wealth. Here we have a trade-off in the form of an inverse relationship between two benefits. This latter trade-off between people and wealth is imposed by the constancy of the total stock and is limited by minimal subsistence per capita wealth at one extreme and by minimal technological requirements for labor to maintain the stock of wealth at the other extreme. Within these limits this trade-off essentially represents the choice of a standard of living. Economics and ecology can at best specify the terms of this trade-off. The actual choice depends on ethical judgments.

In sum, the steady state of wealth and population is maintained by an inflow of low-entropy matter-energy (depletion) and an outflow of an equal quantity of high-entropy matter-energy (pollution). Stocks of wealth and people, like individual organisms, are open systems that feed on low entropy.[22] Many of these relationships are summarized in Figure 1.

The classical economists thought that the steady state would be made necessary by limits on the depletion side (the law of increasing cost or diminishing returns), but the main limits in fact seem to be occurring on the pollution side. In effect, pollution provides another foundation for the law of increasing costs, but has received little attention in this regard, since pollution costs are social, whereas depletion costs are usually private. On the input side the environment is partitioned into spheres of private ownership. Depletion of the environment coincides, to some degree, with depletion of the owner's wealth, and inspires at least a minimum of stewardship. On the output side, however, the waste absorption capacity of the environment is not subject to partitioning and private ownership. Air and water are used freely by all, and the result is a competitive, profligate exploitation—what biologist Garrett Hardin[23] calls "commons effect," and welfare economists call "external diseconomies," and what I like to call the "invisible foot." Adam Smith's "invisible hand" leads private self-interest unwittingly to serve the common good. The "invisible foot" leads private self-interest to kick the common good to pieces. Private ownership and private use under a competitive market give rise to the invisible hand. Public ownership with unrestrained private

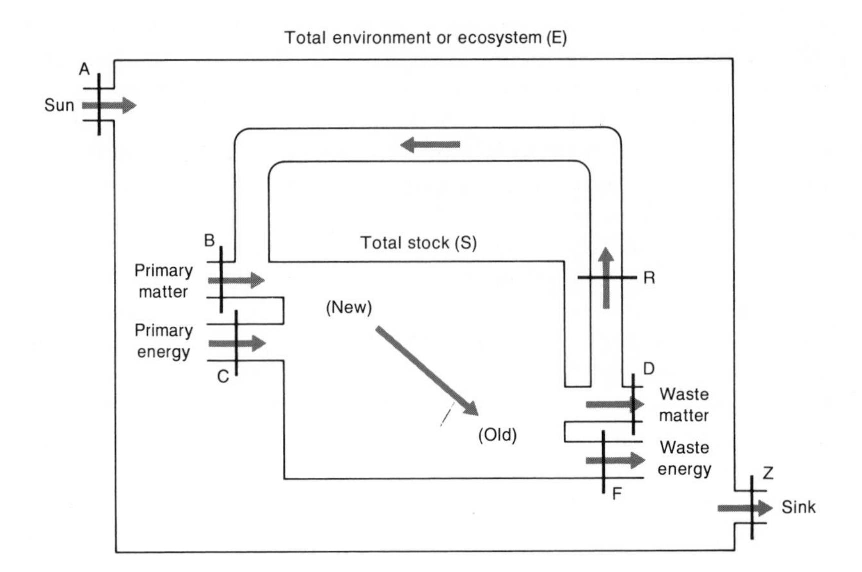

FIGURE 1.
Rectangle (E) is the total ecosystem, which contains the total stock (S) of wealth and people as one of its mutually dependent components. The ecosystem imports energy from outer space (sun) and exports waste heat to outer space (sink).

The stock contains matter in which a considerable amount of available energy is stored (mined coal, oil in oil tanks, water on high ground, living things, wood products, etc.) as well as matter in which virtually no available energy is stored. Matter and energy in the stock must be separately maintained. The stock is maintained in a steady state when B is equal to D and C is equal to F. Throughput is defined only for the steady state, where throughput equals both input (B plus C) and output (D plus F).

From the second law of thermodynamics we know that energy cannot be recycled. Matter may be recycled (R), but only by using more energy (and matter) to do it. In the diagram energy moves only from left to right, whereas matter moves in both directions.

For a constant S the lower the rate of throughput the more durable or longer-lived is the total stock. For a given throughput, the lower the rate of recycling (R), the more durable are the individual commodities. The optimum durability of an individual commodity is attained when the marginal production cost of increased durability equals the marginal recycling cost of not increasing durability further. "Cost" is total ecological cost and is extremely difficult to measure.

Both the size of the stock and the rate of throughput must not be so large relative to the total environment that they obstruct the natural ecological processes which form the biophysical foundations of wealth. Otherwise the total stock (S) and its associated throughput become a cancer which kills the total organism (E).

use gives rise to the invisible foot. Public ownership with public restraints on use gives rise to the visible hand (and foot) of the planner. Depletion has been partially restrained by the invisible hand, while pollution has been encouraged by the invisible foot. It is therefore not surprising to find limits occurring mainly on the pollution side—which, of course, is not to deny depletion limits.

It is interesting that the first school of economists, the physiocrats, emphasized the dependence of man on nature. Only the "natural" activity of agriculture was for them capable of producing a net product of value. Indeed, the word "physiocracy" meant "rule of nature." Something of the physiocrats' basic vision, if not their specific theories, is badly needed in economics today.

ECONOMIC AND SOCIAL IMPLICATIONS OF THE STEADY STATE

The economic and social implications of the steady state are enormous and revolutionary. The physical flows of production and consumption must be *minimized, not maximized* subject to some minimum population and standard of living.[24] The central concept must be the stock of wealth, not as presently, the flow of income and consumption. Furthermore the stock must not grow. For several reasons the important issue of the steady state will be distribution, not production. The problem of relative shares can no longer be avoided by appeals to growth. The argument that everyone should be happy as long as his absolute share of the wealth increases, regardless of his relative share, will no longer be available. Absolute and relative shares will move together, and the division of physical wealth will be a zero sum game. Also the arguments justifying inequality in wealth as necessary for savings, investment, and growth will lose their force. With production flows (which are really *costs* of maintaining the stock) kept low, the focus will be on the distribution of the stock of wealth, not on the distribution of the flow of income. Marginal productivity theories and "justifications" pertain only to flows, and therefore are not available to explain or "justify" the distribution of stock ownership. It is hard to see how ethical appeals to equal shares can be countered. Also, even though physical stocks remain constant, increased income in the form of leisure will result from continued technological improvements. How will it be distributed, if not according to some ethical norm of equality? The steady state would make fewer demands on our environmental resources, but much greater demands on our moral resources. In the past a good case could be made that leaning too heavily on scarce moral resources, rather than relying on abundant self-interest, was the road to serfdom. But in an age of rockets, hydrogen bombs, cybernetics, and genetic control, there is simply no substitute for moral resources, and no alternative to relying on them, whether they prove sufficient or not.

On the question of maximizing versus minimizing the flow of production, there is an interesting analogy with ecological succession. Young ecosystems (early stages of succession) are characterized by a high production efficiency, and mature ecosystems (late stages of succession) are characterized by a high maintenance efficiency. For a given B (biomass stock) young ecosystems tend to maximize P (production flow), giving a high production efficiency P/B, whereas mature ecosystems tend to minimize P for a given B, thus attaining a high maintenance efficiency, B/P. According to ecologist Eugene P. Odum, young ecosystems seem to emphasize production, growth, and quantity, whereas mature ecosystems emphasize protection, stability, and quality.[25] For the young, the flow of production is the quantitative source of growth, and is maximized. For the mature, the flow of production is the maintenance cost of protecting the stability and quality of the stock, and is minimized. If we conceive of the human economy as an ecosystem moving from an earlier to a later stage of succession (from the "cowboy economy" to the "spaceman economy" as Boulding puts it), then we would expect, by analogy, that production, growth, and quantity would be replaced by protective maintenance, stability, and quality, respectively, as the major social goals. The cardinal virtues of the past become the cardinal sins of the present.

With constant physical stocks economic growth must be in nonphysical goods: services and leisure.[26] Taking the benefits of technological progress in the form of increased leisure is a reversal of the historical practice of taking the benefits mainly in the form of goods, and has extensive social implications. In the past, economic development has increased the physical output of a day's work while the number of hours in a day has, of course, remained constant, with the result that the opportunity cost of a unit of time in terms of goods has risen. Time is worth more goods, a good is worth less time. As time becomes more expensive in terms of goods, fewer activities are "worth the time." We become goods-rich and time-poor. Consequently we crowd more activities and more consumption into the same period of time in order to raise the return on nonwork time so as to bring it into equality with the higher returns on work time, thereby maximizing the total returns to total time. This gives rise to what Staffan Linder has called the "harried leisure class."[27] Not only do we use work time more efficiently, but also personal consumption time, and we even try to be "efficient in our sleep" by attempting subconscious learning. Time-intensive activities (friendships, care of the aged and children, meditation, and reflection) are sacrified in favor of commodity-intensive activities (consumption). At some point people will feel rich enough to afford more time-intensive activities, even at the higher price. But advertising, by constantly extolling the value of material-intensive commodities, postpones this point. From an ecological view, of course, this is exactly the reverse of what is called for. What is needed is a low relative price of time in terms of material commodities. Then time-intensive activities will be substituted for material-intensive activities. To become less materialistic in our habits we must raise the relative price of matter. Keeping physical stocks constant and using technology to increase leisure time will do just that. Thus a policy of nonmaterial growth, or leisure-only growth, in addition to being necessary for keeping physical stocks constant, has the further beneficial effect of encouraging a more generous expenditure of time and a more careful use of physical goods. A higher relative price of material-intensive goods may at first glance be thought to encourage their production. But material goods require material inputs, so that costs as well as revenues would increase, thus eliminating profit incentives to expand.

In the 1930s Bertrand Russell proposed a policy of leisure growth rather than commodity growth, and viewed the unemployment question in terms of the distribution of leisure. The following words are from his delighful essay "In Praise of Idleness."

> Suppose that, at a given moment, a certain number of people are engaged in the manufacture of pins. They make as many pins as the world needs, working (say) eight hours a day. Someone makes an invention by which the same number of men can make twice as many pins as before. But the world does not need twice as many pins. Pins are already so cheap that hardly any more will be bought at a lower price. In a sensible world, everybody concerned in the manufacture of pins would take to working four hours instead of eight, and everything else would go on as before. But in the actual world this would be thought demoralizing. The men still work eight hours, there are too many pins, some employers go bankrupt, and half the men previously concerned in making pins are thrown out of work. There is, in the end, just as much leisure as on the other plan, but half the men are totally idle while half are still overworked. In this way it is insured that the unavoidable leisure shall cause misery all round instead of being a universal source of happiness. Can anything more insane be imagined?[28]

In addition to this strategy of leisure-only growth, and the resulting reinforcement of an increased price of material-intensity relative to time-intensity, we can internalize some pollution costs by charging pollution taxes. Economic efficiency requires only that a price be placed on environmental amenities—it does not tell us who should pay the price. The producer may claim that the use of the environment to absorb waste products is a right that all organisms and firms must of necessity enjoy, and whoever wants air and water to be cleaner than it is at any given time should pay for it. Consumers may argue that the use of the environment as a source of clean inputs of air and water takes precedence over its use as a sink, and that whoever makes the environment dirtier than it otherwise would be should be the one to pay. Again the issue becomes basically one of distribution—not what the price should be but who should pay it. The fact that the price takes the form of a tax automatically decides who will receive it—the government. But this raises more distribution issues; and the "solutions" to these problems are ethical, not technical.

Another possibility of nonmaterial growth is to redistribute wealth from the low utility uses of the rich to the high utility uses of the poor, thereby increasing total "social utility." Joan Robinson has noted that this egalitarian implication of the law of diminishing marginal utility was "sterilized . . . mainly by slipping from utility to physical output as the object to be maximized."[29] As we move back from physical output to nonphysical utility, the egalitarian implications become "unsterilized."

Economic growth has kept at bay two closely related problems. First, growth is necessary to maintain full employment. Only if it is possible for nearly everyone to have a job can the income-through-jobs ethic of distribution remain workable. Second, growth takes the edge off of distributional conflicts—if everyone's absolute share of income is increasing there is a tendency not to fight over relative shares, especially since such fights may interfere with growth and even lead to a lower absolute share for all. But these problems cannot be kept at bay forever, because growth cannot continue indefinitely.

Growth, by allowing full employment, permits the old principles of distribution (income-through-jobs link) to continue in effect. But with no growth in physical stocks, and a policy of using technological progress to increase leisure, full employment and income-through-jobs are no longer workable mechanisms for distribution. Furthermore, we add a new dimension to the distribution problem—how to distribute leisure. The point is that distribution issues must be squarely faced and not left to work themselves out as the by-product of full-employment policies aimed at promoting growth.

A stationary population, with low birth and death rates, would imply a greater percentage of old people than in the present growing population, though hardly a geriatric society as some youth worshippers claim. The average age, assuming the current U.S. mortality holds, would change from twenty-seven to thirty-seven. One hears much nonsense about the conservatism and reactionary character of older populations and the progressive dynamism of younger populations, but a simple comparison of Sweden (old but hardly reactionary) with Brazil (young but hardly progressive) should make us cautious about such facile relationships. It is also noted that the age pyramid of a stationary U.S. population would be essentially rectangular up to about age fifty, and then would rapidly taper off, and that the age "pyramid" would no longer be roughly congruent with the pyramid of authority in hierarchical organizations, with the result that the general correlation between increasing age and increasing authority would not hold for very many people. Quite true, but a salutary result could well be that more people will seek their personal fulfillment outside the structure of hierarchical organizations, and that fewer people would rise to levels of their incompetence within bureaucracies. Since old people do not work, this further accentuates the distribution problem. However, the percentage of children will diminish, so, in effect there will be mainly a change in the direction that payments are transferred. More of the earnings of working adults will be transferred to the old, and less to children.

What institutions will provide the control necessary to keep the stocks of wealth and people constant, with the minimum sacrifice of individual freedom? This, I submit, is the question we should be struggling with. It would be far too simpleminded to blurt out "socialism" as the answer, since socialist states are as badly afflicted with growthmania as capitalist states. The Marxist eschatology of the classless society is based on the premise of complete abundance; consequently, economic growth is exceedingly important in socialist theory and practice. Also, population growth, for the orthodox Marxist, cannot present problems under socialist institutions. This latter tenet has weakened a bit in recent years, but the first continues in full force. However, it is equally simpleminded to believe that the present big capital, big labor, big government, big military type of private profit capitalism is capable of the required foresight and restraint, and that the addition of a few pollution and severance taxes here and there will solve the problem. The issues are much deeper, and inevitably impinge on the distribution of income and wealth.

All economic systems are subsystems within the big biophysical system of ecological interdependence. The ecosystem provides a set of physical constraints to which all economic systems must conform. The facility with which an economic system can adapt to these constraints is a major, if neglected, criterion for comparing economic systems. This neglect is understandable because in the past, ecological constraints showed no likelihood of becoming effective. But population growth, growth in the physical stock of wealth, and growth in the power of technology all combine to make ecological constraints effective. Perhaps this common set of constraints will be one more factor favoring convergence of economic systems.

Why do people produce junk and cajole other people into buying it? Not out of any innate love for junk or hatred of the environment, but simply in order to earn an income. If, with the prevailing distribution of wealth, income, and power, production governed by the profit motive results in the output of great amounts of noxious junk, then something is wrong with the distribution of wealth and power, the profit motive, or both. We need some principle of income distribution independent of and supplementary to the income-through-jobs link.[30] Perhaps a start in this direction was made by Oskar Lange in his *On the Economic Theory of Socialism*[31] in which he attempted to combine some socialist principles of distribution with the allocative efficiency advantages of the market system. However, at least as much remains to be done here as remains to be done in designing institutions for stabilizing population. But before much progress can be made on these issues, we must recognize their necessity and blow the whistle on growthmania.

AN EMERGING POLITICAL ECONOMY OF FINITE WANTS AND NONGROWTH

Although the ideas expressed by Mill have been totally dominated by growthmania, there is a growing number of economists who have frankly expressed their disenchantment with the growth ideology. Arguments stressing ecologically sound limits to wealth and population have been made by Boulding and by Spengler (both past presidents of the American Economic Association).[32] Recently E. J. Mishan, Tibor Scitovsky, and Staffan Linder have made penetrating antigrowth arguments.[33] There is also much in Galbraith that is antigrowth—at least against growth of commodities the want for which must be manufactured along with the product.[34]

In spite of these beginnings, most economists are still hung up on the assumption of infinite wants, or the postulate of nonsatiety as the mathematical economists call it. Any single want can be satisfied, but all wants in the aggregate cannot be. Wants are infinite in number if not in intensity, and the satisfaction of some wants stimulates other wants. If wants are infinite, growth is always justified—or so it would seem.

Even while accepting the foregoing hypothesis, one could still object to growthmania on the grounds that, given the completely inadequate definition of GNP, "growth" simply means the satisfaction of ever more trivial wants, while simultaneously creating ever more powerful externalities which destroy ever more important environmental amenities. To defend ourselves against these externalities we produce even more, and instead of subtracting the purely defensive expenditures we add them! For example, the medical bills paid for treatment of cigarette-induced cancer and pollution-induced emphysema are added to GNP when in a welfare sense they should clearly be subtracted. This should be labeled "swelling," not "growth." Also the satisfaction of wants created by brainwashing and "hogwashing" the public over the mass media represent mostly swelling. A policy of maximizing GNP is practically equivalent to a policy of maximizing depletion and pollution.

One may hesitate to say "maximizing" pollution on the grounds that the production inflow into the stock can be greater than the consumption outflow as long as the stock increases as it does in our growing economy. To the extent that wealth becomes more durable, the production of waste can be kept low by expanding the stock. But is this in fact what happens? In the present system if one wants to maximize production one must have a market for it. Increasing the durability of goods reduces the replacement demand. The faster things wear out, the greater can be the flow of production and income. To the extent that consumer apathy and weakening competition permit, there is every incentive to minimize durability. Planned obsolescence and programmed self-destruction and other waste-making practices, so well discussed by Vance Packard, are the logical result of maximizing a marketed physical flow.[35] If we must maximize something it should be the stock of wealth, not the flow—but with full awareness of the ecological limits that constrain this maximization.

But why this perverse emphasis on flows, this "flow fetishism" of standard economic theory? Again, I believe the underlying issue is distribution. There is no theoretical explanation, much less justification, for the distribution of the stock of wealth. It is a historical datum. But the distribution of the flow of income is at least partly explained by marginal productivity theory, which at times is even misinterpreted as a justification. Everyone gets a part of the flow, call it wages, interest, rent, or profit—and it all looks rather fair. But not everyone owns a piece of the stock, and that does not seem quite so fair. Looking only at the flow helps to avoid disturbing thoughts.

Even the common-sense argument for infinite wants—that the rich seem to enjoy their high consumption—cannot be generalized without committing the fallacy of composition. If all earned the same high income, a consumption limit occurs sooner than if only a minority had high incomes. The reason is that a large part of the consumption by plutocrats is consumption of personal services rendered by the poor, which would not be available if all were rich. Plutocrats can easily spend large sums on consumption, since all the maintenance work of the household can be done by others. By hiring the poor to maintain and even purchase commodities for them, the rich devote their limited consumption time only to the most pleasurable aspects of consumption. The rich only ride their horses; they do not clean, comb, saddle, and feed them, nor do they clean out the stable. If all did their own maintenance work, consumption would perforce be less. Time sets a limit to consumption.

The big difficulty with the infinite wants assumption, however, is that pointed out by Keynes, who in spite of the use made of his theories in

support of growth, was certainly no advocate of unlimited growth, as seen in the following quotation:

> Now it is true that the needs of human beings may seem to be insatiable. But they fall into two classes—those needs which are absolute in the sense that we feel them whatever the situation of our fellow human beings may be, and those which are relative in the sense that we feel them only if their satisfaction lifts us above, makes us feel superior to, our fellows. Needs of the second class, those which satisfy the desire for superiority, may indeed be insatiable; for the higher the general level, the higher still are they. But this is not so true of the absolute needs—a point may soon be reached, much sooner perhaps than we are all of us aware of, when those needs are satisfied in the sense that we prefer to devote our further energies to non-economic purposes.[36]

For Keynes, real absolute needs are those that can be satisfied, and do not require inequality and invidious comparison for their very existence; relative wants are the wants of vanity and are insatiable. Lumping the two categories together and speaking of "infinite wants" in general can only muddy the waters. The same distinction is implicit in the quotation from Mill, who spoke disparagingly of "consuming things which give little or no pleasure except as representative of wealth."

Some two and a half millennia before Keynes, the Prophet Isaiah, in a discourse on idolatry, developed the theme more fully.

> [Man] cuts down cedars; or he chooses a holm tree or an oak and lets it grow strong among the trees of the forest; he plants a cedar and the rain nourishes it. Then it becomes fuel for a man; and he takes a part of it and warms himself, he kindles a fire and bakes bread; also he makes a god and worships it, he makes a graven image and falls down before it. Half of it he burns in the fire; over the half he eats flesh, he roasts meat and is satisfied; also he warms himself and says, "Aha, I am warm, I have seen the fire!" And the rest of it he makes into a god, his idol; and he falls down to it and worships it; he prays to it and says, "Deliver me, for thou art my god!"
>
> They know not, nor do they discern; for he has shut their eyes so that they cannot see, and their minds so that they cannot understand. No one considers, nor is there knowledge or discernment to say, "Half of it I burned in the fire, I also baked bread on its coals, I roasted flesh and have eaten; and shall I make the residue of it an abomination? Shall I fall down before a block of wood?" He feeds on ashes, a deluded mind has led him astray, and he cannot deliver himself or say, "Is there not a lie in my right hand?" [Isa. 44:14–20]

The first half of the tree burned for warmth and food, the finite absolute wants of Keynes, the bottom portion of GNP devoted to basic wants—these are all approximately synonymous. The second or surplus half of the tree used to make an idol, Keynes's infinite relative wants or wants of vanity, the top or surplus (growing) portion of GNP used to satisfy marginal wants—are also synonymous. Futhermore the surplus half of the tree used to make an idol, an abomination, is symbolic of the use made of the economic surplus throughout history of enslaving and coercing other men by gaining control over the economic surplus and obliging men to "fall down before a block of wood." The controllers of the surplus may be a priesthood that controls physical idols made from the surplus, and used to extract more surplus in the form of offerings and tribute. Or they may be feudal lords who through the power given by possession of the land extract a surplus in the form of rent and the *corvée;* or capitalists (state or private) who use the surplus in the form of capital to gain more surplus in the form of interest and quasi-rents. If growth must cease, the surplus becomes less important, and so do those who control it. If the surplus is not to lead to growth, then it must be consumed, and ethical demands for equal participation in the consumption of the surplus could not be countered by arguments that inequality is necessary for accumulation. Accumulation in excess of depreciation, and the privileges attached thereto, would not exist.

We no longer speak of "worshiping idols." Instead of "idols" we have an abomination called "GNP," large parts of which, however, bear such revealing names as Apollo, Poseidon, and Zeus. Instead of "worshiping" the idol, we "maximize" it. The idol has become rather more abstract and conceptual and rather less concrete and material, while the mode of adoration has become technical rather than personal. But fundamentally idolatry remains idolatry, and we cry out to the growing surplus, "Deliver me, for thou art my god!" Instead we should pause and ask with Isaiah, "Is there not a lie in my right hand?"

NOTES AND REFERENCES

1. Thomas S. Kuhn, *The Structure of Scientific Revolutions*, Chicago: University of Chicago Press, 1969. Second Edition.
2. Arthur Koestler, *The Sleepwalkers*, New York: Macmillan Co., 1968.
3. Michael Polanyi, *Personal Knowledge*, New York: Harper and Row, 1964.
4. Evesy Domar, "Expansion and Employment," *American Economic Review*, March 1947, pp. 34–55.
5. This, of course, is a *physical* axiom. If a "quantity" has no physical dimensions it is not limited by physical finitude. Thus "psychic income" or welfare may increase forever. But the physical stock that yields want-satisfying services, and the physical flows which maintain that stock are limited. What about GNP? If we choose to measure "GNP" in such a way that it reflects total want satisfaction, then presumably it could increase forever. However this is

emphatically *not* the way we measure GNP at present. Prices (exchange values) and quantities are the basis of GNP. Prices bear no relation whatsoever to total utility or want satisfaction. Quantity probably has borne a direct relation to welfare in the past. Whether it still does today in affluent countries is very debatable. But in any event quantities are limited by physical considerations. Even quantities of "services rendered" have some irreducible physical dimension. It is always some *thing* that yields a service—e.g., a machine or a skilled person.

6. *Science*, November 19, 1971, pp. 847–848.
7. Thomas S. Kuhn, *op cit.*, p. 92.
8. The high professional reputations of Boulding and Georgescu-Roegen are based on their many contributions within the orthodox paradigm. Their work outside that paradigm has probably diminished rather than enhanced their academic prestige.
9. Fertility refers to actual reproduction as opposed to fecundity, which refers to reproductive potential or capacity. One measure of fertility is the Gross Reproduction Rate, defined in note 10.
10. GRR is roughly the ratio of one generation to the preceding generation, assuming that all children born survive to the end of their reproductive life. It is usually defined in terms of females only. The length of a generation is the mean age of mothers at childbirth.
11. United Nations, *Population Bulletin of the United Nations*, No. 7, 1963, New York: UN, 1965.
12. Goran Ohlin, *Population Control and Economic Development*, Paris: Development Centre of the Organization for Economic Cooperation and Development, 1967.
13. According to Robert E. Baldwin: "In the 1957–58 to 1963–64 period, the less developed nations maintained a 4.7 percent annual growth rate in gross national product compared to a 4.4 percent rate in the developed economies. The gap in per capita income widened because population increased at only 1.3 percent annually in the developed countries compared to a 2.4 percent annual rate in the less developed economies." (*Economic Development and Growth*, New York: Wiley, 1966, p. 8).
14. The term *stationary state* has been burdened with two distinct meanings in economics. The classical meaning is that of an actual state of affairs toward which the real world is supposed to be evolving; that is, a teleological or eschatological concept. The neoclassical sense of the term is entirely mechanistic —an epistemologically useful fiction like an ideal gas or frictionless machine— and describes an economy in which tastes and techniques are constant. The latter sense is more current in economics today, but the fomer meaning is the relevant one in this discussion.
15. J. S. Mill, *Principles of Political Economy*, Vol. II, London: John W. Parker and Son, 1857, pp. 320–326, with omissions.
16. All quotes in this paragraph are from Mark Blaug, *Economy Theory in Retrospect*, Homewood, Ill.: Richard D. Irwin, 1968, pp. 214–221. Blaug's views are, I think, representative of orthodox economists.
17. By "stock" is meant a quantity measured at a point in time; for example, a population census or a balance sheet of assets and liabilities as of a certain date. By "flow" is meant a quantity measured across some actual or conceptual boundary over a period of time; for example, births and deaths per year or an income and loss statement for a given year.

   The boundary lines separating the stock of wealth from the rest of the physical world may sometimes be fuzzy. But the main criterion is that physical wealth must in some way have been transformed by man to increase its usefulness over its previous state as primary matter or energy. For example, coal in the ground is primary matter and energy, coal in the inventory of firms and households is physical wealth, coal after use in the form of carbon dioxide and soot is waste matter. The heat produced by the coal is part usable and part unusable. Eventually all the heat becomes unusable or waste heat, but while it is usable it is a part of the physical stock of wealth. For some purposes one may wish to define proven reserves in mines as part of wealth, but that presents no problems.

18. Staffan B. Linder, *The Harried Leisure Class*, New York: Columbia University Press, 1970.
19. A. J. Lotka, *Elements of Mathematical Biology*, New York: Dover Publications, 1957. Republication. See especially Chapter 24.
20. Report of the Committee for Environmental Information, before Joint Congressional Committee on Atomic Energy, January 29, 1970. Quoted in "The Space Available Report of the Committee for Environmental Information," *Environment*, March 1970, p. 7.
21. Herman E. Daly, "On Economics as a Life Science," *Journal of Political Economy*, July, 1968, pp. 392–406.
22. Erwin Schroedinger, *What Is Life?* New York: Macmillan, 1945.
23. Garrett Hardin, "The Tragedy of the Commons," *Science*, December 13, 1968, pp. 1243–1248. Reprinted in this volume on pages 133–148.
24. Kenneth E. Boulding, "The Economics of the Coming Spaceship Earth," *in* Henry Jarrett, ed., *Environmental Quality in a Growing Economy*, Baltimore: Johns Hopkins Press, 1966. Reprinted in this volume on pages 121–132.
25. Eugene P. Odum, "The Strategy of Ecosystem Development," *Science*, April 18, 1969.
26. Services are included in GNP and are not in themselves physical outputs. However, increasing service outputs often require increases in physical inputs to the service sector, so that there is an indirect physical component. Leisure is not counted in GNP, and more physical inputs are not necessarily required as the amount of leisure is increased.
27. Staffan B. Linder, *op. cit.*
28. Bertrand Russell, *In Praise of Idleness and Other Essays*, London: Allen and Unwin, Ltd., 1935, pp. 16–17.
29. Joan Robinson, *Economic Philosophy*, London: C. A. Watts and Co., Ltd., 1962, p. 55.
30. Robert Theobald, *Free Men and Free Markets*, Garden City, N.Y.: Doubleday, 1965.
31. Oskar Lange, *On the Economic Theory of Socialism*, ed. Benjamin E. Lippincott, New York: McGraw-Hill, 1964.
32. Kenneth E. Boulding, *op. cit;* J. J. Spengler, Public Address, Yale Forestry School, Summer 1969.
33. E. J. Mishan, *The Costs of Economic Growth*, New York: Praeger, 1967; Tibor Scitovsky, "What Price Economic Growth," *Papers on Welfare and Growth*, Stanford, Calif.: Stanford University Press, 1964; Staffan B. Linder, *op. cit.*
34. J. K. Galbraith, *The Affluent Society*, Boston: Houghton Mifflin, 1958.
35. Vance Packard, *The Waste Makers*, New York: Pocket Books, 1963.
36. J. M. Keynes, "Economic Possibilities for Our Grandchildren," *Essays in Persuasion*, New York: Norton, 1963 (originally published 1931).

I

BIOPHYSICAL CONSTRAINTS ON ECONOMIC GROWTH

INTRODUCTION

"All flesh is grass," said the Prophet Isaiah. That is probably the most concise statement ever made of the ecological constraints on human life. But such visions of unity and wholeness have been fragmented by the specialization of modern thought. The economist's abstract world of commodities, with its laws of motion and equilibrium, has very few points of contact left with "grass," and is even in danger of losing touch with "flesh." Seemingly, economics has become detached from its own biophysical foundations. Standard textbooks do little to counteract this trend, representing the economic process—according to economist Nicholas Georgescu-Roegen—with a mechanistic diagram of a circular flow, "a pendulum movement between production and consumption within a completely closed system." In modern economic growth theory aggregate production functions generally ignore nature and natural resources completely. Physical scientists, such as M. King Hubbert, find this neglect rather perplexing:

> One speaks of the rate of growth of GNP. I haven't the faintest idea what this means when I try to translate it into coal, and oil, and iron, and the other physical quantities which are required to run an industry. So far as I have been able to find out, the quantity GNP is a monetary bookkeeping entity. It obeys the laws of money. It can be expanded or diminished, created or destroyed, but it does not obey the laws of physics.[1]

Even though GNP is an abstract entity, it is a value *index* of an aggregate of *physical* quantities. Value is the product of prices times those quantities. In calculating real GNP and its growth rate, we hold constant both absolute and relative prices for the purpose of isolating and measuring *quantitative* change. Although GNP cannot be expressed in

1. References for this introduction will be found on page 36.

simple physical units, it remains an index of physical quantities and therefore should be very much subject to laws of physics. Economic models that ignore this dependence are grossly deficient and are in large part responsible for our present ecological crisis.

Earlier thinkers have called attention to this deficiency and some of their words bear repeating. J. A. Hobson, a British economic heretic of the late nineteenth and early part of the twentieth century (familiar to economics students for his theory of underconsumption, which influenced Keynes, and his theory of imperialism, which influenced Lenin), noted that

> . . . All serviceable organic activities consume tissue and expend energy, the biological costs of the services they render. Though this economy may not correspond in close quantitative fashion to a pleasure and pain economy or to any conscious valuation, it must be taken as the groundwork for that conscious valuation. For most economic purposes we are well-advised to prefer the organic test to any other test of welfare, bearing in mind that many organic costs do not register themselves easily or adequately in terms of conscious pain or disutility, while organic gains are not always interpretable in conscious enjoyment.[2]

The mathematical biologist A. J. Lotka, noted for his contributions to population demography in the early years of the twentieth century, expressed a similar insight in the following words:

> Underlying our economic manifestations are biological phenomena which we share in common with other species; and . . . the laying bare and clearly formulating of the relations thus involved—in other words the analysis of biophysical foundations of economics—is one of the problems coming within the program of physical biology.[3]

Clearly, Hobson and Lotka saw the importance of natural bases for economic thinking.

And so do the authors in the first part of this volume. The articles here deal with the "biophysical foundations of economics" and the "groundwork for conscious valuation." A major contribution to reuniting economics with its biophysical foundations has been made by Nicholas Georgescu-Roegen in his book *The Entropy Law and the Economic Process* (Harvard University Press, 1971). The first article in this part is essentially the introduction to that book. According to Georgescu-Roegen, the major link which connects economics to its biophysical foundations is the entropy law, the second law of thermodynamics.

Generally, entropy may be considered the measure of unavailable energy within a closed thermodynamic system. The energy that is free for man to use is available energy, of low entropy. Energy becomes unavailable to man—it is of high entropy—when it has been dissipated throughout a thermodynamic system, when, in effect, it has become "bound" by equilibrium with the system of which it is part. The second law of thermodynamics states that the entropy of a closed thermodynamic system continuously increases: the order of such a system steadily turns into disorder. The crucial point of Georgescu-Roegen's thesis is how he defines "closed thermodynamic systems." Not only are these as small as single heat engines—study of which gave rise to the discipline of thermodynamics—the whole earth itself is a thermodynamic system, within which are stocks and flows of energy that mankind attempts to economize. A net increase of order within a system requires inputs of external energy. Entropy is a deep and perplexing concept, even for physicists. Georgescu-Roegen's exposition is clear and accessible to the layman, and his article contains so many important ideas in so short a space that readers will find new insights through several readings.

Preston Cloud's article on mineral resources provides a factual, concrete discussion of the physical foundations of economics, the materials that generate human and mechanical energy, and thus it serves as a complement to Georgescu-Roegen's theoretical discussion. In addition, Cloud analyzes the basic premises of the "cornucopian faith" of the economic-growth-men. This symbol—the goat's horn spilling forth abundance—is apprioriately picturesque, chiefly because of its unreality. Further discussion of the biophysical foundations and carrying capacity is found in Part III, in the article by Jørgen Randers and Donella Meadows, although the main focus there is on ethical implications. Nevertheless, readers will find it meaningful to compare the conclusions of Randers and Meadows with the facts Cloud outlines here.

The following two articles, by Paul Ehrlich and John Holdren and by Leon Kass, emphasize the "bio" aspect of the biophysical foundations. Ehrlich and Holdren emphasize the role of population growth in causing environmental degradation, and argue against downplaying what have, to some, seemed like independent considerations—the roles of per capita consumption and technology. Interrelations among these factors are given careful attention. Ehrlich and Holdren examine five theorems that strip away many preconceived notions about population, environment, the impact of population *on* environment, and the nature of solutions to the problem of population impact.

Shifting the focus from the macro level of populations to the micro level of genetics, Leon Kass raises some very probing questions concerning our management of the part of our biophysical foundation that is the most important of all: the human gene pool. It is clear that avoidance of ecological catastrophe will require profound changes in human behavior, a fact Randers and Meadows will show. But coincidentally with this increasing demand for behavioral change, genetics is promising to increase the supply of behavior-changing techniques. The "new biology" of which Kass writes will not merely change behavior, it will alter the very *capacity* to behave—not content to engineer a new engine, it seeks to engineer a new engineer! This is perhaps the ultimate "technological fix." Should economic growth and technology create a world toward which the nature of man rebels, we will be offered the "logical" solution: change the nature of man! The game played by the Sorcerer's Apprentice could be escalated to a precipitous and far more dangerous height. The last essay in this book, by C. S. Lewis, returns to this theme, arguing that the stakes in this new game could well be "the abolition of man," not by ecocatastrophe, but by the banishment of value and spontaneity from the stage on which life and evolution are played out.

REFERENCES

1. M. K. Hubbert *in* F. Fraser Darling and John P. Milton, eds., *Future Environments of North America.* Garden City, New York, The Natural History Press, 1966, p. 291.
2. J. A. Hobson, *Economics and Ethics.* Boston, D. C. Heath and Co., 1929, p. xxi.
3. A. J. Lotka, *Elements of Mathematical Biology.* New York, Dover Publications, 1957.

1

THE ENTROPY LAW AND THE ECONOMIC PROBLEM

Nicholas Georgescu-Roegen

I

A curious event in the history of economic thought is that, years after the mechanistic dogma has lost its supremacy in physics and its grip on the philosophical world, the founders of the neoclassical school set out to erect an economic science after the pattern of mechanics—in the words of Jevons, as "*the mechanics of utility and self-interest.*"[1] And while economics has made great strides since, nothing has happened to deviate economic thought from the mechanistic epistemology of the forefathers of standard economics. A glaring proof is the standard textbook representation of the economic process by a circular diagram, a pendulum movement between production and consumption within a completely closed system.[2] The situation is not different with the analytical pieces that adorn the standard economic literature; they, too, reduce

1. Notes and references for this reading will be found on page 48–49.

"The Entropy Law and the Economic Problem" appeared previously in The University of Alabama *Distinguished Lecture Series*, No. 1, 1971. Reprinted by permission of the author and The University of Alabama.

the economic process to a self-sustained mechanical analogue. The patent fact that between the economic process and the material environment there exists a continuous mutual influence which is history-making carries no weight with the standard economist. And the same is true of Marxist economists, who swear by Marx's dogma that everything nature offers man is a spontaneous gift.[3] In Marx's famous diagram of reproduction, too, the economic process is represented as a completely circular and self-sustaining affair.[4]

Earlier writers, however, pointed in another direction, as did Sir William Petty in arguing that labor is the father and nature is the mother of wealth.[5] The entire economic history of mankind proves beyond question that nature, too, plays an important role in the economic process as well as in the formation of economic value. It is high time, I believe, that we should accept this fact and consider its consequences for the economic problem of mankind. For, as I shall endeavor to show in this paper, some of these consequences have an exceptional importance for the understanding of the nature and the evolution of man's economy.

II

Some economists have alluded to the fact that man can neither create nor destroy matter or energy[6]—a truth which follows from the principle of conservation of matter-energy, alias the first law of thermodynamics. Yet no one seems to have been struck by the question—so puzzling in the light of this law—"what then does the economic process do?" All that we find in the cardinal literature is an occasional remark that man can produce only utilities, a remark which actually accentuates the puzzle. How is it possible for man to produce something material, given the fact that he cannot produce either matter or energy?

To answer this question, let us consider the economic process as a whole and view it only from the purely physical viewpoint. What we must note first of all is that this process is a partial process which, like all partial processes, is circumscribed by a boundary across which matter and energy are exchanged with the rest of the material universe.[7] The answer to the question of what this *material* process does is simple: it neither produces nor consumes matter-energy; it only absorbs matter-energy and throws it out continuously. This is what pure physics teaches us. However, economics—let us say it high and loud—is not pure physics, not even physics in some other form. We may trust that even the fiercest partisan of the position that natural resources have nothing to do with value will admit in the end that there is a difference between what goes into the economic process and what comes out of it. To be sure, this difference can be only qualitative.

An unorthodox economist—such as myself—would say that what goes into the economic process represents *valuable natural resources* and what is thrown out of it is *valueless waste*. But this qualitative difference is confirmed, albeit in different terms, by a particular (and peculiar) branch of physics known as thermodynamics. From the viewpoint of thermodynamics, matter-energy enters the economic process in a state of *low entropy* and comes out of it in a state of *high entropy*.[8]

To explain in detail what entropy means is not a simple task. The notion is so involved that, to trust an authority on thermodynamics, it is "not easily understood even by physicists."[9] To make matters worse not only for the layman, but for everyone else as well, the term now circulates with several meanings, not all associated with a physical coordinate.[10] The 1965 edition of *Webster's Collegiate Dictionary* has three entries under "entropy." Moreover, the definition pertaining to the meaning relevant for the economic process is likely to confuse rather than enlighten the reader: "a measure of unavailable energy in a closed thermodynamic system so related to the state of the system that a change in the measure varies with change in the ratio of the increment of heat taken in the absolute temperature at which it is absorbed." But (as if intended to prove that not all progress is for the better) some older editions supply a more intelligible definition. "A measure of the unavailable energy in a thermodynamic system"—as we read in the 1948 edition—cannot satisfy the specialist but would do for general purposes. To explain (again in broad lines) what unavailable energy means is now a relatively simple task.

Energy exists in two qualitative states—*available* or *free* energy, over which man has almost complete command, and *unavailable* or *bound* energy, which man cannot possibly use. The chemical energy contained in a piece of coal is free energy because man can transform it into heat or, if he wants, into mechanical work. But the fantastic amount of heat-energy contained in the waters of the seas, for example, is bound energy. Ships sail on top of this energy, but to do so they need the free energy of some fuel or of the wind.

When a piece of coal is burned, its chemical energy is neither decreased nor increased. But the initial free energy has become so dissipated in the form of heat, smoke and ashes that man can no longer use it. It has been degraded into bound energy. Free energy means energy that displays a differential level, as exemplified most simply by the difference of temperatures between the inside and the outside of a boiler. Bound energy is, on the contrary, chaotically dissipated energy. This difference may be expressed in yet another way. Free energy implies some ordered structure, comparable with that of a store in which all meat is on one counter, vegetables on another, and so on. Bound energy is energy dissipated in disorder, like the same store after being struck by a tornado. This is why entropy is also defined as a measure of disorder. It fits the fact that a copper sheet represents a lower entropy than the copper ore from which it was produced.

The distinction between free and bound energy is certainly an anthropomorphic one. But this fact need not trouble a student of man, nay, even a student of matter in its simple form. Every element by which man seeks to get in mental contact with actuality can be but anthropomorphic. Only, the case of thermodynamics happens to be more striking. The point is that it was the economic distinction between things having an economic value and waste which prompted the thermodynamic distinction, not conversely. Indeed, the discipline of thermodynamics grew out of a memoir in which the French engineer Sadi Carnot (1824) studied for the first time the *economy* of heat engines. Thermodynamics thus began as a physics of economic value and has remained so in spite of the numerous subsequent contributions of a more abstract nature.

III

Thanks to Carnot's memoir, the elementary fact that heat moves by itself only from the hotter to the colder body acquired a place among the truths recognized by physics. Still more important was the consequent recognition of the additional truth that once the heat of a closed system has diffused itself so that the temperature has become uniform throughout the system, the movement of the heat cannot be reversed without external intervention. The ice cubes in a glass of water, once melted, will not form again by themselves. In general, the free heat-energy of a closed system continuously and irrevocably degrades itself into bound energy. The extension of this property from heat-energy to all other kinds of energy led to the second law of thermodynamics, alias the entropy law. This law states that the entropy (i.e., the amount of bound energy) of a closed system continuously increases or that the order of such a system steadily turns into disorder.

The reference to a closed system is crucial. Let us visualize a closed system, a room with an electric stove and a pail of water that has just been boiled. What the entropy law tells us is, first, that the heat of the boiled water will continuously dissipate into the system. Ultimately, the system will attain thermodynamic equilibrium—a state in which the temperature is uniform throughout (and all energy is bound). This applies to every kind of energy in a closed system. The free chemical energy of a piece of coal, for instance, will ultimately become degraded into bound energy even if the coal is left in the ground. Free energy will do so in any case.

The law also tells us that once thermodynamic equilibrium is reached, the water will not start boiling by itself.[11] But, as everyone knows, we can make it boil again by turning on the stove. This does not mean, however, that we have defeated the entropy law. If the entropy of the room has been decreased as the result of the temperature differential created by boiling the water, it is only because some low entropy (free energy) was brought into the system from the outside. And if we include the electric plant in the system, the entropy of this new system must have decreased, as the entropy law states. This means that the decrease in the entropy of the room has been obtained only at the cost of a greater increase in entropy elsewhere.

Some writers, impressed by the fact that living organisms remain almost unchanged over short periods of time, have set forth the idea that life eludes the entropy law. Now, life may have properties that cannot be accounted for by the natural laws, but the mere thought that it may violate some law of matter (which is an entirely different thing) is sheer nonsense. The truth is that every living organism strives only to maintain its own entropy constant. To the extent to which it achieves this, it does so by sucking low entropy from the environment to compensate for the increase in entropy to which, like every material structure, the organism is continuously subject. But the entropy of the entire system—consisting of the organism and its environment—must increase. Actually, the entropy of a system must increase faster if life is present than if it is absent. The fact that any living organism fights the entropic degradation of its own material structure may be a characteristic property of life, not accountable by material laws, but it does not constitute a violation of these laws.

Practically all organisms live on low entropy in the form found immediately in the environment. Man is the most striking exception: he cooks most of his food and also transforms natural resources into mechanical work or into various objects of utility. Here again, we should not let ourselves be misled. The entropy of copper metal is lower than the entropy of the ore from which it was refined, but this does not mean that man's *economic* activity eludes the entropy law. The refining of the ore causes a more than compensating increase in the entropy of the surroundings. Economists are fond of saying that we cannot get something for nothing. The entropy law teaches us that the rule of biological life and, in man's case, of its economic continuation is far harsher. In entropy terms, the cost of any biological or economic enterprise is always greater than the product. In entropy terms, any such activity necessarily results in a deficit.

IV

The statement made earlier—that, from a purely physical viewpoint, the economic process only transforms valuable natural resources (low entropy) into waste (high entropy)—is thus completely vindicated. But the puzzle of why such a process should go on is still with us. And it will remain a puzzle as long as we do not see that the true economic output of the economic process is not a material flow of waste, but an immaterial flux: the enjoyment of life. If we do not recognize the existence of this flux, we are not in the economic world. Nor do we have a complete picture of the economic process if we ignore the fact that this flux—which, as an entropic feeling, must characterize life at all levels—exists only as long as it can continuously feed itself on environmental low entropy. And if we go one step further, we discover that every object of economic value—be it a fruit just picked from a tree, or a piece of clothing, or furniture, etc.—has a highly ordered structure, hence, a low entropy.[12]

There are several lessons to be derived from this analysis. The first lesson is that man's economic struggle centers on environmental low entropy. Second, environmental low entropy is scarce in a different sense than Ricardian land. Both Ricardian land and the coal deposits are available in limited amounts. The difference is that a piece of coal can be used only once. And, in fact, the entropy law is the reason why an engine (even a biological organism) ultimately wears out and must be replaced by a *new* one, which means an additional tapping of environmental low entropy.

Man's continuous tapping of natural resources is not an activity that makes no history. On the contrary, it is the most important long-run element of mankind's fate. It is because of the irrevocability of the entropic degradation of matter-energy that, for instance, the peoples from the Asian steppes, whose economy was based on sheep-raising, began their Great Migration over the entire European continent at the beginning of the first millennium. The same element—the pressure on natural resources—had, no doubt, a role in other migrations, including that from Europe to the New World. The fantastic efforts made for reaching the moon may also reflect some vaguely felt hope of obtaining access to additional sources of low entropy. It is also because of the particular scarcity of environmental low entropy that ever since the dawn of history man has continuously sought to invent means for sifting low entropy better. In most (though not in all) of man's inventions one can definitely see a progessively better economy of low entropy.

Nothing could, therefore, be further from the truth than the notion that the economic process is an isolated, circular affair—as Marxist and standard analysis represent it. The economic process is solidly anchored to a material base which is subject to definite constraints. It is because of these constraints that the economic process has a unidirectional irrevocable evolution. In the economic world only money circulates back and forth between one economic sector and another (although, in truth, even the bullion slowly wears out and its stock must be continuously replenished from the mineral deposits). In retrospect it appears that the economists of both persuasions have succumbed to the worst economic fetishism—money fetishism.

V

Economic thought has always been influenced by the economic issues of the day. It also has reflected—with some lag—the trend of ideas in the natural sciences. A salient illustration of this correlation is the very fact that, when economists began ignoring the natural environment in representing the economic process, the event reflected a turning point in the temper of the entire scholarly world. The unprecedented achievements of the Industrial Revolution so amazed everyone with what man might do with the aid of machines that the general attention became confined to the factory. The landslide of spectacular scientific discoveries triggered by the new technical facilities strengthened this general awe for the power of technology. It also induced the literati to overestimate and, ultimately, to oversell to their audiences the powers of science. Naturally, from such a pedestal one could not even conceive that there is any real obstacle inherent in the human condition.

The sober truth is different. Even the lifespan of the human species represents just a blink when compared with that of a galaxy. So, even with progress in space travel, mankind will remain confined to a speck of space. Man's biological nature sets other limitations as to what he can do. Too high or too low a temperature is incompatible with his existence. And so are many radiations. It is not only that he cannot reach up to the stars, but he cannot even reach down to an individual elementary particle, nay, to an individual atom.

Precisely because man has felt, however unsophisticatedly, that his life depends on scarce, irretrievable low entropy, man has all along nourished the hope that he may eventually discover a self-perpetuating force. The discovery of electricity enticed many to believe that the hope was actually fulfilled. Following the strange marriage of thermodynamics with mechanics, some began seriously thinking about schemes to unbind bound energy.[13] The discovery of atomic energy spread another wave of sanguine hopes that, this time, we have truly gotten hold of a self-perpetuating power. The shortage of electricity which plagues New York and is gradually extending to other cities should suffice to sober us up. Both the nuclear theorists and the operators of atomic plants vouch that it all boils down to a problem of cost, which in the perspective of this paper means a problem of a balance sheet in entropy terms.

With natural scientists preaching that science can do away with all limitations felt by man and with the economists following suit in not relating the analysis of the economic process to the limitations of man's material environment, no wonder that no one realized that we cannot produce "better and bigger" refrigerators, automobiles, or jet planes, without producing also "better and bigger" waste. So, when everyone (in the countries with "better and bigger" industrial production) was, literally, hit in the face by pollution, scientists as well as economists were taken by surprise. But even now no one seems to see that the cause of all this is that we have failed to acknowledge the entropic nature of the economic process. A convincing proof is that the various authorities on pollution now to try to sell us, on the one hand, the idea of machines and chemical reactions that produce no waste, and, on the other, salvation through a perpetual recycling of waste. There is no denial that, in principle at least, we can recycle even the gold dispersed in the sand of the seas just as we can recycle the boiling water in my earlier example. But in both cases we must use an additional amount of low entropy much greater than the decrease in the entropy of what is recycled. There is no free recycling just as there is no wasteless industry.

VI

The globe to which the human species is bound floats, as it were, within the cosmic store of free energy, which may be even infinite. But for the reasons mentioned in the preceding section, man cannot have access to all this fantastic amount, nor to all possible forms of free energy. Man cannot, for example, tap directly the immense thermonuclear energy of the sun. The most important impediment (valid also for the industrial use of the "hydrogen bomb") is that no material container can resist the temperature of massive thermonuclear reactions. Such reactions can occur only in free space.

The free energy to which man can have access comes from two distinct sources. The first source is a *stock*, the stock of free energy of the mineral deposits in the bowels of the earth. The second source is a *flow*, the flow of solar radiation intercepted by the earth. Several differences between these two sources should be well marked. Man has almost complete command over the terrestrial dowry; conceivably, we may use it all within a single year. But, for all practical purposes, man has no control over the flow of solar radiation. Neither can he use the flow of the future *now*. Another asymmetry between the two sources pertains to their specific roles. Only the terrestrial source provides us with the low entropy materials from which we manufacture our most important implements. On the other hand, solar radiation is the primary source of all life on earth, which begins with chlorophyll photosynthesis. Finally, the terrestrial stock is a paltry source in comparison with that of the sun. In all probability, the active life of the sun—during which the earth will receive a flow of solar energy of significant intensity—will last another five billion years.[14] But hard to believe though it may be, the entire terrestrial stock could only yield a few days of sunlight.[15]

All this casts a new light on the population problem, which is so topical today. Some students are alarmed at the possibility that the world population will reach seven billion by 2000 A.D.—the level predicted by United Nations demographers. On the other side of the fence, there are those who, like Colin Clark, claim that with a proper administration of resources the earth may feed as many as forty-five billion people.[16] Yet no population expert seems to have raised the far more vital question for mankind's future: How long can a given world population—be it of one billion or of forty-five billion—be maintained? Only if we raise this question can we see how complicated the population problem is. Even the analytical concept of optimum population, on which many population studies have been erected, emerges as an inept fiction.

What has happened to man's entropic struggle over the last two hundred years is a telling story in this respect. On the one hand, thanks to the spectacular progress of science man has achieved an almost miraculous level of economic development. On the other hand, this development has forced man to push his tapping of terrestrial sources to a staggering degree (witness offshore oil-drilling). It has also sustained a population growth which has accentuated the struggle for food and, in some areas, brought this pressure to critical levels. The solution, advocated unanimously, is an increased mechanization of agriculture. But let us see what this solution means in terms of entropy.

In the first place, by eliminating the traditional partner of the farmer—the draft animal—the mechanization of agriculture allows the entire land area to be allocated to the production of food (and to fodder only to the extent of the need for meat). But the ultimate and the most important result is a shift of the low entropy input from the solar to the terrestrial source. The ox or the water buffalo—which derive their mechanical power from the solar radiation caught by chlorophyll photosynthesis—is replaced by the tractor—which is produced and operated with the aid of terrestrial low entropy. And the same goes for the shift from manure to artificial fertilizers. The upshot is that the mechanization of agriculture is a solution which, though inevitable in the present impasse, is antieconomical in the long run. Man's biological existence is made to depend in the future more and more upon the scarcer of the two sources of low entropy. There is also the risk that mechanized agriculture may trap the human species in a cul-de-sac because of the possibility that some of the biological species involved in the other method of farming will be forced into extinction.

Actually, the problem of the economic use of the terrestrial stock of low entropy is not limited to the mechanization of agriculture only: it is the main problem for the fate of the human species. To see this, let S denote the present stock of terrestrial low entropy and let r be some average annual amount of depletion. If we abstract (as we can safely do here) from the slow degradation of S, the *theoretical* maximum number of years until the complete exhaustion of that stock is S/r. This is also the number of years until the *industrial* phase in the evolution of mankind will forcibly come to its end. Given the fantastic disproportion between S and the flow of solar energy that reaches the globe annually, it is beyond question that, even with a very parsimonious use of S, the industrial phase of man's evolution will end long before the sun will cease to shine. What will happen then (if the extinction of the human species is not brought about earlier by some totally resistant bug or some insidious chemical) is hard to say. Man could continue to live by reverting to the stage of a berry-picking species—as he once was. But, in the light of what we know about evolution, such an evolutionary reversal does not seem probable. Be that as it may, the fact remains that the higher the degree of economic development, the greater must be the annual depletion r and, hence, the shorter becomes the expected life of the human species.

VII

The upshot is clear. Every time we produce a Cadillac, we irrevocably destroy an amount of low entropy that could otherwise be used for producing a plow or a spade. In other words, every time we produce a Cadillac, we do it at the cost of decreasing the number of human lives in the future. Economic development through industrial abundance may be a blessing for us now and for those who will be able to enjoy it in the near future, but it is definitely against the interest of the human species as a whole, if its interest is to have a lifespan as long as is compatible with its dowry of low entropy. In this paradox of economic development we can see the price man has to pay for the unique privilege of being able to go beyond the biological limits in his struggle for life.

Biologists are fond of repeating that natural selection is a series of fantastic blunders since future conditions are not taken into account. The remark, which implies that man is wiser than nature and should take over her job, proves that man's vanity and the scholar's self-confidence will never know their limits. For the race of economic development that is the hallmark of modern civilization leaves no doubt about man's lack of foresight. It is only because of his biological nature (his inherited instincts) that man cares for the fate of only some of his immediate descendants, generally not beyond his great-grandchildren. And there is neither cynicism nor pessimism in believing that, even if made aware of the entropic problem of the human species, mankind would not be willing to give up its present luxuries in order to ease the life of those humans who will live ten thousand or even one thousand years from now. Once man expanded his biological powers by means of industrial artifacts, he became *ipso facto* not only dependent on a very scarce source of life support but also addicted to industrial luxuries. It is as if the human species were determined to have a short but exciting life. Let the less ambitious species have a long but uneventful existence.

Issues such as those discussed in these pages pertain to long-run forces. Because these forces act extremely slowly we are apt to ignore their existence or, if we recognize them, to belittle their importance. Man's nature is such that he is always interested in what will happen until tomorrow, not in thousands of years from now. Yet it is the slow-acting forces that are the more fateful in general. Most people die not because of some quickly acting force—such as a pneumonia or an automobile accident—but because of the slow-acting forces that cause aging. As a Jain philospher remarked, man begins to die at birth. The point is that it would not be hazardous to venture some thoughts about the distant future of man's economy any more than it would be to predict in broad lines the life of a newly born child. One such thought is that the increased pressure on the stock of mineral resources created by the modern fever of industrial development, together with the mounting problem of making pollution less noxious (which places additional demands on the same stock), will necessarily concentrate man's attention on ways to make greater use of solar radiation, the more abundant source of free energy.

Some scientists now proudly claim that the food problem is on the verge of being completely solved by the imminent conversion on an industrial scale of mineral oil into food protein—an inept thought in view of what we know about the entropic problem. The logic of this problem justifies instead the prediction that, under the pressure of necessity, man will ultimately turn to the contrary conversion, of vegetable products into gasoline (if he will still have any use for it).[17] We may also be quasi-certain that, under the same pressure, man will discover means by which to transform solar radiation into motor power directly. Certainly, such a discovery will represent the greatest possible breakthrough for man's entropic problem, for it will bring under his command also the more abundant source of life support. Recycling and pollution purification would still consume low entropy, but not from the rapidly exhaustible stock of our globe.

NOTES AND REFERENCES

1. W. Stanley Jevons, *The Theory of Political Economy* (4th edn., London, 1924), p. 21.
2. For examples, R. T. Bye, *Principles of Economics* (5th edn., New York, 1956), p. 253; G. L. Bach, *Economics* (2nd edn., Englewood Cliffs, N. J., 1957), p. 60; J. H. Dodd, C. W. Hasek, T. J. Hailstones, *Economics* (Cincinnati, 1957), p. 125; R. M. Havens, J. S. Henderson, D. L. Cramer, *Economics* (New York, 1966), p. 49; Paul A. Samuelson, *Economics* (8th edn., New York, 1970), p. 42.
3. Karl Marx, *Capital* (3 vols., Chicago, 1906–1933), I, 94, 199, 230, and *passim.*
4. *Ibid.*, II, ch. XX.
5. *The Economic Writings of Sir William Petty*, ed. C. H. Hull (2 vols., Cambridge, Eng., 1899), II, 377. Curiously, Marx went along with Petty's idea; but he claimed that nature only "helps to create use-value without contributing to the formation of exchange value." Karl Marx, *Capital*, I, 227. See also *ibid.*, p. 94.
6. For example, Alfred Marshall, *Principles of Economics* (8th edn., New York, 1924), p. 63.
7. On the problem of the analytical representation of a process, see N. Georgescu-Roegen, *The Entropy Law and the Economic Process* (Cambridge, Mass., 1971), pp. 211-231.
8. This distinction together with the fact that no one would exchange some natural resources for waste disposes of Marx's assertion that "no chemist has ever discovered exchange value in a pearl or a diamond." Karl Marx, *Capital*, I, 95.

9. D. ter Harr, "The Quantum Nature of Matter and Radiation," in *Turning Points in Physics*, ed. R. J. Blin-Stoyle *et al.* (Amsterdam, 1959), p. 37.
10. One meaning that has recently made the term extremely popular is "the amount of information." For an argument that this term is misleading and for a critique of the alleged connection between information and physical entropy, see N. Georgescu-Roegen, *The Entropy Law and the Economic Process*, Appendix B.
11. This position calls for some technical elaboration. The opposition between the entropy law—with its unidirectional qualitative change—and mechanics—where everything can move either forward or backward while remaining self-identical—is accepted without reservation by every physicist and philosopher of science. However, the mechanistic dogma retained (as it still does) its grip on scientific activity even after physics recanted it. The result was that mechanics was soon brought into thermodynamics in the company of randomness. This is the strangest possible company, for randomness is the very antithesis of the deterministic nature of the laws of mechanics. To be sure, the new edifice (known as statistical mechanics) could not include mechanics under its roof and, at the same time, exclude reversibility. So, statistical mechanics must teach that a pail of water may start boiling by itself, a thought which is slipped under the rug by the argument that the miracle has not been observed because of its extremely small probability. This position has fostered the belief in the possibility of converting bound into free energy or, as P. W. Bridgman wittily put it, of bootlegging entropy. For a critique of the logical fallacies of statistical mechanics and of the various attempts to patch them, see N. Georgescu-Roegen, *The Entropy Law and the Economic Process*, ch. VI.
12. This does not mean that everything of low entropy necessarily has economic value. Poisonous mushrooms, too, have a low entropy. The relation between low entropy and economic value is similar to that between economic value and price. An object can have a price only if it has economic value, and it can have economic value only if its entropy is low. But the converse is not true.
13. See note 11, above.
14. George Gamow, *Matter, Earth, and Sky* (Englewood Cliffs, N. J., 1958), pp. 493 f.
15. Four days, according to Eugene Ayres, "Power from the Sun," *Scientific American*, August 1950, p. 16. The situation is not changed even if we admit that the calculations might be in error by as much as one thousand times.
16. Colin Clark, "Agricultural Productivity in Relation to Population," in *Man and His Future*, ed. G. Wolstenholme (Boston, 1963), p. 35.
17. That the idea is not far-fetched is proved by the fact that in Sweden, during World War II, automobiles were driven by the poor gas obtained by heating wood with wood.

2

MINERAL RESOURCES IN FACT AND FANCY

Preston Cloud

Optimism and imagination are happy human traits. They often make bad situations appear tolerable or even good. Man's ability to imagine solutions, however, commonly outruns his ability to find them. What does he do when it becomes clear that he is plundering, overpopulating, and despoiling his planet at such a horrendous rate that it is going to take some kind of a big leap, and soon, to avert irreversible degradation?

The inventive genius of man has got him out of trouble in the past. Why not now? Why be a spoil-sport when brilliant, articulate, and well-intentioned men assure us that all we need is more technology? Why? Because the present crisis is exacerbated by four conditions that reinforce each other in a very undesirable manner: (1) the achievements of medical technology which have brought on the run-away imbalance between birth and death rates; (2) the hypnotic but unsustainable national dream of an ever-increasing real Gross National Product based on obsolescence and waste; (3) the finite nature of the earth and particularly its accessible

"Mineral Resources in Fact and Fancy" was originally published in *Environment: Resources, Pollution and Society*, William W. Murdoch, ed. Sinauer Associates, Inc. 1971. Reprinted by permission of the publisher.

mineralized crust; and (4) the increased risk of irreversible spoilation of the environment which accompanies overpopulation, overproduction, waste, and the movement of ever-larger quantities of source rock for ever-smaller proportions of useful minerals.

Granted the advantages of big technological leaps, therefore, provided they are in the right direction, I see real hope for permanent long-range solutions to our problems as beginning with the taking of long-range views of them. Put in another way, we should not tackle vast problems with half-vast concepts. We must build a platform of scientific and social comprehension, while concurrently endeavoring to fill the rut of ignorance, selfishness, and complacency with knowledge, restraint, and demanding awareness on the part of an enlightened electorate. And we must not be satisfied merely with getting the United States or North America through the immediate future, critical though that will be. We must consider what effects current and proposed trends and actions will have on the world as a whole for several generations hence, and how we can best influence those trends favorably the world over. Above all, we must consider how to preserve for the yet unborn the maximum flexibility of choices consistent with meeting current and future crises.

NATURE AND GEOGRAPHY OF RESOURCES

Man's concept of resources, to be sure, depends on his needs and wants, and thus to a great degree on his locale and place in history, on what others have, and on what he knows about what they have and what might be possible for him to obtain. Food and fiber from the land, and food and drink from the waters of the earth have always been indispensable resources. So have the human beings who have utilized these resources and created demands for others—from birch bark to beryllium, from buffalo hides to steel and plastic. It is these other resources, the ones from which our industrial society has been created, to which my remarks are directed. I refer, in particular, to the nonrenewable or wasting resources—mineral fuels which are converted into energy plus carbon, nuclear fuels, and the metals, chemicals, and industrial materials of geological origin which to some extent can be and even are recycled but which tend to become dispersed and wasted.

All such resources, except those that are common rocks whose availability and value depend almost entirely on economic factors plus fabrication, share certain peculiarities that transcend economics and limit technology and even diplomacy. They occur in local concentrations that may exceed their crustal abundances by thousands of times, and particular resources tend to be clustered within geochemical or metallogenic provinces from which others are excluded. Some parts of the earth are rich in mineral raw materials and others are poor.

No part of the earth, not even on a continent-wide basis, is self-sufficient in all critical metals. North America is relatively rich in molybdenum and poor in tin, tungsten, and manganese, for instance, whereas Asia is comparatively rich in tin, tungsten, and manganese and, apparently, less well supplied with molybdenum. The great bulk of the world's gold appears to be in South Africa, which has relatively little silver but a good supply of platinum. Cuba and New Caledonia have well over half the world's total known reserves of nickel. The main known reserves of cobalt are in the Congo Republic, Cuba, New Caledonia, and parts of Asia. Most of the world's mercury is in Spain, Italy, and parts of the Sino-Soviet bloc. Industrial diamonds are still supplied mainly by the Congo.

Consider tin. Over half the world's currently recoverable reserves are in Indonesia, Malaya, and Thailand, and much of the rest is in Bolivia and the Congo. Known North American reserves are negligible. For the United States loss of access to extracontinental sources of tin is not likely to be offset by economic factors or technological changes that would permit an increase in potential North American production, even if present production could be increased by an order of magnitude. It is equally obvious that other peculiarities in the geographical distribution of the world's geological resources will continue to encourage interest both in trading with some ideologically remote nations and in seeking alternative sources of supply.

RECOVERABLE MINERAL RESERVES

Consider now some aspects of the apparent lifetimes of estimated recoverable reserves of a selection of critical mineral resources and the position of the United States with regard to some of these. The selected resources are those for which suitable data are available.

Figure 1 shows such lifetimes for different groups of metals and mineral fuels at current minable grades and rates of consumption. No allowance is made for increase of populations, or for increased rates of consumption which, in the United States, tend to increase at twice the rate of population growth. Nor is allowance made for additions to reserves that will result from discovery of submarine deposits, use of submarginal grades, or imports—which may reduce but will not eliminate the impact of growth factors. Data are updated from the U.S. Bureau of Mines compendia *Mineral Facts and Problems* and its *Minerals Year-*

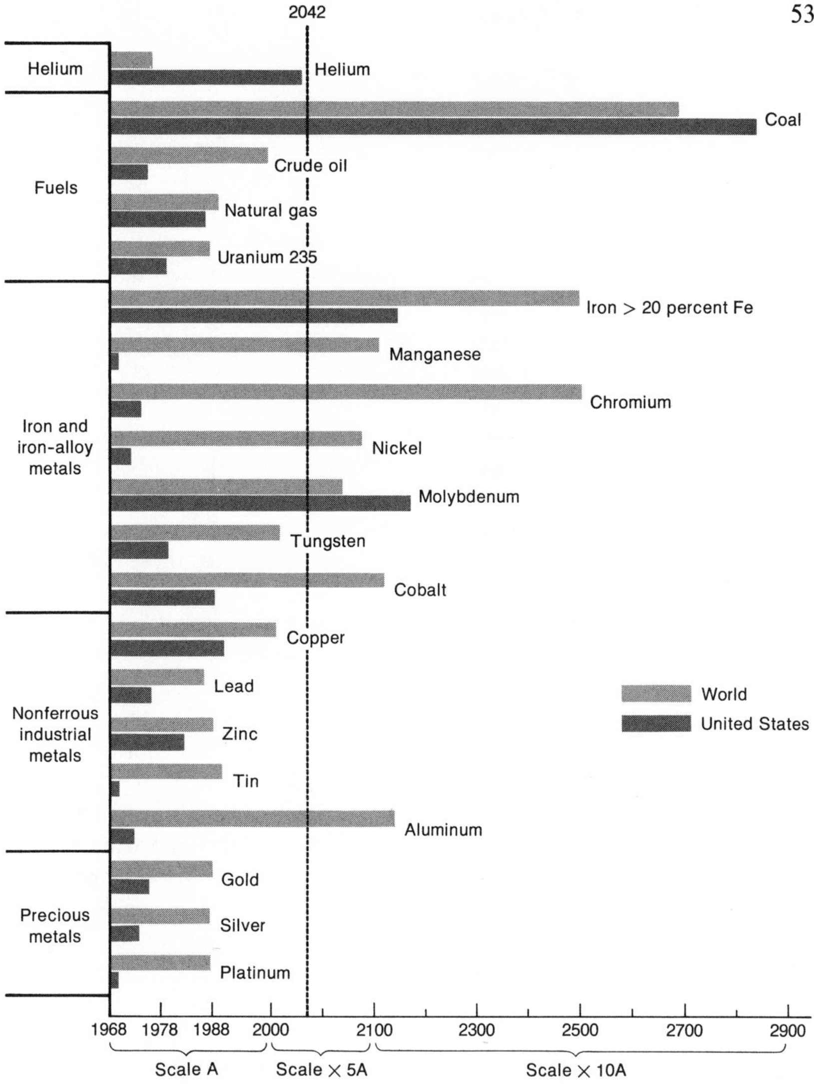

FIGURE 1.
Mineral reserve lifetimes. Apparent lifetimes of known recoverable reserves of twenty mineral commodities at currently minable grades and existing rates of consumption. (Except for helium, whose lifetime is estimated from U.S. Bureau of Mines data on reserves, conservation practices, and expected increases in demand.) Such lifetimes tend to increase with new discoveries and technological advances and to decrease with increasing population and per capita consumption rates, but resources to left of vertical dashed line are in obvious danger of depletion.

books, as summarized by Flawn.[1] The light bars represent lifetimes of world reserves for a stable population of roughly 3.5×10^9 at current rates of use. The heavy bars represent similar data for a United States population of about 200 million. Actual availability of some such commodities to the United States will, of course, be extended by imports from abroad, just as that of others will be reduced by population growth, increased per capita demands, and perhaps by political changes. The dashed vertical line represents the year 2042. This is chosen as a reference line because it marks that point in the future which is just as distant from the present as the invention of the airplane and the discovery of radioactivity are in the past.

The prospect is hardly conducive to unrestrained optimism. Of the commodities considered some are in very short supply. Only eleven for the world and four for the United States persist beyond the turn of the century; and only eight for the world and three for the United States extend beyond 2042. I do not suggest that we equate these lines with revealed truth. Time will prove some too short and others perhaps too long. New reserves will be found, lower-grade reserves will become minable for economic or technological reasons, substitutes will be discovered or synthesized, and some critical materials can be conserved by waste control and recycling. The crucial questions are: (1) How do we reduce these generalities to specifics? (2) Can we do so fast enough to sustain current rates of consumption? (3) Can we increase and sustain production of industrial materials at a rate sufficient to meet the rising expectations of a world population of three-and-a-half billion, growing with a doubling time of about thirty to thirty-five years, and for how long? (4) If the answer to the last question is no, what then?

A more local way of viewing the situation is to compare the position of the United States or North America with other parts of the world. Figures 2 to 4 show such a comparison for sixteen commodities with our favorite measuring stick, the USSR plus China. Figure 2 shows the more cheerful side of the coin. The United States is a bit ahead in petroleum, lignite, and phosphate, and neither we nor Asia have much chromium—known reserves are practically all in South Africa and Rhodesia. Figure 3, however, shows the USSR plus China to have a big lead in zinc, mercury, potash, and bauxite. And Figure 4 shows similar leads in tungsten, copper, iron, and coal.

Again there are brighter aspects to the generally unfavorable picture. Ample local low-grade sources of alumina other than bauxite are available with metallurgical advances and at a price. The U.S. coal supply is not in danger of immediate shortage. Potassium can be extracted from sea water. And much of the world's iron is in friendly hands, including

---

1. References and suggestions for further reading will be found on page 74–75.

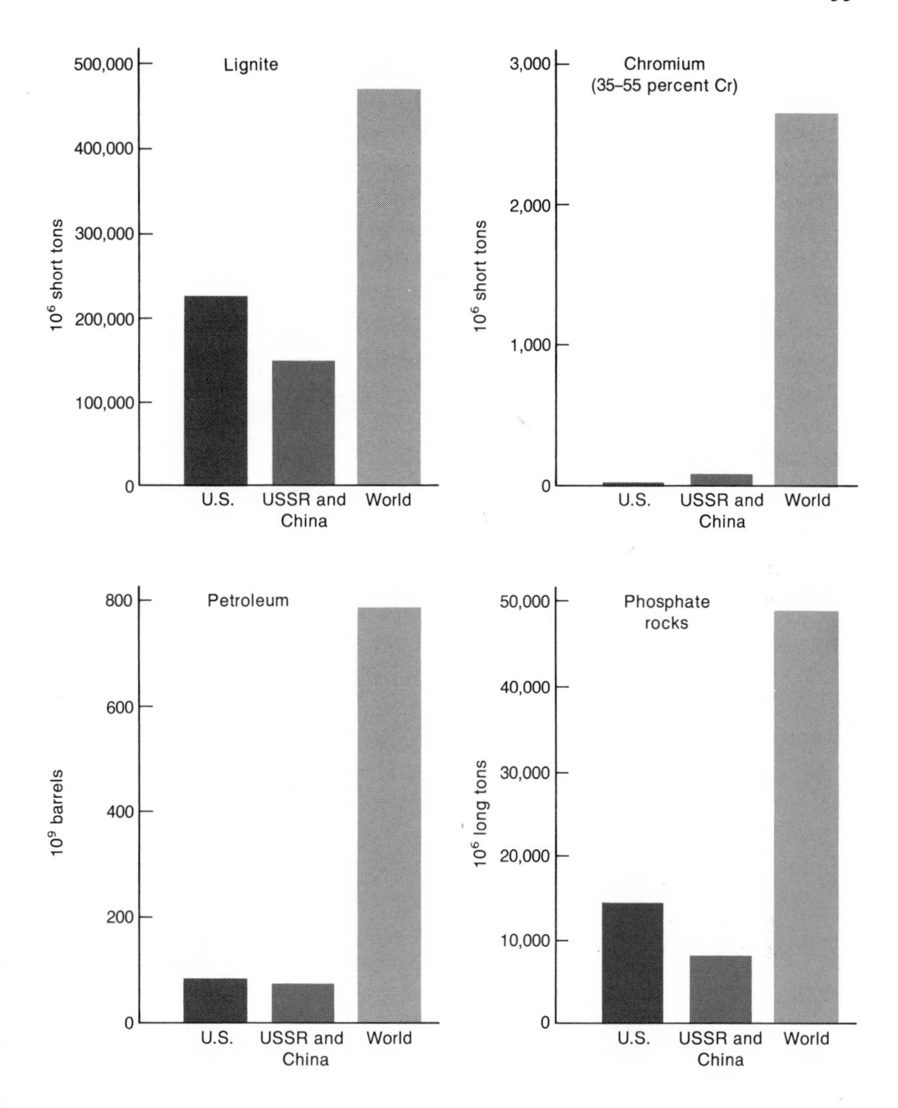

FIGURE 2.
Distribution of recoverable mineral resources. Estimated recoverable reserves of minerals (above sea level) for which U.S. reserve estimates exceed, equal, or fall only slightly below those of the USSR plus Mainland China. [Source: Data on lignite, chromium, phosphate from Flawn, *Mineral Resources* (see reference 1), on petroleum from M. K. Hubbert, *Resources and Man* (see reference 7).]

those of our good neighbor Canada and our more distant friend Australia.

No completely safe source is visible, however, for mercury, tungsten, and chromium. Lead, tin, zinc, and the precious metals appear to be in short supply throughout the world. And petroleum and natural gas will be exhausted or nearly so within the lifetimes of many of those alive today

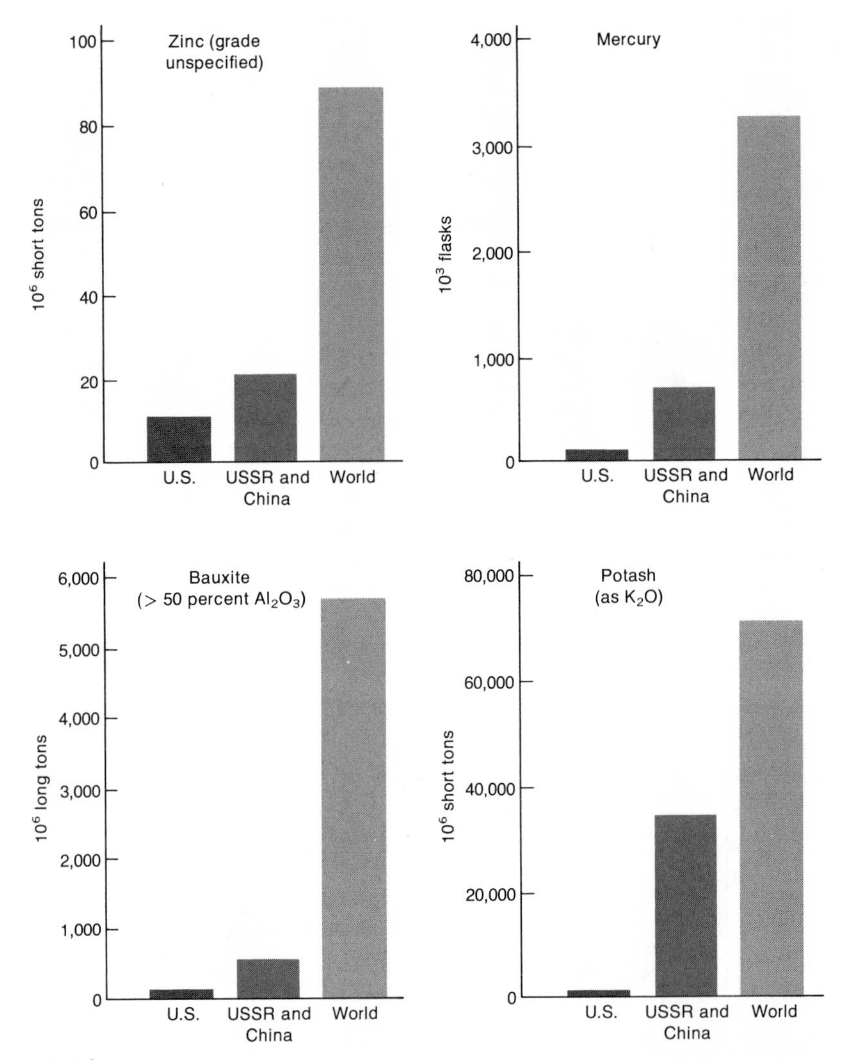

FIGURE 3.
Distribution of recoverable mineral resources. Estimated recoverable reserves of four minerals (above sea level) for which U.S. reserve estimates are less than those of the USSR plus Mainland China. [Source: Flawn, *Mineral Resources*.]

unless we decide to conserve them for petrochemicals and plastics. Even the extraction of liquid fuels from oil shales and "tar sands," or by hydrogenation of coal, will not meet energy requirements over the long term. If they were called upon to supply all the liquid fuels and other products now produced by the fractionation of petroleum, for instance, the sug-

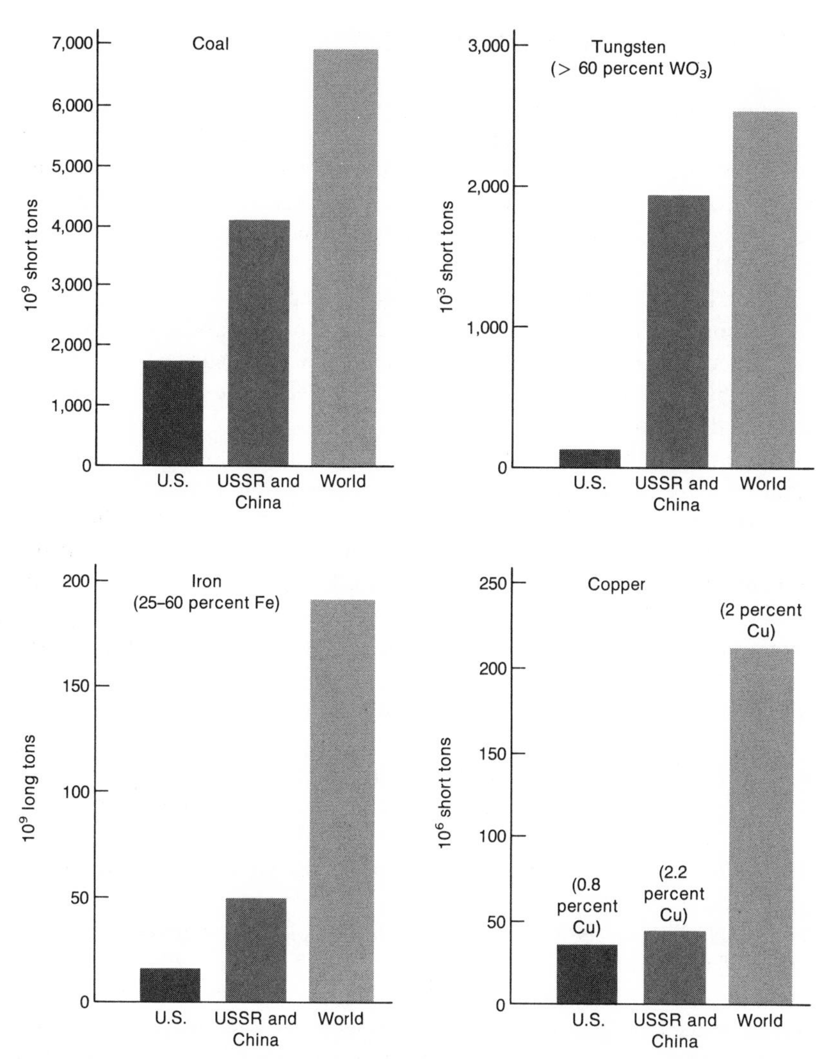

FIGURE 4.
Distribution of recoverable mineral resources. Estimated recoverable reserves of four additional minerals (above sea level) for which U.S. reserve estimates are less than those of the USSR plus Mainland China. [Source: Data on iron, tungsten, and copper from Flawn, *Mineral Resources*, on coal from Paul Averitt, 1969, *U.S. Geological Survey Bull.* 1275.]

gested lifetime for coal, the reserves of which are probably the most accurately known of all mineral products, would be drastically reduced below that indicated in Figure 1—and such a shift will be needed to a yet unknown degree before the end of the century.

THE CORNUCOPIAN PREMISES

In view of these alarming prospects, why do intelligent men of good faith seem to assure us that there is nothing to be alarmed about? It can only be because they visualize a completely nongeological solution to the problem, or because they take a very short-range view of it, or because they are compulsive optimists or are misinformed, or some combination of these things.

Let me first consider some of the basic concepts that might give rise to a cornucopian view of the earth's mineral resources and the difficulties that impede their unreserved acceptance. Then I will suggest some steps that might be taken to minimize the risks or slow the rates of mineral-resource depletion.

The central dilemma of all cornucopian premises is, of course, how to sustain an exponential increase of anything—people, mineral products, industrialization, or solid currency—on a finite resource base. This is, as everyone must realize, obviously impossible in the long run and will become increasingly difficult in the short run. For great though the mass of the earth is, well under 0.1 percent of that mass is accessible to us by any imaginable means (the entire crust is only about 0.4 percent of the total mass of the earth) and this relatively minute accessible fraction, as we have seen and shall see, is very unequally mineralized.

But the cornucopians are not naive or mischievous people. On what grounds do they deny the restraints and belittle the difficulties?

The six main premises from which their conclusions follow are:

Premise I. The promise of essentially inexhaustible cheap useful energy from nuclear sources.

Premise II. The thesis that economics is the sole factor governing availability of useful minerals and metals.

Premise III. The fallacy of essentially uninterrupted variation from ore of a metal to its average crustal abundance, which is inherent in Premise II; and from which emanates the strange and misleading notion that quantity of a resource available is essentially an inverse exponential function of its concentration.

Premise IV. The crucial assumption of population control, without which there can be no future worth living for most of the world (or, worse, the belief that quanitity of people is of itself the ultimate good, which, astounding as it may seem, is still held by a few people who ought to know better).[2]

Premise V. The concept of the "technological fix."

Premise VI. The naive and unsupported faith that if all else fails the sea will supply our needs.

Now these are appealing premises, several of which contain large elements of both truth and hope. Why do I protest their unreserved acceptance? I protest because, in addition to elements of truth, they also contain assumptions that are gross oversimplifications, outright errors, or are not demonstrated. I warn because their uncritical acceptance contributes to a dangerous complacency toward problems that will not be solved by a few brilliant technological breakthroughs, a wider acceptance of deficit economy, or fallout of genius from unlimited expansion of population. They will be solved only by intensive, wide-ranging, and persistent scientific and engineering investigation, supported by new social patterns and wise legislation.

I will discuss these premises in the order cited.

Premise I

The concept of essentially inexhaustible cheap useful energy from nuclear sources offers by all odds the most promising prospect of sweeping changes in the mineral resource picture.[3] We may be on the verge of developing a workable breeder reactor just in time to sustain an energy-hungry world facing the imminent exhaustion of traditional energy sources. Such a development, it has been persuasively stated, will also banish many problems of environmental pollution and open up unlimited reserves of metals in common crustal rocks. There are, unhappily, some flaws in this delightful picture, of which it is important to be aware.

Uranium 235 is the only naturally occurring spontaneously fissionable source of nuclear power. When a critical mass of uranium is brought together, the interchange of neutrons back and forth generates heat and continues to do so as long as the ^{235}U lasts. In the breeder reactor some of the free neutrons kick common ^{235}U over to plutonium 239, which is fissionable and produces more neutrons, yielding heat and accelerating the breeder reaction. Even in existing reactors some breeding takes place, and, if a complete breeding system could be produced, the amount of energy available from uranium alone would be increased about 140-fold. If thorium also can be made to breed, energy generated could be increased about 400-fold over that now attainable. This would extend the lifetime of visible energy resources at demands anticipated by 1980 by perhaps 1000 to 3000 years and gain time to work on contained nuclear fusion.

The problem is that it will require about 275,000 short tons of \$6.00 to \$10.00 per pound uranium oxide (U_3O_8) (not ore, not uranium) to fuel reactors now on order to 1980, plus another 400,000 tons to sustain them until the turn of the century, burning only ^{235}U with currently available enrichments from slow breeding. Only about 310,000 of the 675,000 tons of uranium needed is known to be available at this price, although known geologic conditions indicate the possibility of another 350,000 tons. Thus we now appear to be somewhat short of the U_3O_8 needed to produce the hoped-for 150,000 megawatts of nuclear energy on a sustained basis from 1985 until the end of the century without a functioning breeder reactor. Unless we find more uranium, or pay more money for it, or get a functioning complete breeder reactor or contained nuclear fusion within ten or fifteen years, the energy picture will be far from bright, especially in view of the fact that other nations from whom we might purchase uranium are eager to develop their own nuclear energy plants. There is good reason to hope that the breeder will come, and after it, contained fusion, *if* the ^{235}U holds out—but there is no room for complacency.

If and when the breeder reactor or contained fusion does become available as a practicable energy source, however, how will this help with mineral resources? It is clear immediately that it will take pressure off the fossil fuels so that it will become feasible, and should become the law, to reserve them for petrochemicals, plastics, essential liquid propellants, and other special purposes not served by nuclear fuels. It is also clear that cheap massive transportation, or direct transmittal of large quantities of cheap electric power to, or its generation at, distant sources will bring the mineral resources of remote sites to the market place—either as bulk ore for processing or as the refined or partially refined product.

What is not clear is how this very cheap energy will bring about the extraction of thinly dispersed metals in large quantity from common rock. The task is very different from the recovery of liquid fuels or natural gas by nuclear fracturing. The procedure usually suggested is the breakup of rock in place at depth with a nuclear blast, followed by hydrometallurgical or chemical mining. The problems, however, are great. Complexing solutions in large quantity, also from natural resources, must be brought into contact with the particles desired. This means that the enclosing rock must be fractured to that particle size. Then other substances, unsought, may use up and dissipate valuable reagents. Or the solvent reagents may escape to ground waters and become contaminants. Underground electrolysis is no more promising in dealing with very low concentrations. And the bacteria that catalyze reactions of metallurgical interest are all aerobic, so that, in addition to having access to the particles of interest, they must also be provided with a source of oxygen underground if they are to work there.

Indeed the energy used in breaking rock for the removal of metals is not now a large fraction of mining cost in comparison with that of labor and capital. The big expense is in equipping and utilizing manpower, and, although cheap energy will certainly reduce manpower requirements, it will probably never adequately substitute for the intelligent man with the pick at the mining face in dealing with vein and many replacement deposits, where the sought-after materials are irregularly concentrated in limited spaces. There are also limits to the feasible depths of open-pit mining, which would be by all odds the best way to mine common rock. Few open-pit mines now reach much below about 1500 feet. It is unlikely that such depths can be increased by as much as an order of magnitude. Moreover, the quantity of rock removable decreases exponentially with depth because pit circumference must decrease downward to maintain stable walls.

It may also not be widely realized by nongeologists that many types of ore bodies have definite floors or pinch-out downward, so that extending exploitative operations to depth gains no increase in ore produced. Even where mineralization does extend to depth, of course, exploitability is ultimately limited by temperature and rock failure.

Then there is the problem of reducing radioactivity so that ores can be handled and the refined product utilized without harm—not to mention heat dispersal (which in some but not all situations could itself be a resource) and the disposal of waste rock and spent reagents.

Altogether the problems are sufficiently formidable that it would be foolhardy to accept them as resolved in advance of a working efficient breeder reactor plus a demonstration that either cheap electricity or nucear explosions will significantly facilitate the removal of metals from any common rock.

A pithy comment from Peter Flawn's book on *Mineral Resources*[4] is appropriate here. It is to the effect that "average rock will never be mined." It is the uncommon features of a rock that make it a candidate for mining! Even with a complete nuclear technology, sensible people will seek, by geological criteria, to choose and work first those rocks or ores that show the highest relative recoverable enrichments in the desired minerals.

The reality is that even the achievement of a breeder reactor offers no guarantee of unlimited mineral resources in the face of geologic limitations and expanding populations with increased per capita demands, even over the middle term. To assume such for the long term would be sheer folly.

Premise II

The thesis that economics is the sole, or at least the dominant, factor governing availability of useful minerals and metals is one of those vexing part-truths which has led to much seemingly fruitless discussion between economists and geologists. This proposition bears examination.

It seems to have its roots in that interesting economic index known as the Gross National Product (GNP). No one seems to have worked out exactly what proportion of the GNP is in some way attributable to the mineral resource base. It does, however, appear that the dollar value of the raw materials themselves is small compared to the total GNP, and that it has decreased proportionately over time to something like two percent of the present GNP. From this it is logically deduced that the GNP could, if necessary, absorb a severalfold increase in cost of raw materials. The gap in logic comes when this is confused with the notion that all that is necessary to obtain inexhaustible quantities of any substance is either to raise the price or to increase the volume of rock mined. In support of such a notion, of course, one can point to diamond, which in the richest deposit ever known occurred in a concentration of only 1 to 25 million, but which, nevertheless, has continued to be available. The flaw is not only that we cannot afford to pay the price of diamond for many substances, but also that no matter how much rock we mine we can't get diamonds out of it if there were none there in the first place.

Daniel Bell[5] comments on the distorted sense of relations that emerges from the cumulative nature of GNP accounting. Thus, when a mine is developed, the costs of the new facilities and payroll become additions to the GNP, whether the ore is sold at a profit or not. Should the mine wastes at the same time pollute a stream, the costs of cleaning up the stream or diverting the wastes also become additions to the GNP. Similarly if you hire someone to wash the dishes this adds to GNP, but if your wife does them it doesn't count.

From this it results that mineral raw materials and housework are not very impressive fractions of the GNP. What seems to get lost sight of is what a mess we would be in without either!

Assuming an indefinite extension of their curves and continuance of access to foreign markets, economists appear to be on reasonably sound grounds in postulating the relatively long-term availability of certain sedimentary, residual, and disseminated ores, such as those of iron, aluminum, and perhaps copper. What many of them do not appreciate is that the type of curve that can with some reason be applied to such deposits and metals is by no means universally applicable. This difficulty is aggravated by the fact that conventional economic indexes minimize the vitamin-like quality for the economy as a whole of the raw materials whose enhancement in value through beneficiation, fabrication, and exchange accounts for such a large part of the material assets of society.

In a world that wants to hear only good news some economists are perhaps working too hard to emancipate their calling from the epithet of "dismal science," but not all of them. One voice from the wilderness of hyperoptimism and over-consumption is that of Kenneth Boulding[6] who observes (as the reader will find on page 127 of this volume) that "the essential measure of the success of the economy is not production and consumption at all, but the nature, extent, quality, and complexity of the total capital stock, including in this the state of the human bodies and minds included in the system." Until this concept penetrates widely into the councils of government and the conscience of society, there will continue to be a wide gap between the economic aspects of national and industrial policy and the common good, and the intrinsic significance of raw materials will remain inadequately appreciated.

Economic geology, which in its best sense brings all other fields of geology to bear on resource problems, is concerned particularly with questions of how certain elements locally attain geochemical concentrations that greatly exceed their crustal abundance and with how this knowledge can be applied to the discovery of new deposits and the delineation of reserves. Economics and technology play equally important parts with geology itself in determining what deposits and grades it is practicable to exploit. Neither economics, nor technology, nor geology can make an ore deposit where the desired substance is absent or exists in insufficient quantity.

The reality is that economics per se, powerful though it can be when it has material resources to work with, is not all powerful. Indeed, without material resources to start with, no matter how small a fraction of the GNP they may represent, economics is of no consequence at all. The current orthodoxy of economic well-being through obsolescence, overconsumption, and waste will prove, in the long term, to be a cruel and a preposterous illusion.

Premise III

Premise III, the postulate of essentially uninterrupted variation from ore to average crustal abundance, is seldom if ever stated in that way, but it is inherent in Premise II. It could almost as well have been treated under Premise II; but it is such an important and interesting idea, whether true or false, that separate consideration is warranted.

If the postulated continuous variation were true for mineral resources in general, volume of "ore" (not metal) produced would be an exponential inverse function of grade mined, the handling of lower grades would be compensated for by the availability of larger quantities of elements sought, and reserve estimates would depend only on the accuracy with which average crustal abundances were known. Problems in extractive metallurgy, of course, are not considered in such an outlook.

This delightfully simple picture would supplant all other theories of ore deposits, invalidate the foundations of geochemistry, divest geology of much of its social relevance, and place the fate of the mineral industry squarely in the hands of economists and nuclear engineers.

Unfortunately this postulate is simply untrue in a practical sense for many critical minerals and is only crudely true, leaving out metallurgical problems, for particular metals, like iron and aluminum, whose patterns approach the predicted form.[7] Sharp discontinuities exist in the abundances of mercury, tin, nickel, molybdenum, tungsten, manganese, cobalt, diamond, the precious metals, and even such staples as lead and zinc, for example. But how many prophets of the future are concerned about where all the lead or cadmium will come from for all those electric automobiles that are supposed to solve the smog problem?

Helium is a good example of a critical substance in short supply. Although a gas which has surely at some places diffused in a continuous spectrum of concentrations, particular concentrations of interest as a source of supply appear from published information to vary in a stepwise manner. Here I draw mainly on data summarized by H. W. Lipper.[8] Although an uncommon substance, helium serves a variety of seemingly indispensable uses. A bit less than half of the helium now consumed in the United States is used in pressurizing liquid fueled missiles and space ships. Shielded-arc welding is the next largest use, followed closely by its use in producing controlled atmospheres for growing crystals for transistors, processing fuels for nuclear energy, and cooling vacuum pumps. Only about 5.5 percent of the helium consumed in the United States is now being used as a lifting gas. It plays an increasingly important role, however, as a coolant for nuclear reactors and a seemingly indispensable one in cryogenics and superconductivity. In the latter role, it could control the feasibility of massive long-distance transport of nuclear-generated electricity. High-helium low-oxygen breathing mixtures may well be critical to man's long-range success in attempting to operate at great depths in the exploration and exploitation of the sea. Other uses are in research, purging, leak detection, chromatography, and so on.

Helium thus appears to be a very critical element, as the Department of the Interior has recognized in establishing its helium-conservation program. What are the prospects that there will be enough helium in 2042?

The only presently utilized source of helium is in natural gas, where it occurs at a range of concentrations from as high as 8.2 percent by volume to zero. The range, however, in particular gas fields of significant volume, is apparently not continuous. Dropping below the one field (Pinta Dome) that shows an 8.2 percent concentration, we find a few small isolated fields (Mesa and Hogback, New Mexico) that contain about 5.5 percent helium, and then several large fields (for example, Hugoton and Texas Panhandle) with a range of 0.3 to 1.0 percent helium. Other large natural gas fields contain either no helium or show it only in quantities of less than 5 parts per 10,000. From the latter there is a long jump down to the atmosphere with a concentration of only 1 part per 200,000.

Present annual demand for helium is about 900 million cubic feet, with a projected increase in demand approaching 2 billion cubic feet annually by about 1990. It will be possible to meet such an accelerated demand for a limited time only as a result of Interior's current purchase and storage program, which will augment recovery from natural gas then being produced. As now foreseen, if increases in use do not outrun estimates, conservation and continued recovery of helium from natural gas reserves will meet needs to somewhat beyond the turn of the century. When known and expected discoveries of reserves of natural gas are exhausted, the only potential sources of new supply will be from the atmosphere, as small quantities of ^{3}He from nuclear reactor technology, or by synthesis from hydrogen—a process whose practical feasibility and adequacy remain to be established.

Spending even a lot more money to produce more helium from such sources under existing technology just may not be the best or even a very feasible way to deal with the problem. Interior's conservation program should be enlarged and extended, under compulsory legislation if necessary. New sources must be sought. Research into possible substitutions, recovery and reuse, synthesis, and extraction from the atmosphere must be accelerated—now while there is still time. And we must be prepared to curtail, if necessary, activities which waste the limited helium reserves. Natural resources are the priceless heritage of all the people, including those yet to be born; their waste cannot be tolerated.

Problems of the adequacy of reserves obtain for many other substances, especially under the escalating demands of rising populations and expectations, and it is becoming obvious to many geologists that time is running out. Dispersal of metals which could be recycled should be controlled. Unless industry and the public undertake to do this voluntarily, legislation should be generated to define permissible mixes of material and disposal of "junk" metal. Above all the wastefulness of war and preparation for it must be terminated if reasonable options for posterity are to be preserved.

The reality is that a healthy mineral resource industry, and therefore a healthy industrial economy, can be maintained only on a firm base of geologic knowledge, and geochemical and metallurgical understanding of the distribution and limits of metals, mineral fuels, and chemicals in the earth's crust and hydrosphere.

Premise IV

The assumption that world populations will soon attain and remain in a state of balance is central to all other premises. Without this the rising expectations of the poor are doomed to failure, and the affluent can remain affluent only by maintaining existing shameful discrepancies. Taking present age structures and life expectancies of world populations into account, it seems certain that, barring other forms of catastrophe, world population will reach six or seven billion by about the turn of the century, regardless of how rapidly family planning is accepted and practiced.

On the most optimistic assumptions, this is probably close to the maximum number of people the world can support on a reasonably sustained basis, even under strictly regularized conditions, at a general level of living roughly comparable to that now enjoyed in Western Europe. It would, of course, be far better to stabilize at a much smaller world population. In any case, much greater progress than is as yet visible must take place over much larger parts of the world before optimism on the prospects of voluntary global population control at any level can be justified. And even if world population did level off and remain balanced at about seven billion, it would probably take close to 100 years of intensive, enlightened, peaceful effort to lift all mankind to anywhere near the current level of Western Europe or even much above the level of chronic malnutrition and deprivation.

This is not to say that we must therefore be discouraged and withdraw to ineffectual diversions. Rather it is a challenge to focus with energy and realism on seeking a truly better life for all men living and yet unborn and on keeping the latter to the minimum. On the other hand, an uncritical optimism, just for the sake of that good feeling it creates, is a luxury the world cannot, at this juncture, afford.

A variation of outlook on the population problem which, surprisingly enough, exists among a few nonbiological scholars is that quantity of people is of itself a good thing. The misconception here seems to be that frequency of effective genius will increase, even exponentially, with increasing numbers of people and that there is some risk of breeding out to a merely high level of mediocrity in a stabilized population. The extremes of genius and idiocy, however, appear in about the same frequency at birth from truly heterogeneous gene pools regardless of size. What is unfortunate, among other things, about overly dense concentrations of people is that this leads not only to reduced likelihood of the identification of mature genius, but to drastic reductions in the development of potential genius, owing to malnutrition in the weaning years and early youth, accompanied by retardation of both physical and mental growth. If we are determined to turn our problems over to an elite corps of mental prodigies a more sure-fire method is at hand. Nuclear transplant from various adult tissue cells into fertilized ova whose own nuclei have been removed has already produced identical copies of amphibian nucleus-donors and can probably do the same in man.[9] Thus we appear to be on the verge of being able to make as many "xerox" copies as we want or need of any particular genius as long as we can get a piece of his or her nucleated tissue and find eggs and incubators for the genome aliquots to develop in. Female geniuses would be the best because (with a little help) they could copy themselves!

The reality is that without real population control and limitation of demand all else is drastically curtailed, not to say lost. And the prospect that such limitations may take place voluntarily is not bright. The most fundamental freedom should be the right not to be born into a world of want and smothering restriction. I am convinced that we must give up (or have taken away from us) the right to have as many children as we want, or see all other freedoms lost for them. Nature, to be sure, will restore a dynamic balance between our species and the world ecosystem if we fail to do so ourselves—by famine, pestilence, plague, or war. It seems, but is not, unthinkable that this should happen. If it does, of course, mineral resources may then be or appear to be relatively unlimited in relation to demand for them.

Premise V

The notion of the "technological fix" expresses a view that is at once full of hope and full of risk. It is a gripping thought to contemplate a world set free by nuclear energy. Imagine soaring cities of aluminum, plastic, and thermopane where all live in peace and plenty at unvarying temperature and without effort, drink distilled water, feed on produce grown from more distilled water in coastal deserts, and flit from heliport to heliport in capsules of uncontaminated air. Imagine having as many children as you want, who, of course, will grow up seven stories above the ground and under such germ-free conditions that they will need to wear breathing masks if they ever do set foot in a park or a forest. Imagine a world in which there is no balance of payments problem, no banks, or money, and such mundane affairs as acquiring a shirt or a wife are handled for us by central computer systems. Imagine, if you like, a world in which the only problem is boredom, all others being solved by the state-maintained system of genius-technologists produced by transfer of nuclei from the skin cells of certified gene donors to the previously fertilized ova of final contestants in the annual ideal-pelvis contest. Imagine the problem of getting out of this disease-free world gracefully at the age of 110 when you just can't stand it any longer!

Of course this extreme view may not appeal to people not conditioned to think in those terms. But the risk of slipping bit by bit into such a smothering condition as one of the better possible outcomes is inherent in any proposition that encourages or permits people or industries to believe that they can leave their problems to the invention of technological fixes by someone else.

Although the world ecosystem has been in a constant state of flux throughout geologic time, in the short and middle term it is essentially homeostatic. That is to say, it tends to obey Le Châtelier's general principle—when a stress is applied to a system such as to perturb a state of near equilibrium, the system tends to react in such a way as to restore the equilibrium. But large parts of the world ecosystem have probably already undergone or are in danger of undergoing irreversible changes. We cannot continue to plunder and pollute it without serious or even deadly consequences.

Consider what would be needed in terms of conventional mineral raw materials merely to raise the level of all 3.6 billion people now living in the world to the average of the 200 million now living in the United States. In terms of present staple commodities, it can be estimated[10] that this would require a "standing crop" of about 30 billion tons or iron, 500 million tons of lead, 330 million tons of zinc, and 50 million tons of tin. This is about 100 to 200 times the present annual production of these commodities. Annual power demands would, of course, increase proportionately. To support the doubled populations expected by the year 2000 at the same level would require, of course, a doubling of all the above numbers or substitute measures. The iron needed could probably be produced over a long period of time, perhaps even by the year 2000, given a sufficiently large effort. But once in circulation, merely to replace losses due to oxidation, friction, and dispersal, not counting production of new iron for larger populations, would take around 200,000 tons of new iron every year, or a drastic curtailment of losses below the present rate of one percent every two or three years. And the molybdenum needed to convert the iron to steel could become a serious limiting factor. The quantities of lead, zinc, and tin also called for far exceed all measured, indicated, and inferred world reserves of these metals.

This exercise gives a crude measure of the pressures that mineral resources will be under. It seems likely, to be sure, that substitutions, metallurgical research, and other technological advances will come to our aid, and that not all peoples of the world will find a superfluity of obsolescing gadgets necessary for the good life. But this is balanced by the equal likelihood that world population will not really level off at six-and-a-half or seven billion and that there will be growing unrest to share the material resources that might lead at least to an improved standard of living. The situation is also aggravated by the attendant problems of disposal of mine wastes and chemically and thermally polluted waters on a vast scale.

The "technological fix," as its informed proponents well understand, is not a panacea but an anesthetic. It may keep the patient quiet long enough to decide what the best long-range course of treatment may be, or even solve *some* of his problems permanently, but it would be tragic to forget that a broader program of treatment and recuperation is necessary. The flow of science and technology has always been fitful, and population control is a central limiting factor in what can be achieved. It will require much creative insight, hard work, public enlightenment, and good fortune to bring about the advances in discovery and analysis, recovery and fabrication, wise use and conservation of materials, management and recovery of wastes, and substitution and synthesis that will be needed to keep the affluent comfortable and bring the deprived to tolerable levels. It will probably also take some revision of criteria for self-esteem, achievement, and pleasure if the gap between affluent and deprived is to be narrowed and demand for raw materials kept within bounds that will permit man to enjoy a future as long as his past, and under conditions that would be widely accepted as agreeable.

The reality is that the promise of the "technological fix" is a meretricious premise, full of glittering appeal but devoid of heart and comprehension of the environmental and social problems. Technology and "hard" science we must have, in sustained and increasing quality, and in quantities relevant to the needs of man—material, intellectual, and spiritual. But in dealing with the problems of resources in relation to man, let us not lose sight of the fact that this is the province of the environmental and social sciences. A vigorous and perceptive technology will be an essential handmaiden in the process, but it is a risky business to put the potential despoilers of the environment in charge of it.

Premise VI

What, finally, about marine mineral resources, often proposed as a veritable cornucopia, waiting only to be harvested?[11] This notion is so widely accepted that it is worth considering in some detail what we actually know about prospective mineral resources from the sea.

In 1964, mineral production from the sea represented about ten percent of the total known value of the specific products recovered and about five percent of the entire world mineral output. Sizable quantities of oil and gas, sulfur, magnesium, bromine, salt, oyster shells, tin, and sand and gravel are currently being produced from the sea.[12] What are the future prospects for these as well as for other substances not now being recovered in quantity?

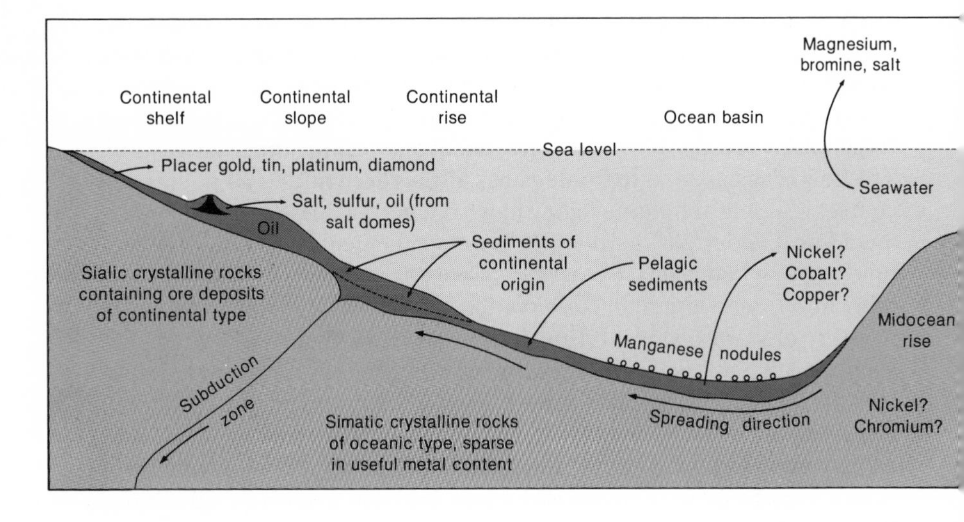

FIGURE 5.
Marine mineral resources. Sites of possible marine mineral resources. Chart is highly diagrammatic and not to scale.

Mineral and chemical resources from the sea may be found among the following (see also Figure 5).

1. Seawater.
2. Placer deposits within or beneath now-submerged beach or stream deposits.
3. Sediments other than placers, and sedimentary rocks that overlie crystalline rocks (a) on the continental shelves and slopes (about fifteen percent of the total sea floor), and (b) beyond the continental margins (about eighty-five percent of the total sea floor; the truly oceanic realm).
4. Crystalline rock exposed at the sea floor or lying beneath sediments (a) on the continental margins, and (b) beyond the continental margins.

Seawater. The sea contains about 1.3 billion cubic kilometers of seawater—an amount so large that quantities of dissolved substances are large even where their concentrations are small. Yet recovery of such substances accounts for little more than two percent of current production of marine minerals and chemicals. Only magnesium, bromine, and common salt are now being extracted in substantial quantities, and, for them, the seas do contain reserves that can be considered to be "inexhaustible" under any foreseeable pressures.

At the other extreme of accessibility is the 10 billion metric tons of gold in seawater—about 0.0013 troy ounce of gold in every million liters of water. Although capable people and corporations have worked intensively at the problem, the amount of gold so far reported to have been extracted from seawater is trivial.

Sixty-four of the ninety naturally occurring elements now known on earth have been detected in seawater. Of these only fifteen occur in quantities of more than 1.8 kilograms per million liters. Only nine, all of them among the first fifteen in abundance, represent 1965 values of more than $2.50 per million liters (chlorine, sodium, magnesium, sulfur, calcium, potassium, bromine, lithium, and rubidium). These nine (or their salts), plus boron, fluorine, and iodine, offer the best promise for direct recovery from seawater through ion exchange, biological concentration, or more novel processes.

Omitting these twelve, and very few others, the metal elements we are likely to have greatest need to extract from seawater offer little promise for direct recovery.

Placer deposits. Placer deposits now offshore were formed by gravitational segregation in and beneath former beach and stream deposits when the sea stood lower or the land higher. The outer limit at which such deposits can be expected is about 100 to 130 meters, the approximate position of the beach when Pleistocene glaciation was at its peak.

Diamonds, gold, and tin are being recovered from submarine placers (the diamonds, up to 1967 at least, at a cost in excess of their value). Approximate 1964 global values, omitting cost of recovery, were as follows: diamonds, $4 million; tin, about $21 million; gold, unknown.

Submarine placers of tough heavy metals such as gold, tin, and platinum offer the best prospects for the practicable recovery of mineral resources from the sea other than magnesium (from seawater) and oil and gas (from continental shelf sediments).

Sediments. Continental-shelf sediments and salt-dome structures that penetrate them account for nearly ninety-eight percent of the mineral and chemical wealth currently produced from within and beneath the sea—by far the greater part of this being oil and gas. About seventeen percent of the world's petroleum and natural gas now comes from offshore, nearly half the fields and about one-fourth the production being adjacent to the United States.

From data available in 1965, it has been estimated that about 700 to 1000 billion barrels of liquid fuels are potentially recoverable from offshore areas worldwide, which is about equal to or somewhat more than that remaining to be discovered and produced on land.

The oil-producing salt domes in the Gulf of Mexico also yield sulfur. More than five percent of the world's sulfur now comes from such sources.

Current reserves, however, will have been depleted by about 1990, and new discoveries or other sources will have to take up the slack.

Sediments and sedimentary rocks beyond the continental shelves and slopes are strikingly different from those that mantle and comprise the continental margins. Here is where we find the curious and geologically interesting manganese nodules and crusts. Despite the extravagant claims that have been made, however, their prospects for future mineral production remain to be established.

Crystalline rocks. Finding and exploiting mineralized crystalline rocks on the sea floor—even on the continental shelves—involves the same problems as on land, and many more. Although it is clear from geological data that the substructure of the shelf and slope is of a continental rather than an oceanic type, and that mineral deposits comparable to those found on the adjacent land are to be expected, problems peculiar to the region hamper their discovery and exploitation. Nevertheless, it seems statistically certain that ore deposits exist in crystalline rocks somewhere on or beneath the continental shelves. How many of them will eventually be discovered and worked is another question.

Beyond the continental margins the difficulties increase. The crystalline rocks of the ocean basins appear to be mainly basalts, probably limited both in the variety of included minerals and in the degree of enrichment to be found. Nickel, chromium, copper, and platinum may be present, but the first submarine ore of any is yet to be found. Iron and magnesium are probably the most abundant metal elements in the oceanic rocks, but such ores, if any, could not compete with sources from dry land and from seawater.

Mineral and chemical resources of the sea that will be significant for man over the next half century are those that can be extracted from seawater or recovered from the seabed of the continental shelf (and perhaps the oceanic rises). About five percent of the world's known production of geological wealth came from the shelves and seawater in 1964 and the trend is upwards. Oil and gas are by far the most important products, although their duration at expected rates of consumption will be limited. Seawater can supply ample magnesium and bromine, as well as common salt and some other substances. It will, however, supply few important metal elements other than magnesium, sodium, potassium, iodine, and perhaps strontium and boron. Oyster shells (used in the recovery of magnesium and for road metal, and by no means an inexhaustible resource) are being taken from the shallower parts of the shelves in relatively large quantities. The use of nearshore submarine sand and gravel, not yet large, will probably increase as coastal cities expand over and use up other local sources.

The sediments of the continental shelves and the crystalline rocks beneath them can be expected to produce mineral commodities similar to those of the immediately adjacent land. One way of guessing the magnitude of such resources is to reflect the hundred-fathom depthline across the shoreline. It then defines an onshore area equivalent to the continental shelf and having roughly similar geology. For the equivalent on-shore area in the United States (in 1966 dollars), the total cumulative value of minerals extracted since the beginning of the U.S. mineral industry, is about $160 billion, exclusive of oil and gas, or $240 billion with oil and gas. Because of geological differences from the land, and other obstacles that complicate discovery and recovery in the subsea environment, however, this figure is doubtless considerably larger than what we can expect from the continental shelves.

The ocean basins beyond the continental margin are not promising places to seek mineral resources.

A "mineral cornucopia" beneath the sea exists only in hyperbole. What is actually won from it will be the result of persistent imaginative research, inspired invention, bold and skillful experiment, and intelligent application and management—and such resources as are found will come mostly from the continental shelves, slopes, and rises. Whether they will be large or small remains to be seen. It is a fair guess that they will be substantial; but if present concepts of earth structure and of seafloor composition and history are correct, minerals from the seabed are not likely to compare with those yet to be recovered from the emerged lands. As for seawater itself, despite its volume and the quantities of dissolved salts it contains, it can supply few of the substances considered essential to modern industry.

THE NUB OF THE MATTER

The realities of mineral distribution, in a nutshell, are that it is neither inconsiderable nor limitless, and that we just don't know yet, in the detail required for considered weighting of comprehensive long-range alternatives, where or how the critical lithophilic elements are concentrated. Stratigraphically controlled substances such as the fossil fuels, and, to a degree, iron and alumina, we can comprehend and estimate within reasonable limits. Reserves, grades, locations, and recoverability of many critical metals, on the other hand, are affected by a much larger number of variables. We in North America began to develop our rich natural endowment of mineral resources at an accelerated pace before the rest of the world. Thus it stands to reason that, to the extent we are unable to meet needs by imports, we will feel the pinch sooner than countries like the USSR with a larger component of virgin mineral lands.

In some instances nuclear energy or other technological fixes may buy time to seek better solutions or will even solve a problem permanently. But sooner or later man must come to terms with his environment and its limitations. The sooner the better. The year 2042, by which time even current rates of consumption will have exhausted presently known recoverable reserves of perhaps half the world's now useful metals, is only as far from the present as the invention of the airplane and the discovery of radioactivity. In the absence of real population control or catastrophe there could be fifteen billion people on earth by then! Much that is difficult to anticipate can happen in the meanwhile, to be sure, and to center faith in a profit-motivated technology and refuse to look beyond a brief "foreseeable future" is a choice widely made. Against this we must weigh the consequences of error or thoughtless inaction and the prospects of identifying constructive alternatives for deliberate courses of long-term action, or inaction, that will affect favorably the long-range future. It is well to remember that to do nothing is equally to make a choice.

REFERENCES AND SUGGESTIONS FOR FURTHER READING

References

This discussion is adapted, with permission of the editors and publishers, from a 1968 paper by the author: "Realities of Mineral Distribution." *The Texas Quarterly* (Summer 1968), pp. 103–206.

1. P. Flawn, *Mineral Resources* (Rand McNally, Chicago, 1966), 406 pp.
2. C. Clark, *Population Growth and Land Use* (Macmillan, New York, 1967), 406 pp.
3. A. Weinberg, and G. Young, "The Nuclear Energy Revolution." *Proc. Natl. Acad. Sci.* (*U.S.*), 57, 1–15. (1966).
4. P. Flawn, *op. cit.*, p. 14.
5. D. Bell, "Notes on the Post-Industrialist Society II." *The Public Interest*, No. 7 (1967), pp. 102–118.
6. K. E. Boulding, "The Economics of the Coming Spaceship Earth." In *Environmental Quality in a Growing Economy* (H. Jarrett, ed.), Resources for the Future (John Hopkins Press, Baltimore, 1966), 146 pp. Reprinted on pages 121–132, of this volume.
7. National Academy of Sciences, Committee on Resources and Man. *Resources and Man* (W. H. Freeman and Company, San Francisco, 1969), 259 pp.

8. H. W. Lipper, "Helium." In *Mineral Facts and Problems*, pp. 429–440. U.S. Bureau of Mines, Bull. 630 (1965), 1118 pp. B. J. Moore, "Helium." Preprint from 1968 *Bureau of Mines Minerals Yearbook* (1969), 4 pp.
9. J. Lederberg, "Experimental Genetics and Human Evolution." *Bull. Atomic Scientists* 22, 1–11. (1966).
10. H. Brown and others, *The Next Hundred Years* (Viking Press, New York, 1957), 193 pp.; *The Next Ninety Years* (California Inst. of Technology Press, Pasadena, 1957), 186 pp.
11. J. L. Mero, *The Mineral Resources of the Sea* (Elsevier, New York, 1965), 312 pp.
12. K. O. Emery, "Geological Methods for Locating Mineral Deposits on the Ocean Floor," *Marine Technol. Soc., Trans. 2d Marine Technol. Soc. Conf.*, (1966), pp. 24–43. National Academy of Sciences, Committee on Resources and Man (1969). *Op. cit.* Bascom, W. 1967. "Mining the Ocean Depths": *Geosci. News*, I: 10–11, 26–28.

For Further Reading

H. Brown, *The Challenge of Man's Future* (Viking Press, New York, 1954), 290 pp.

M. Clawson, ed., *Natural Resources and International Development* (John Hopkins Press, Baltimore, 1964), 475 pp.

P. Cloud, "Our Disappearing Earth Resources," *Science Year* (1969), pp. 166–181.

H. H. Landsberg, *Natural Resources of U.S. Growth* (John Hopkins Press, Baltimore, 1964), 256 pp.

T. S. Lovering, *Minerals in World Affairs* (Prentice-Hall, Englewood Cliffs, N. J., 1943), 394 pp.

C. Park, *Affluence in Jeopardy* (Freeman, Cooper & Co., San Francisco, 1968), 368 pp.

B. J. Skinner, *Earth Resources* (Prentice-Hall, Englewood Cliffs, N. J., 1969), 150 pp.

U.S. Bureau of Mines, *Mineral Facts and Problems*, Bureau of Mines, Bull. 630 (1965), 1118 pp.

3

IMPACT OF POPULATION GROWTH

Paul R. Ehrlich and John P. Holdren

The interlocking crises in population, resources, and environment have been the focus of countless papers, dozens of prestigious symposia, and a growing avalanche of books. In this wealth of material, several questionable assertions have been appearing with increasing frequency. Perhaps the most serious of these is the notion that the size and growth rate of the U.S. population are only minor contributors to this country's adverse impact on local and global environments.[1] We propose to deal with this and several related misconceptions here, before persistent and unrebutted repetition entrenches them in the public mind—if not the scientific literature. Our discussion centers around five theorems which we believe are demonstrably true and which provide a framework for realistic analysis:

1. Population growth causes a *disproportionate* negative impact on the environment.

---

1. Notes and references for this reading will be found on page 87–89.

"Impact of Population Growth," from *Science*, Vol. 171, pp. 1212–1217, 26 March 1971.

2. Problems of population size and growth, resource utilization and depletion, and environmental deterioration must be considered jointly and on a global basis. In this context, population control is obviously not a panacea—it is necessary but not alone sufficient to see us through the crisis.

3. Population density is a poor measure of population pressure, and redistributing population would be a dangerous pseudosolution to the population problem.

4. "Environment" must be broadly construed to include such things as the physical environment of urban ghettos, the human behavioral environment, and the epidemiological environment.

5. Theoretical solutions to our problems are often not operational and sometimes are not solutions.

We now examine these theorems in some detail.

POPULATION SIZE AND PER CAPITA IMPACT

In an agricultural or technological society, each human individual has a negative impact on his environment. He is responsible for some of the simplification (and resulting destabilization) of ecological systems which results from the practice of agriculture.[2] He also participates in the utilization of renewable and nonrenewable resources. The total negative impact of such a society on the environment can be expressed, in the simplest terms, by the relation

$$I = P \cdot F$$

where P is the population, and F is a function which measures the per capita impact. A great deal of complexity is subsumed in this simple relation, however. For example, F increases with per capita consumption if technology is held constant, but may decrease in some cases if more benign technologies are introduced in the provision of a constant level of consumption. (We shall see in connection with theorem 5 that there are limits to the improvements one should anticipate from such "technological fixes.")

Pitfalls abound in the interpretation of manifest increases in the total impact I. For instance, it is easy to mistake changes in the composition of resource demand or environmental impact for absolute per capita increases, and thus to underestimate the role of the population multiplier. Moreover, it is often assumed that population size and per capita impact are independent variables, when in fact they are not. Consider, for example, the 1970 article by Coale,[3] in which he disparages the role of U.S. population growth in environmental problems by noting that since 1940 "population has increased by fifty percent, but per capita use of electricity has been multiplied several times." This argument contains both the fallacies to which we have just referred.

First, a closer examination of very rapid increases in many kinds of consumption shows that these changes reflect a shift among alternatives within a larger (and much more slowly growing) category. Thus the 760 percent increase in electricity consumption from 1940 to 1969[4] occurred in large part because the electrical *component* of the energy budget was (and is) increasing much faster than the budget itself. (Electricity comprised twelve percent of the U.S. energy consumption in 1940 versus twenty-two percent today.) The total energy production, a more important figure than its electrical component in terms of resources and the environment, increased much less dramatically—140 percent from 1940 to 1969. Under the simplest assumption (that is, that a given increase in population size accounts for an exactly proportional increase in production), this would mean that thirty-eight percent of the increase in energy production during this period is explained by population growth (the actual population increase from 1940 to 1969 was fifty-three percent). Similar considerations reveal the imprudence of citing, say, aluminum consumption to show that population growth is an "unimportant" factor in resource use. Certainly, aluminum consumption has swelled by over 1400 percent since 1940, but much of the increase has been due to the substitution of aluminum for steel in many applications. Thus a fairer measure is combined consumption of aluminum and steel, which has risen only 117 percent since 1940. Again, under the simplest assumption, population growth accounts for forty-five percent of the increase.

The "simplest assumption" is not valid, however, and this is the second flaw in Coale's example (and in his thesis). In short, he has failed to recognize that per capita consumption of energy and resources, and the associated per capita impact on the environment, are themselves functions of the population size. Our previous equation is more accurately written

$$I = P \cdot F(P)$$

displaying the fact that impact can increase faster than linearly with population. Of course, whether F (P) is an increasing or decreasing function of P depends in part on whether diminishing returns or economies of scale are dominant in the activities of importance. In populous, industrial nations such as the United States, most economies of scale are already being exploited; we are on the diminishing returns part of most of the important curves.

As one example of diminishing returns, consider the problem of providing nonrenewable resources such as minerals and fossil fuels to a growing population, even at fixed levels of per capita consumption. As the richest supplies of these resources and those nearest to centers of use are consumed, we are obliged to use lower-grade ores, drill deeper, and extend our supply networks. All these activities increase our per capita use of energy and our per capita impact on the environment. In the case of partly renewable resources such as water (which is effectively non-renewable when groundwater supplies are mined at rates far exceeding natural recharge), per capita costs and environmental impact escalate dramatically when the human population demands more than is locally available. Here the loss of free-flowing rivers and other economic, esthetic, and ecological costs of massive water-movement projects represent increased per capita diseconomies directly stimulated by population growth.

Diminishing returns are also operative in increasing food production to meet the needs of growing populations. Typically, attempts are made both to overproduce on land already farmed and to extend agriculture to marginal land. The former requires disproportionate energy use in obtaining and distributing water, fertilizer, and pesticides. The latter also increases per capita energy use, since the amount of energy invested per unit yield increases as less desirable land is cultivated. Similarly, as the richest fisheries stocks are depleted, the yield per unit effort drops, and more and more energy per capita is required to maintain the supply.[5] Once a stock is depleted it may not recover—it may be nonrenewable.

Population size influences per capita impact in ways other than diminishing returns. As one example, consider the oversimplified but instructive situation in which each person in the population has links with every other person—roads, telephone lines, and so forth. These links involve energy and materials in their construction and use. Since the number of links increases much more rapidly than the number of people,[6] so does the per capita consumption associated with the links.

Other factors may cause much steeper positive slopes in the per capita impact function, F (P). One such phenomenon is the *threshold effect*. Below a certain level of pollution trees will survive in smog. But, at some point, when a small increment in population produces a small increment in smog, living trees become dead trees. Five hundred people may be able to live around a lake and dump their raw sewage into the lake, and the natural systems of the lake will be able to break down the sewage and keep the lake from undergoing rapid ecological change. Five hundred and five people may overload the system and result in a "polluted" or eutrophic lake. Another phenomenon capable of causing near-discontinuities is the *synergism*. For instance, as cities push out into farmland, air pollution increasingly becomes a mixture of agricultural chemicals with power plant and automobile effluents. Sulfur dioxide from the city paralyzes the cleaning mechanisms of the lungs, thus increasing the residence time of potential carcinogens in the agricultural chemicals. The joint effect may be much more than the sum of the individual effects. Investigation of synergistic effects is one of the most neglected areas of environmental evaluation.

Not only is there a connection between population size and per capita damage to the environment, but the cost of maintaining environmental quality at a given level escalates disproportionately as population size increases. This effect occurs in part because costs increase very rapidly as one tries to reduce contaminants per unit volume of effluent to lower and lower levels (diminishing returns again!). Consider municipal sewage, for example. The cost of removing eighty to ninety percent of the biochemical and chemical oxygen demand, ninety percent of the suspended solids, and sixty percent of the resistant organic matter by means of secondary treatment is about eight cents per 1000 gallons (3785 liters) in a large plant.[7] But if the volume of sewage is such that its nutrient content creates a serious eutrophication problem (as is the case in the United States today), or if supply considerations dictate the reuse of sewage water for industry, agriculture, or groundwater recharge, advanced treatment is necessary. The cost ranges from two to four times as much as for secondary treatment (seventeen cents per 1000 gallons for carbon absorption; thirty-four cents per 1000 gallons for disinfection to yield a potable supply). This dramatic example of diminishing returns in pollution control could be repeated for stack gases, automobile exhausts, and so forth.

Now consider a situation in which the limited capacity of the environment to absorb abuse requires that we hold man's impact in some sector constant as population doubles. This means *per capita effectiveness* of pollution control in this sector must double (that is, effluent per person must be halved). In a typical situation, this would yield doubled per capita costs, or quadrupled total costs (and probably energy consumption) in this sector for a doubling of population. Of course, diminishing returns and threshold effects may be still more serious: we may easily have an eightfold increase in control costs for a doubling of population. Such arguments leave little ground for the assumption, popularized by Barry Commoner[8] and others, that a one percent rate of population growth spawns only one percent effects.

It is to be emphasized that the possible existence of "economies of scale" does not invalidate these arguments. Such savings, if available at all, would apply in the case of our sewage example to a change in the amount of effluent to be handled at an installation of a given type. For most technologies, the United States is already more than populous enough to achieve such economies and is doing so. They are accounted for in our example by citing figures for the largest treatment plants of each type. Population growth, on the other hand, forces us into quantitative *and* qualitative changes in how we handle each unit volume of effluent—what fraction and what kinds of material we remove. Here economies of scale do not apply at all, and diminishing returns are the rule.

THE GLOBAL CONTEXT

We will not deal in detail with the best example of the global nature and interconnections of population resource and environmental problems—namely, the problems involved in feeding a world in which ten to twenty million people starve to death annually,[9] and in which the population is growing by some seventy million people per year. The ecological problems created by high-yield agriculture are awesome[10] and are bound to have a negative feedback on food production. Indeed, the Food and Agriculture Organization of the United Nations has reported that in 1969 the world suffered its first absolute decline in fisheries yield since 1950. It seems likely that part of this decline is attributable to pollution originating in terrestrial agriculture.

A second source of the fisheries decline is, of course, overexploitation of fisheries by the developed countries. This problem, in turn, is illustrative of the situation in regard to many other resources, where similarly rapacious and shortsighted behavior by the developed nations is compromising the aspirations of the bulk of humanity to a decent existence. It is now becoming more widely comprehended that the United States alone accounts for perhaps thirty percent of the nonrenewable resources consumed in the world each year (for example, thirty-seven percent of the energy, twenty-five percent of the steel, twenty-eight percent of the tin, and thirty-three percent of the synthetic rubber).[11] This behavior is in large part inconsistent with American rhetoric about "developing" the countries of the Third World. *We* may be able to afford the technology to mine lower grade deposits when we have squandered the world's rich ores, but the underdeveloped countries, as their needs grow and their means remain meager, will not be able to do so. Some observers argue that the poor countries are today economically dependent on our use of their resources, and indeed that economists in these countries complain that world demand for their raw materials is too low.[12] This proves only that their economists are as shortsighted as ours.

It is abundantly clear that the entire context in which we view the world resource pool and the relationships between developed and underdeveloped countries must be changed, if we are to have any hope of achieving a stable and prosperous existence for all human beings. It cannot be stated too forcefully that the developed countries (or, more accurately, the overdeveloped countries) are the principal culprits in the consumption and dispersion of the world's nonrenewable resources[13] as well as in appropriating much more than their share of the world's protein. Because of this consumption, and because of the enormous negative impact on the global environment accompanying it, the population growth in these countries must be regarded as the most serious in the world today.

In relation to theorem 2 we must emphasize that, even if population growth were halted, the present population of the world could easily destroy civilization as we know it. There is a wide choice of weapons—from unstable plant monocultures and agricultural hazes to DDT, mercury, and thermonuclear bombs. If population size were reduced, and per capita consumption remained the same (or increased), we would still quickly run out of vital, high-grade resources or generate conflicts over diminishing supplies. Racism, economic exploitation, and war will not be eliminated by population control (of course, they are unlikely to be eliminated without it).

POPULATION DENSITY AND DISTRIBUTION

Theorem 3 deals with a problem related to the inequitable utilization of world resources. One of the commonest errors made by the uninitiated is to assume that population density (people per square mile) is the critical measure of overpopulation or underpopulation. For instance, Wattenberg states that the United States is not very crowded by "international standards" because Holland has eighteen times the population density.[14] We call this notion "the Netherlands fallacy." The Netherlands actually requires large chunks of the earth's resources and vast areas of land not within its borders to maintain itself. For example, it is the second largest per capita importer of protein in the world, and it imports sixty-three percent of its cereals, including one hundred percent of its corn and rice. It also imports all of its cotton, seventy-seven percent of its wool, and all of its iron ore, antimony, bauxite, chromium, copper, gold, lead, magnesite, manganese, mercury, molybdenum, nickel, silver, tin, tungsten, vanadium, zinc, phosphate rock (fertilizer), potash (fertilizer), asbestos, and diamonds. It produces energy equivalent to some twenty million metric tons of coal and consumes the equivalent of over forty-seven million metric tons.[15]

A certain preoccupation with density as a useful measure of overpopulation is apparent in the article by Coale.[16] He points to the existence of urban problems such as smog in Sydney, Australia, "even though the total population of Australia is about twelve million in an area eighty percent as big as the United States," as evidence that environmental problems are unrelated to population size. His argument would be more persuasive if problems of population *distribution* were the only ones with environmental consequences, and if population distribution were unrelated to resource distribution and population size. Actually, since the carrying capacity of the Australian continent is far below that of the United States, one would *expect* distribution problems—of which Sydney's smog is one symptom—to be encountered at a much lower total population there. Resources, such as water, are in very short supply, and people cluster where resources are available. (Evidently, it cannot be emphasized enough that carrying capacity includes the availability of a wide variety of resources in addition to space itself, and that population pressure is measured relative to the carrying capacity. One would expect water, soils, or the ability of the environment to absorb wastes to be the limiting resource in far more instances than land area.)

In addition, of course, many of the most serious environmental problems are essentially independent of the way in which population is distributed. These include the global problems of weather modification by carbon dioxide and particulate pollution, and the threats to the biosphere posed by man's massive inputs of pesticides, heavy metals, and oil.[17] Similarly, the problems of resource depletion and ecosystem simplification by agriculture depend on how many people there are and their patterns of consumption, but not in any major way on how they are distributed.

Naturally, we do not dispute that smog and most other familiar urban ills are serious problems, or that they are related to population distribution. Like many of the difficulties we face, these problems will not be cured simply by stopping population growth; direct and well-conceived assaults on the problems themselves will also be required. Such measures may occasionally include the redistribution of population, but the considerable difficulties and costs of this approach should not be underestimated. People live where they do not because of a perverse intention to add to the problems of their society but for reasons of economic necessity, convenience, and desire for agreeable surroundings. Areas that are uninhabited or sparsely populated today are presumably that way because they are deficient in some of the requisite factors. In many cases, the remedy for such deficiencies—for example, the provision of water and power to the wastelands of central Nevada—would be extraordinarily expensive in dollars, energy, and resources and would probably create environmental havoc. (Will we justify the rape of Canada's rivers to "colonize" more of our western deserts?)

Moving people to more "habitable" areas, such as the central valley of California or, indeed, most suburbs, exacerbates another serious problem—the paving over of prime farmland. This is already so serious in California that, if current trends continue, about fifty percent of the best acreage in the nation's leading agricultural state will be destroyed by the year 2020.[18] Encouraging that trend hardly seems wise.

Whatever attempts may be made to solve distribution-related problems, they will be undermined if population growth continues, for two reasons. First, population growth and the aggravation of distribution problems are correlated—part of the increase will surely be absorbed in urban areas that can least afford the growth. Indeed, barring the unlikely prompt reversal of present trends, most of it will be absorbed there. Second, population growth puts a disproportionate drain on the very financial resources needed to combat its symptoms. Economist Joseph Spengler has estimated that four percent of national income goes to support our one percent per year rate of population growth in the United States.[19] The four percent figure now amounts to about $30 billion per year. It seems safe to conclude that the faster we grow the less likely it is that we will find the funds either to alter population distribution patterns or to deal more comprehensively and realistically with our problems.

THE MEANING OF ENVIRONMENT

Theorem 4 emphasizes the comprehensiveness of the environment crisis. All too many people think in terms of national parks and trout streams when they say "environment." For this reason many of the suppressed people of our nation consider ecology to be just one more "racist shuck."[20] They are apathetic or even hostile toward efforts to avert further environmental and sociological deterioration, because they have no reason to believe they will share the fruits of success.[21] Slums, cockroaches, and rats are ecological problems, too. The correction of ghetto conditions in Detroit is neither more nor less important than saving the Great Lakes—both are imperative.

We must pay careful attention to sources of conflict both within the United States and between nations. Conflict within the United States blocks progress toward solving our problems; conflict among nations can easily "solve" them once and for all. Recent laboratory studies on human beings support the anecdotal evidence that crowding may increase aggressiveness in human males.[22] These results underscore long-standing suspicions that population growth, translated through the inevitable uneven distribution into physical crowding, will tend to make the solution of all of our problems more difficult.

As a final example of the need to view "environment" broadly, note that human beings live in an epidemiological environment which deteriorates with crowding and malnutrition—both of which increase with population growth. The hazard posed by the prevalence of these conditions in the world today is componded by man's unprecedented mobility: potential carriers of diseases of every description move routinely and in substantial numbers from continent to continent in a matter of hours. Nor is there any reason to believe that modern medicine has made widespread plague impossible.[23] The Asian influenza epidemic of 1968 killed relatively few people only because the virus *happened* to be nonfatal to people in otherwise good health, not because of public health measures. Far deadlier viruses, which easily could be scourges without precedent in the population at large, have on more than one occasion been confined to research workers largely by good luck (for example, the Marburgvirus incident of 1967[24] and the Lassa fever incident of 1970[25]).

SOLUTIONS: THEORETICAL AND PRACTICAL

Theorem 5 states that theoretical solutions to our problems are often not operational, and sometimes are not solutions. In terms of the problem of feeding the world, for example, technological fixes suffer from limitations in scale, lead time, and cost.[26] Thus potentially attractive theoretical approaches—such as desalting seawater for agriculture, new irrigation systems, high-protein diet supplements—prove inadequate in practice. They are too little, too late, and too expensive, or they have sociological costs which hobble their effectiveness.[27] Moreover, many aspects of our technological fixes, such as synthetic organic pesticides, and inorganic nitrogen fertilizers, have created vast environmental problems which seem certain to erode global productivity and ecosystem stability.[28] This is not to say that important gains have not been made through the application of technology to agriculture in the poor countries, or that further technological advances are not worth seeking. But it must be stressed that even the most enlightened technology cannot relieve the necessity of grappling forthrightly and promptly with population growth (as Norman Borlaug aptly observed on being notified of his Nobel Prize for development of the new wheats).[29]

Technological attempts to ameliorate the environmental impact of population growth and rising per capita affluence in the developed countries suffer from practical limitations similar to those just mentioned. Not only do such measures tend to be slow, costly, and insufficient in scale, but in addition they most often *shift* our impact rather than remove it. For example, our first generation of smog-control devices increased emissions of oxides of nitrogen while reducing those of hydrocarbons and carbon monoxide. Our unhappiness about eutrophication has led to the replacement of phosphates in detergents with compounds like NTA—nitrilotriacetic acid—which has carcinogenic breakdown products and apparently enhances teratogenic effects of heavy metals.[30] And our distaste for lung diseases apparently induced by sulfur dioxide inclines us to accept the hazards of radioactive waste disposal, fuel reprocessing, routine low-level emissions of radiation, and an apparently small but finite risk of catastrophic accidents associated with nuclear fission power plants. Similarly, electric automobiles would simply shift part of the environmental burden of personal transportation from the vicinity of highways to the vicinity of power plants.

We are not suggesting here that electric cars, or nuclear power plants, or substitutes for phosphates are inherently bad. We argue that they, too, pose environmental costs which must be weighed against those they eliminate. In many cases the choice is not obvious, and in *all* cases there will be some environmental impact. The residual per capita impact, after all the best choices have been made, must then be multiplied by the population engaging in the activity. If there are too many people, even the most wisely managed technology will not keep the environment from being overstressed.

In contending that a change in the way we use technology will invalidate these arguments, Commoner[31] claims that our important environmental problems began in the 1940s with the introduction and rapid spread of certain "synthetic" technologies: pesticides and herbicides, inorganic fertilizers, plastics, nuclear energy, and high-compression gasoline engines. In so arguing, he appears to make two unfounded assumptions. The first is that man's pre-1940 environmental impact was innocuous and, without changes for the worse in technology, would have remained innocuous even at a much larger population size. The second assumption is that the advent of the new technologies was independent of the attempt to meet human needs and desires in a growing population. Actually, man's record as a simplifier of ecosystems and plunderer of resources can be traced from his probable role in the extinction of many Pleistocene mammals,[32] through the destruction of the soils of Mesopotamia by salination and erosion, to the deforestation of Europe in the Middle Ages and the American dustbowls of the 1930s, to cite only some highlights. Man's contemporary arsenal of synthetic technological bludgeons indisputably magnifies the potential for disaster, but these were evolved in some measure to *cope* with population pressures, not independently of them. Moreover, it is worth noting that, of the four enviromental threats viewed by the prestigious Williamstown study[33] as globally significant, three are associated with pre-1940 technologies which have simply increased in scale (heavy metals, oil in the seas, and carbon dioxide and particulates in the atmosphere, the latter probably due in considerable part to agriculture[34]). Surely, then, we can anticipate that supplying food, fiber, and metals for a population even larger than today's will have a profound (and destabilizing) effect on the global ecosystem under *any* set of technological assumptions.

CONCLUSION

John Platt has aptly described man's present predicament as "a storm of crisis problems."[35] Complacency concerning any component of these problems—sociological, technological, economic, ecological—is unjustified and counterproductive. It is time to admit that there are no monolithic solutions to the problems we face. Indeed, population control, the redirection of technology, the transition from open to closed resource cycles, the equitable distribution of opportunity and the ingredients of prosperity must *all* be accomplished if there is to be a future worth having. Failure in any of these areas will surely sabotage the entire enterprise.

In connection with the five theorems elaborated here, we have dealt at length with the notion that population growth in industrial nations such as the United States is a minor factor, safely ignored. Those who so argue often add that, anyway, population control would be the slowest to take effect of all possible attacks on our various problems, since the inertia in attitudes and in the age structure of the population is so considerable. To conclude that this means population control should be assigned low priority strikes us as curious logic. Precisely because population is the most difficult and slowest to yield among the components of environmental deterioration, we must start on it at once. To ignore population today because the problem is a tough one is to commit ourselves to even gloomier prospects twenty years hence, when most of the "easy" means to reduce per capita impact on the environment will have been exhausted. The desperate and repressive measures for population control which might be contemplated then are reason in themselves to proceed with foresight, alacrity, and compassion today.

NOTES AND REFERENCES

1. A. J. Coale, *Science* 170, 132 (1970). B. Commoner, *Saturday Rev.* 53, 50 (1970); *Humanist* 30, 10 (1970).
2. For a general discussion, see P. R. Ehrlich and A. H. Ehrlich, *Population, Resources, Environment* (W. H. Freeman and Company, San Francisco, 1970), chap. 7. More technical treatments of the relationship between complexity

and stability may be found in R. H. MacArthur, *Ecology* 36, 533 (1955); D. R. Margalef, *Gen. Syst.* 3, 3671 (1958); E. G. Leigh, Jr., *Proc. Nat. Acad. Sci. U.S.* 53, 777 (1965); and O. T. Loucks, "Evolution of Diversity, Efficiency, and Stability of a Community," paper delivered at AAAS meeting, Dallas, Texas, 30 December 1968.

3. A. J. Coale, *op. cit.*
4. The figures used in this paragraph are all based on data in *Statistical Abstract of the United States 1970* (U.S. Department of Commerce) (Government Printing Office, Washington, D.C., 1970).
5. A dramatic example of this effect is given in R. Payne's analysis of the whale fisheries [*N.Y. Zool. Soc. Newsl.* (November 1968)]. The graphs in Payne's paper are reproduced in Ehrlich and Ehrlich, *op. cit.*
6. If N is the number of people, then the number of links is N(N—1)/2, and the number of links per capita is (N—1)/2.
7. These figures and the others in this paragraph are from *Cleaning Our Environment: The Chemical Basis for Action* (American Chemical Society, Washington, D.C., 1969), pp. 95–162.
8. B. Commoner, *Saturday Review*, *op. cit.*; *Humanist*, *op. cit.* In his unpublished testimony before the President's Commission on Population Growth and the American Future (17 November 1970), Commoner acknowledged the operation of diminishing returns, threshold effects, and so on. Since such factors apparently do not account for *all* of the increase in per capita impact on the environment in recent decades, however, Commoner drew the unwarranted conclusion that they are negligible.
9. R. Dumont and B. Rosier, *The Hungry Future* (Praeger, New York, 1969), pp. 34–35.
10. L. Brown, *Sci. Amer.* 223, 160 (1970), Offprint 1196; P. R. Ehrlich, *War on Hunger* 4, 1 (1970). See also the sources listed at 2 above.
11. These figures are based on data from the *United Nations Statistical Yearbook 1969* (United Nations, New York, 1969), with estimates added for the consumption by Mainland China when none were included.
12. A. J. Coale, *op. cit.*
13. The notion that dispersed resources, because they have not left the planet, are still available to us, and the hope that mineral supplies can be extended indefinitely by the application of vast amounts of energy to common rock have been the subject of lively debate elsewhere. See. for example, the articles by P. Cloud, T. Lovering, A. Weinberg, *Texas Quart.* 11, 103, 127, 90 (Summer 1968). (Cloud's contribution to this volume is based on his article in *Texas Quart.*). See also *Resources and Man* (National Academy of Sciences) (W. H. Freeman and Company, San Francisco, 1969). While the pessimists seem to have had the better of this argument, the entire matter is academic in the context of the rate problem we face in the next thirty years. Over that time period, at least, cost, lead time, and logistics will see to it that industrial economies and dreams of development stand or fall with the availability of high-grade resources.
14. B. Wattenberg, *New Republic* 162, 18 (4 April and 11 April 1970).
15. These figures are from *United Nations Statistical Yearbook 1969*, as described in note 11, from the *FAO Trade Yearbook*, the *FAO Production Yearbook* (United Nations, New York, 1968), and from G. Borgstrom, *Too Many* (Collier-Macmillan, Toronto, Ont., 1969).
16. A. J. Coale, *op. cit.*

17. *Man's Impact on the Global Environment, Report of the Study of Critical Environmental Problems* (M.I.T. Press, Cambridge, Mass., 1970).
18. *A Model of Society, Progress Report of the Environmental Systems Group* (Univ. of California Institute of Ecology, Davis, April 1969).
19. J. J. Spengler, in *Population: The Vital Revolution*, R. Freedman, Ed. (Doubleday, New York, 1964), p. 67.
20. R. Chrisman, *Scanlan's* 1, 46 (August 1970).
21. A more extensive discussion of this point is given in an article by P. R. Ehrlich and A. H. Ehrlich, in *Global Ecology: Readings Toward a Rational Strategy for Man*, J. P. Holdren and P. R. Ehrlich, Eds. (Harcourt, Brace, Jovanovich, New York, 1971).
22. J. L. Freedman, A. Levy, J. Price, R. Welte, M. Katz, P. R. Ehrlich, in preparation.
23. J. Lederberg, *Washington Post* (15 March and 22 March 1970).
24. C. Smith, D. Simpson, E. Bowen, I. Zlotnik, *Lancet* 1967-II, 1119, 1128 (1967).
25. J. Lederberg, *op. cit.;* Associated Press wire service, 2 February 1970.
26. P. R. Ehrlich and J. P. Holdren, *BioScience* 19, 1065 (1969).
27. See L. Brown [*Seeds of Change* (Praeger, New York, 1970)] for a discussion of unemployment problems exacerbated by the Green Revolution.
28. G. Woodwell, *Science* 168, 429 (1970).
29. *New York Times*, 22 October 1970, p. 18; *Newsweek* 76, 50 (2 November 1970).
30. S. Epstein, *Environment* 12, No. 7, 2 (September, 1970); *New York Times* service, 17 November 1970.
31. B. Commoner, *Saturday Rev., op. cit.; Humanist, op. cit.;* see also comment about Commoner's unpublished testimony at 8, above.
32. G. S. Krantz, *Amer. Sci.* 58, 164 (March–April 1970).
33. *Op. cit.*, see note 17.
34. R. A. Bryson and W. M. Wendland, in *Global Effects of Environmental Pollution*, S. F. Singer, Ed. (Springer-Verlag, New York, 1970).
35. J. Platt, *Science* 166, 1115 (1969).

4

THE NEW BIOLOGY: WHAT PRICE RELIEVING MAN'S ESTATE?

Leon R. Kass

Recent advances in biology and medicine suggest that we may be rapidly acquiring the power to modify and control the capacities and activities of men by direct intervention and manipulation of their bodies and minds. Certain means are already in use or at hand, others await the solution of relatively minor technical problems, while yet others, those offering perhaps the most precise kind of control, depend upon further basic research. Biologists who have considered these matters disagree on the question of how much how soon, but all agree that the power for "human engineering," to borrow from the jargon, is coming and that it will probably have profound social consequences.

These developments have been viewed both with enthusiasm and with alarm; they are only just beginning to receive serious attention. Several biologists have undertaken to inform the public about the technical possibilities, present and future. Practitioners of social science "futurology" are attempting to predict and describe the likely social consequences of and public responses to the new technologies. Lawyers and

"The New Biology: What Price Relieving Man's Estate?" From *Science*, Vol. 174, pp. 779–788, 19 November 1971.

legislators are exploring institutional innovations for assessing new technologies. All of these activities are based upon the hope that we can harness the new technology of man for the betterment of mankind.

Yet this commendable aspiration points to another set of questions, which are, in my view, sorely neglected—questions that inquire into the meaning of phrases such as the "betterment of mankind." A *full* understanding of the new technology of man requires an exploration of ends, values, standards. What ends will or should the new techniques serve? What values should guide society's adjustments? By what standards should the assessment agencies assess? Behind these questions lie others: what is a good man, what is a good life for man, what is a good community? This article is an attempt to provoke discussion of these neglected and important questions.

While these questions about ends and ultimate ends are never unimportant or irrelevant, they have rarely been more important or more relevant. That this is so can be seen once we recognize that we are dealing here with a group of technologies that are in a decisive respect unique: the object upon which they operate is man himself. The technologies of energy or food production, of communication, of manufacture, and of motion greatly alter the implements available to man and the conditions in which he uses them. In contrast, the biomedical technology works to change the user himself. To be sure, the printing press, the automobile, the television, and the jet airplane have greatly altered the conditions under which and the way in which men live; but men as biological beings have remained largely unchanged. They have been, and remain, able to accept or reject, to use and abuse these technologies; they choose, whether wisely or foolishly, the ends to which these technologies are means. Biomedical technology may make it possible to change the inherent capacity for choice itself. Indeed, both those who welcome and those who fear the advent of "human engineering" ground their hopes and fears in the same prospect: *that man can for the first time recreate himself.*

Engineering the engineer seems to differ in kind from engineering his engine. Some have argued, however, that biomedical engineering does not differ qualitatively from toilet training, education, and moral teachings—all of which are forms of so-called "social engineering," which has man as its object, and is used by one generation to mold the next. In reply, it must at least be said that the techniques which have hitherto been employed are feeble and inefficient when compared to those on the horizon. This quantitative difference rests in part on a qualitative difference in the means of intervention. The traditional influences operate by speech or by symbolic deeds. They pay tribute to man as the animal who lives by speech and who understands the meanings of actions. Also, their effects are, in general, reversible, or at least subject to attempts at reversal. Each person has greater or lesser power to accept or reject or abandon them. In contrast, biomedical engineering circumvents the human context of speech and meaning, bypasses choice, and goes directly to work to modify the human material itself. Moreover, the changes wrought may be irreversible.

In addition, there is an important practical reason for considering the biomedical technology apart from other technologies. The advances we shall examine are fruits of a large, humane project dedicated to the conquest of disease and the relief of human suffering. The biologist and physician, regardless of their private motives, are seen, with justification, to be the well-wishers and benefactors of mankind. Thus, in a time in which technological advance is more carefully scrutinized and increasingly criticized, biomedical developments are still viewed by most people as benefits largely without qualification. The price we pay for these developments is thus more likely to go unrecognized. For this reason, I shall consider only the dangers and costs of biomedical advance. As the benefits are well known, there is no need to dwell upon them here. My discussion is deliberately partial.

I begin with a survey of the pertinent technologies. Next, I will consider some of the basic ethical and social problems in the use of these technologies. Then, I will briefly raise some fundamental questions to which these problems point. Finally, I shall offer some very general reflections on what is to be done.

THE BIOMEDICAL TECHNOLOGIES

The biomedical technologies can be usefully organized into three groups, according to their major purpose: (1) control of death and life, (2) control of human potentialities, and (3) control of human achievement. The corresponding technologies are (1) medicine, especially the arts of prolonging life and of controlling reproduction, (2) genetic engineering, and (3) neurological and psychological manipulation. I shall briefly summarize each group of techniques.

1. Control of death and life. Previous medical triumphs have greatly increased average life expectancy. Yet other developments, such as organ transplantation or replacement, and research into aging, hold forth the promise of increasing not just the average, but also the maximum life expectancy. Indeed, medicine seems to be sharpening its tools to do battle with death itself, as if death were just one more disease.

More immediately and concretely, available techniques of prolonging life—respirators, cardiac pacemakers, artificial kidneys—are already in the lists against death. Ironically, the success of these devices in forestalling death has introduced confusion in determining that death has, in fact, occurred. The traditional signs of life—heartbeat and respiration—can now be maintained entirely by machines. Some physicians are now busily trying to devise so-called "new definitions of death," while others maintain that the technical advances show that death is not a concrete event at all, but rather a gradual process, like twilight, incapable of precise temporal localization.

The real challenge to death will come from research into aging and senescence, a field just entering puberty. Recent studies suggest that aging is a genetically controlled process, distinct from disease, but one that can be manipulated and altered by diet or drugs. Extrapolating from animal studies, some scientists have suggested that a decrease in the rate of aging might also be achieved simply by effecting a very small decrease in human body temperature. According to some estimates, by the year 2000 it may be technically possible to add from twenty to forty useful years to the period of middle life.

Medicine's success in extending life is already a major cause of excessive population growth: death control points to birth control. Although we are already technically competent, new techniques for lowering fertility and chemical agents for inducing abortion will greatly enhance our powers over conception and gestation. Problems of definition have been raised here as well. The need to determine when individuals acquire enforceable legal rights gives society an interest in the definition of human life and of the time when it begins. These matters are too familiar to need elaboration.

Technologies to conquer infertility proceed alongside those to promote it. The first successful laboratory fertilization of human egg by human sperm was reported in 1969.[1] In 1970, British scientists learned how to grow human embryos in the laboratory up to at least the blastocyst stage (that is, to the age of one week).[2] We may soon hear about the next stage, the successful reimplantation of such an embryo into a woman previously infertile because of oviduct disease. The development of an artificial placenta, now under investigation, will make possible full laboratory control of fertilization and gestation. In addition, sophisticated biochemical and cytological techniques of monitoring the "quality" of the fetus have been and are being developed and used. These developments not only give us more power over the generation of human

---

1. Notes and references for this reading will be found on page 110–113.

life, but make it possible to manipulate and to modify the quality of the human material.

2. Control of human potentialities. Genetic engineering, when fully developed, will wield two powers not shared by ordinary medical practice. Medicine treats existing individuals and seeks to correct deviations from a norm of health. Genetic engineering, in contrast, will be able to make changes that can be transmitted to succeeding generations and will be able to create new capacities, and hence to establish new norms of health and fitness.

Nevertheless, one of the major interests in genetic manipulation is strictly medical: to develop treatments for individuals with inherited diseases. Genetic disease is prevalent and increasing, thanks partly to medical advances that enable those affected to survive and perpetuate their mutant genes. The hope is that normal copies of the appropriate gene, obtained biologically or synthesized chemically, can be introduced into defective individuals to correct their deficiencies. This *therapeutic* use of genetic technology appears to be far in the future. Moreover, there is some doubt that it will ever be practical, since the same end could be more easily achieved by transplanting cells or organs that could compensate for the missing or defective gene product.

Far less remote are technologies that could serve *eugenic* ends. Their development has been endorsed by those concerned about a general deterioration of the human gene pool and by others who believe that even an undeteriorated human gene pool needs upgrading. Artificial insemination with selected donors, the eugenic proposal of Herman Muller,[3] has been possible for several years because of the perfection of methods for long-term storage of human spermatozoa. The successful maturation of human oocytes in the laboratory and their subsequent fertilization now make it possible to select donors of ova as well. But a far more suitable technique for eugenic purposes will soon be upon us—namely, nuclear transplantation, or cloning. Bypassing the lottery of sexual recombination, nuclear transplantation permits the asexual reproduction or copying of an already developed individual. The nucleus of a mature but unfertilized egg is replaced by a nucleus obtained from a specialized cell of an adult organism or embryo (for example, a cell from the intestines or the skin). The egg with its transplanted nucleus develops as if it had been fertilized and, barring complications, will give rise to a normal adult organism. Since almost all the hereditary material (DNA) of a cell is contained within its nucleus, the renucleated egg and the individual into which it develops are genetically identical to the adult organism that was the source of the donor nucleus. Cloning could be used to produce sets of unlimited numbers of genetically identical individuals, each set derived from a single parent. Cloning has been successful in amphibians and is now being tried in mice; its extension to man merely requires the solution of certain technical problems.

Production of man-animal chimeras by the introduction of selected nonhuman material into developing human embryos is also expected. Fusion of human and nonhuman cells in tissue culture has already been achieved.

Other, less direct means for influencing the gene pool are already available, thanks to our increasing ability to identify and diagnose genetic diseases. Genetic counselors can now detect biochemically and cytologically a variety of severe genetic defects (for example, Mongolism, Tay-Sachs disease) while the fetus is still *in utero*. Since treatments are at present largely unavailable, diagnosis is often followed by abortion of the affected fetus. In the future, more sensitive tests will also permit the detection of heterozygote carriers, the unaffected individuals who carry but a single dose of a given deleterious gene. The eradication of a given genetic disease might then be attempted by aborting all such carriers. In fact, it was recently suggested that the fairly common disease cystic fibrosis could be completely eliminated over the next forty years by screening all pregnancies and aborting the seventeen million unaffected fetuses that will carry a single gene for this disease. Such zealots need to be reminded of the consequences should each geneticist be allowed an equal assault on his favorite genetic disorder, given that each human being is a carrier for some four to eight such recessive, lethal genetic diseases.

3. Control of human achievement. Although human achievement depends at least in part upon genetic endowment, heredity determines only the material upon which experience and education impose the form. The limits of many capacities and powers of an individual are indeed genetically determined, but the nurturing and perfection of these capacities depend upon other influences. Neurological and psychological manipulation hold forth the promise of controlling the development of human capacities, particularly those long considered most distinctively human: speech, thought, choice, emotion, memory, and imagination.

These techniques are now in a rather primitive state because we understand so little about the brain and mind. Nevertheless, we have already seen the use of electrical stimulation of the human brain to produce sensations of intense pleasure and to control rage, the use of brain surgery (for example, frontal lobotomy) for the relief of severe anxiety, and the use of aversive conditioning with electric shock to treat sexual perversion. Operant-conditioning techniques are widely used, apparently with success, in schools and mental hospitals. The use of so-called consciousness-expanding and hallucinogenic drugs is widespread, to say nothing of tranquilizers and stimulants. We are promised drugs to modify memory, intelligence, libido, and aggressiveness.

The following passages from a recent book by the Yale University neurophysiologist José Delgado—a book instructively entitled *Physical Control of the Mind: Toward a Psychocivilized Society*—should serve to make this discussion more concrete. In the early 1950s, it was discovered that, with electrodes placed in certain discrete regions of their brains, animals would repeatedly and indefatigably press levers to stimulate their own brains, with obvious resultant enjoyment. Even starving animals preferred stimulating these so-called pleasure centers to eating. Delgado comments on the electrical stimulation of a similar center in a human subject.[4]

> The patient reported a pleasant tingling sensation in the left side of her body 'from my face down to the bottom of my legs.' She started giggling and making funny comments, stating that she enjoyed the sensation 'very much.' Repetition of these stimulations made the patient more communicative and flirtatious, and she ended by openly expressing her desire to marry the therapist.

And one further quotation from Delgado.[5]

> Leaving wires inside of a thinking brain may appear unpleasant or dangerous, but actually the many patients who have undergone this experience have not been concerned about the fact of being wired, nor have they felt any discomfort due to the presence of conductors in their heads. Some women have shown their feminine adaptability to circumstances by wearing attractive hats or wigs to conceal their electrical headgear, and many people have been able to enjoy a normal life as out-patients, returning to the clinic periodically for examination and stimulation. In a few cases in which contacts were located in pleasurable areas, patients have had the opportunity to stimulate their own brains by pressing the button of a portable instrument, and this procedure is reported to have therapeutic benefits.

It bears repeating that the sciences of neurophysiology and psychopharmacology are in their infancy. The techniques that are now available are crude, imprecise, weak, and unpredictable, compared to those that may flow from a more mature neurobiology.

BASIC ETHICAL AND SOCIAL PROBLEMS IN THE USE OF BIOMEDICAL TECHNOLOGY

After this cursory review of the powers now and soon to be at our disposal, I turn to the questions concerning the use of these powers. First, we must recognize that questions of use of science and technology are always moral and political questions, never simply technical ones. All private or public decisions to develop or to use biomedical technology—and decisions *not* to do so—inevitably contain judgments about value. This is true even if the values guiding those decisions are not articulated or made clear, as indeed they often are not. Second, the value judgments cannot be derived from biomedical science. This is true even if scientists themselves make the decisions.

These important points are often overlooked for at least three reasons.

1. They are obscured by those who like to speak of "the control of nature by science." It is men who control, not that abstraction "science." Science may provide the means, but men choose the ends; the choice of ends comes from beyond science.

2. Introduction of new technologies often appears to be the result of no decision whatsoever, or of the culmination of decisions too small or unconscious to be recognized as such. What can be done is done. However, someone is deciding on the basis of some notions of desirability, no matter how self-serving or altruistic.

3. Desires to gain or keep money and power no doubt influence much of what happens, but these desires can also be formulated as reasons and then discussed and debated.

Insofar as our society has tried to deliberate about questions of use, how has it done so? Pragmatists that we are, we prefer a utilitarian calculus: we weigh "benefits" against "risks," and we weigh them for both the individual and "society." We often ignore the fact that the very definitions of "a benefit" and "a risk" are themselves based upon judgments about value. In the biomedical areas just reviewed, the benefits are considered to be self-evident: prolongation of life, control of fertility and of population size, treatment and prevention of genetic disease, the reduction of anxiety and aggressiveness, and the enhancement of memory, intelligence, and pleasure. The assessment of risk is, in general, simply pragmatic—will the technique work effectively and reliably, how much will it cost, will it do detectable bodily harm, and who will complain if we proceed with development? As these questions are familiar and congenial, there is no need to belabor them.

The very pragmatism that makes us sensitive to considerations of economic cost often blinds us to the larger social costs exacted by biomedical advances. For one thing, we seem to be unaware that we may not be able to maximize all the benefits, that several of the goals we are promoting conflict with each other. On the one hand, we seek to control population growth by lowering fertility; on the other hand, we develop techniques to enable every infertile woman to bear a child. On the one hand, we try to extend the lives of individuals with genetic disease; on the other, we wish to eliminate deleterious genes from the human population.

I am not urging that we resolve these conflicts in favor of one side or the other, but simply that we recognize that such conflicts exist. Once we do, we are more likely to appreciate that most "progress" is heavily paid for in terms not generally included in the simple utilitarian calculus.

To become sensitive to the larger costs of biomedical progress, we must attend to several serious ethical and social questions. I will briefly discuss three of them: (1) questions of distributive justice, (2) questions of the use and abuse of power, and (3) questions of self-degradation and dehumanization.

DISTRIBUTIVE JUSTICE

The introduction of any biomedical technology presents a new instance of an old problem—how to distribute scarce resources justly. We should assume that demand will usually exceed supply. Which people should receive a kidney transplant or an artificial heart? Who should get the benefits of genetic therapy or of brain stimulation? Is "first-come, first-served" the fairest principle? Or are certain people "more worthy," and if so, on what grounds?

It is unlikely that we will arrive at answers to these questions in the form of deliberate decisions. More likely, the problem of distribution will continue to be decided ad hoc and locally. If so, the consequence will probably be a sharp increase in the already far too great inequality of medical care. The extreme case will be longevity, which will probably be, at first, obtainable only at great expense. Who is likely to be able to buy it? Do conscience and prudence permit us to enlarge the gap between rich and poor, especially with respect to something as fundamental as life itself?

Questions of distributive justice also arise in the earlier decisions to acquire new knowledge and to develop new techniques. Personnel and facilities for medical research and treatment are scarce resources. Is the development of a new technology the best use of the limited resources, given current circumstances? How should we balance efforts aimed at prevention against those aimed at cure, or either of these against efforts to redesign the species? How should we balance the delivery of available levels of care against further basic research? More fundamentally, how should we balance efforts in biology and medicine against efforts to eliminate poverty, pollution, urban decay, discrimination, and poor education? This last question about distribution is perhaps the most profound. We should reflect upon the social consequences of seducing many of our brightest young people to spend their lives locating the biochemical defects in rare genetic diseases, while our more serious problems go begging. The current squeeze on money for research provides us with an opportunity to rethink and reorder our priorities.

Problems of distributive justice are frequently mentioned and discussed, but they are hard to resolve in a rational manner. We find them especially difficult because of the enormous range of conflicting values and interests that characterizes our pluralistic society. We cannot agree—unfortunately, we often do not even try to agree—on standards for just distribution. Rather, decisions tend to be made largely out of a clash of competing interests. Thus, regrettably, the question of how to distribute justly often gets reduced to who shall decide how to distribute. The question about justice has led us to the question about power.

THE USE AND ABUSE OF POWER

We have difficulty recognizing the problems of the exercise of power in the biomedical enterprise because of our delight with the wondrous fruits it has yielded. This is ironic because the notion of power is absolutely central to the modern conception of science. The ancients conceived of science as the *understanding* of nature, pursued for its own sake. We moderns view science as power, as *control* over nature; the conquest of nature "for the relief of man's estate" was the charge issued by Francis Bacon, one of the leading architects of the modern scientific project.[6]

Another source of difficulty is our fondness for speaking of the abstraction "Man." I suspect that we prefer to speak figuratively about "Man's power over Nature" because it obscures an unpleasant reality about human affairs. It is in fact particular men who wield power, not Man. What we really mean by "Man's power over Nature" is a power exercised by some men over other men, with a knowledge of nature as their instrument.

While applicable to technology in general, these reflections are especially pertinent to the technologies of human engineering, with which men deliberately exercise power over future generations. An excellent discussion of this question is found in *The Abolition of Man*, by C. S. Lewis.[7] (The reader will find Lewis's full essay, from which the following extract is taken, reprinted on pages 321–332.)

> It is, of course, a commonplace to complain that men have hitherto used badly, and against their fellows, the powers that science has given them. But that is not the point I am trying to make. I am not speaking of particular corruptions and abuses which an increase of moral virtue would cure: I am considering what the thing called "Man's power over Nature" must always and essentially be. . . .
>
> In reality, of course if any one age really attains, by eugenics and scientific

> education, the power to make its descendants what it pleases, all men who live after it are the patients of that power. They are weaker, not stronger: for though we may have put wonderful machines in their hands, we have preordained how they are to use them. . . . The real picture is that of one dominant age . . . which resists all previous ages most successfully and dominates all subsequent ages most irresistibly, and thus is the real master of the human species. But even within this master generation (itself an infinitesimal minority of the species) the power will be exercised by a minority smaller still. Man's conquest of Nature, if the dreams of some scientific planners are realized, means the rule of a few hundreds of men over billions upon billions of men. There neither is nor can be any simple increase of power on Man's side. Each new power won *by* man is a power *over* man as well. Each advance leaves him weaker as well as stronger. In every victory, besides being the general who triumphs, he is also the prisoner who follows the triumphal car.

Please note that I am not yet speaking about the problem of the misuse or abuse of power. The point is rather that the power which grows is unavoidably the power of only some men, and that the number of powerful men decreases as power increases.

Specific problems of abuse and misuse of specific powers must not, however, be overlooked. Some have voiced the fear that the technologies of genetic engineering and behavior control, though developed for good purposes, will be put to evil uses. These fears are perhaps somewhat exaggerated, if only because biomedical technologies would add very little to our highly developed arsenal for mischief, destruction, and stultification. Nevertheless, any proposal for large-scale human engineering should make us wary. Consider a program of positive eugenics based upon the widespread practice of asexual reproduction. Who shall decide what constitutes a superior individual worthy of replication? Who shall decide which individuals may or must reproduce, and by which method? These are questions easily answered only for a tyrannical regime.

Concern about the use of power is equally necessary in the selection of means for desirable or agreed-upon ends. Consider the desired end of limiting population growth. An effective program of fertility control is likely to be coercive. Who should decide the choice of means? Will the program penalize "conscientious objectors"?

Serious problems arise simply from obtaining and disseminating information, as in the mass screening programs now being proposed for detection of genetic disease. For what kinds of disorders is compulsory screening justified? Who shall have access to the data obtained, and for what purposes? To whom does information about a person's genotype belong? In ordinary medical practice, the patient's privacy is protected by the doctor's adherence to the principle of confidentiality. What will protect his privacy under conditions of mass screening?

More than privacy is at stake if screening is undertaken to detect psychological or behavioral abnormalities. A recent proposal, tendered and supported high in government, called for the psychological testing of all six-year-olds to detect future criminals and misfits. The proposal was rejected; current tests lack the requisite predictive powers. But will such a proposal be rejected if reliable tests become available? What if certain genetic disorders, diagnosable in childhood, can be shown to correlate with subsequent antisocial behavior? For what degree of correlation and for what kinds of behavior can mandatory screening be justified? What use should be made of the data? Might not the dissemination of the information itself undermine the individual's chance for a worthy life and contribute to his so-called antisocial tendencies?

Consider the seemingly harmless effort to redefine clinical death. If the need for organs for transplantation is the stimulus for redefining death, might not this concern influence the definition at the expense of the dying? One physician, in fact, refers in writing to the revised criteria for declaring a patient dead as a "new definition of heart donor eligibility."[8]

Problems of abuse of power arise even in the acquisition of basic knowledge. The securing of a voluntary and informed consent is an abiding problem in the use of human subjects in experimentation. Gross coercion and deception are now rarely a problem; the pressures are generally subtle, often related to an intrinsic power imbalance in favor of the experimentalist.

A special problem arises in experiments on or manipulations of the unborn. Here it is impossible to obtain the consent of the human subject. If the purpose of the intervention is therapeutic—to correct a known genetic abnormality, for example—consent can reasonably be implied. But can anyone ethically consent to nontherapeutic interventions in which parents or scientists work their wills or their eugenic visions on the child-to-be? Would not such manipulation represent in itself an abuse of power, independent of consequences?

There are many clinical situations which already permit, if not invite, the manipulative or arbitrary use of powers provided by biomedical technology: obtaining organs for transplantation, refusing to let a person die with dignity, giving genetic counselling to a frightened couple, recommending eugenic sterilization for a mental retardate, ordering electric shock for a homosexual. In each situation, there is an opportunity to violate the will of the patient or subject. Such opportunities have generally existed in medical practice, but the dangers are becoming increasingly serious. With the growing complexity of the technologies, the technician gains in authority, since he alone can understand what he is doing. The patient's lack of knowledge makes him deferential and often inhibits him from speaking up when he feels threatened. Physicians *are* sometimes troubled by their increasing power, yet they feel they cannot avoid its exercise. "Reluctantly," one commented to me, "we shall have to play God." With what guidance and to what ends I shall consider later. For the moment, I merely ask: "By whose authority?"

While these questions about power are pertinent and important, they are in one sense misleading. They imply an inherent conflict of purpose between physician and patient, between scientist and citizen. The discussion conjures up images of master and slave, of oppressor and oppressed. Yet it must be remembered that conflict of purpose is largely absent, especially with regard to general goals. To be sure, the purposes of medical scientists are not always the same as those of the subjects experimented on. Nevertheless, basic sponsors and partisans of biomedical technology are precisely those upon whom the technology will operate. The will of the scientist and physician is happily married to (rather, is the offspring of) the desire of all of us for better health, longer life, and peace of mind.

Most future biomedical technologies will probably be welcomed, as have those of the past. Their use will require little or no coercion. Some developments, such as pills to improve memory, control mood, or induce pleasure, are likely to need no promotion. Thus, even if we should escape from the dangers of coercive manipulation, we shall still face large problems posed by the voluntary use of biomedical technology, problems to which I now turn.

VOLUNTARY SELF-DEGRADATION AND DEHUMANIZATION

Modern opinion is sensitive to problems of restriction of freedom and abuse of power. Indeed, many hold that a man can be injured only by violating his will. But this view is much too narrow. It fails to recognize the great dangers we shall face in the use of biomedical technology, dangers that stem from an excess of freedom, from the uninhibited exercises of will. In my view, our greatest problem will increasingly be one of voluntary self-degradation, or willing dehumanization.

Certain desired and perfected medical technologies have already had some dehumanizing consequences. Improved methods of resuscitation have made possible heroic efforts to "save" the severely ill and injured. Yet these efforts are sometimes only partly successful; they may succeed in salvaging individuals with severe brain damage, capable of only a less-than-human, vegetating existence. Such patients, increasingly found in the intensive care units of university hospitals, have been denied a death with dignity. Families are forced to suffer seeing their loved ones so reduced, and are made to bear the burdens of a protracted death watch.

Even the ordinary methods of treating disease and prolonging life have impoverished the context in which men die. Fewer and fewer people die in the familiar surroundings of home or in the company of family and friends. At that time of life when there is perhaps the greatest need for human warmth and comfort, the dying patient is kept company by cardiac pacemakers and defibrillators, respirators, aspirators, oxygenators, catheters, and his intravenous drip.

But the loneliness is not confined to the dying patient in the hospital bed. Consider the increasing number of old people who are still alive, thanks to medical progress. As a group, the elderly are the most alienated members of our society. Not yet ready for the world of the dead, not deemed fit for the world of the living, they are shunted aside. More and more of them spend the extra years medicine has given them in "homes for senior citizens," in chronic hospitals, in nursing homes—waiting for the end. We have learned how to increase their years, but we have not learned how to help them enjoy their days. And yet, we bravely and relentlessly push back the frontiers against death.

Paradoxically, even the young and vigorous may be suffering because of medicine's success in removing death from their personal experience. Those born since penicillin represent the first generation ever to grow up without the experience or fear of probable unexpected death at an early age. They look around and see that virtually all of their friends are alive. A thoughtful physician, Eric Cassell, has remarked on this in "Death and the Physician"[9]:

> While the gift of time must surely be marked as a great blessing, the *perception* of time, as stretching out endlessly before us, is somewhat threatening. Many of us function best under deadlines, and tend to procrastinate when time limits are not set. . . . Thus, this unquestioned boon, the extension of life, and the removal of the threat of premature death, carries with it an unexpected anxiety: the anxiety of an unlimited future.
>
> In the young, the sense of limitless time has apparently imparted not a feeling of limitless opportunity, but increased stress and anxiety, in addition to the anxiety which results from other modern freedoms: personal mobility, a wide range of occupational choice, and independence from the limitations of class and familial patterns of work. . . . A certain aimlessness (often ringed around with great social consciousness) characterizes discussions about their own aspirations. The future is endless, and their inner demands seem minimal. Although it may appear uncharitable to say so, they seem to be acting in a way best described as "childish"—particularly in their lack of time sense. They behave as though there were no tomorrow, or as though the time limits imposed by the biological facts of life had become so vague for them as to be nonexistent.

Consider next the coming power over reproduction and genotype. We endorse the project that will enable us to control numbers and to treat individuals with genetic disease. But our desires outrun these defensible goals. Many would welcome the chance to become parents without the inconvenience of pregnancy; others would wish to know in advance the characteristics of their offspring (sex, height, eye color, intelligence); still others would wish to design these characteristics to suit their tastes. Some scientists have called for the use of the new technologies to assure the "quality" of all new babies.[10] As one obstetrician put it: "The business of obstetrics is to produce *optimum* babies." But the price to be paid for the "optimum baby" is the transfer of procreation from the home to the laboratory and its coincident transformation into manufacture. Increasing control over the product is purchased by the increasing depersonalization of the process. The complete depersonalization of procreation (possible with the development of an artificial placenta) shall be, in itself, seriously dehumanizing, no matter how optimum the product. It should not be forgotten that human procreation not only issues new human beings, but is itself a human activity.

Procreation is not simply an activity of the rational will. It is a more complete human activity precisely because it engages us bodily and spiritually, as well as rationally. Is there perhaps some wisdom in that mystery of nature which joins the pleasure of sex, the communication of love, and the desire for children in the very activity by which we continue the chain of human existence? Is not biological parenthood a built-in "mechanism," selected because it fosters and supports in parents an adequate concern for and commitment to their children? Would not the laboratory production of human beings no longer be *human* procreation? Could it keep human parenthood human?

The dehumanizing consequences of programmed reproduction extend beyond the mere acts and processes of life-giving. Transfer of procreation to the laboratory will no doubt weaken what is presently for many people the best remaining justification and support for the existence of marriage and the family. Sex is now comfortably at home outside of marriage; child rearing is progressively being given over to the state, the schools, the mass media, and the child-care centers. Some have argued that the family, long the nursery of humanity, has outlived its usefulness. To be sure, laboratory and governmental alternatives might be designed for procreation and child rearing, but at what cost?

This is not the place to conduct a full evaluation of the biological family. Nevertheless, some of its important virtues are, nowadays, too often overlooked. The family is rapidly becoming the only institution in an increasingly impersonal world where each person is loved not for what he does or makes, but simply because he is. The family is also the institution where most of us, both as children and as parents, acquire a sense of continuity with the past and a sense of commitment to the future. Without the family, we would have little incentive to take an interest in anything after our own deaths. These observations suggest that the elimination of the family would weaken ties to past and future, and would throw us, even more than we are now, to the mercy of an impersonal, lonely present.

Neurobiology and psychobiology probe most directly into the distinctively human. The technological fruit of these sciences is likely to be both more tempting than Eve's apple and more "catastrophic" in its result.[11] One need only consider contemporary drug use to see what people are willing to risk or sacrifice for novel experiences, heightened perceptions, or just "kicks." The possibility of drug-induced, instant, and effortless gratification will be welcomed. Recall the possibilities of voluntary self-stimulation of the brain to reduce anxiety, to heighten pleasure, or to create visual and auditory sensations unavailable through the peripheral sense organs. Once these techniques are perfected and safe, is there much doubt that they will be desired, demanded, and used?

What ends will these techniques serve? Most likely, only the most elemental, those most tied to the bodily pleasures. What will happen to thought, to love, to friendship, to art, to judgment, to public-spiritedness in a society with a perfected technology of pleasure? What kinds of creatures will we become if we obtain our pleasure by drug or electrical stimulation without the usual kind of human efforts and frustrations? What kind of society will we have?

We need only consult Aldous Huxley's prophetic novel *Brave New World* for a likely answer to these questions. There we encounter a society dedicated to homogeneity and stability, administered by means of instant gratifications and peopled by creatures of human shape but of stunted humanity. They consume, fornicate, take "soma," and operate the machinery that makes it all possible. They do not read, write, think, love, or govern themselves. Creativity and curiosity, reason and passion, exist only in a rudimentary and multilated form. In short, they are not men at all.

True, our techniques, like theirs, may in fact enable us to treat schizophrenia, to alleviate anxiety, to curb aggressiveness. We, like they, may indeed be able to save mankind from itself, but probably only at the cost of its humanness. In the end, the price of relieving man's estate might well be the abolition of man.[12]

There are, of course, many other routes leading to the abolition of man. There are many other and better known causes of dehumanization. Disease, starvation, mental retardation, slavery, and brutality—to name just a few—have long prevented many, if not most, people from living a fully human life. We should work to reduce and eventually to eliminate these evils. But the existence of these evils should not prevent us from appreciating that the use of the technology of man, uninformed by wisdom concerning proper human ends, and untempered by an appropriate humility and awe, can unwittingly render us all irreversibly less than human. For, unlike the man reduced by disease or slavery, the people dehumanized à la *Brave New World* are not miserable, do not know that they are dehumanized, and, what is worse, would not care if they knew. They are, indeed, happy slaves, with a slavish happiness.

SOME FUNDAMENTAL QUESTIONS

The practical problems of distributing scarce resources, of curbing the abuses of power, and of preventing voluntary dehumanization point beyond themselves to some large, enduring, and most difficult questions: the nature of justice and the good community, the nature of man and the good for man. My appreciation of the profundity of these questions and my own ignorance before them makes me hesitant to say any more about them. Nevertheless, previous failures to find a shortcut around them have led me to believe that these questions must be faced if we are to have any hope of understanding where biology is taking us. Therefore, I shall try to show in outline how I think some of the larger questions arise from my discussion of dehumanization and self-degradation.

My remarks on dehumanization can hardly fail to arouse argument. It might be said, correctly, that to speak about dehumanization presupposes a concept of "the distinctively human." It might also be said, correctly, that to speak about wisdom concerning proper human ends presupposes that such ends do in fact exist and that they may be more or less accessible to human understanding, or at least to rational inquiry. It is true that neither presupposition is at home in modern thought.

The notion of the "distinctively human" has been seriously challenged by modern scientists. Darwinists hold that man is, at least in origin, tied to the subhuman; his seeming distinctiveness is an illusion or, at most, not very important. Biochemists and molecular biologists extend the challenge by blurring the distinction between the living and the nonliving. The laws of physics and chemistry are found to be valid and are held to be sufficient for explaining biological systems. Man is a collection of molecules, an accident on the stage of evolution, endowed by chance with the power to change himself, but only along determined lines.

Psychoanalysts have also debunked the "distinctly human." The essence of man is seen to be located in those drives he shares with other animals—pursuit of pleasure and avoidance of pain. The so-called "higher functions" are understood to be servants of the more elementary, the more base. Any distinctiveness or "dignity" that man has consists of his superior capacity for gratifying his animal needs.

The idea of "human good" fares no better. In the social sciences, historicists and existentialists have helped drive this question underground.

The former hold all notions of human good to be culturally and historically bound, and hence mutable. The latter hold that values are subjective: each man makes his own, and ethics becomes simply the cataloging of personal tastes.

Such appear to be the prevailing opinions. Yet there is nothing novel about reductionism, hedonism, and relativism; these are doctrines with which Socrates contended. What is new is that these doctrines seem to be vindicated by scientific advance. Not only do the scientific notions of nature and of man flower into verifiable predictions, but they yield marvelous fruit. The technological triumphs are held to validate their scientific foundations. Here, perhaps, is the most pernicious result of technological progress—more dehumanizing than any actual manipulation of technique, present or future. We are witnessing the erosion, perhaps the final erosion, of the idea of man as something splendid or divine, and its replacement with a view that sees man, no less than nature, as simply more raw material for manipulation and homogenization. Hence, our peculiar moral crisis. We are in turbulent seas without a landmark precisely because we adhere more and more to a view of nature and of man which both gives us enormous power and, at the same time, denies all possibility of standards to guide its use. Though well equipped, we know not who we are nor where we are going. We are left to the accidents of our hasty, biased, and ephemeral judgments.

Let us not fail to note a painful irony: our conquest of nature has made us the slaves of blind chance. We triumph over nature's unpredictabilities only to subject ourselves to the still greater unpredictability of our capricious wills and our fickle opinions. That we have a method is no proof against our madness. Thus, engineering the engineer as well as the engine, we race our train we know not where.[13]

While the disastrous consequences of ethical nihilism are insufficient to refute it, they invite and make urgent a reinvestigation of the ancient and enduring questions of what is a proper life for a human being, what is a good community, and how are they achieved.[14] We must not be deterred from these questions simply because the best minds in human history have failed to settle them. Should we not rather be encouraged by the fact that they considered them to be the most important questions?

As I have hinted before, our ethical dilemma is caused by the victory of modern natural science with its nonteleological view of man. We ought therefore to reexamine with great care the modern notions of nature and of man, which undermine those earlier notions that provide a basis for ethics. If we consult our common experience, we are likely to discover some grounds for believing that the questions about man and human good are far from closed. Our common experience suggests many difficulties for the modern "scientific view of man." For example, this view fails to account for the concern for justice and freedom that appears to be characteristic of all human societies.[15] It also fails to account for or to explain the fact that men have speech and not merely voice, that men can choose and act and not merely move or react. It fails to explain why men engage in moral discourse, or, for that matter, why they speak at all. Finally, the "scientific view of man" cannot account for scientific inquiry itself, for why men seek to know. Might there not be something the matter with a knowledge of man that does not explain or take account of his most distinctive activities, aspirations, and concerns?[16]

Having gone this far, let me offer one suggestion as to where the difficulty might lie: in the modern understanding of knowledge. Since Bacon, as I have mentioned earlier, technology has increasingly come to be the basic justification for scientific inquiry. The end is power, not knowledge for its own sake. But power is not only the end. It is also an important *validation* of knowledge. One definitely knows that one knows only if one can make. Synthesis is held to be the ultimate proof of understanding.[17] A more radical formulation holds that one knows only what one makes: knowing *equals* making.

Yet therein lies a difficulty. If truth be the power to change or to make the object studied, then of what do we have knowledge? If there are no fixed realities, but only material upon which we may work our wills, will not "science" be merely the "knowledge" of the transient and the manipulatable? We might indeed have knowledge of the laws by which things change and the rules for their manipulation, but no knowledge of the things themselves. Can such a view of "science" yield any knowledge about the nature of man, or indeed, about the nature of anything? Our questions appear to lead back to the most basic of questions: What does it mean to know? What is it that is knowable?[18]

We have seen that the practical problems point toward and make urgent certain enduring, fundamental questions. Yet while pursuing these questions, we cannot afford to neglect the practical problems as such. Let us not forget Delgado and the "psychocivilized society." The philosophical inquiry could be rendered moot by our blind, confident efforts to dissect and redesign ourselves. While awaiting a reconstruction of theory, we must act as best we can.

WHAT IS TO BE DONE?

First, we sorely need to recover some humility in the face of our awesome powers. The arguments I have presented should make apparent the folly of arrogance, of the presumption that we are wise enough to remake ourselves. Because we lack wisdom, caution is our urgent need. Or to put it another way, in the absence of that "ultimate wisdom," we can be wise enough to know that we are not wise enough. When we lack sufficient wisdom to do, wisdom consists in not doing. Caution, restraint, delay, abstention are what this second-best (and, perhaps, only) wisdom dictates with respect to the technology for human engineering.

If we can recognize that biomedical advances carry significant social costs, we may be willing to adopt a less permissive, more critical stance toward new developments. We need to reexamine our prejudice not only that all biomedical innovation is progress, but also that it is inevitable. Precedent certainly favors the view that what can be done will be done, but is this necessarily so? Ought we not to be suspicious when technologists speak of coming developments as automatic, not subject to human control? Is there not something contradictory in the notion that we have the power to control all the untoward consequences of a technology, but lack the power to determine whether it should be developed in the first place?

What will be the likely consequences of the perpetuation of our permissive and fatalistic attitude toward human engineering? How will the large decisions be made? Technocratically and self-servingly, if our experience with previous technologies is any guide. Under conditions of laissez-faire, most technologists will pursue techniques, and most private industries will pursue profits. We are fortunate that, apart from the drug manufacturers, there are at present in the biomedical area few large industries that influence public policy. Once these appear, the voice of "the public interest" will have to shout very loudly to be heard above their whisperings in the halls of Congress. These reflections point to the need for institutional controls.

Scientists understandably balk at the notion of the regulation of science and technology. Censorship is ugly and often based upon ignorant fear; bureaucratic regulation is often stupid and inefficient. Yet there is something disingenuous about a scientist who professes concern about the social consequences of science, but who responds to every suggestion of regulation with one or both of the following: "No restrictions on scientific research," and "Technological progress should not be curtailed." Surely, to suggest that *certain* technologies ought to be regulated or forestalled is not to call for the halt of *all* technological progress (and says nothing at all about basic research). Each development should be considered on its own merits. Although the dangers of regulation cannot be dismissed, who, for example, would still object to efforts to obtain an effective, complete, global prohibition on the development, testing, and use of biological and nuclear weapons?

The proponents of laissez-faire ignore two fundamental points. They ignore the fact that not to regulate is as much a policy decision as the opposite, and that it merely postpones the time of regulation. Controls will eventually be called for—as they are now being demanded to end environmental pollution. If attempts are not made early to detect and diminish the social costs of biomedical advances by intelligent institutional regulation, the society is likely to react later with more sweeping, immoderate, and throttling controls.

The proponents of laissez-faire also ignore the fact that much of technology is already regulated. The federal government is already deep in research and development (for example, space, electronics, and weapons) and is the principal sponsor of biomedical research. One may well question the wisdom of the direction given but one would be wrong in arguing that technology cannot survive social control. Clearly, the question is not control versus no control, but rather what kind of control, when, by whom, and for what purpose.

Means for achieving international regulation and control need to be devised. Biomedical technology can be no nation's monopoly. The need for international agreements and supervision can readily be understood if we consider the likely American response to the successful asexual reproduction of 10,000 Mao Tse-tungs.

To repeat, the basic short-term need is caution. Practically, this means that we should shift the burden of proof to the *proponents* of a new biomedical technology. Concepts of "risk" and "cost" need to be broadened to include some of the social and ethical consequences discussed earlier. The probable or possible harmful effects of the widespread use of a new technique should be anticipated and introduced as "costs" to be weighed in deciding about the *first* use. The regulatory institutions should be encouraged to exercise restraint and to formulate the grounds for saying "no." We must all get used to the idea that biomedical technology makes possible many things we should never do.

But caution is not enough. Nor are clever institutional arrangements. Institutions can be little better than the people who make them work. However worthy our intentions, we are deficient in understanding. In the *long* run, our hope can only lie in education: in a public educated about the meanings and limits of science and enlightened in its use of technology; in scientists better educated to understand the relationships between science and technology on the one hand, and ethics and politics on the other; in human beings who are as wise in the latter as they are clever in the former.

NOTES AND REFERENCES

1. R. G. Edwards, B. D. Bavister, P. C. Steptoe, *Nature* 221, 632 (1969).
2. R. G. Edwards, P. C. Steptoe, J. M. Purdy, *ibid.* 227, 1307 (1970).
3. H. J. Muller, *Science* 134, 643 (1961).
4. J. M. R. Delgado, *Physical Control of the Mind: Toward a Psychocivilized Society* (Harper & Row, New York, 1969), p. 185.

5. *Ibid.*, p. 88.
6. F. Bacon, *The Advancement of Learning, Book I*, H. G. Dick, Ed. (Random House, New York, 1955), p. 193.
7. C. S. Lewis, *The Abolition of Man* (Macmillan, New York, 1965), pp. 69–71. Reprinted on pp. 321–332 of this volume.
8. D. D. Rutstein, *Daedalus* (Spring 1969), p. 523. Quotation is from p. 526.
9. E. J. Cassell, *Commentary* (June 1969), p. 73. Quotation is from p. 76.
10. B. Glass, *Science* 171, 23 (1971).
11. It is, of course, a long-debated question as to whether the fall of Adam and Eve ought to be considered "catastrophic," or more precisely, whether the Hebrew tradition considered it so. I do not mean here to be taking sides in this quarrel by my use of the term "catastrophic," and, in fact, tend to line up on the negative side of the questions, as put above. Curiously, as Aldous Huxley's *Brave New World* (Harper & Row, New York, 1969) suggests, the implicit goal of the biomedical technology could well be said to be the reversal of the Fall and a return of man to the hedonic and immortal existence of the Garden of Eden. Yet I can point to at least two problems. First, the new Garden of Eden will probably have no gardens; the received, splendid world of nature will be buried beneath asphalt, concrete, and other human fabrications, a transformation that is already far along. (Recall that in *Brave New World* elaborate consumption-oriented, mechanical amusement parks—featuring, for example, centrifugal bumble-puppy—had supplanted wilderness and even ordinary gardens.) Second, the new inhabitant of the new "Garden" will have to be a creature for whom we have no precedent, a creature as difficult to imagine as to bring into existence. He will have to be simultaneously an innocent like Adam and a technological wizard who keeps the "Garden" running. (I am indebted to Dean Robert Goldwin, St. John's College, for this last insight.)
12. Some scientists naively believe that an engineered increase in human intelligence will steer us in the right direction. Surely we have learned by now that intelligence, whatever it is and however measured, is not synonymous with wisdom and that, if harnessed to the wrong ends, it can cleverly perpetrate great folly and evil. Given the activities in which many, if not most, of our best minds are now engaged, we should not simply rejoice in the prospect of enhancing IQ. On what would this increased intelligence operate? At best, the programming of further increases in IQ. It would design and operate techniques for prolonging life, for engineering reproduction, for delivering gratifications. With no gain in wisdom, our gain in intelligence can only enhance the rate of our dehumanization.
13. The philosopher Hans Jonas has made the identical point: "Thus the slow-working accidents of nature, which by the very patience of their small increments, large numbers, and gradual decisions, may well cease to be 'accident' in outcome, are to be replaced by the fast-working accidents of man's hasty and biased decisions, not exposed to the long test of the ages. His uncertain ideas are to set the goals of generations, with a certainty borrowed from the presumptive certainty of the means. The latter presumption is doubtful enough, but this doubtfulness becomes secondary to the prime question that arises when man indeed undertakes to 'make himself': in what image of his own devising shall he do so, even granted that he can be sure of the means? In fact, of course, he can be sure of neither, not of the end, nor of the means, once he enters the realm where he plays with the roots of life. Of one thing only can he be sure: of his power to move the foundations and to cause incalculable and irreversible consequences. Never was so much power coupled with so little guidance for its use." [*J. Cent. Conf. Amer. Rabbis* (January 1968), p.

27.] These remarks demonstrate that, contrary to popular belief, we are not even on the right road toward a rational understanding of and rational control over human nature and human life. It is indeed the height of irrationality triumphantly to pursue rationalized technique, while at the same time insisting that questions of ends, values, and purposes lie beyond rational discourse.

14. It is encouraging to note that these questions are seriously being raised in other quarters—for example, by persons concerned with the decay of cities or the pollution of nature. There is a growing dissatisfaction with ethical nihilism. In fact, its tenets are unwittingly abandoned, by even its staunchest adherents, in any discussion of "what to do." For example, in the biomedical area, everyone, including the most unreconstructed and technocratic reductionist, finds himself speaking about the use of powers for "human betterment." He has wandered unawares onto ethical ground. One cannot speak of "human betterment" without considering what is meant by *the human* and by the related notion of *the good for man*. These questions can be avoided only by asserting that practical matters reduce to tastes and power, and by confessing that the use of the phrase "human betterment" is a deception to cloak one's own will to power. In other words, these questions can be avoided only by ceasing to discuss.
15. Consider, for example, the widespread acceptance, in the legal systems of very different societies and cultures, of the principle and the practice of third-party adjudication of disputes. And consider why, although many societies have practiced slavery, no slaveholder has preferred his own enslavement to his own freedom. It would seem that some notions of justice and freedom, as well as right and truthfulness, are constitutive for any society, and that a concern for these values may be a fundamental characteristic of "human nature."
16. Scientists may, of course, continue to believe in righteousness or justice or truth, but these beliefs are not grounded in their "scientific knowledge" of man. They rest instead upon the receding wisdom of an earlier age.
17. This belief, silently shared by many contemporary biologists, has recently been given the following clear expression: "One of the acid tests of understanding an object is the ability to put it together from its component parts. Ultimately, molecular biologists will attempt to subject their understanding of all structure and function to this sort of test by trying to synthesize a cell. It is of some interest to see how close we are to this goal." [P. Handler, Ed., *Biology and the Future of Man* (Oxford Univ. Press, New York, 1970), p. 55.]
18. When a version of this article was presented publicly before its appearance in *Science*, it was criticized by one questioner as being "antiscientific." He suggested that my remarks "were the kind that gave science a bad name." He went on to argue that, far from being the enemy of morality, the pursuit of truth was itself a highly moral activity, perhaps the highest. The relation of science and morals is a long and difficult question with an illustrious history, and it deserves a more extensive discussion than space permits. However, because some readers may share the questioner's response, I offer a brief reply. First, on the matter of reputation, we should recall that the pursuit of truth may be in tension with keeping a good name (witness Oedipus, Socrates, Galileo, Spinoza, Solzhenitsyn). For most of human history, the pursuit of truth (including "science") was not a reputable activity among the many, and was, in fact, highly suspect. Even today, it is doubtful whether more than a few appreciate knowledge as an end in itself. Science has acquired a "good name" in recent times largely because of its technological fruit; it is therefore

to be expected that a disenchantment with technology will reflect badly upon science. Second, my own attack has not been directed against science, but against the use of *some* technologies and, even more, against the unexamined belief—indeed, I would say, superstition—that all biomedical technology is an unmixed blessing. I share the questioner's belief that the pursuit of truth is a highly moral activity. In fact, I am inviting him and others to join in a pursuit of truth about whether all these new technologies are really good for us. This is a question that merits and is susceptible of serious intellectual inquiry. Finally, we must ask whether what we call "science" has a monopoly on the pursuit of truth. What is "truth"? What is knowable, and what does it mean to know? Surely, these are also questions that can be examined. Unless we do so, we shall remain ignorant about what "science" is and about what it discovers. Yet "science"—that is, modern natural science—cannot begin to answer them; they are philosophical questions, the very ones I am trying to raise at this point in the text.

II

THE SOCIAL WORLD AND ADJUSTMENT TO A STEADY STATE

INTRODUCTION

Although biophysical constraints on economic growth are the more easily recognizable, social and moral constraints are likely to be the more stringent. In other words, the economic steady state will be desirable socially long before physical limitations will make it a necessity. For example, the social problem of safeguarding plutonium from use by criminals is more likely to limit the growth of use of the breeder reactor than are the physical problems of thermal pollution and low level radiation. The articles here in Part II, but also in the third part, focus mainly on social and moral constraints to economic growth, and on the social problems which would be encountered in making a transition from a growing economy to a stationary economy. What social institutions will allow us to reach and maintain a steady state with the least sacrifice of individual freedom? Might we even be able to increase individual freedom? Which dimensions of freedom can be expanded and which must be contracted? These are typical of the questions raised, if not always answered, by the authors of the articles throughout the rest of the book.

Although the articles in Part II vary greatly in their approaches, they seem to share a tacit paradigm that is very different from the paradigm of orthodox economics. Presently, economic theory begins with nonphysical parameters (technology, preferences, and distribution of wealth and income are all established beforehand as "givens") and inquires how the physical variables of quantities produced and resources used must be adjusted to fit an equilibrium (or an "equilibrium rate of growth") determined by these nonphysical parameters. The nonphysical conditions are given, and physical magnitudes must adjust. The new paradigm, however, begins with physical parameters (a finite world, complex biophysical interrelations, the immutability of laws of thermodynamics) and inquires how the nonphysical variables of technology, distribution, and life styles can be brought into a feasible and just equilibrium with the complex biophysical system of which we are a part. The physical magnitudes are given, and the nonphysical patterns of life become variables. The "adjustment" that mankind must make is therefore an adjustment to a new realization of physical and biophysical limitations, for it is as though these limitations have come to symbolize a general sense of closure: man, peering through the window into the universe, has been made all the more aware of the finite sphere that is his own room within that universe. The shift in outlook to an economic view in which man's activities are obedient to the physical limitations of his globe is captured very well in the following quote by Arnold Toynbee:

> More and more people are coming to realize that the growth of material wealth, which the British industrial revolution set going, and which the modern British-made ideology has presented as being mankind's proper paramount objective, cannot in truth be the "wave of the future." Nature is going to compel posterity to revert to a stable state on the material plane and to turn to the realm of the spirit for satisfying man's hunger for infinity.[1]

We have already read about nature compelling posterity to revert to a stable state, and in the last part of the book we will read what various authors have to say about values, the realm of the spirit where man's hunger for infinity has at least some chance of being satisfied. For now, however, we shall read about the social adjustments necessary for achieving Toynbee's "stable state on the material plane."

The first article of Part II, by economist Kenneth Boulding, has by now become a classic. In it Boulding contrasts various "systems"—for examples, biological systems, or systems of matter, energy, and information—that are either "open" or "closed." An open system maintains some structure in the midst of the flow of throughput, taking inputs and giving outputs. Closed systems, on the other hand, are like self-contained closed loops, generating their own inputs and outputs from internal stock. As man has pressed closer to his terrestrial limits, the earth has seemed to become less of an open and more of a closed system. To symbolize the economics of the old, limitless, open world, Boulding uses the term "cowboy economy." As a result of a kind of ecological succession, the closed earth of the future makes necessary the replacement of the linear cowboy economy with what Boulding calls a "spaceman economy." Not only are these terms picturesque, they are very apt, and readers will find that several other authors make reference to them.

The article by biologist Garrett Hardin is likewise a modern classic,

---

1. Notes for this introduction will be found on page 120.

a forceful, frequently cited presentation of problems arising from private exploitation of a "commonwealth." The commons Hardin refers to is, symbolically, a pastureland that is killed off by the overgrazing that results when every herdsman increases his herd by the additional animals each thinks the pasture can support. Clearly the symbol describes the real effects of uncontrolled population growth and diminishing resources. Moreover, though "commons" problems can be analyzed, it is likely there are no technical solutions to them. Hardin thinks a social policy of "mutual coercion, mutually agreed upon" might soften this aspect of the tragedy of the commons by controlling the freedom of the individual to bring ruin to all.

In the third article I attempt to build on ideas advanced by Boulding, Georgescu-Roegen, John Stuart Mill (the early originator of the concept of a "stationary state"), and others, in elucidating the steady-state economy, which has potential for altering the nature of presently insoluble problems. The institution of three interrelated social conditions is suggested to bring about the transition: constant population, constant physical wealth, and control of distribution.

Warren Johnson focuses his attention on the last of these and suggests that an institution not originally designed to meet the environmental crisis—the guaranteed annual income—could nevertheless have important and beneficial environmental effects.

Richard England and Barry Bluestone, two active members of the Union for Radical Political Economy,[2] analyze the problems of class conflict and vested interests, which are considerably sharpened by the closure of material growth. For example, precisely *who* benefits most from environmental protection measures? Probably the poor pay more for them, and receive less. The ironic dilemma in the view of England and Bluestone is that government regulation may be ineffective as long as government and corporations cooperate in the regulatory process, and that underdeveloped nations may turn out to provide the world's final, grim "commons" to which corporate interests will turn should environmental protection measures restrict them elsewhere.

Evidently Hardin is right. Not all who understand the need for change are sufficiently moved to apply those changes to themselves. Political scientist William Ophuls, building on Garrett Hardin's article and generalizing the analysis of the "commons," points out that the features of what Hardin explicated as the tragedy of unlimited freedom in a commons were of central concern to the English philospher Thomas Hobbes. So Hobbes's thought and his tragic sense of life are tremendously relevant to our present crisis. Perhaps Hobbes's view of mankind was harsher than Hardin's is: Hobbes would have established an autocratic "Leviathan" to implement controls for the best interests of mankind, rather than "mutual coercion, mutually agreed upon." Ophuls admits the concept is not appealing. But will world finitude ultimately force a choice between Leviathan and oblivion?

Beginning with Buddhist rather than Hobbesian assumptions about the nature of man, E. F. Schumacher analyzes a pattern of economic behavior which is consistent with Buddhist values, and shows that it is remarkably consistent with ecological requirements in that it emphasizes the attainment of given ends with minimum means. The Buddhist belief in nonviolence, for example, enjoins Buddhists against ravaging the earth of its nonrenewable resources, and though Western countries are apt to look upon expenditure of human labor as something to be minimized, in Buddhist economies human work is an aim to be achieved for itself.

Walter Weisskopf analyzes the conflict between economic growth and existential balance, and explains the historical developments, rooted in classical economics, that lead to overemphasis on the former. He further shows that the concept of an equilibrium among all levels in the hierarchy of needs was an important part of the economics of Alfred Marshall, the founder of neoclassical economics, which, had it not been neglected, might have prevented the excesses of growth fetishism that cause us such problems today. The articles by Schumacher and Weisskopf —touching as they do on the values that form the bases for economic systems—could well have been placed in Part III, about values, but their inclusion here is out of deference to the fact that both authors are economists. Both are discussing society as it is influenced by economic thinking.

The final article of this part shifts attention from the possibilities of a better world back to the actualities of the present world. Specifically how much ground lies between the economic growth policies of the present and the steady-state policies we wish to adopt? Taking the steadfast adherence of our country's electric power industry to growthmania as a case study, I consider critically the specific arguments about the needs for energy growth on which they rest their case.

NOTES

1. Arnold Toynbee, *The Observer*, London, June 11, 1972.
2. URPE, founded in 1968, is an association of teachers, students, and economists working together toward economic change. Its headquarters are in Ann Arbor, Michigan.

5

THE ECONOMICS OF THE COMING SPACESHIP EARTH

Kenneth E. Boulding

We are now in the middle of a long process of transition in the nature of the image which man has of himself and his environment. Primitive men, and to a large extent also men of the early civilizations, imagined themselves to be living on a virtually illimitable plane. There was almost always somewhere beyond the known limits of human habitation, and over a very large part of the time that man has been on earth, there has been something like a frontier. That is, there was always some place else to go when things got too difficult, either by reason of the deterioration of the natural environment or a deterioration of the social structure in places where people happened to live. The image of the frontier is probably one of the oldest images of mankind, and it is not surprising that we find it hard to get rid of.

Gradually, however, man has been accustoming himself to the notion of the spherical earth and a closed sphere of human activity. A few unusual spirits among the ancient Greeks perceived that the earth was a sphere. It was only with the circumnavigations and the geographical

---

"The Economics of the Coming Spaceship Earth." From *Environmental Quality in a Growing Economy*, published for Resources for the Future, Inc.

explorations of the fifteenth and sixteenth centuries, however, that the fact that the earth was a sphere became at all widely known and accepted. Even in the nineteenth century, the commonest map was Mercator's projection, which visualizes the earth as an illimitable cylinder, essentially a plane wrapped around the globe, and it was not until the Second World War and the development of the air age that the global nature of the planet really entered the popular imagination. Even now we are very far from having made the moral, political, and psychological adjustments which are implied in this transition from the illimitable plane to the closed sphere.

Economists in particular, for the most part, have failed to come to grips with the ultimate consequences of the transition from the open to the closed earth. One hesitates to use the terms "open" and "closed" in this connection, as they have been used with so many different shades of meaning. Nevertheless, it is hard to find equivalents. The open system, indeed, has some similarities to the open system of von Bertalanffy,[1] in that it implies that some kind of structure is maintained in the midst of a throughput from inputs to outputs. In a closed system, the outputs of all parts of the system are linked to the inputs of other parts. There are no inputs from outside and no outputs to the outside; indeed, there is no outside at all. Closed systems, in fact, are very rare in human experience, in fact almost by definition unknowable, for if there are genuinely closed systems around us, we have no way of getting information into them or out of them; and hence if they are really closed, we would be quite unaware of their existence. We can only find out about a closed system if we participate in it. Some isolated primitive societies may have approximated to this, but even these had to take inputs from the environment and give outputs to it. All living organisms, including man himself, are open systems. They have to receive inputs in the shape of air, food, water, and give off outputs in the form of effluvia and excrement. Deprivation of input of air, even for a few minutes, is fatal. Deprivation of the ability to obtain any input or to dispose of any output is fatal in a relatively short time. All human societies have likewise been open systems. They receive inputs from the earth, the atmosphere, and the waters, and they give outputs into these reservoirs; they also produce inputs internally in the shape of babies and outputs in the shape of corpses. Given a capacity to draw upon inputs and to get rid of outputs, an open system of this kind can persist indefinitely.

There are some systems—such as the biological phenotype, for instance the human body—which cannot maintain themselves indefinitely by inputs and outputs because of the phenomenon of aging. This process

1. References for this reading will be found on page 132.

is very little understood. It occurs, evidently, because there are some outputs which cannot be replaced by any known input. There is not the same necessity for aging in organizations and in societies, although an analogous phenomenon may take place. The structure and composition of an organization or society, however, can be maintained by inputs of fresh personnel from birth and education as the existing personnel ages and eventually dies. Here we have an interesting example of a system which seems to maintain itself by the self-generation of inputs, and in this sense is moving toward closure. The input of people (that is, babies) is also an output of people (that is, parents).

Systems may be open or closed in respect to a number of classes of inputs and outputs. Three important classes are matter, energy, and information. The present world economy is open in regard to all three. We can think of the world economy or "econosphere" as a subset of the "world set," which is the set of all objects of possible discourse in the world. We then think of the state of the econosphere at any one moment as being the total capital stock, that is, the set of all objects, people, organizations, and so on, which are interesting from the point of view of the system of exchange. This total stock of capital is clearly an open system in the sense that it has inputs and outputs, inputs being production which adds to the capital stock, outputs being consumption which subtracts from it. From a material point of view, we see objects passing from the noneconomic into the economic set in the process of production, and we similarly see products passing out of the economic set as their value becomes zero. Thus we see the econosphere as a material process involving the discovery and mining of fossil fuels, ores, etc., and at the other end a process by which the effluents of the system are passed out into noneconomic reservoirs—for instance, the atmosphere and the oceans—which are not appropriated and do not enter into the exchange system.

From the point of view of the energy system, the econosphere involves inputs of available energy in the form, say, of water power, fossil fuels, or sunlight, which are necessary in order to create the material throughput and to move matter from the noneconomic set into the economic set or even out of it again; and energy itself is given off by the system in a less available form, mostly in the form of heat. These inputs of available energy must come either from the sun (the energy supplied by other stars being assumed to be negligible) or it may come from the earth itself, either through its internal heat or through its energy of rotation or other motions, which generate, for instance, the energy of the tides. Agriculture, a few solar machines, and water power use the current available energy income. In advanced societies this is supplemented very extensively by the use of fossil fuels, which represent, as it were, a capital stock of stored-up sunshine. Because of this capital stock of energy, we have been able to maintain an energy input into the system, particularly over the last two centuries, much larger than we would have been able to do with existing techniques if we had had to rely on the current input of available energy from the sun or the earth itself. This supplementary input, however, is by its very nature exhaustible.

The inputs and outputs of information are more subtle and harder to trace, but also represent an open system, related to, but not wholly dependent on, the transformations of matter and energy. By far the larger amount of information and knowledge is self-generated by the human society, though a certain amount of information comes into the sociosphere in the form of light from the universe outside. The information that comes from the universe has certainly affected man's image of himself and of his environment, as we can easily visualize if we suppose that we lived on a planet with a total cloud-cover that kept out all information from the exterior universe. It is only in very recent times, of course, that the information coming in from the universe has been captured and coded into the form of a complex image of what the universe is like outside the earth; but even in primitive times, man's perception of the heavenly bodies has always profoundly affected his image of earth and of himself. It is the information generated within the planet, however, and particularly that generated by man himself, which forms by far the larger part of the information system. We can think of the stock of knowledge, or as Teilhard de Chardin called it, the "noosphere," and consider this as an open system, losing knowledge through aging and death and gaining it through birth and education and the ordinary experience of life.

From the human point of view, knowledge, or information, is by far the most important of the three systems. Matter only acquires significance and only enters the sociosphere or the econosphere insofar as it becomes an object of human knowledge. We can think of capital, indeed, as frozen knowledge or knowledge imposed on the material world in the form of improbable arrangements. A machine, for instance, originates in the mind of man, and both its construction and its use involve information processes imposed on the material world by man himself. The cumulation of knowledge, that is, the excess of its production over its consumption, is the key to human development of all kinds, especially to economic development. We can see this preeminence of knowledge very clearly in the experiences of countries where the material capital has been destroyed by a war, as in Japan and Germany. The knowledge of the people was not destroyed, and it did not take long, therefore, certainly not more than ten years, for most of the material capital to be reestablished again. In a country such as Indonesia, however, where the knowledge did not exist, the material capital did not come into being either. By "knowledge" here I mean, of course, the whole cognitive structure, which includes valuations and motivations as well as images of the factual world.

The concept of entropy, used in a somewhat loose sense, can be applied to all three of these open systems. In material systems, we can distinguish between entropic processes, which take concentrated materials and diffuse them through the oceans or over the earth's surface or into the atmosphere, and antientropic processes, which take diffuse materials and concentrate them. Material entropy can be taken as a measure of the uniformity of the distribution of elements and, more uncertainly, compounds and other structures on the earth's surface. There is, fortunately, no law of increasing material entropy, as there is in the corresponding case of energy, as it is quite possible to concentrate diffused materials if energy inputs are allowed. Thus the processes for fixation of nitrogen from the air, processes for the extraction of magnesium or other elements from the sea, and processes for the desalinization of sea water are antientropic in the material sense, though the reduction of material entropy has to be paid for by inputs of energy and also inputs of information, or at least a stock of information in the system. In regard to matter, therefore, a closed system is conceivable, that is, a system in which there is neither increase nor decrease in material entropy. In such a system all outputs from consumption would constantly be recycled to become inputs for production, as for instance, nitrogen in the nitrogen cycle of the natural ecosystem.

In the energy system there is, unfortunately, no escape from the grim second law of thermodynamics; and if there were no energy inputs into the earth, any evolutionary or developmental process would be impossible. The large energy inputs which we have obtained from fossil fuels are strictly temporary. Even the most optimistic predictions expect the easily available supply of fossil fuels to be exhausted in a mere matter of centuries at present rates of use. If the rest of the world were to rise to American standards of power consumption, and still more if world population continues to increase, the exhaustion of fossil fuels would be even more rapid. The development of nuclear energy has improved this picture, but has fundamentally altered it, at least in present technologies, for fissionable material is still relatively scarce. If we should achieve the economic use of energy through fusion, of course, a much larger source of energy materials would be available, which would expand the time horizons of supplementary energy input into an open social system by perhaps tens to hundreds of thousands of years. Failing this, however, the time is not very far distant, historically speaking, when man will once more have to retreat to his current energy input from the sun, even though with increased knowledge this could be used much more effectively than in the past. Up to now, certainly, we have not got very far with the technology of using current solar energy, but the possibility of substantial improvements in the future is certainly high. It may be, indeed, that the biological revolution which is just beginning will produce a solution to this problem, as we develop artificial organisms which are capable of much more efficient transformation of solar energy into easily available forms than any that we now have. As Richard Meier has suggested, we may run our machines in the future with methane-producing algae.[2]

The question of whether there is anything corresponding to entropy in the information system is a puzzling one, though of great interest. There are certainly many examples of social systems and cultures which have lost knowledge, especially in transition from one generation to the next, and in which the culture has therefore degenerated. One only has to look at the folk culture of Appalachian migrants to American cities to see a culture which started out as a fairly rich European folk culture in Elizabethan times and which seems to have lost skills, adaptability, folk tales, songs, and almost everything that goes up to make richness and complexity in a culture, in the course of about ten generations. The American Indians on reservations provide another example of such degradation of the information and knowledge system. On the other hand, over a great part of human history, the growth of knowledge in the earth as a whole seems to have been almost continuous, even though there have been times of relatively slow growth and times of rapid growth. As it is knowledge of certain kinds that produces the growth of knowledge in general, we have here a very subtle and complicated system, and it is hard to put one's finger on the particular elements in a culture which make knowledge grow more or less rapidly, or even which make it decline. One of the great puzzles in this connection, for instance, is why the takeoff into science, which represents an "acceleration," or an increase in the rate of growth of knowledge in European society in the sixteenth century, did not take place in China, which at that time (about 1600) was unquestionably ahead of Europe, and one would think even more ready for the breakthrough. This is perhaps the most crucial question in the theory of social development, yet we must confess that it is very little understood. Perhaps the most significant factor in this connection is the existence of "slack" in the culture, which permits a divergence from established patterns and activity which is not merely devoted to reproducing the existing society but is devoted to changing it. China was perhaps too well organized and had too little slack in its society to produce the kind of acceleration which we find in the somewhat poorer and less well organized but more diverse societies of Europe.

The closed earth of the future requires economic principles which are somewhat different from those of the open earth of the past. For the sake of picturesqueness, I am tempted to call the open economy the "cowboy economy," the cowboy being symbolic of the illimitable plains and also associated with reckless, exploitative, romantic, and violent behavior, which is characteristic of open societies. The closed economy of the future might similarly be called the "spaceman" economy, in which the earth has become a single spaceship, without unlimited reservoirs of anything, either for extraction or for pollution, and in which, therefore, man must find his place in a cyclical ecological system which is capable of continuous reproduction of material form even though it cannot escape having inputs of energy. The difference between the two types of economy becomes most apparent in the attitude towards consumption. In the cowboy economy, consumption is regarded as a good thing and production likewise; and the success of the economy is measured by the amount of the throughput from the "factors of production," a part of which, at any rate, is extracted from the reservoirs of raw materials and noneconomic objects, and another part of which is output into the reservoirs of pollution. If there are infinite reservoirs from which material can be obtained and into which effluvia can be deposited, then the throughput is at least a plausible measure of the success of the economy. The Gross National Product is a rough measure of this total throughput. It should be possible, however, to distinguish that part of the GNP which is derived from exhaustible and that which is derived from reproducible resources, as well as that part of consumption which represents effluvia and that which represents input into the productive system again. Nobody, as far as I know, has ever attempted to break down the GNP in this way, although it would be an interesting and extremely important exercise, which is unfortunately beyond the scope of this paper.

By contrast, in the spaceman economy, throughput is by no means a desideratum, and is indeed to be regarded as something to be minimized rather than maximized. The essential measure of the success of the economy is not production and consumption at all, but the nature, extent, quality, and complexity of the total capital stock, including in this the state of the human bodies and minds included in the system. In the spaceman economy, what we are primarily concerned with is stock maintenance, and any technological change which results in the maintenance of a given total stock with a lessened throughput (that is, less production and consumption) is clearly a gain. This idea that both production and consumption are bad things rather than good things is very strange to economists, who have been obsessed with the income-flow concepts to the exclusion, almost, of capital-stock concepts.

There are actually some very tricky and unsolved problems involved in the questions as to whether human welfare or well-being is to be regarded as a stock or a flow. Something of both these elements seems actually to be involved in it, and as far as I know there have been practically no studies directed towards identifying these two dimensions of human satisfaction. Is it, for instance, eating that is a good thing, or is it being well fed? Does economic welfare involve having nice clothes, fine houses, good equipment, and so on, or is to be measured by the depreciation and the wearing out of these things? I am inclined myself to regard the stock concept as most fundamental, that is, to think of being well fed as more important than eating, and to think even of so-called services as essentially involving the restoration of a depleting psychic capital. Thus I have argued that we go to a concert in order to restore a psychic condition which might be called "just having gone to a concert," which, once established, tends to depreciate. When it depreciates beyond a certain point, we go to another concert in order to restore it. If it depreciates rapidly, we go to a lot of concerts; if it depreciates slowly, we go to a few. On this view, similarly, we eat primarily to restore bodily homeostasis, that is, to maintain a condition of being well fed, and so on. On this view, there is nothing desirable in consumption at all. The less consumption we can maintain a given state with, the better off we are. If we had clothes that did not wear out, houses that did not depreciate, and even if we could maintain our bodily condition without eating, we would clearly be much better off.

It is this last consideration, perhaps, which makes one pause. Would we, for instance, really want an operation that would enable us to restore all our bodily tissues by intravenous feeding while we slept? Is there not, that is to say, a certain virtue in throughput itself, in activity itself, in production and consumption itself, in raising food and in eating it? It would certainly be rash to exclude this possibility. Further interesting problems are raised by the demand for variety. We certainly do not want a constant state to be maintained; we want fluctuations in the state. Otherwise there would be no demand for variety in food, for variety in scene, as in travel, for variety in social contact, and so on. The demand for variety can, of course, be costly, and sometimes it seems to be too costly to be tolerated or at least legitimated, as in the case of marital partners, where the maintenance of a homeostatic state in the family is usually regarded as much more desirable than the variety and excessive throughput of the libertine. There are problems here which the economics profession has neglected with astonishing singlemindedness. My own attempts to call attention to some of them, for instance, in two articles, as far as I can judge, produced no response whatever; and economists continue to think and act as if production, consumption, throughput, and the GNP were the sufficient and adequate measure of economic success.

It may be said, of course, why worry about all this when the spaceman economy is still a good way off (at least beyond the lifetimes of any now living), so let us eat, drink, spend, extract and pollute, and be as merry as we can, and let posterity worry about the spaceship earth. It is always a little hard to find a convincing answer to the man who says, "What has posterity ever done for me?" and the conservationist has always had to fall back on rather vague ethical principles postulating identity of the individual with some human community or society which extends not only back into the past but forward into the future. Unless the individual identifies with some community of this kind, conservation is obviously "irrational." Why should we not maximize the welfare of this generation at the cost of posterity? "*Après nous, le déluge*" has been the motto of not insignificant numbers of human societies. The only answer to this, as far as I can see, is to point out that the welfare of the individual depends on the extent to which he can identity himself with others, and that the most satisfactory individual identity is that which identifies not only with a community in space but also with a community extending over time from the past into the future. If this kind of identity is recognized as desirable, then posterity has a voice, even if it does not have a vote; and in a sense, if its voice can influence votes, it has votes too. This whole problem is linked up with the much larger one of the determinants of the morale, legitimacy, and "nerve" of a society, and there is a great deal of historical evidence to suggest that a society which loses its identity with posterity and which loses its positive image of the future loses also its capacity to deal with present problems, and soon falls apart.[4]

Even if we concede that posterity is relevant to our present problems, we still face the question of time-discounting and the closely related question of uncertainty-discounting. It is a well-known phenomenon that individuals discount the future, even in their own lives. The very existence of a positive rate of interest may be taken as at least strong supporting evidence of this hypothesis. If we discount our own future, it is certainly not unreasonable to discount posterity's future even more, even if we do give posterity a vote. If we discount this at five percent per annum, posterity's vote or dollar halves every fourteen years as we look into the future, and after even a mere hundred years it is pretty small—only about one-and-a-half cents on the dollar. If we add another five percent for uncertainty, even the vote of our grandchildren reduces almost to insignificance. We can argue, of course, that the ethical thing to do is not to discount the future at all, that time-discounting is mainly the result of myopia and perspective, and hence is an illusion which the moral man should not tolerate. It is a very popular illusion, however, and one that must certainly be taken into consideration in the formulation of policies. It explains, perhaps, why conservationist policies almost have to be sold under some other excuse which seems more urgent, and why, indeed, necessities which are visualized as urgent, such as defense, always seem to hold priority over those which involve the future.

All these considerations add some credence to the point of view which says that we should not worry about the spaceman economy at all, and that we should just go on increasing the GNP and indeed the Gross World Product, or GWP, in the expectation that the problems of the future can be left to the future, that when scarcities arise, whether this is of raw materials or of pollutable reservoirs, the needs of the then present will determine the solutions of the then present, and there is no use giving ourselves ulcers by worrying about problems that we really do not have to solve. There is even high ethical authority for this point of view in the New Testament, which advocates that we should take no thought for tomorrow and let the dead bury their dead. There has always been something rather refreshing in the view that we should live like the birds, and perhaps posterity is for the birds in more senses than one; so perhaps we should all call it a day and go out and pollute something cheerfully. As an old taker of thought for the morrow, however, I cannot quite accept this solution; and I would argue, furthermore, that tomorrow is not only very close, but in many respects it is already here. The shadow of the future spaceship, indeed, is already falling over our spendthrift merriment. Oddly enough, it seems to be in pollution rather than in exhaustion that the problem is first becoming salient. Los Angeles has run out of air, Lake Erie has become a cesspool, the oceans are getting full of lead and DDT, and the atmosphere may become man's major problem in another generation, at the rate at which we are filling it up with gunk. It is, of course, true that at least on a microscale, things have been worse at times in the past. The cities of today, with all their foul air and polluted waterways, are probably not as bad as the filthy cities of the pretechnical age. Nevertheless, that fouling of the nest which has been typical of man's activity in the past on a local scale now seems to be extending to the whole world society; and one certainly cannot view with equanimity the present rate of pollution of any of the natural reservoirs, whether the atmosphere, the lakes, or even the oceans.

I would argue strongly also that our obsession with production and consumption to the exclusion of the "state" aspects of human welfare distorts the process of technological change in a most undesirable way. We are all familiar, of course, with the wastes involved in planned obsolescence, in competitive advertising, and in poor quality of consumer goods. These problems may not be so important as the "view with alarm" school indicates, and indeed the evidence at many points is conflicting. New materials especially seem to edge towards the side of improved durability, such as, for instance, neolite soles for footwear, nylon socks, wash and wear shirts, and so on. The case of household equipment and automobiles is a little less clear. Housing and building construction generally almost certainly has declined in durability since the Middle Ages, but this decline also reflects a change in tastes towards flexibility and fashion and a need for novelty, so that it is not easy to assess. What is clear is that no serious attempt has been made to assess the impact over the whole of economic life of changes in durability, that is, in the ratio of capital in the widest possible sense to income. I suspect that we have underestimated, even in our spendthrift society, the gains from increased durability, and that this might very well be one of the places where the price system needs correction through government-sponsored research and development. The problems which the spaceship earth is going to present, therefore, are not all in the future by any means, and a strong case can be made for paying much more attention to them in the present than we now do.

It may be complained that the considerations I have been putting forth relate only to the very long run, and they do not much concern our immediate problems. There may be some justice in this criticism, and my main excuse is that other writers have dealt adequately with the more immediate problems of deterioration in the quality of the environment. It is true, for instance, that many of the immediate problems of pollution of the atmosphere or of bodies of water arise because of the failure of the price system, and many of them could be solved by corrective taxation. If people had to pay the losses due to the nuisances which they create, a good deal more resources would go into the prevention of nuisances. These arguments involving external economies and diseconomies are familiar to economists and there is no need to recapitulate them. The law of torts is quite inadequate to provide for the correction of the price system which is required, simply because where damages are widespread and their incidence on any particular person is small, the ordinary remedies of the civil law are quite inadequate and inappropriate. There needs, therefore, to be special legislation to cover these cases, and though such legislation seems hard to get in practice, mainly because of the widespread and small personal incidence of the injuries, the technical problems involved are not insuperable. If we were to adopt in principle a law for tax penalties for social damages, with an apparatus for making assessments under it, a very large proportion of current pollution and deterioration of the environment would be prevented. There are tricky problems of equity involved, particularly where old established nuisances create a kind of "right by purchase" to perpetuate themselves, but these are problems again which a few rather arbitrary decisions can bring to some kind of solution.

The problems which I have been raising in this paper are of larger scale and perhaps much harder to solve than the more practical and immediate problems of the above paragraph. Our success in dealing with the larger problems, however, is not unrelated to the development of skill in the solution of the more immediate and perhaps less difficult problems. One can hope, therefore, that as a succession of mounting crises, especially in pollution, arouse public opinion and mobilize support for the solution of the immediate problems, a learning process will be set in motion which will eventually lead to an appreciation of and perhaps solutions for the larger ones. My neglect of the immediate problems, therefore, is in no way intended to deny their importance, for unless we make at least a beginning on a process for solving the immediate problems we will not have much chance of solving the larger ones. On the other hand, it may also be true that a long-run vision, as it were, of the deep crisis which faces mankind may predispose people to taking more interest in the immediate problems and to devote more effort for their solution. This may sound like a rather modest optimism, but perhaps a modest optimism is better than no optimism at all.

REFERENCES

1. Ludwig von Bertalanffy, *Problems of Life* (New York: John Wiley and Sons, 1952).
2. Richard L. Meier, *Science and Economic Development* (New York: John Wiley and Sons, 1956).
3. Kenneth E. Boulding, "The Consumption Concept in Economic Theory," *American Economic Review*, 35:2 (May 1945), pp. 1–14; and "Income or Welfare?," *Review of Economic Studies*, 17 (1949–50), pp. 77–86.
4. Fred L. Polak, *The Image of the Future*, Vols. I and II, translated by Elise Boulding (New York: Sythoff, Leyden and Oceana, 1961).

6

THE TRAGEDY OF THE COMMONS

Garrett Hardin

At the end of a thoughtful article on the future of nuclear war, Wiesner and York[1] concluded that: "Both sides in the arms race are . . . confronted by the dilemma of steadily increasing military power and steadily decreasing national security. *It is our considered professional judgment that this dilemma has no technical solution.* If the great powers continue to look for solutions in the area of science and technology only, the result will be to worsen the situation."

I would like to focus your attention not on the subject of the article (national security in a nuclear world) but on the kind of conclusion they reached, namely that there is no technical solution to the problem. An implicit and almost universal assumption of discussions published in professional and semipopular scientific journals is that the problem under discussion has a technical solution. A technical solution may be defined as one that requires a change only in the techniques of the natural

1. References for this reading will be found on pages 147–148.

"The Tragedy of the Commons." From *Science*, Vol. 162, pp. 1243–1248, 13 December 1968.

sciences, demanding little or nothing in the way of change in human values or ideas of morality.

In our day (though not in earlier times) technical solutions are always welcome. Because of previous failures in prophecy, it takes courage to assert that a desired technical solution is not possible. Wiesner and York exhibited this courage; publishing in a science journal, they insisted that the solution to the problem was not to be found in the natural sciences. They cautiously qualified their statement with the phrase, "It is our considered professional judgment. . . ." Whether they were right or not is not the concern of the present article. Rather, the concern here is with the important concept of a class of human problems which can be called "no technical solution problems," and, more specifically, with the identification and discussion of one of these.

It is easy to show that the class is not a null class. Recall the game of tick-tack-toe. Consider the problem, "How can I win the game of tick-tack-toe?" It is well known that I cannot, if I assume (in keeping with the conventions of game theory) that my opponent understands the game perfectly. Put another way, there is no "technical solution" to the problem. I can win only by giving a radical meaning to the word "win." I can hit my opponent over the head; or I can drug him; or I can falsify the records. Every way in which I "win" involves, in some sense, an abandonment of the game, as we intuitively understand it. (I can also, of course, openly abandon the game—refuse to play it. This is what most adults do.)

The class of "No technical solution problems" has members. My thesis is that the "population problem," as conventionally conceived, is a member of this class. How it is conventionally conceived needs some comment. It is fair to say that most people who anguish over the population problem are trying to find a way to avoid the evils of overpopulation without relinquishing any of the privileges they now enjoy. They think that farming the seas or developing new strains of wheat will solve the problem—technologically. I try to show here that the solution they seek cannot be found. The population problem cannot be solved in a technical way, any more than can the problem of winning the game of tick-tack-toe.

WHAT SHALL WE MAXIMIZE?

Population, as Malthus said, naturally tends to grow "geometrically," or, as we would now say, exponentially. In a finite world this means that the per capita share of the world's goods must steadily decrease. Is ours a finite world?

A fair defense can be put forward for the view that the world is infinite; or that we do not know that it is not. But, in terms of the practical problems that we must face in the next few generations with the foreseeable technology, it is clear that we will greatly increase human misery if we do not, during the immediate future, assume that the world available to the terrestrial human population is finite. "Space" is no escape.[2]

A finite world can support only a finite population; therefore, population growth must eventually equal zero. (The case of perpetual wide fluctuations above and below zero is a trivial variant that need not be discussed.) When this condition is met, what will be the situation of mankind? Specifically, can Bentham's goal of "the greatest good for the greatest number" be realized?

No—for two reasons, each sufficient by itself. The first is a theoretical one. It is not mathematically possible to maximize for two (or more) variables at the same time. This was clearly stated by von Neumann and Morgenstern,[3] but the principle is implicit in the theory of partial differential equations, dating back at least to D'Alembert (1717–1783).

The second reason springs directly from biological facts. To live, any organism must have a source of energy (for example, food). This energy is utilized for two purposes: mere maintenance and work. For man, maintenance of life requires about 1600 kilocalories a day ("maintenance calories"). Anything that he does over and above merely staying alive will be defined as work, and is supported by "work calories" which he takes in. Work calories are used not only for what we call work in common speech; they are also required for all forms of enjoyment, from swimming and automobile racing to playing music and writing poetry. If our goal is to maximize population it is obvious what we must do: We must make the work calories per person approach as close to zero as possible. No gourmet meals, no vacations, no sports, no music, no literature, no art. . . . I think that everyone will grant, without argument or proof, that maximizing population does not maximize goods. Bentham's goal is impossible.

In reaching this conclusion I have made the usual assumption that it is the acquisition of energy that is the problem. The appearance of atomic energy has led some to question this assumption. However, given an infinite source of energy, population growth still produces an inescapable problem. The problem of the acquisition of energy is replaced by the problem of its dissipation, as J. H. Fremlin has so wittily shown.[4] The arithmetic signs in the analysis are, as it were, reversed; but Bentham's goal is still unobtainable.

The optimum population is, then, less than the maximum. The difficulty of defining the optimum is enormous; so far as I know, no one has seriously tackled this problem. Reaching an acceptable and stable solution will surely require more than one generation of hard analytical work—and much persuasion.

We want the maximum good per person; but what is good? To one person it is wilderness, to another it is ski lodges for thousands. To one it is estuaries to nourish ducks for hunters to shoot; to another it is factory land. Comparing one good with another is, we usually say, impossible because goods are incommensurable. Incommensurables cannot be compared.

Theoretically this may be true; but in real life incommensurables *are* commensurable. Only a criterion of judgment and a system of weighting are needed. In nature the criterion is survival. Is it better for a species to be small and hideable, or large and powerful? Natural selection commensurates the incommensurables. The compromise achieved depends on a natural weighting of the values of the variables.

Man must imitate this process. There is no doubt that in fact he already does, but unconsciously. It is when the hidden decisions are made explicit that the arguments begin. The problem for the years ahead is to work out an acceptable theory of weighting. Synergistic effects, nonlinear variation, and difficulties in discounting the future make the intellectual problem difficult, but not (in principle) insoluble.

Has any cultural group solved this practical problem at the present time, even on an intuitive level? One simple fact proves that none has: there is no prosperous population in the world today that has, and has had for some time, a growth rate of zero. Any people that has intuitively identified its optimum point will soon reach it, after which its growth rate becomes and remains zero.

Of course, a positive growth rate might be taken as evidence that a population is below its optimum. However, by any reasonable standards, the most rapidly growing populations on earth today are (in general) the most miserable. This association (which need not be invariable) casts doubt on the optimistic assumption that the positive growth rate of a population is evidence that it has yet to reach its optimum.

We can make little progress in working toward optimum population size until we explicitly exorcize the spirit of Adam Smith in the field of practical demography. In economic affairs, *The Wealth of Nations* (1776) popularized the "invisible hand," the idea that an individual who "intends only his own gain," is, as it were, "led by an invisible hand to promote . . . the public interest."[5] Adam Smith did not assert that this was invariably true, and perhaps neither did any of his followers. But he contributed to a dominant tendency of thought that has ever since interfered with positive action based on rational analysis, namely, the tendency to assume that decisions reached individually will, in fact, be the best decisions for an entire society. If this assumption is correct it justifies the continuance of our present policy of laissez-faire in reproduction. If it is correct we can assume that men will control their individual fecundity so as to produce the optimum population. If the assumption is not correct, we need to reexamine our individual freedoms to see which ones are defensible.

THE TRAGEDY OF FREEDOM IN A COMMONS

The rebuttal to the invisible hand in population control is to be found in a scenario first sketched in a little-known pamphlet[6] in 1833 by a mathematical amateur named William Forster Lloyd (1794–1852). We may well call it "the tragedy of the commons," using the word "tragedy" as the philosopher Whitehead used it:[7] "The essence of dramatic tragedy is not unhappiness. It resides in the solemnity of the remorseless working of things." He then goes on to say, "This inevitableness of destiny can only be illustrated in terms of human life by incidents which in fact involve unhappiness. For it is only by them that the futility of escape can be made evident in the drama."

The tragedy of the commons develops in this way. Picture a pasture open to all. It is to be expected that each herdsman will try to keep as many cattle as possible on the commons. Such an arrangement may work reasonably satisfactorily for centuries because tribal wars, poaching, and disease keep the numbers of both man and beast well below the carrying capacity of the land. Finally, however, comes the day of reckoning, that is, the day when the long-desired goal of social stability becomes a reality. At this point, the inherent logic of the commons remorselessly generates tragedy.

As a rational being, each herdsman seeks to maximize his gain. Explicitly or implicitly, more or less consciously, he asks, "What is the utility to *me* of adding one more animal to my herd?" This utility has one negative and one positive component.

1. The positive component is a function of the increment of one animal. Since the herdsman receives all the proceeds from the sale of the additional animal, the positive utility is nearly +1.
2. The negative component is a function of the additional overgrazing created by one more animal. Since, however, the effects of overgrazing are shared by all the herdsmen, the negative utility for any particular decision-making herdsman is only a fraction of −1.

Adding together the component partial utilities, the rational herdsman concludes that the only sensible course for him to pursue is to add another animal to his herd. And another; and another. . . . But this is the conclusion reached by each and every rational herdsman sharing a commons. Therein is the tragedy. Each man is locked into a system that compels him to increase his herd without limit—in a world that is limited. Ruin is the destination toward which all men rush, each pursuing his own best interest in a society that believes in the freedom of the commons. Freedom in a commons brings ruin to all.

Some would say that this is a platitude. Would that it were! In a sense, it was learned thousands of years ago, but natural selection favors the forces of psychological denial.[8] The individual benefits as an individual from his ability to deny the truth even though society as a whole, of which he is a part, suffers. Education can counteract the natural tendency to do the wrong thing, but the inexorable succession of generations requires that the basis for this knowledge be constantly refreshed.

A simple incident that occurred a few years ago in Leominster, Massachusetts, shows how perishable the knowledge is. During the Christmas shopping season the parking meters downtown were covered with plastic bags that bore tags reading: "Do not open until after Christmas. Free parking courtesy of the mayor and city council." In other words, facing the prospect of an increased demand for already scarce space, the city fathers reinstituted the system of the commons. (Cynically, we suspect that they gained more votes than they lost by this retrogressive act.)

In an approximate way, the logic of the commons has been understood for a long time, perhaps since the discovery of agriculture or the invention of private property in real estate. But it is understood mostly only in special cases which are not sufficiently generalized. Even at this late date, cattlemen leasing national land on the western ranges demonstrate no more than an ambivalent understanding, in constantly pressuring federal authorities to increase the head count to the point where overgrazing produces erosion and weed dominance. Likewise, the oceans of the world continue to suffer from the survival of the philosophy of the commons. Maritime nations still respond automatically to the shibboleth of the "freedom of the seas." Professing to believe in the "inexhaustible resources of the oceans," they bring species after species of fish and whales closer to extinction.[9]

The National Parks present another instance of the working out of the tragedy of the commons. At present, they are open to all, without limit. The parks themselves are limited in extent—there is only one Yosemite Valley—whereas population seems to grow without limit. The values that visitors seek in the parks are steadily eroded. Plainly, we must soon cease to treat the parks as commons or they will be of no value to anyone.

What shall we do? We have several options. We might sell them off as private property. We might keep them as public properity, but allocate the right to enter them. The allocation might be on the basis of wealth, by the use of an auction system. It might be on the basis of merit, as defined by some agreed-upon standards. It might be by lottery. Or it might be on a first-come, first-served basis, administered to long queues. These, I think, are all the reasonable possibilities. They are all objectionable. But we must choose—or acquiesce in the destruction of the commons that we call our National Parks.

POLLUTION

In a reverse way, the tragedy of the commons reappears in problems of pollution. Here it is not a question of taking something out of the commons, but of putting something in—sewage, or chemical, radioactive, and heat wastes into water; noxious and dangerous fumes into the air; and distracting and unpleasant advertising signs into the line of sight. The calculations of utility are much the same as before. The rational man finds that his share of the cost of the wastes he discharges into the commons is less than the cost of purifying his wastes before releasing them. Since this is true for everyone, we are locked into a system of "fouling our own nest," so long as we behave only as independent, rational, free-enterprisers.

The tragedy of the commons as a food basket is averted by private property, or something formally like it. But the air and waters surrounding us cannot readily be fenced, and so the tragedy of the commons as a cesspool must be prevented by different means, by coercive laws or taxing devices that make it cheaper for the polluter to treat his pollutants than to discharge them untreated. We have not progressed as far with the solution of this problem as we have with the first. Indeed, our particular concept of private property, which deters us from exhausting the positive resources of the earth, favors pollution. The owner of a factory on the bank of a stream—whose property extends to the middle of the stream—often has difficulty seeing why it is not his natural right to muddy the waters flowing past his door. The law, always behind the times, requires elaborate stitching and fitting to adapt it to this newly perceived aspect of the commons.

The pollution problem is a consequence of population. It did not much matter how a lonely American frontiersman disposed of his waste. "Flowing water purifies itself every ten miles," my grandfather used to say, and the myth was near enough to the truth when he was a boy, for there were not too many people. But as population became denser, the natural chemical and biological recycling processes became overloaded, calling for a redefinition of property rights.

HOW TO LEGISLATE TEMPERANCE?

Analysis of the pollution problem as a function of population density uncovers a not generally recognized principle of morality, namely: *the morality of an act is a function of the state of the system at the time it is performed.*[10] Using the commons as a cesspool does not harm the general public under frontier conditions, because there is no public; the same behavior in a metropolis is unbearable. A hundred and fifty years ago a plainsman could kill an American bison, cut out only the tongue for his dinner, and discard the rest of the animal. He was not in any important sense being wasteful. Today, with only a few thousand bison left, we would be appalled at such behavior.

In passing, it is worth noting that the morality of an act cannot be determined from a photograph. One does not know whether a man killing an elephant or setting fire to the grassland is harming others until one knows the total system in which his act appears. "One picture is worth a thousand words," said an ancient Chinese; but it may take 10,000 words to validate it. It is as tempting to ecologists as it is to reformers in general to try to persuade others by way of the photographic shortcut. But the essence of an argument cannot be photographed: it must be presented rationally—in words.

That morality is system-sensitive escaped the attention of most codifiers of ethics in the past. "Thou shalt not . . ." is the form of traditional ethical directives which make no allowance for particular circumstances. The laws of our society follow the pattern of ancient ethics, and therefore are poorly suited to governing a complex, crowded, changeable world. Our epicyclic solution is to augment statutory law with administrative law. Since it is practically impossible to spell out all the conditions under which it is safe to burn trash in the back yard or to run an automobile without smog-control, by law we delegate the details to bureaus. The result is administrative law, which is rightly feared for an ancient reason —*Quis custodiet ipsos custodes?*—"Who shall watch the watchers themselves?" John Adams said that we must have "a government of laws and not men." Bureau administrators, trying to evaluate the morality of acts in the total system, are singularly liable to corruption, producing a government by men, not laws.

Prohibition is easy to legislate (though not necessarily to enforce);

but how do we legislate temperance? Experience indicates that it can be accomplished best through the mediation of administrative law. We limit possibilities unnecessarily if we suppose that the sentiment of *Quis custodiet* denies us the use of administrative law. We should rather retain the phrase as a perpetual reminder of fearful dangers we cannot avoid. The great challenge facing us now is to invent the corrective feedbacks that are needed to keep custodians honest. We must find ways to legitimate the needed authority of both the custodians and the corrective feedbacks.

FREEDOM TO BREED IS INTOLERABLE

The tragedy of the commons is involved in population problems in another way. In a world governed solely by the principle of "dog eat dog"—if indeed there ever was such a world—how many children a family had would not be a matter of public concern. Parents who bred too exuberantly would leave fewer descendants, not more, because they would be unable to care adequately for their children. David Lack and others have found that such a negative feedback demonstrably controls the fecundity of birds.[11] But men are not birds, and have not acted like them for millenniums, at least.

If each human family were dependent only on its own resources; *if* the children of improvident parents starved to death; *if*, thus, overbreeding brought its own "punishment" to the germ line—*then* there would be no public interest in controlling the breeding of families. But our society is deeply committed to the welfare state,[12] and hence is confronted with another aspect of the tragedy of the commons.

In a welfare state, how shall we deal with the family, the religion, the race, or the class (or indeed any distinguishable and cohesive group) that adopts overbreeding as a policy to secure its own aggrandizement?[13] To couple the concept of freedom to breed with the belief that everyone born has an equal right to the commons is to lock the world into a tragic course of action.

Unfortunately this is just the course of action that is being pursued by the United Nations. In late 1967, some thirty nations agreed to the following:[14]

> The Universal Declaration of Human Rights describes the family as the natural and fundamental unit of society. It follows that any choice and decision with regard to the size of the family must irrevocably rest with the family itself, and cannot be made by someone else.

It is painful to have to deny categorically the validity of this right;

denying it, one feels as uncomfortable as a resident of Salem, Massachusetts, who denied the reality of witches in the seventeenth century. At the present time, in liberal quarters, something like a taboo acts to inhibit criticism of the United Nations. There is a feeling that the United Nations is "our last and best hope," that we shouldn't find fault with it; we shouldn't play into the hands of the archconservatives. However, let us not forget what Robert Louis Stevenson said: "The truth that is suppressed by friends is the readiest weapon of the enemy." If we love the truth we must openly deny the validity of the Universal Declaration of Human Rights, even though it is promoted by the United Nations. We should also join with Kingsley Davis[15] in attempting to get Planned Parenthood-World Population to see the error of its ways in embracing the same tragic ideal.

CONSCIENCE IS SELF-ELIMINATING

It is a mistake to think that we can control the breeding of mankind in the long run by an appeal to conscience. Charles Galton Darwin made this point when he spoke on the centennial of the publication of his grandfather's great book. The argument is straightforward and Darwinian.

People vary. Confronted with appeals to limit breeding, some people will undoubtedly respond to the plea more than others. Those who have more children will produce a larger fraction of the next generation than those with more susceptible consciences. The difference will be accentuated, generation by generation.

In C. G. Darwin's words: "It may well be that it would take hundreds of generations for the progenitive instinct to develop in this way, but if it should do so, nature would have taken her revenge, and the variety *Homo contracipiens* would become extinct and would be replaced by the variety *Homo progenitivus*."[16]

The argument assumes that conscience or the desire for children (no matter which) is hereditary—but hereditary only in the most general formal sense. The result will be the same whether the attitude is transmitted through germ cells, or exosomatically, to use A. J. Lotka's term. (If one denies the latter possibility as well as the former, then what's the point of education?) The argument has here been stated in the context of the population problem, but it applies equally well to any instance in which society appeals to an individual exploiting a commons to restrain himself for the general good—by means of his conscience. To make such an appeal is to set up a selective system that works toward the elimination of conscience from the race.

PATHOGENIC EFFECTS OF CONSCIENCE

The long-term disadvantage of an appeal to conscience should be enough to condemn it; but it has serious short-term disadvantages as well. If we ask a man who is exploiting a commons to desist "in the name of conscience," what are we saying to him? What does he hear?—not only at the moment but also in the wee small hours of the night when, half asleep, he remembers not merely the words we used but also the nonverbal communication cues we gave him unawares? Sooner or later, consciously or subconsciously, he senses that he has received two communications, and that they are contradictory: (1, the intended communication) "If you don't do as we ask, we will openly condemn you for not acting like a responsible citizen"; (2, the unintended communication) "If you *do* behave as we ask, we will secretly condemn you for a simpleton who can be shamed into standing aside while the rest of us exploit the commons."

Everyman then is caught in what Bateson has called a "double bind." Bateson and his co-workers have made a plausible case for viewing the double bind as an important causative factor in the genesis of schizophrenia.[17] The double bind may not always be so damaging, but it always endangers the mental health of anyone to whom it is applied. "A bad conscience," said Nietzsche, "is a kind of illness."

To conjure up a conscience in others is tempting to anyone who wishes to extend his control beyond the legal limits. Leaders at the highest level succumb to this temptation. Has any President during the past generation failed to call on labor unions to moderate voluntarily their demands for higher wages, or to steel companies to honor voluntary guidelines on prices? I can recall none. The rhetoric used on such occasions is designed to produce feelings of guilt in noncooperators.

For centuries it was assumed without proof that guilt was a valuable, perhaps even an indispensable, ingredient of the civilized life. Now, in this post-Freudian world, we doubt it.

Paul Goodman speaks from the modern point of view when he says: "No good has ever come from feeling guilty, neither intelligence, policy, nor compassion. The guilty do not pay attention to the object but only to themselves, and not even to their own interests, which might make sense, but to their anxieties."[18]

One does not have to be a professional psychiatrist to see the consequences of anxiety. We in the Western world are just emerging from a dreadful two-centuries-long Dark Ages of Eros that was sustained partly by prohibition laws, but perhaps more effectively by the anxiety-generating mechanisms of education. Alex Comfort has told the story well in *The Anxiety Makers;*[19] it is not a pretty one.

Since proof is difficult, we may even concede that the results of anxiety may sometimes, from certain points of view, be desirable. The larger question we should ask is whether, as a matter of policy, we should ever encourage the use of a technique the tendency (if not the intention) of which is psychologically pathogenic. We hear much talk these days of responsible parenthood; the coupled words are incorporated into the titles of some organizations devoted to birth control. Some people have proposed massive propaganda campaigns to instill responsibility into the nation's (or the world's) breeders. But what is the meaning of the word responsibility in this context? Is it not merely a synonym for the word conscience? When we use the word responsibility in the absence of substantial sanctions are we not trying to browbeat a free man in a commons into acting against his own interest? Responsibility is a verbal counterfeit for a substantial *quid pro quo*. It is an attempt to get something for nothing.

If the word responsibility is to be used at all, I suggest that it be in the sense Charles Frankel uses it.[20] "Responsibility," says this philosopher, "is the product of definite social arrangements." Notice that Frankel calls for social arrangements—not propaganda.

MUTUAL COERCION MUTUALLY AGREED UPON

The social arrangements that produce responsibility are arrangements that create coercion, of some sort. Consider bank robbing. The man who takes money from a bank acts as if the bank were a commons. How do we prevent such action? Certainly not be trying to control his behavior solely by a verbal appeal to his sense of responsibility. Rather than rely on propaganda we follow Frankel's lead and insist that a bank is not a commons; we seek the definite social arrangements that will keep it from becoming a commons. That we thereby infringe on the freedom of would-be robbers we neither deny nor regret.

The morality of bank robbing is particularly easy to understand because we accept complete prohibition of this activity. We are willing to say "Thou shalt not rob banks," without providing for exceptions. But temperance also can be created by coercion. Taxing is a good coercive device. To keep downtown shoppers temperate in their use of parking space we introduce parking meters for short periods, and traffic fines for longer ones. We need not actually forbid a citizen to park as long as he wants to; we need merely make it increasingly expensive for him to do so. Not prohibition, but carefully biased options are what we offer him. A Madison Avenue man might call this persuasion; I prefer the greater candor of the word coercion.

Coercion is a dirty word to most liberals now, but it need not forever be so. As with the four-letter words, its dirtiness can be cleansed away by exposure to the light, by saying it over and over without apology or embarrassment. To many, the word coercion implies arbitrary decisions of distant and irresponsible bureaucrats; but this is not a necessary part of its meaning. The only kind of coercion I recommend is mutual coercion, mutually agreed upon by the majority of the people affected.

To say that we mutually agree to coercion is not to say that we are required to enjoy it, or even to pretend we enjoy it. Who enjoys taxes? We all grumble about them. But we accept compulsory taxes because we recognize that voluntary taxes would favor the conscienceless. We institute and (grumblingly) support taxes and other coercive devices to escape the horror of the commons.

An alternative to the commons need not be perfectly just to be preferable. With real estate and other material goods, the alternative we have chosen is the institution of private property coupled with legal inheritance. Is this system perfectly just? As a genetically trained biologist I deny that it is. It seems to me that, if there are to be differences in individual inheritance, legal possession should be perfectly correlated with biological inheritance—that those who are biologically more fit to be the custodians of property and power should legally inherit more. But genetic recombination continually makes a mockery of the doctrine of "like father, like son" implicit in our laws of legal inheritance. An idiot can inherit millions, and a trust fund can keep his estate intact. We must admit that our legal system of private property plus inheritance is unjust—but we put up with it because we are not convinced, at the moment, that anyone has invented a better system. The alternative of the commons is too horrifying to contemplate. Injustice is preferable to total ruin.

It is one of the peculiarities of the warfare between reform and the status quo that it is thoughtlessly governed by a double standard. Whenever a reform measure is proposed it is often defeated when its opponents triumphantly discover a flaw in it. As Kingsley Davis has pointed out,[21] worshippers of the status quo sometimes imply that no reform is possible without unanimous agreement, an implication contrary to historical fact. As nearly as I can make out, automatic rejection of proposed reforms is based on one of two unconscious assumptions: (1) that the status quo is perfect; or (2) that the choice we face is between reform and no action; if the proposed reform is imperfect, we presumably should take no action at all, while we wait for a perfect proposal.

But we can never do nothing. That which we have done for thousands of years is also action. It also produces evils. Once we are aware that the status quo is action, we can then compare its discoverable advantages and disadvantages with the predicted advantages and disadvantages of the proposed reform, discounting as best we can for our lack of experience. On the basis of such a comparison, we can make a rational decision which will not involve the unworkable assumption that only perfect systems are tolerable.

RECOGNITION OF NECESSITY

Perhaps the simplest summary of this analysis of man's population problems is this: the commons, if justifiable at all, is justifiable only under conditions of low-population density. As the human population has increased, the commons has had to be abandoned in one aspect after another.

First we abandoned the commons in food gathering, enclosing farm land and restricting pastures and hunting and fishing areas. These restrictions are still not complete throughout the world.

Somewhat later we saw that the commons as a place for waste disposal would also have to be abandoned. Restrictions on the disposal of domestic sewage are widely accepted in the Western world; we are still struggling to close the commons to pollution by automobiles, factories, insecticide sprayers, fertilizing operations, and atomic energy installations.

In a still more embryonic state is our recognition of the evils of the commons in matters of pleasure. There is almost no restriction on the propagation of sound waves in the public medium. The shopping public is assaulted with mindless music, without its consent. Our government is paying out billions of dollars to create supersonic transport which will disturb 50,000 people for every one person who is whisked from coast to coast three hours faster. Advertisers muddy the airwaves of radio and television and pollute the view of travelers. We are a long way from outlawing the commons in matters of pleasure. Is this because our Puritan inheritance makes us view pleasure as something of a sin, and pain (that is, the pollution of advertising) as the sign of virtue?

Every new enclosure of the commons involves the infringement of somebody's personal liberty. Infringements made in the distant past are accepted because no contemporary complains of a loss. It is the newly proposed infringements that we vigorously oppose; cries of "rights" and "freedom" fill the air. But what does "freedom" mean? When men mutually agreed to pass laws against robbing, mankind became more free, not less so. Individuals locked into the logic of the commons are free only to bring on universal ruin; once they see the necessity of mutual coercion, they become free to pursue other goals. I believe it was Hegel who said, "Freedom is the recognition of necessity."

The most important aspect of necessity that we must now recognize, is the necessity of abandoning the commons in breeding. No technical solution can rescue us from the misery of overpopulation. Freedom to breed will bring ruin to all. At the moment, to avoid hard decisions many of us are tempted to propagandize for conscience and responsible parenthood. The temptation must be resisted, because an appeal to independently acting consciences selects for the disappearance of all conscience in the long run, and an increase in anxiety in the short.

The only way we can preserve and nurture other and more precious freedoms is by relinquishing the freedom to breed, and that very soon. "Freedom is the recognition of necessity"—and it is the role of education to reveal to all the necessity of abandoning the freedom to breed. Only so, can we put an end to this aspect of the tragedy of the commons.

REFERENCES

1. J. B. Wiesner and H. F. York, *Sci. Amer.* 211 (No. 4), 27 (1964), Offprint 319.
2. G. Hardin, *J. Hered.* 50, 68 (1959); S. von Hoernor, *Science* 137, 18 (1962).
3. J. von Neumann and O. Morgenstern. *Theory of Games and Economic Behavior* (Princeton Univ. Press, Princeton, N. J., 1947), p. 11.
4. J. H. Fremlin, *New Sci.*, No. 415 (1964), p. 285.
5. A. Smith, *The Wealth of Nations* (Modern Library, New York, 1937), p. 423.
6. W. F. Lloyd, *Two Lectures on the Checks to Population* (Oxford Univ. Press, Oxford, England, 1833), reprinted (in part) *in* G. Hardin, ed., *Population, Evolution, and Birth Control*, 2nd edition (W. H. Freeman and Company, San Francisco, 1969), p. 28.
7. A. N. Whitehead, *Science and the Modern World* (Mentor, New York, 1948), p. 17.
8. G. Hardin, ed., *Population, Evolution, and Birth Control*, 2nd edition (W. H. Freeman and Company, San Francisco, 1969), p. 46.
9. S. McVay, *Sci. Amer.* 216 (No. 8), 13 (1966). Offprint 1046.
10. J. Fletcher, *Situation Ethics* (Westminster, Philadelphia, 1966).
11. D. Lack, *The Natural Regulation of Animal Numbers* (Clarendon Press, Oxford, 1954).
12. H. Girvetz, *From Wealth to Welfare* (Stanford Univ. Press, Stanford, Calif., 1950).
13. G. Hardin, *Perspec. Biol. Med.* 6, 366 (1963).
14. U. Thant, *Int. Planned Parenthood News*, No. 168 (February 1968), p. 3.
15. K. Davis, *Science* 158, 730 (1967).
16. S. Tax, ed., *Evolution after Darwin* (Univ. of Chicago Press, Chicago, 1960), vol. 2, p. 469.

17. G. Bateson, D. D. Jackson, J. Haley, J. Weakland, *Behav. Sci.* 1, 251 (1956).
18. P. Goodman, *New York Rev. Books* 10 (8), 22 (23 May 1968).
19. A. Comfort, *The Anxiety Makers* (Nelson, London, 1967).
20. C. Frankel, *The Case for Modern Man* (Harper, New York, 1955), p. 203.
21. J. D. Roslansky, *Genetics and the Future of Man* (Appleton-Century-Crofts, New York, 1966), p. 177.

7

THE STEADY-STATE ECONOMY: TOWARD A POLITICAL ECONOMY OF BIOPHYSICAL EQUILIBRIUM AND MORAL GROWTH

Herman E. Daly

"There is nothing in front but a flat wilderness of standardization either by Bolshevism or Big Business. But it is strange that some of us should have seen sanity, if only in a vision, while the rest go forward chained eternally to enlargement without liberty and progress without hope."
G. K. Chesterton

GROWTHMANIA

The fragmentation of knowledge and people by excessive specialization, the disequilibrium between the human economy and the natural ecosystem, the congestion and pollution of our spatial dimension of existence, the congestion and pollution of our temporal dimension of existence with the resulting state of harried drivenness and stress—all these evils and more are symptomatic of the basic malady of growthmania.

"Growthmania" is an insufficiently pejorative term for the paradigm or mind-set that always puts growth in first place—the attitude that there

---

Originally titled "The Stationary-State Economy: Toward a Political Economy of Biophysical Equilibrium and Moral Growth." From The University of Alabama *Distinguished Lecture Series*, No. 2, 1971. Reprinted by permission of The University of Alabama. This version has been revised and expanded.

is no such thing as enough, that cannot conceive of too much of a good thing. It is the set of unarticulated preconceptions which allows the President's Council of Economic Advisers to say, "If it is agreed that economic output is a good thing it follows by definition that there is not enough of it."[1] As a sop to environmentalists the Council does admit that "growth of GNP has its costs, and beyond some point they are not worth paying."[2] But instead of raising the obvious question—"What determines this point of optimal GNP, and how do we know when we have reached it?"—the Council merely pontificates that "the existing propensities of the population and the policies of the government constitute claims upon GNP itself that can only be satisfied by rapid economic growth." That of course is merely to restate the problem, not to give a solution. Apparently these "existing propensities and policies" are beyond discussion. That is growthmania. Brezhnev, Castro, and Franco receive much the same advice from their respective Councils of Economic Advisers. Growthmania is ecumenical.

The answer to the avoided question "When do the costs of growth in GNP outweigh the benefits?" is contained in the question itself. This occurs when the decreasing marginal benefit of extra GNP becomes less than the increasing marginal cost. The marginal benefit is measured by the market value of extra goods and services—i.e., the increment in GNP itself in value units. But what statistical series measures the cost? Answer: *none!* That is growthmania; literally not counting the costs of growth.

But the worst is yet to come. We take the real costs of increasing GNP as measured by the defensive expenditures incurred to protect ourselves from the *unwanted* side effects of production, and *add* these expenditures to GNP rather than subtract them. We count the real costs as benefits—this is hyper-growthmania. Since the net benefit of growth can never be negative with this Alice-in-Wonderland accounting system, the rule becomes "grow forever" or at least until it kills you—and then count your funeral expenses as further growth. This is terminal hyper-growthmania. Is the water table falling? Dig deeper wells, build bigger pumps, and up goes GNP! Mines depleted? Build more expensive refineries to process lower grade ores, and up goes GNP! Soil depleted? Produce more fertilizer, etc. As we press against the carrying capacity of our physical environment, these "extra-effort" and "defensive" expenditures (which are really costs masquerading as benefits) will loom larger and larger. As more and more of the finite physical world is converted into wealth, less and less is left over as nonwealth—i.e., the nonwealth physical world becomes scarce, and in becoming scarce it gets a price and thereby becomes wealth. This creates the illusion of becoming better off, when in

1. Notes and references for this reading will be found on pages 173–174.

actuality we are becoming worse off. We may already have passed the point where the marginal cost of growth exceeds the marginal benefit. This suspicion is increased by looking at who absorb the costs and who receive the benefits. We all get some of each, but not equal shares. Who buys a second car or a third TV? Who lives in the most congested, polluted areas? The benefits of growth go mainly to the rich, the costs go mainly to the poor. That statement is based on casual empiricism—we do not have social accounts which allow us to say precisely who receive the benefits and who absorb the costs of growth, a fact which is itself very revealing. Ignorance, if not blissful, is often politically expedient.

Growthmania is the paradigm upon which stand the models and policies of our current political economy. The answer to every problem is growth.

For example:

1. Poverty? Grow more to provide more employment for the poor and more tax revenues for welfare programs.
2. Unemployment? Invest and grow to bolster aggregate demand and employment.
3. Inflation? Grow by raising productivity so that more goods will be chased by the same number of dollars and prices will fall.
4. Balance of payments? Grow more and increase productivity in order to increase exports. Cutting imports is seen only as a short-run stopgap, not a solution.
5. Pollution and depletion? Grow so we will be rich enough to afford the cost of cleaning up and of discovering new resources and technologies.
6. War? We must grow to be strong and have *both* guns and butter.

The list could be extended, but it can also be summarized in one sentence: The way to have your cake and eat it too is to make it grow.

Growthmania is the attitude in economic theory that begins with the theological assumption of infinite wants, and then with infinite hubris goes on to presume that the original sin of infinite wants has its redemption vouchsafed by the omnipotent savior of technology, and that the first commandment is to produce more and more goods for more and more people, world without end. And that this is not only possible, but desirable.

Environmental degradation is an iatrogenic disease induced by economic physicians who treat the basic malady of unlimited wants by prescribing unlimited economic growth. We experience environmental degradation in the form of increased scarcity of clean air, pure water, relaxed moments, etc. But the only way the growthmania paradigm knows to deal with scarcity is to recommend growth. Yet one certainly does not cure a treatment-induced disease by increasing the treatment dosage! Nevertheless the usual recommendation for combating pollution is to grow more because "a rising GNP will enable the nation more easily to bear the costs of eliminating pollution."[3] Such a view is patently inept.

The growth paradigm has outlived its usefulness. It is a senile ideology that should be unceremoniously retired into the history of economic doctrines. In the terminology of Thomas Kuhn's book, *The Structure of Scientific Revolutions*, the growth paradigm has been more than exhausted by the normal science puzzle-solving research done within its confines. Political economy must enter a period of revolutionary science to establish a new paradigm to guide a new period of normal science. Just as mercantilism gave way to physiocracy, physiocracy to classical laissez-faire, laissez-faire to Keynesianism, Keynesianism to the neoclassical growth synthesis—so the current neoclassical growthmania must give way to a new paradigm. What will the new paradigm be? I submit that it must be very similar to an idea from classical economics that never attained the status of a paradigm, except for a brief chapter in John Stuart Mill's *Principles of Political Economy*. This idea is that of the steady-state economy.

THE STEADY STATE

What is meant by a "steady-state economy"?

Why is it necessary?

How can it be attained?

The first two questions are relatively easy and have been dealt with elsewhere.[4] Hence they will be treated rapidly. The third question is extremely difficult, and will be the main focus of attention.

The steady state is defined as an economy in which the total population and the total stock of physical wealth are maintained constant at some desired levels by a "minimal" rate of maintenance throughput (i.e., by birth and death rates that are equal at the lowest feasible level, and by physical production and consumption rates that are equal at the lowest feasible level). The first part of the definition (constant stocks) goes back to John Stuart Mill, and the second part ("minimal" flow of throughput) goes back to 1949 vintage Kenneth Boulding. Minimizing throughput implies maximizing the average life expectancy of a member of the stock.[5]

Why is the steady state necessary? Not for the reasons given by the classical economists who saw increasing rent and interest eliminating profit and thus the incentive for "progress." Rather, the necessity follows immediately from physical first principles. The world is finite, the ecosystem is a steady state. The human economy is a subsystem of the steady-state ecosystem. Therefore at some level and over some time period the subsystem must also become a steady state, at least in its physical dimensions of people and physical wealth. The steady-state economy is therefore a physical necessity. One may counter this by arguing that we always have the alternative of extinction, and that therefore the steady state is a moral choice, not a physical necessity. But even this is mistaken. Extinction itself is a steady state, the special case of zero stocks maintained by a zero throughput. The choice of stock levels and rates of maintenance throughput requires value judgments, but the attainment of a steady state at some level is a physical necessity.

Our definition of "steady state" is much closer to the classical than to the neoclassical definition of the term. The neoclassical definition of steady state assumes constant wants and technology (nonphysical parameters) and investigates the adjustment of physical variables to the nonphysical parameters. Our definition assumes constant physical wealth and population (physical parameters) and inquires how the nonphysical variables of wants (including the ethical want for "better wants") and technology can be sensibly adjusted to the physical parameters. Furthermore, the neoclassical concept is an epistemological fiction useful mainly as a first step in the analysis of a growing economy. It is in no sense a target for policy or a real state toward which the economy actually tends. Our concept is not an epistemological fiction, but an attempt to describe in broad outlines a real and necessary future state of society.

The above differences represent a paradigm shift in the sense of Thomas Kuhn. The steady-state paradigm will not be easily accepted by those who have been trained in and worked within the growth paradigm. But the arguments are too logical and too simple to be resisted for long, and the weight of anomaly under which the old paradigm is groaning will eventually crush it. An example of a simple argument that cannot be long resisted is the following. All reasonable men by now accept the ultimate necessity of zero population growth. But in addition to the population of human bodies (the stock of endosomatic capital) we must consider the population of extensions of the human body (exosomatic capital). Bicycles and automobiles are extensions of man's legs; hammers and pliers are extensions of his arms and hands; pots and pans and ovens are extensions of his digestive system; the telephone and phonograph extend man's ears; the TV extends his eyes; clothing and buildings extend his skin, etc. Both endosomatic and exosomatic capital are necessary to maintain life. More importantly both endosomatic and exosomatic capital stocks are physical open systems that maintain themselves by continually importing low entropy matter-energy from the environment and exporting high entropy matter-energy back to the environment.[6] The same physical laws that limit the population of organisms apply with equal force to the population of extensions of organisms. If the first limitation is admitted, how can the second be denied?

In sum the steady state is necessary. It must be the norm. But once we have attained a steady state at some level of population and wealth, we are not forever frozen at that level. As values and technology evolve we may find that a different level is both possible and desirable. But the growth (or decline) required to get to the new level is a temporary adjustment process, not a norm. At present the momentum of growth in population and capital pushes our technological and moral development. In the steady-state paradigm, technological and moral evolution would precede and lead growth instead of being pushed. Growth would always be seen as a temporary passage from one steady state to another, not as the norm of a "healthy" economy.

When we raise the third question, how to attain the steady state, things become more difficult. First we must give operational definitions to the specific goals contained in the definition of steady state. Second, we must specify the technologies, social institutions, and moral values which are in harmony with and supportive of the steady state.

To define more clearly the goal of the steady state we must face four questions.

1. At what levels should the stocks of wealth and people be maintained constant? Specifying the stock of wealth and of people also specifies the wealth per person or standard of living. In other words the question becomes the old one of what is the optimum population? So far no one has given a definite answer, and I certainly cannot. However, it is sometimes argued that it is vain to advocate a stationary population unless one can specify the optimum level at which the population should become stationary. But I think that puts it backwards. Rather it is vain to speak of an optimum population unless you are first prepared to accept a stationary population—unless you are able and willing to stay at the optimum once you find it. Otherwise knowing the optimum merely enables us to wave goodbye as we pass through it. Furthermore, the optimum population is more likely to be discovered by experience than by a priori thought. We should attain a stationary population at some feasible nearby level. After experiencing it we could then decide whether the optimum level is above or below the current level. Also the optimum may be a welfare plateau spanning a whole range of populations and not just one. It is more important to be able to attain a steady state (at any level) than to know in advance which level is optimal.

2. *What is the optimal level of maintenance throughput for a given level of stocks?* For the time being the answer is probably "as low as possible" or at least "less than at present." If it is good for people to live longer and for goods to last longer, then it is good to reduce the rate of throughput. Under the constraint of present technology perhaps we could advocate minimizing throughput, but as technology increases the potential life expectancy of people and goods we will surely reach a point where optimum life expectancy is less than maximum—or, what is the same thing, optimum throughput is greater than the minimum. But for the present, minimizing throughput makes vastly more sense than the current practice of maximizing it.

3. *What is the optimal time horizon or accounting period over which population and wealth are required to be constant?* Obviously we cannot mean day-to-day constancy and probably not even year-to-year constancy. Related to this is the question of the optimum amplitude of fluctuation around the steady-state mean during the accounting period.

Again, I cannot pretend to be able to answer this question. But it must be pointed out that the question of the proper accounting period is a very general one which applies in equal force to standard economic theory. The fundamental assumption of profit maximization is meaningless unless one specifies the length of the accounting period. Surely we do not maximize daily profits, and often not even yearly profits. Behavior that is "rational" (consistent with profit maximization) over one time period is irrational over another. My favorite example is that of the village idiot who, when offered the choice between a nickel and a dime, always chose the nickel, much to the villagers' continuing amusement. Finally one day a villager said to him, "Look, I know you are not that stupid; you know a dime is worth more than a nickel—why do you always take the nickel?" To which the "idiot" replied "It's obvious—if I took the dime they would stop making the offer!" Idiocy on one time horizon is cleverness on another. But somehow we manage to choose an accounting period and muddle through, and so we could also in a steady state.

Once we have fixed an accounting period, one may then ask how many accounting periods the total system should last. Obviously the carrying capacity of the ecosystem depends not only on the size of the stocks and the rate of maintenance throughput, but also on the length of time over which the stocks are to be carried. This question must at least be implicitly considered in answering questions 1 and 2, since those answers plus the given endowment of nonrenewable resources will determine how long the system can continue.

4. What is the optimal rate of transition from the growing economy to the steady state? We can never attain a steady state in the long run if our efforts to do so kill us in the short run. In the case of population there are interesting trade-offs between speed of attainment of a stationary population versus size of the stationary population and the amplitude of fluctuations in the birth rate induced by the current nonequilibrium age structure.[7]

Once again I do not know the optimum rate of transition. But I think we are very unlikely to exceed it. In any case the sooner we begin deceleration to zero growth the longer we can afford to take and the less disruptive that adjustment will be. The important thing from all points of view is to begin deceleration now. Later we can argue about the optimum rate.

The fact that these four optima cannot be well defined should come as no surprise. In social science all our concepts are dialectical and necessarily imprecise. We may make use of analytical models in which all concepts are given analytically precise definitions that allow logical and mathematical manipulation. But these models are analytical similes or analogies, sometimes useful and sometimes not. They do not remove the dialectical imprecision of our concepts, they merely abstract from it.

As for the above four questions, the immediate directions are clear enough though the optimum magnitudes are vague. We are sometimes too clever in exploiting the imprecision of our knowledge in order to evade moral responsibility for our comfortable inaction.

The questions raised so far seek clearer definitions of the goals of the steady state. A more important set of questions follows concerning the means for attaining the steady-state goals: the appropriate technology, the appropriate social institutions of control for maintaining constant stocks of physical wealth and people and for distributing the constant wealth among the constant population.

The main aim of production technology must, in the steady state, become more analogous to the legitimate aim of medical technology. Just as medical technology seeks (or should seek) to increase average life expectancy, so must production technology seek to increase the durability or "life expectancy" of physical commodities. How? By making individual commodities more durable and designing them for easy repairability, and also by designing for easier recyclability either through manmade closed loops or natural material cycles (biodegradability). High biodegradability may seem to contradict "durability" and in a physical sense it does. But what we are interested in is durability as a part of the stock of wealth, not the durability of garbage. Maximizing durability means maximizing the time matter spends as wealth and minimizing the time it spends as garbage. Our current technology does not aim at maximizing durability. It comes closer to minimizing it, in order not to spoil the market for replacement demand.

One extremely interesting technological possibility from the steady-state perspective is the "fusion torch" idea being pursued by William Gough and Bernard Eastlund of the AEC.[8] An ultrahigh temperature plasma held in a magnetic field is used to provide energy for electric power generation. Garbage is thrown into the plasma, which reduces any material to its basic elements. The elements are then separated and collected electromagnetically and made available for reuse. Although this closes the material cycle there is still the unavoidable problem of thermal pollution. But the idea is to mimimize it by cascading heat downward to lower and lower grade uses. For example the waste heat of power generation would be used for space heating, replacing fossil fuels. There are many technical problems which remain and I am not competent to assess them. But the idea of a fusion torch fits the steady-state paradigm very well, a fact which its proponents consider of great importance.

The above example of "cascading heat downward" illustrates the principle that technology should be so designed as to minimize negative externalities. One way of accomplishing this may be to shift to a smaller plant. Smaller scale and reduced power also increase access to tools and facilitate the distribution of both the benefits of technology and the controls over it. As an example Dr. Ivan Illich convincingly argues that the mobility of the entire population of a country would be increased by substituting cheap, repairable "mechanical donkeys" for expensive automobiles, and by reducing the speed limit from seventy to ten miles per hour!

Moreover, the focus of technological efficiency must shift from increasing output per constant period of labor time to decreasing labor time per constant quantity of output. The fruits of technical progress must be taken in the nonphysical form of increased leisure time.

SOCIAL INSTITUTIONS

The social institutions of control are of three kinds: those for maintaining a constant population, those for maintaining a constant stock of physical wealth, and those governing distribution. In all cases the guiding design principle for social institutions is to provide the necessary control with a minimum sacrifice of personal freedom, to provide macrostability while allowing for microvariability, to combine the macrostatic with the microdynamic.[9]

Constant Population

An ingenious institution for maintaining a constant population has been proposed by Kenneth Boulding.[10] Unfortunately it has been treated more as a joke than as a serious proposal. The idea is to issue licenses to have children directly to individuals. Each person would receive certificates in an amount permitting 1.1 children, or each couple at marriage would receive certificates permitting 2.2 children, or whatever number corresponds to replacement fertility. The licenses could be bought and sold on a free market. Thus macrostability would be attained, and microvariability would be permitted. Furthermore those having more than two children would have to pay for an extra license, those who have fewer than two children would receive payment for their unused license certificates. The right to have children then becomes distributed equally, and market supply and demand then redistributes these rights. People who do not or cannot have children are rewarded financially. People who wish to have more than two are penalized financially. And the subsidies and penalties are handled by the market with no government bureaucracy.

A slight amendment to the plan might be to grant 1.0 certificates to each individual and have these refer not to births but to "survivals." If someone dies before he has a child, then his certificate becomes a part of his estate and is willed to someone else, e.g., his parents, who either use it to have another child, or sell it to someone else. The advantage of this modification is that it offsets existing class differentials in infant and child mortality. Without the modification a poor family desiring two children could end up with two infant deaths and no certificates. The best plan of course is to eliminate class differences in mortality, but in the meantime this modification may make the plan initially easier to accept. Indeed, even in the absence of class differentials the modification has the advantage of building in a "guarantee."

Two other subsidiary advantages might be claimed. First, the genetic burden of infertility is rather arbitrarily and unjustly distributed among couples. The Boulding plan offers at least some compensation to those who draw a fertility blank in the genetic lottery. It partially compensates for a natural inequity. Also, it allows celibates to influence the quality of the next generation through the discretion they exercise in selling or giving their certificates to others, for they could decide to sell or donate the certificates only to those they felt would make good parents.

Let us dispose of two common objections to the plan. First it is argued that it is unjust because the rich have an advantage. Of course the rich always have an advantage, but is their advantage increased or decreased in Boulding's plan? Clearly it is decreased. The effect of the plan on income distribution is equalizing because (1) the new marketable asset is distributed equally, (2) as the rich purchase more certificates and have more children their family per capita incomes are lowered, and as the poor have fewer their family per capita incomes increase. Also from the point of view of the children it is desirable to increase the probability that they will be born rich rather than poor. Whatever injustice there is in the plan stems from the existence of rich and poor, not from Boulding's plan, which actually reduces the degree of injustice. Furthermore, income and wealth distribution are to be controlled by a separate institution, discussed below, so that in the overall system this objection is more fully met.

A more reasonable objection raises the problem of enforcement. What to do with law-breaking parents and their illegal children? What do we do with illegal children today? One possibility is to put the children up for adoption and encourage adoption by paying the adopting parents the market value, plus subsidy if need be, for their license, thus retiring a license from circulation to compensate for the child born without a license. Like any other law breakers the offending parents are subject to punishment. But the punishment need not be drastic or unusual. Of course no law can be enforced if everyone breaks it. The plan presupposes the acceptance of the morality and necessity of the law by a large segment of the public. It also presupposes widespread knowledge of contraceptive practices. But these presuppositions would apply to *any* institution of population control, except the most coercive. The moral issue is of such critical importance that it will be considered separately later.

Choice may be influenced in two ways: by controlling or "rigging" the objective conditions of choice (prices and incomes in a broad sense), or by manipulating the subjective conditions of choice (preferences). Boulding's plan imposes straightforward objective constraints and does not presumptuously attempt to manipulate peoples' preferences. Changed preferences due to individual example and moral conversion are in no way ruled out. If preferences should change so that, on the average, the population desired replacement fertility, the price of a certificate would approach zero and the objective constraint would automatically vanish. The moral basis of the plan is that everyone is treated equally, yet there is no insistence upon conformity of preferences, this being the great drawback of "voluntary" plans that rely on official moral suasion. Some people, God bless them, will never be persuaded, and their individual nonconformity wrecks the moral basis (equal treatment) of "voluntary" programs.

Constant Physical Wealth

The guiding principle is the same as in the case of population: to combine macrostability with microvariability, or macrostatics with microdynamics. The strategic point at which to impose macro control seems to me to be the rate of depletion of material resources. If we control aggregate depletion, then by the law of conservation of matter and energy, we also control aggregate pollution. J. H. Dales has suggested a scheme of pollution quotas, which has great merit (see his *Pollution, Property, and Prices*, University of Toronto Press, 1968). However, putting the quotas on depletion rather than pollution seems preferable. How such an institution might work is outlined below.

Let quotas be set on new depletion of each of the basic resources, both renewable and nonrenewable, during a given time. The legal right to deplete to the amount of the quota for each resource would be auctioned off by the government at the beginning of each time period, in conveniently divisible units, to private firms, individuals, and public enterprises. After purchase from the government the quota rights would be freely transferable by sale or gift. As population growth and economic growth press against resources, the prices of the depletion quotas would be driven higher and higher. In the interests of conserving nonrenewable resources and optimal exploitation of renewable resources, quotas could then be reduced to lower levels, thereby driving the price of the quotas still higher. In this way, the increasing windfall rents resulting from increasing pressure of demand on a fixed supply would be collected by the government through the auctioning of the depletion rights. The government spends the revenues, let us say, by paying a social dividend. Even though the monetary flow is therefore undiminished, the real flow has been physically limited by the resource quotas. All prices of resources and of goods then increase, the prices of resource-intensive goods increase relatively more, and total resource consumption (depletion) is reduced. Moreover, in accordance with the law of conservation of matter-energy, reduction of initial inputs will result in reduction of ultimate outputs (pollution), reducing the aggregate throughput and with it the stress it puts on the ecosystem.

With depletion now made more expensive and with higher prices on final goods, recycling becomes more profitable. As recycling increases pollution is reduced even more. Higher prices make consumers more interested in durability and careful maintenance of wealth. Most importantly, prices now provide a strong incentive to develop new technologies and patterns of consumption that are resource saving. If there is any static inefficiency incurred in setting the rate of depletion outside the market (a doubtful point), it is likely to be more than offset by the dynamic benefits of greater inducements to develop resource-saving technology.

Adjustment of the throughput of depletion and pollution flows to long-run ecologically sustainable levels can be effected gradually. At first depletion quotas could be set at the preceding year's levels, and if necessary gradually reduced by, say, two percent per year until we reach the "optimal" throughput. Stocks will then adjust to equilibrium with the new throughput. Thereafter the constant stock would be maintained by the constant throughput. As we gradually exhaust nonrenewable resources, quotas for their depletion will approach zero and recycling will become the only source of inputs, at which time, presumably, the ever rising price of the resource will have led to the development of a recycling technology. We should not expect that without depletion quotas the exhaustion of resources would be gradual: most likely it would be sudden. Also, without quotas, less incentive to develop the new technology would exist, in face of the uncertainty that some newly discovered reserves would lower resource prices, making the new technology temporarily uneconomic. When the rate of depletion becomes accepted as a societal parameter, it can be depended on, with the result that uncertainty will be lessened. New discoveries of resources would increase the length of time until exhaustion rather than lower the price of the resources.

The social decision that determines the aggregate rate of depletion through depletion quotas can be regarded as the correction of the failure of the market to bring an end to overexploitation. For renewable resources, quotas can be set at a calculated optimum sustainable yield or maximum rent. The quota on renewable resources must be such as to avoid "eating into our capital," and could be dispensed with for privately owned and well-managed renewable resources, where they would not be needed. Since with nonrenewables mankind is always eating its capital, determining the rate of depletion for these resources should be a collective decision based largely on value judgments once we are below the disaster thresholds, bearing in mind that two considerations argue for lower rates of depletion and higher prices than now prevail: first, the conservationists' moral concern about future generations, and second, the idea that development of resource-saving technology can be induced by high resource prices. The rate at which the stock of terrestrial low entropy should be depleted is fundamentally a moral decision and should be decided on grounds of ethical desirability (stewardship), not technological possibility or present value calculations of profitability. By fixing the rate of depletion, we can force technology to focus more on renewable resources and on the flow source of solar energy, which cannot be increased in the present at the expense of the future, a point brilliantly developed by Nicholas Georgescu-Roegen in "The Entropy Law and the Economic Problem," in this volume. Thus, let technology devote itself to learning how to live off our solar income, rather than our terrestrial capital. Such advances will benefit all generations, not just the present.

The depletion quota plan should appeal both to technological optimists and pessimists. The pessimist should be pleased by the conservation effect of the quotas, while the optimist should be pleased by the price inducement to resource-saving technology. The optimist tells us not to worry about running out of resources because technology embodied in reproducible capital is a "nearly perfect substitute for resources." As we run out of anything prices will rise and substitute methods will be found. If one believes this, then how could one object to quotas, which simply increase the scarcity and prices of resources a bit ahead of schedule in order (a) to achieve the benefits of the new technology sooner, and (b) to conserve resources just in case the new technology is slow in coming?

A further effect of the quota scheme is that factor prices would change, with labor becoming cheaper relative to land and capital. This effect alone would tend to increase employment, which is not a benefit in itself, but is necessary as long as we maintain an income-through-jobs system of distribution. However, reduced aggregate consumption would tend to reduce employment, and might necessitate a reduction in the work week through job sharing or increased reliance on unearned income, such as a social dividend financed out of receipts the auction of resource quotas would provide.

The actual mechanics of quota auction markets for three or four hundred basic resources would present no great problems. The whole process could be computerized since the function of an auctioneer is purely mechanical. Quota auction markets could be vastly simpler, faster, more decentralized, and less subject to fraud and manipulation than today's stock market. Also, differences in the quality and location of resources within the same general category, though ignored at the auction level, will be taken into account in price differentials paid to resource owners by the holders of the auctioned purchase rights.

Assuming a quota depletion system operated within the United States, the scheme could and probably would have to be designed to include imported resources, so the same right to deplete to a quota would be applied to the use of imported resources (though not to the finished goods manufactured from these resources), and thus the market would determine the proportions in which our standard of living is sustained by depletion of foreign as well as national resources. Imported final goods would then be cheaper than U.S.-made goods, assuming other countries do not limit their depletion, and goods made within the U.S. for export would then be more expensive than the domestic goods of foreign countries, thus leading us toward a balance-of-payments deficit. But a fluctuating rate of international exchange of foreign currencies for dollars would restore equilibrium. One might object that limiting our imports of resources will work a hardship on the many underdeveloped countries who export raw materials, an objection that is not clearly valid, for such a policy will also force them to transform their own resources domestically rather than through international trade, since finished goods would not be subject to quotas. In any case it is clear that in the long run we do the underdeveloped countries no favor by using up their resource endowment. Sooner or later they will begin to drive a hard bargain for their nonrenewable resources, and we had best not be too dependent on them.

Such a policy is radical, but less radical than attempting the impossible, i.e., growing forever. It does not expropriate land and capital, but does further restrict their use at an across-the-board level. It provides the necessary macroeconomic control with a minimum sacrifice of microeconomic freedom. It minimizes centralized, quantitative planning and maximizes reliance on decentralized, market decision-making.

The basic difference between depletion quotas and pollution taxes (the latter being a tax on effluents, emissions, and residuals—the usual "solution to pollution" offered by economists) is that the former places macro physical constraints beyond which the market economy may not go, and then leaves the price system alone, whereas the latter sets no physical constraints, seeking by micro intervention to rig all prices in such a way that the market economy will be made to count the costs of all ecological effects of growth and, as a result, stay within proper ecological bounds. The campaign slogan for pollution taxes is "internalize externalities," which means calculating the full social cost of production and including it in the money price of the product, for each commodity.

Unfortunately the problem of setting the correct pollution tax so as truly to internalize externalities is impossible. Many externalities are unmeasurable *in principle* (they involve interpersonal comparisons of well-being), and most are unmeasurable in practice. Indeed, the reason such costs are left out of account by the market in the first place is often that it is impossible (or very expensive) to measure them. Even when external costs (and benefits) can be measured, these often result from more than one polluting activity and an allocation of the joint cost or benefit to each activity is arbitrary. Moreover, by permitting quantities of goods produced to vary without limit, the pollution tax scheme assumes that external costs increase continuously and gradually, that there are no ecological thresholds or trigger relations (whereby a slight additional increase in pollution could trigger massive ecological damage). Unfortunately costs do not increase continuously and gradually, and there are thresholds. In addition, as a tool of micro intervention, pollution taxes require very detailed information and the monitoring of every smokestack, garbage can, and drainpipe in the country. As a practical matter precise internalization could be bypassed and pollution taxes could be applied across the board, as a macroeconomic tool. But monitoring and auditing would still have to take place in individual firms, and many more firms are engaged in polluting than are engaged in depleting.

But even assuming that none of the above difficulties prevail and assuming perfect success at internalizing all hitherto external costs, we find that pollution taxes do not limit growth of the throughput (GNP). They can within limits reduce the resource intensity of a dollar's worth of GNP, but the total volume of GNP (both in dollars and resources) can continue to grow as population growth and economic growth continue. The reason is simple. Every time we "internalize an externality" we increase not only costs, but also incomes. Aggregate expenditure always equals aggregate income. The economy is always "rich" enough to buy as much as it can produce regardless of price. A pollution tax levied on one good could greatly reduce the consumption and throughput of the good. But it does not follow that a general pollution tax levied on all goods could reduce aggregate throughput greatly or continuously. What is true for a part is not necessarily true for the whole (fallacy of composition). If the government accumulated a surplus (by not spending the pollution tax it collected) then growth would be halted. But orthodox, growth-oriented economists will urge government spending, probably even a deficit, in the name of full employment. From the orthodox viewpoint the inability of pollution taxes to limit the GNP-throughput will count as an advantage. But from the steady-state perspective, the best that pollution taxes could do would be to reduce the resource-intensive component of GNP to some minimal percentage level, and to hold it there while the absolute level continues to rise. Internalization of externalities by way of pollution taxes will not keep us from growing beyond ecological bounds.

As a last resort one could forego theoretical optimizing and argue that some pollution taxes are better than no pollution taxes. But even this is doubtful, as it runs afoul of the theorem of second best, which says that when all conditions for an optimum cannot be met, it is not true that the next best strategy is to meet as many of the conditions as possible. But I mention this problem for the benefit of theoretical economists. On practical grounds probably "some pollution taxes are better than no pollution taxes" is a good rule of thumb. Politically, pollution taxes are likely to precede depletion quotas, and there is no point in opposing a step in the right direction no matter how feeble, especially if it is a first step.

Although depletion quotas lack some of the theoretical nicety of pollution taxes, they do offer a number of practical advantages. Entropy is at its minimum at the input (depletion) end of the throughput pipeline, and at its maximum at the output (pollution) end. Therefore it is physically easier to monitor and control depletion than pollution: there are fewer mines, wells, and ports than there are smokestacks, garbage dumps, and drainpipes—not to mention such diffuse emission sources as run-off of insecticides and fertilizers from fields into rivers and lakes, and auto exhausts. Given that there is more leverage in intervening at the input end, should we intervene by way of taxes or quotas? Quotas, if they are auctioned by the government rather than allocated on nonmarket criteria, have an important net advantage over taxes in that they definitely limit aggregate throughput, which is the quantity to be controlled. Taxes exert only an indirect and uncertain limit. It is quite true that given a demand curve, a price plus a tax determines a quantity. But demand curves shift, and are subject to great errors in estimation even when stable. Demand curves for resources could shift up as a result of population increase, change in tastes, increase in income, etc. Every time we increase a price we also increase an income, so that in the aggregate the economy can still purchase exactly as much as before. The government taxes throughput and then spends the tax. On what? On throughput. If government expenditures on each category of throughput were equal to the revenues received from taxing that same category, then the limit on throughput would be cancelled out. If the government taxes resource-intensive items and spends on time-intensive items there will be a reduction in aggregate throughput, but it is hard to say by how much. Furthermore a credit expansion by the banking sector or deficit spending by the government for other purposes could easily offset a tax control. Of course all these activities could be coordinated, but given the limited ability of government administration it seems better not to rely on that. It is quantity that affects the ecosystem, not price, and therefore it is ecologically safer to let errors and unexpected shifts in demand result in price fluctuation rather than in quantity fluctuation. Hence quotas.

The pollution taxes usually recommended would seem, if the above is correct, to intervene at the wrong end with the wrong policy tool. There are, however, limits to the ability of depletion quotas to influence the qualitative nature and spatial location of pollution, and as instruments for fine tuning pollution taxes would be a useful supplement. It is clear that two processes using the same inputs can have qualitatively different pollutions, depending on the nature of the process. At this stage we can no longer influence pollution indirectly via depletion controls, but must control the pollution directly either by pollution taxes or quotas levied on specific microeconomic units. Thus pollution taxes are appropriate for giving the fine details to the basic rough shape of depletion quotas. Just as a sculptor first uses a large blunt chisel to hew the block of marble into something resembling a face, then using the small sharp chisels to put specific features and expressions on the face, so economists should use the macro chisel of depletion quotas to carve out something resembling the face of an ecologically sane economy, then employing the micro chisel of pollution taxes to impart a particular visage. To be misled by theoretical pseudoprecision into shaping a new economy with only the sharp, delicate micro chisel will merely result in a lot of broken chisels that have barely scratched the surface of our task.

Focus on pollution taxes and internalization of externalities is indicative of a peculiar tunnel vision that afflicts economic thought. In an article entitled "The Economist's Approach to Pollution and Its Control,"[11] Professor Robert Solow observes that, "as economic development proceeds many [previously free] resources become scarce. . . . because growing population and increasing production of commodities put more pressure on the limited supply provided by nature. . . . Eventually, as an economy grows, even air and water become scarce." The problem he sees is that external costs arising from the uncharged-for use of these newly scarce resources play havoc with the efficient allocation of resources. The remedy he suggests is "internalization of externalities" so that we each pay the full cost of our consumption. At a theoretical level this is hard to argue with. Professor Solow recognizes operational difficulties, and suggests moving the tax from the pollution end back toward the input end. Yet nowhere within his very sensible and cogent article is there any suggestion that we need not (and cannot) forever continue to turn free resources into scarce resources. It is all very interesting to know that prices can be rigged so as to allocate newly scarce resources "optimally." But that does not mean that we should continue to allow economic growth and population growth to increase the scarcity of clean air and water, silence, noncongested areas, and unhurried moments. We do have the alternative (and long run imperative) of stopping growth in both the population of human organisms and the quantities of extensions of human organisms that make up physical wealth. By contrast, the depletion quota scheme imposes a kind of birth control on objects.

The orthodox view seems to be that as long as we minimize the throughput per unit of GNP, we need not worry about the total number of units. Growth is still paramount. Or perhaps it is assumed that once *all* external costs are fully and accurately accounted in prices—so that marginal *private* cost and benefit coincide with marginal *social* cost and benefit—then individuals will choose to stop increasing production, consumption, and population at the point where marginal social cost equals marginal social benefit. Such an assumption is a good example of the fallacy of misplaced concreteness, which consists in neglecting the degree of abstraction undertaken in the course of considering an actual entity only so far as it exemplifies certain preselected categories of thought.[12]

In an economy in which a choice of labor or leisure would be available on a small margin to all individuals, all of whom were relieved from the pressure to work to ward off insecurity by some minimal holdings of personal wealth, it is possible to imagine everyone opting for leisure after achieving a certain real income. But pollution taxes have little to do with such a limit, and a growth-oriented capitalistic economy allows very little labor-leisure trade-off and very little personal security for most people. Furthermore, ecological limits might be reached before the shift from goods to leisure becomes recognized as important. Nevertheless, assume that pollution taxes enabled us to reach such an optimum state; could our present economy remain there? No, for without growth and net investment, aggregate demand would fall short of capacity, and unemployment would appear. Distribution problems would be greatly intensified. Our system is hooked on growth per se, and does *not* see growth as a temporary *means* of attaining some optimum level of stocks, but as an *end* in itself. Why? Perhaps because, as one prominent economist so bluntly put it in defending growth: "Growth is a substitute for equality of income. So long as there is growth there is hope, and that makes large income differentials tolerable."[13] We are addicted to growth because we are addicted to large inequalities in income and wealth. To paraphrase Marie Antoinette: Let them eat growth. Better yet, let the poor hope to eat growth in the future.

The basic malady is addiction to unlimited growth, growthmania. Pollution taxes are a mere palliative, treating only the symptoms of the disease. Depletion quotas strike at the real trouble, and are radical in the literal sense of getting at the root of things.

Control of Distribution

Distribution is the rock upon which most ships of state, including the steady state, are very likely to run aground. Currently we seek to improve distribution by establishing a minimum standard of living guaranteed by a negative income tax. In the growthmania paradigm there is no upper limit to the standard of living. In the steady-state paradigm there is an upper limit. Furthermore the higher the lower limit below which no one is allowed to fall, the lower must be the upper limit above which no one is allowed to rise. The lower limit has considerable political acceptance, the upper limit does not. But in the steady state the upper limit is a logical necessity. It implies confiscation and redistribution of wealth above a certain limit per person or per family. What does one say to the cries of "destruction of incentive"? Remember—we are no longer anxious to grow in the first place! Also one recalls Jonathan Swift's observation:

> In all well-instituted commonwealths, care has been taken to limit men's possessions; which is done for many reasons, and, among the rest, for one which, perhaps, is not often considered; that when bounds are set to men's desires, after they have acquired as much as the laws will permit them, their private interest is at an end, and they have nothing to do but to take care of the public.[14]

The basic institution for controlling distribution is very simple: set maximum and minimum limits on wealth and income, the maximum limit on wealth being the most important. Such a proposal is in no way an attack on private property. Indeed, as John Stuart Mill argues, it is really a defense of private property:

> Private property, in every defense made of it, is supposed to mean the guarantee to individuals of the fruits of their own labour and abstinence. The guarantee to them of the fruits of the labor and abstinence of others, transmitted to them without any merit or exertion of their own, is not of the essence of the institution, but a mere incidental consequence which, when it reaches a certain height, does not promote, but conflicts with, the ends which render private property legitimate.[15]

According to Mill, private property is legitimated as a bastion against exploitation. But this is true only if everyone owns some minimum amount. Otherwise, when some own a great deal of it and others have very little, private property becomes an *instrument* of exploitation rather than a guarantee against it. It is implicit in this view that private property is legitimate only if there is some distributist institution (like, for example, the Jubilee year of the Old Testament) that keeps inequality of wealth within some tolerable limits. Such an institution is now lacking. The proposed institution of maximum and minimum wealth and income limits would remedy this severe defect and make private property legitimate again. Also it would go a long way toward legitimating the free market, since most of our blundering interference with the price system (e.g., the farm program, the minimum wage) has as its goal an equalizing alteration in the distribution of income and wealth.

Without this legitimation there would be no strong case for extending the market to cover birth quotas and depletion quotas as means of institutionalizing environmental constraints. Thus, such a distributist policy is based on impeccably respectable premises: private property, the free market, opposition to welfare bureaucracies and centralized control. Moreover, it heeds the radicals' call of "power to the people" since it puts the source of power, namely property, in the hands of the many people, rather than in the hands of the few capitalist plutocrats and socialist bureaucrats. What should we call this thing that is neither capitalist nor socialist and that so resembles Jeffersonian democracy? Following G. K. Chesterton let us call it the Distributive State.[16]

But what are the "proper" limits to wealth inequality? "Where do you draw the line?" An answer is necessarily imprecise. However, just because one cannot specify exactly where to draw a line does not mean that no line needs to be drawn, or that one can be drawn anywhere, and much creative thought is dedicated precisely to the task of drawing imprecise lines. On the other hand, Plato was precise in stating that the richest citizens should be four times as wealthy as the poorest. For the sake of political consensus let us propose that the richest be allowed to have, say, twenty times as much as the poorest. Within such limits distribution is governed by market forces. After experiencing a twenty-to-one-ratio for a while we could then intelligently decide how to modify it. Twenty-to-one (or some other) limits would also apply to income, with progressive taxation levied within the limits. Below the lower limit the tax rate becomes negative. Above the upper limit the tax rate becomes 100 percent—in Jonathan Swift's words "private interest is at an end and they have nothing to do but to take care of the public," or tend their own gardens.

Maximum income and wealth would remove many of the incentives to monopoly. Why conspire to corner markets, fix prices, etc., if you cannot keep the loot? As for labor, the minimum property and income would enable the outlawing of strikes, which are rapidly becoming intolerable. Unions would not be needed as a means of confronting the power of concentrated wealth, since wealth would no longer be concentrated. Indeed, the workers would have a share of it and thus would not be at the mercy of an employer. In addition, some limit on corporate size would be needed.

How would such a distributist state look in its specific details? Certainly it would be more complicated than the agrarian vision of three acres and a cow for every sturdy yeoman, with which the idea is often associated. Guaranteeing a minimum limit to wealth is probably not feasible, since one can always spend his wealth, and could hardly expect to have it restored year after year. Therefore, guaranteeing a minimum limit to income would be sufficient. The problems of detail and accounting would be great, but probably no greater than those faced today by the Internal Revenue Service. What is lacking is not technical capability, but the will and the moral commitment.

On Moral Growth

Is the above sketch of a steady state unrealistic and idealistic? On the contrary, it is in broad characteristics the only realistic possibility. The present economy is literally unrealistic because in its disregard for natural laws it is attempting the impossible. The steady-state paradigm, unlike growthmania, is realistic because it takes the physical laws of nature as its first premise.

Let us assume for a moment that the necessity of the steady state and the above outline of its appropriate technologies and social institutions are accepted. Logic and necessity are not sufficient to bring about social reform. The philospher Leibnitz observed that,

> If geometry conflicted with our passions and interests as much as do ethics, we would contest it and violate it as much as we do ethics now, in spite of all the demonstrations of Euclid and Archimedes, which would be labeled paralogisms and dreams.[17]

Leibnitz is surely correct. However logical and necessary the above outline of the steady state, it is, on the assumption of static morality, nothing but a dream. The physically steady economy absolutely requires moral growth beyond the present level.

Economists and other social scientists of positivistic bias seem to consider appeals to morality as cheating, as an admission of intellectual defeat, like bending the pieces of a jigsaw puzzle. In economics there is a long and solid tradition of regarding moral resources as static and too scarce to be relied upon. In the words of the great British economist Alfred Marshall, "progress chiefly depends on the extent to which the *strongest* and not merely the *highest* forces of human nature can be utilized for the increase of social good."[18]

Presumably self-interest is stronger and more abundant than brotherhood. Presumably "progress" and "social good" can be defined independently of the driving motive of society.

Another British economist, D. H. Robertson, once asked the illuminating question: What is it that economists economize? His answer was "love, the scarcest and most precious of all resources."[19] Paul Samuelson quotes Robertson approvingly in the latest edition of *Economics*, his influential textbook. Nor are economists alone in ruling out reliance on moral resources. The reader will recall from the previous reading that in his "Tragedy of the Commons" the biologist Garrett Hardin identifies a class of problems with no technical solution.[20] He rules out moral solutions as self-eliminating on a somewhat farfetched evolutionary analogy, and advocates a political solution: mutual coercion mutually agreed upon. This is fine, but where is the mutual agreement to come from if not from shared values, from a convincing morality? Political scientist Beryl Crowe, in revisiting the tragedy of the commons, argues that the set of no-technical-solution problems coincides with the set of no-political-solution problems and that Hardin's "mutual coercion mutually agreed upon" is politically impossible.[21] Between them they present a convincing case that "commons problems" will not be solved technically nor politically, assuming static morality. Mutual coercion does not substitute for, but presupposes, moral growth.

Going back to Robertson's repulsive but correct idea that economists economize love, one may ask, "How"? Mainly by maximizing growth. Let there be more for everyone year after year so that we need never face up to sharing a fixed total. Unequal distribution can be justified as necessary for saving, incentive, and hence, growth. This must continue, otherwise the problem of sharing a fixed total will place too heavy a strain on our precious resource of love, which is so scarce that it must never be used. I am reminded of Lord Thomas Balough's statement that one purpose of economic theory is to make those who *are* comfortable *feel* comfortable.

To paraphrase the above, we are told "Don't worry about today's inequities, but anxiously fix your attention on tomorrow's larger total income." Compare that with the Sermon on the Mount: "Do not be anxious about tomorrow, for tomorrow will be anxious for itself. Let the day's own evil be sufficient for the day." The morality of the steady state is that of the Sermon on the Mount. Growthmania requires the negation of that morality. If we give our first attention to the evils of the day we will have moral growth, though not so much economic growth. If we anxiously give our first attention to tomorrow's larger income we will have economic growth but little or no moral growth. Since economic growth is reaching physical limits anyway we may now find the Sermon on the Mount more appealing and easier to accept.

The same idea is stated in Alexander Solzhenitsyn's *Cancer Ward*, in the chapter entitled "Idols of the Market Place," in which the position of "ethical socialism" is advocated. The main theme is "ethics first and economics afterwards"—a theme which finds as little acceptance in the Soviet Union as it does in the United States, perhaps even less. The following words are from the character Shulubin (page 443):

> Happiness is a mirage—as for the so-called "happiness of future generations" it is even more of a mirage. Who knows anything about it? Who has spoken with these future generations? Who knows what idols they will worship? Ideas of what happiness is have changed too much through the ages. No one should have the effrontery to try to plan it in advance. When we have enough loaves of white bread to crush them under our heels, when we have enough milk to choke us, we still won't be in the least happy. But if we share the things we don't have enough of, we can be happy today! If we care only about "happiness" and about reproducing our species, we shall merely crowd the earth senselessly and create a terrifying society. . . .

There are other sources of moral support for the steady state besides the Sermon on the Mount. From the Old Testament we have two creation myths, the Priestly and the Yawistic, one which gives value to creation only with reference to man, and one which gives value to creation independently of man. In Western thought the first tradition has dominated, but the other is there waiting to receive its proper emphasis. Also Aldo Leopold's "land ethic" is extremely appealing and would serve admirably as the moral foundation of the steady state. Finally Karl Marx's materialism and objection to the alienation of man from nature can be enlisted as a moral foundation of the steady state. Marx recognized that nature is the "inorganic body of man" and not just a pile of neutral stuff to be dominated.[22]

In writing this chapter, I've considered the steady state only at a national level. Clearly the world as a whole must eventually adjust to a steady state. Perhaps ultimately this recognition will promote unity among nations—or conversely the desire for unity may promote the recognition. However, when nations cannot even agree to limit the stock of "bads" through disarmament it is hard to be optimistic about their limiting the stocks of "goods." There is no alternative except to try, but national efforts need not wait for international agreement.

Finally, one rather subtle, yet very powerful, moral force can be enlisted in support of the steady-state paradigm. That is wholeness. If the truth is the whole, as Hegel claimed, then our current splintered knowledge is so far from truth that it is hardly worth learning. I believe this is why many of our best university students do not work very hard at their studies. Why continue mining the deep, narrow, disciplinary shafts sunk into man's totality by the intellectual fragment-makers? Why deepen the tombs in which we have buried the wholeness of knowledge? Why increase the separation of people by filling separate heads with separate fragments of knowledge? The malaise reflected in these questions is very grave, and is, in my view, a major reason for the new surge of interest in ecology. Ecology is whole. It brings together the broken, analyzed, alienated, fragmented pieces of man's image of the world. Ecology is also a fad, but when the fad passes, the movement toward wholeness must continue. Unless the physical, the social, and the moral dimensions of our knowledge are integrated in a unified paradigm offering a vision of wholeness, no solutions to our problems are likely. John Stuart Mill's idea of the stationary state seems to me to offer such a paradigm.

NOTES AND REFERENCES

1. *Economic Report of the President, 1971.* p. 92.
2. *Ibid*, p. 88.
3. Neil Jacoby, "The Environmental Crisis," *The Center Magazine*, Vol. III, No. 6, November–December 1970.
4. See K. E. Boulding, "The Economics of the Coming Spaceship Earth" *in* Henry Jarrett, ed., *Environmental Quality in a Growing Economy*, Baltimore: Johns Hopkins Press, 1966; reprinted in this volume on pages 121–132. See also the introduction to this volume.
5. The slower the water flows through a tank of fixed size, the longer the time an average drop spends in the tank.
6. For a brilliant and extensive development of this theme see N. Georgescu-Roegen, *The Entropy Law and the Economic Process*, Cambridge, Mass.: Harvard University Press, 1971. The essay printed on pages 37–49 of this volume is a short summary treatment.
7. See Thomas Frejka, "Reflections on the Demographic Conditions Needed to Establish a United States Stationary Population Growth," *Population Studies*, November, 1968.
8. William Gough and Bernard Eastlund, "The Prospects of Fusion Power," *Scientific American*, February, 1971.

9. See Daniel B. Luten, "Teleoeconomics: The Microdynamic, Macrostatic Economy," Department of Geography, University of California, Berkeley (Mimeo).
10. Kenneth E. Boulding, *Economics As A Science*, New York: McGraw-Hill, 1970, p. 149.
11. Robert Solow, "The Economist's Approach to Pollution and Its Control," *Science*, August 6, 1971.
12. We might select "yellowness" and "four-wheeled-ness" as defining characteristics of a bus, but the fallacy of misplaced concreteness prevents us from repeating the old saying, "If Grandmother were yellow and had four wheels, she'd be a bus." Likewise, from the concrete interdependencies of life we might abstract those pecuniary links which operate through a market as the defining characteristics of all interdependence, and then we go off in all directions painting "internal" and hanging a price tag on everything in the ecosystem. But alas, the ecosystem is not just a market economy *writ large* any more than Grandmother is a bus.
13. Henry C. Wallich, "Zero Growth," *Newsweek*, January 24, 1972, p. 62.
14. Jonathan Swift, "Thoughts on Various Subjects," reprinted in *The Literature of England*, G. B. Woods et al., eds., New York: Scott, Foresman and Company, 1958, p. 1003.
15. John Stuart Mill, "Of Property," in *Principles of Political Property*, Volume II, London, John Parker and Son, 1857, Chapter I.
16. G. K. Chesterton, *The Outline of Sanity*, Methuen and Co., Ltd., London, 1926.
17. Leibnitz quoted in A. Sauvy, *The General Theory of Population*, New York: Basic Books, 1970, p. 270.
18. Alfred Marshall, quoted in D. H. Robertson, *Economic Commentaries*, London: Staples Press Ltd., 1956, p. 148.
19. D. H. Robertson, *Economic Commentaries*, op. cit., p. 154.
20. Garrett Hardin, "The Tragedy of the Commons," *Science*, December 13, 1968. Reprinted in this volume on pp. 133–148.
21. Beryl Crowe, "The Tragedy of the Commons Revisited," *Science*, November 28, 1969.
22. Karl Marx, *Karl Marx's Early Writings*, Translated and edited by T. B. Bottomore, New York: McGraw-Hill, 1963, p. 127.

8

THE GUARANTEED INCOME AS AN ENVIRONMENTAL MEASURE

Warren A. Johnson

It is ironic that one of the major consequences of the almost continuous economic growth since World War II has been the steady deterioration of the environment. Our incomes and standard of living have increased significantly so that the private worlds of most Americans are now complete with expansive homes and gardens, full garages, kitchens, and closets. Nearly all urban areas have seen the construction of luxury apartments, country clubs, residential areas, marinas, shopping centers, and office buildings. While the private sector has prospered, the public sector has been neglected; and that part of our environment that is not privately owned has declined in quality, beset with air and water pollution, noise, crime, congested roads and freeways, and crowded recreation areas. Industrial agriculture has diminished the viability of rural life, forcing people to cities that are already so large that the quality of urban life has diminished too.

But if the result of sustained economic growth has not been altogether satisfying, it is still considered to be far better than the only alternatives that are generally visualized: unemployment, recession, and eventually

---

"The Guaranteed Income as an Environmental Measure." From *Economic Growth vs. The Environment*, Warren A. Johnson and John Hardesty, eds. Wadsworth Publishing Company, Inc. 1971. Reprinted by permission of the author and publisher.

depression. Economists are confident they understand what is necessary for continued prosperity and high employment—real economic growth of something like four percent per year. Such a rate of growth can be maintained, in theory, through judicious application of governmental spending and taxing power, supplemented by monetary controls. Politicians are sometimes reluctant to apply the measures that economists prescribe, as when President Johnson tried to finance simultaneously the Vietnam War and domestic social welfare programs without increasing taxes. And sometimes economists disagree on the stringency of economic controls to be applied, mainly how much unemployment is an acceptable price to pay for reducing inflation. But at no time is the basic necessity of economic growth disputed: growth adequate to maintain full employment without inflation.

Growth has generally been considered synonymous with progress, with health and vitality. Stability, on the other hand, has usually been associated with stagnation. The first qualms about the value of growth have been about population. Encouraged by calculations of how many years it would take to reach standing room only, the goal of stopping population growth has been rapidly accepted. But while ingenious mathematics has been applied to population growth, it is only recently that similar thoughts have been turned toward economic growth. It has been young people primarily, who, so lacking in economic responsibility and blissfully unremembering of the Great Depression, point out that what most economists look on as economic health is in itself death by obesity, sooner or later. The mathematics is inexorable; if all goes according to our best hopes and a steady four percent annual growth is maintained, this would mean a doubling in seventeen years, a quadrupling in thirty-four, and an eightfold increase in fifty-one years. This is a much faster rate of increase than population, which in the United States will double in around seventy years at present growth rates. Maintaining growth requires a feverish pace of resource extraction and use of energy, generates many types of pollution, and requires new technologies and continued urbanization, all of which create the specter of ecological armageddon. Both economic growth and population growth will have to be stopped sooner or later in order to achieve a stable balance with our environment. The only question is when.

For the most part, the fear of runaway inflation or depression—particularly the latter—is the motivating force in our economic policies. The scale of social breakdown, of the human suffering and humiliation during the Great Depression, is closely related to the unanimous feeling in the United States that it cannot be allowed to happen again, at all costs. So now the economists find themselves with undreamed-of power in the federal government, for they are the major tacticians in the struggle to maintain full employment without inflation. And since growth is necessary to achieve this objective, growth we shall have. All the major participants in the political process—the administration, business, and labor—agree on this, to the degree that there is no basic ideological difference between them, only skirmishes over how the end product, the wealth created by the economy, shall be divided among the participants. Underlying the whole process is the concept of economic responsibility, which has come to perform the same social function that religious faith played in medieval Europe: disobedience might call forth the wrath of God (runaway inflation or depression), while pious acts can be trusted to lead to heaven (a cornucopia of consumer goods and services). For the most part, environmental problems will be considered a necessary part of our way of life, to be tolerated in order to obtain what we are conditioned to believe is the good life. After all, nothing is all good, and surely ours is a better life than has ever been realized before, all things considered.

Historically, the vastness of our land has allowed us to exercise our propensity to escape from our problems, and our economic system has encouraged this behavior. Initially this meant abandoning eroded farms or logged-over forest land. Now it means leaving our central cities to decay, strangled by declining employment and tax revenues, by increasing welfare costs and crime, by anachronistic transportation systems, and by racial polarization. Out of sight, out of mind; most of the affluent move to the suburbs and the new resort communities, where life is easier and residents are free from taxation to support the high costs of the central city. There they are able to provide lavish private environments for themselves, occupying their time with golf, gardening, relaxing, and entertaining friends. These private worlds are where our loyalties are; the real world, the larger environment, is disowned. Environmental problems, especially the urban ones, are seen as too massive and pervasive to solve. There will be talk of strong regulation and some conscience money as well, both primarily to search for technological solutions which are much easier to apply than solutions that require social change. But our tendency toward privatism suggests that we will not make the massive commitments necessary to make our cities a source of pride and satisfaction.

THE BASIC ECONOMIC PROBLEM

In order to keep everyone employed it is necessary to consume everything that the labor force can produce; consumption must equal production at full employment. If production exceeds consumption, goods pile up on shelves and in warehouses, and plants lay off labor. Workers without paychecks don't buy much, so sales fall off, which leads to other workers being laid off, and the whole thing can degenerate into a recession or depression. Recently we experienced the other side of the problem where, because of Vietnam War expenditures, not enough could be produced to meet all the demands, so prices for available goods were bid up by consumers, hence inflation. But as production of materials for Vietnam is reduced and returning GIs look for jobs, the persistent problem of unemployment has returned. In this situation, conservation measures that put people out of work, like shutting down polluting factories, stopping the construction of power plants, reducing the consumption of scarce fossil fuels or the production of environmentally damaging consumer goods—all of which put workers out of jobs—will have an increasingly hard time gaining acceptance. Only job-producing conservation measures, such as the construction of sewage treatment plants or the development and production of air pollution control devices will find the going easy. It should be noted that, within this framework, the GNP is useful primarily as a measure of the number of jobs the economy can generate rather than some abstract measure of human welfare.

Why is continued growth necessary? Why can't we just stay where we are? Because a good portion of our work force is employed through investment in new industrial plants, office buildings, freeways, schools, and houses. If these new facilities were not needed, a lot of workers would be unemployed. (Population growth is valuable in this context because it sustains demand for goods and services.) The second reason why growth is so essential is that the productivity of the average worker is increasing, primarily through automation. New products must be developed and consumption increased to keep pace with this increased productivity, or workers are laid off. So the government's role is to see to it that money is pumped into the economy when a recession threatens, to make sure that consumption and employment are maintained. Unfortunately, economic activity usually requires an urban location to be competitive, uses resources and energy, and generates pollution, and additional problems are created in the process of using and disposing of the things produced. Most services of the private sector of the economy are also based on goods, in marketing, retailing, and servicing them.

An analogy can be made between our economy and a speeding train. It is an extraordinarily powerful and efficient train, and it is traveling very fast already. It works beautifully except for this odd characteristic of having to keep speeding up all the time. Already, for a number of would-be passengers the train is going too fast for them to get on, and a number of the riders are not enjoying the frantic trip the way they expected they would and want to get off or at least slow down, while just a few are beginning to wonder how fast the train will ultimately have to go, and whether it can get the increasing amounts of fuel, water, and air it needs to keep going. It is a finite world.

The objective, of course, is to control the machine so that it will not have to speed up all the time, to set it at whatever speed is most desirable and can be maintained, or even to operate several trains at different speeds for various life styles of different travelers.

Overproduction is the major source of the problem; we work too much, given our level of technology. This could theoretically be overcome without unemployment if everyone worked less and less as productivity increased and new investment declined. Unfortunately, this alternative is being rejected at present. The long decline in the average number of hours worked per week has bottomed out and has even started back up over forty hours, primarily because workers are taking second jobs. Either there are still so many things people want to buy, or the problems of paying for what they have are so difficult, or they do not know what to do with the increased spare time that is as desirable as the extra income. Time is money, and to most people, free time isn't worth the money they could be making.

Galbraith has suggested an alternative to the overproduction of consumer goods and services—the reallocation of resources from private consumption to public endeavors, including improvement of the environment. Instead of more cars, public rapid transit systems would be built. Instead of the market-directed expansion of existing cities we would build new cities. Instead of more summer homes, there would be more parks and recreation areas. Instead of private services, public services would be expanded, in education, in aid to the disadvantaged, the sick, the mentally ill, and the aged. It is very logical, and federal funds will probably increase in some of these areas but certainly not at the expense of private consumption. Taxes, if anything, will also be reduced rather than raised because of our bias toward privatism. Tax money, for the most part, is seen as money down the drain, as money that goes mainly for someone else's welfare. Many public expenditures primarily benefit the affluent, although we are reluctant to admit it. Urban renewal, freeways, defense, and law enforcement all gain strong support from the broad middle class compared to public housing, public transportation, aid to the educationally handicapped, or urban parks. Most of us already have our own private parks around our houses and our own private transportation systems. Money spent on our own homes is not really spent but invested, and can be enjoyed while we own it, and then we can recoup our investment when we move. Unfortunately, we do not think of public facilities as our own, something to be proud of, cared for, and encouraged. Nowadays there is far more talk of tax revolts than higher taxes for the expanded government expenditures that would be necessary to redirect the growth of the economy in ways the market does not now support.

Establishment economists rightly discern this lack of public spirit among us while agreeing that there are deficiencies in the public environment that need attention and money. Their rebuttal to Galbraith's proposal, however, is that the only way to get the necessary government funds is to encourage rapid economic growth, to get the additional tax revenues that a higher GNP will generate. But this certainly has not worked in the last twenty years. The undesirable social and environmental effects of economic growth have grown much faster than tax revenues for financing solutions. Today we can barely provide funds for basic governmental functions such as education and welfare, let alone all the vast new needs for reconstructing decaying central cities, building new transportation systems, and acquiring parks and open space. Yet the GNP is now more than three times higher than it was twenty years ago. Instead of experiencing an abundance of tax revenues for the enhancement of the environment, we are losing ground rapidly. Is there any reason to believe the future will be otherwise?

Even if, for some unanticipated reason, we find ourselves with vast sums of public money, we may not be able to spend it effectively because measures to improve the environment impinge on so many private interests. Rapid transit threatens the auto and oil interests, public housing interferes with the private housing market, and acquiring land for parks or open space eliminates the developer and the craft unions. This is very different from spending for defense or space, where few if any economic interests are adversely effected while many benefit. What might be called modern environmental conservation, on the other hand, goes against much of the grain of our economic society; it requires strong governmental powers or heavy expenditures, the benefits are largely public rather than private, and it inhibits economic growth, the overriding objective of the system. These factors suggest that the deterioration of the environment will continue unless some way can be found to modify existing economic forces and to control the acceleration of the economy.

THE GUARANTEED INCOME

It would seem that some very basic changes are necessary. It is the objective here to suggest one, that of changing the nature of the work that our society permits and supports. At present, a prerequisite of almost all jobs is that they be economically "efficient," which generally means a high level of productivity and an urban location. Couldn't this prerequisite be relaxed? Couldn't we permit uneconomic forms of work in uneconomic locations? The classic situation is the small farmer who is being forced off the land or onto welfare roles by efficient industrial agriculture. Another would be the socially committed young person who cannot find a way to help the people who most need help and still subsist himself. Encouraging uneconomic forms of work in new ways may be the most straightforward method of slowing economic output, while broadening the range of opportunities for meaningful work at the same time. Significantly, the process that could lead to a true guaranteed income has begun in the form of President Nixon's Family Assistance Program. Its probability of coming into being seems fairly good, certainly as good, if not better, than the strong government regulations or expenditures that would be necessary to reverse the deterioration of the environment under the conditions of continued rapid growth.

For the most part, the guaranteed income has been considered as a welfare measure for those who are unable to work or who cannot find a job, and as a supplement to the incomes of the working poor. In the context of our environmental problems, however, the justification for the guaranteed income is that it offers a positive incentive for reduced production, for slowing the speed of our economic train. To consider the guaranteed income as a device for discouraging economic growth among the nonpoor majority of this country is in no way intended to denigrate the importance of the measure for those who live in poverty in our affluent society. Nor would the environmental effect be the same; among the poor it would almost certainly lead to increased work and consumption, the things the poor now need. But the effect of the guaranteed income on the poor is a subject in itself, one which is under intense study elsewhere. Here the subject is mainstream American society, where the economic machine has been fashioned that is taking us so rapidly in the direction of environmental deterioration.

In this context, a guaranteed income with a basic allowance of around $4,000 a year for a family of four could perform three important functions. It could (1) expand the opportunities for public service, (2) support the development of new methods of livelihood appropriate to an age where it is no longer necessary or even useful for everyone to have an economically efficient job, and (3) it could discourage economic growth while still providing a flexible device for maintaining the stability of our economic system.

Expanding Opportunities for Service

There is nothing more disheartening than to be asked by a young person what jobs are available to help with the social and environmental problems of our cities, rural areas, or reservations. For the most part, the opportunities for those with social concerns are in large, bureaucratic social welfare agencies where "professional" roles are prescribed, innovation is difficult, and heavy workloads lead to superficiality and coldness toward the poor, the aged, the unwanted children, the mentally disturbed. There are great needs in education, and there are many who want to teach, but not enough funds are available to put the two together. The guaranteed income would let students, ghetto residents, or anyone else with the motivation apply their energy and imagination to our social problems. Unstructured and flexible, it is the kind of situation that young people and ethnic groups have utilized effectively in recent years.

Fostering the Development of New Methods of Livelihood

The number of individuals looking for an opportunity for meaningful public service will not be large enough to get our accelerating economic machine under control. New methods of livelihood must also be developed. This trend is already well underway as the young especially, but others as well, attempt to escape the lonely and threatening world of competition and commercialism to find more satisfying ways. This is an uphill struggle, to a degree at least, because of the economic problems involved, unless special talents or outside financial resources are available. In the city, there are more diverse income possibilities, but costs of living are higher, public transportation is poor, and recreation is expensive or otherwise limited. The guaranteed income would almost certainly foster a movement back to rural areas because of the prospects for independence, offering inexpensive housing, the opportunity to raise at least part of one's food, and the use of wood, wind, or sun for energy. The small amounts of land needed for subsistence agriculture are relatively inexpensive. The guaranteed income would almost certainly contribute to the efforts of the Black Muslims and previously CORE to escape from the entrapment of urban ghettos. And if the surveys are correct that tell of large numbers of urban Americans who would like to return to small towns and the countryside, then the movement away from the cities would cover a broad spectrum of the urban population.

Probably the greatest problem for these emigrants will be their conditioning to fast-paced urban life and the loss of the rural skills of their forebears. It cannot be expected to be an easy transition, but at least they would have time to make mistakes and learn. The quality of the rural environment may initially decline as emigrants from urban areas learn new skills and new life styles evolve. The cultural (and environmental) shocks entailed in this process can at least be balanced against the avoidance of the cultural shock that occurs when people from depressed rural areas try to survive in the city without proper education or the support of kinfolk and neighbors. Both groups, however, those who stay on the land and those who move to it, would contribute to an easing of the problems of the cities.

One of the greatest benefits of the guaranteed income may very well be the encouragement it would offer for the reestablishment of community on a functional basis. With a low income, individuals would be encouraged to rely on community provision of some of their needs, as has been the case through most of the history of man. Community has declined recently because it serves no purpose when everyone has such a high standard of living that he can provide all of his needs on his own. But this privatism is what makes suburbia so uninteresting; there are few public places where people can work together, watch children play, or strike up a conversation. Suburban streets are quiet, save for a few children, and sidewalks are not even built in some of the new developments. The result is that wives can't wait to get out and get a job, to see people, and to join the major source of action in our society. The guaranteed income would re-create the age-old conditions that fostered a viable and enriching community, a real need for cooperation and community provision of services and facilities.

Efforts to reinvigorate rural communities must be considered as valuable efforts to reestablish time-honored elements of civilization, a functioning community and a real interaction with nature. But there must be an infinite number of ways in which people for whom the city remains the center of gravity, could use a guaranteed income. Adoption of the guaranteed income would not have to be permanent, but could be an interlude in one's working career, before college or after, or an encouragement to leave a dull, dead-end job and train for a more satisfying one. Would-be craftsmen could quit their jobs and become working artisans. The guaranteed income would encourage labor intensive activity rather than the resource and energy intensive activities now encouraged. Each person, in considering the future, would have the opportunity to incorporate the guaranteed income in planning his life, balancing off the advantages of a job at high pay with the broadened opportunities of the guaranteed, but lower, income. Unlike President Nixon's present proposal, however, the guaranteed income would have to be available to anyone, not just those with a family who cannot get a job. If it were available to all, the guaranteed income would probably have better support from mainstream America, since everyone would be potential beneficiaries. At the same time, it would be less of a paternalistic welfare measure for the poor who are forced to depend on it. And jobs vacated by middle class workers might become available to the poor and unemployed, a most desirable effect.

Liberal education might also see a renaissance once the harsh demands of making a living were muted. Today, that query of "What will you do with a degree in art (or English or religions)?" has a real terror in it for students. Many of us have known a bright and sensitive student who wanted to be a poet or a musician but was not sufficiently confident in his abilities to take the brave step, realizing that the chances for making a living at it were almost nil. Because of the nature of jobs presently available and the competition for them, our educational system has become almost exclusively vocational and specialized, and the humanities have been virtually eclipsed at a time when they are needed more than ever. It could be expected that a whole new thrust in education would develop in response to the establishment of the guaranteed income, training in which the need for work would be balanced with other needs that are not now being met by our educational system.

The guaranteed income could function as a universal form of financial support for higher education. At present, scholarships are available to only a miniscule number of students, and loans are drying up, especially for undergraduates, while tuition and expenses are rising. A $1,000 guaranteed income would not solve all of the student's financial needs, but it would be a significant help.

In effect, what the guaranteed income would do would be to let people live the way they wanted to. For those who prefer the fast-paced, competitive, high-style life, this opportunity would be largely undiminished, and financial support would be available to obtain the education necessary to participate. For those who find this way of life unsatisfying, whatever the reason, the guaranteed income would provide the minimum resources to strike out in other directions. Hopefully, this would offer an incentive adequate enough to break our dependence on economic growth and put us on a track with greater evolutionary potential. It is frequently predicted that in the relatively near future only a fraction of the labor force will be needed to produce all of our basic needs. In such a situation why should everyone be forced into work that is economically productive but not socially or environmentally productive? Young people growing up in today's world are faced with what could be called economic tyranny. Well-paying jobs in large organizations are available, complete with all the elements generally referred to as the rat race. Other than something like the Peace Corps or VISTA, however, there are few other alternatives except dropping out completely. But economic tyranny being what it is, this is a very difficult alternative because food, medical care, and other needs are still expensive. At present, there is little middle ground; for the most part, you are either in the system or out of it, and for many individuals neither alternative is very satisfying. The guaranteed income would offer a major new alternative. Hopefully, as new methods of livelihood were developed, economic solutions demonstrated, and communities established, the impact of the guaranteed income would grow so that a number of ecological niches that are now vacant would be occupied.

A Flexible Device for Maintaining Economic Health without the Necessity of Growth

Even though the major long-run objective of the guaranteed income is to limit production and to remove the necessity of maintaining continuous economic growth, it is still absolutely essential that our economic system be maintained in a healthy state. Its productiveness is what permits the luxury of a guaranteed income in the first place (as well as creating the urgency for it). The requirement that total production of goods and services equals demand still holds, although now it is not at the previous level of full employment but at the lower level of the number of workers who wish to remain in economically productive jobs. But what happens if too many want to work, or too few, so that the desired amount of production is not maintained? The guaranteed income provides an effective device to help balance this equation; the government could raise or lower the amount of income guaranteed. For instance, if we should someday achieve a measure of peace which permitted dismantling a good portion of the military-industrial complex, the guaranteed income would be raised to encourage workers away from jobs, to take up the slack. Anytime unemployment became a problem, the guaranteed income could be raised, not only to attract workers but also to increase consumer expenditures. Thus, as productivity increases in the future, the guaranteed income would tend to rise, increasing its capacity to attract and absorb increased numbers of people just at the time when this would be necessary.

Lowering the guaranteed income, however, would cause problems, especially for people who have no other choice than the guaranteed income and who have families and bills for rent, food, and clothing. It is true that a reduction in the guaranteed income should be necessary only when there was a shortage of labor, so jobs would be available at the same time, but many recipients of the guaranteed income would be families without fathers, the incapacitated, and the elderly. A floor on the guaranteed income, limiting the amount it could be reduced to, could be a safeguard beyond which other government expenditures would have to be cut or taxes raised. Hopefully, the increased stability of an economy that does not have to grow continuously would reduce the economic fluctuations that would require changes in the guaranteed income. But still, the opportunity to vary the level of the income guaranteed would always be necessary, along with varying taxes and governmental spending, to maintain economic stability. People on a guaranteed income would have to accept the possibility of varying levels of income as a necessary part of life, in much the same way that the employed face varying job and income situations.

PROSPECTS FOR A GUARANTEED ANNUAL INCOME

President Nixon's proposal for a Family Assistance Program is a significant step in the direction of a guaranteed income, even though the income provided is very low and is restricted to families with children and to those who can prove they cannot obtain a job. Opposition so far has been mainly from the Chamber of Commerce, and less openly from a few big city mayors who would prefer federal funds coming through the cities rather than directly to the recipients. It is also criticized by representatives of the poor who object to the low level of income provided and the coercive nature of the work and job training requirements. Opposition by conservatives has been limited, so far, mainly because Nixon's proposal anticipated this opposition and guarded against it while emphasizing the measure's definite advantages in providing incentives to work and to hold families together compared to present welfare programs.

However, if Nixon's proposal passed, and was subsequently expanded and liberalized into a full guaranteed income, it would then become a greater threat to traditional attitudes toward work and its rewards. The role of many welfare agencies would also be threatened, which would lead to the intense and uncompromising opposition that occurs whenever jobs are threatened. And the failures bound to occur with the first efforts to utilize the guaranteed income would receive full coverage in the media. It is impossible to anticipate what might happen during this critical stage. An optimistic scenario might include the difficulty of reducing the guaranteed income at this point because of the recession it would cause, or because middle class constituencies wanted to maintain it if unemployment intensified, or because state and local governments were dependent on federal financing and unwilling to support a more limited federal program which shifts responsibility back to state and local budgets. Key support would come from the large producers of consumer goods, whose main concern is not with a shortage of labor but with an adequate demand for their products; they would be the ones ending up with much of the guaranteed income anyway. The National Association of Manufacturers is now supporting the proposal for a Family Assistance Program.

Initially, the level of the guaranteed income would probably be determined more by the composition of the federal budget than by abrupt changes in taxes. The amount of money spent for such programs as defense and space, not the tax level, is the important factor. To keep the magnitude of the costs of a guaranteed income in perspective, consider that $60 billion of the Department of Defense's annual $80 billion appropriation could provide sixty million people—thirty percent of our population—with a guaranteed income of $4,000 for a family of four! A "peace scare," which now throws terror into millions of workers paid by DOD funds, could be utilized to increase slowly the guaranteed income while DOD funds were reduced. In the long run, however, after reducing the governmental expenditures that are largely to provide employment, it would seem that corporation taxes would be the logical source of revenue to finance the guaranteed income. As automation replaces workers, the new machines would be taxed to support the workers displaced, thus translating increased productivity into fewer economically productive jobs rather than increased consumption, as at present. The transition to the guaranteed income should be slow so that major social dislocations could be avoided and satisfactory ways to use the guaranteed income could evolve. The development of the guaranteed income should be slow, but if it was also a fitful and fluctuating development, anxieties and hardships would result. And it would be tragic if a preliminary program was terminated completely at a time of retrenchment and reaction, before it had time to stimulate a broad response.

There is no denying that there would be many problems. When the guaranteed income is first offered there might be disequilibrium in the labor market due to job resignations, but most of these jobs would be filled again when the restrictions of a low income were realized and other satisfying activities proved hard to find. If jobs with the lowest wages were widely vacated, especially the menial and repetitious, the pay for these jobs would have to be raised to get them done, to tempt workers back. Higher pay for such workers as agricultural laborers and janitors is only economic justice, but beyond that the upper level of the guaranteed income would have to be set carefully, and not be so high that work patterns would be altered excessively before social and economic conditions were ready. The more gradual the introduction of the guaranteed income the less would be the fluctuations in the labor market, although the impact would also be delayed.

One problem that demographers anticipate is an increase in the birth rates. Enjoying one's children is a pleasure that could be indulged in more fully on a guaranteed income; some people might wish to have children around much of the time, especially if they would mean increased income as well. Stabilizing the population, of course, is the other essential for survival in a livable world, along with stabilizing the economy, so positive steps would have to be taken to resist any trend toward increased birth rates. The obvious step would be to reduce the support for each additional child beyond the second to influence family planning. Perhaps, instead of each family's having more children, community enjoyment of children would develop, as in Europe, where townsfolk take great delight in the children playing in the streets, parks, and squares.

The most serious problem in the adoption of the guaranteed income would involve our real psychological dependence on work. For most of us, work is an outlet for the psychic energy generated by our active society, and because social status and rewards have been based on how productive one is, the ability to enjoy oneself has lost prestige, and its cultivation has declined. Work has had a tendency to become an end in itself, rather than something that supports other equally desirable elements of life. We have large voids in our lives which in older societies were filled with festivals, religious rites, folk arts, music, dancing, and just knowing how to relax. Older societies also had large amounts of essential work to round out their lives. It can be assumed that we need a certain measure of meaningful work, that without it we are troubled by alienation and bordeom, by an existential vacuum. Man evolved as a working animal, to secure food, shelter, and warmth. To find satisfying work and to balance it with other elements of life may be a very difficult task. Let us hope that the opportunities for "uneconomic" work offered by the guaranteed income will stimulate fruitful results.

It is ironic that work, the one element we have depended on for most of our psychic income and have developed to a very high degree, is now becoming less useful and is even beginning to jeopardize our future. Our economic institutions and behavior are rapidly becoming obsolete and perilous. But since change in human behavior is difficult, it is important that the process of establishing a stable relationship with our environment be started as quickly as possible.

So often it seems that people have a tendency to underestimate the rate of change we are experiencing, failing to see that a very different future is being created. The rate of change today is unprecedented. Just a little over fifty years ago the Model T was introduced, and, as is commonly the case, only the benevolent aspects of the new technology were identified; Henry Ford saw it as a way to let Americans get out to God's green countryside. No one foresaw that the car would foster suburban sprawl that would bury the nearby countryside, lead to the decay of city life, consume vast quantities of resources, and become the major source of air pollution. Undesirable consequences are now appearing from the most humane technological advances; the control of disease in underdeveloped countries is leading to the far more terrible problems of unabated population growth and, inevitably, it seems, to death by starvation for many millions of people. For some time now it has been evident that it is the very nature of our technological achievements that is causing stress; it is because DDT is such an effective biocide, because machines can replace so much human labor, because the private car is such a flexible form of transportation, and because the concentration of economic activities in urban areas is so productive that our world is being disturbed now as never before. Most environmental measures now being considered have the uncomfortable air of being only stopgap measures, largely directed toward technological changes, which will have to be superseded by hoped-for technological breakthroughs, perhaps again and again as we continue to strain the limits of the environment, both physically and socially. The evolutionary potential of this line of action is definitely limited.

Yet the same technology provides us with vast power if it could be applied to support necessary social changes. The guaranteed income is one tool that seems to fit our social and environmental imbalances with remarkable directness, permitting economic behavior consistent with our technology but not tied desperately to it. It offers the possibility of balance and stability over the long run in our relation with the environment, if accompanied by a stabilized population.

In short, it has evolutionary potential.

9

ECOLOGY AND SOCIAL CONFLICT

Richard England and Barry Bluestone

During recent years, the symptoms of environmental deterioration have become increasingly visible and ominous, and public recognition of an "ecological crisis" has become increasingly widespread. The crusade for environmental protection has already attracted substantial popular support in America, particularly among young middle-class whites, and has emerged as a liberal reform movement of some importance. The serious political danger in these developments is that the liberal formulations that have dominated public discussion obscure the root causes of environmental decay and imply prescriptions that are likely to fail in the long run.

Unfortunately, many academic economists have attempted to reduce the ecological problem to a narrowly defined technical exercise, which ignores the broad range of social and political changes a viable solution will require. Reflecting the neoclassical approach of Alfred Marshall

"Ecology and Social Conflict." Published by permission of the authors. Our thanks go to Eric Chester, Stephan Michelson, Craig Morgan, Marilyn Myers, and the Ann Arbor URPE Seminar in Political Economy for their critical comments on an earlier version of this essay.

and A. C. Pigou,[1] the growing literature on the economics of pollution control is concerned almost solely with the search for an "efficient" set of product prices which will account for the social, as well as the private, costs of production.[2] Most academic economists have not yet recognized that their traditional analyses are inadequate and that the very fabric of the private enterprise system must be questioned. The fact is the growing stress between man and his natural environment requires a complete reexamination of economic goals, organization of production and consumption, and the distribution of political and economic power.

THE ORTHODOX PERSPECTIVE

The emerging consensus among academic economists is that the deterioration of the American environment arises from the failure of a capitalist economy to "internalize externalities"; that is, the failure to account for all the costs of production, including such things as waste disposal. In an economy based on private property rights and the profit motive, a single business organizes its productive activities in order to keep its *private* production costs to a minimum. In the absence of public regulation or profit incentives, corporate owners and managers normally ignore the *social* costs (or externalities) of the production processes of their firm because it is in their financial interest to do so.[3] The total costs of production include environmental losses borne by society, and the total production costs exceed the monetary costs incurred by the individual firm. Orthodox economists normally view these social costs of economic activity as a residual, small by comparison with private costs. Consequently the presumed solution to the environmental crisis consists more in patching up the existing system than in redesigning basic economic institutions.

The solution to the ecological crisis proposed most frequently is simply a new federal excise tax. Orthodox economists advocate that government environmental agencies be instructed to measure the amount of pollution discharged into the environment by both producers and consumers and that a pollution tax, or an "effluent tax" be levied on each unit of pollution. The tax rate for each type of pollution would depend on the expected severity of its environmental effects. Those who discharge mildly obnoxious gases would, for instance, be taxed lightly, whereas those who dump highly toxic materials would be taxed at prohibitively high rates. Neoclassical economics predicts that three complementary effects would result from such a pollution tax. (1) The higher prices of private goods that generate significant social costs would

---

1. Notes and references for this reading will be found on pages 209–214.

induce some people to buy smaller quantities of these pollution-creating products. (2) Business firms would invent and adopt cleaner production techniques in an attempt to reduce their pollution tax payments. (3) The revenue from the pollution tax could be earmarked to reduce pollution at its source, clean it up once it is in the environment, or financially reimburse those who suffer its effects.[4] Ideally, the economists' solution would reduce the total amount of pollution to an "optimal" level, where the benefits of further pollution abatement would not justify the costs of further pollution control.

On the surface this diagnosis and prescription may appear sound. Except for the administrative problem of measuring benefits and costs, "internalizing the externalities" appears to solve, or at least contain, the ecological crisis. The operation of a pollution tax is conceptually simple and apparently requires a minimum amount of change in existing political and social institutions.[5] In strictly economic terms, it moves the whole economy toward a more "efficient" pattern of production where the price of every item produced reflects its full social cost of production.

On further investigation, however, the neoclassical analysis of the environmental question is found to be seriously inadequate for a number of reasons. It obscures the social conflict inherent in both the present environmental situation and the proposed tax reform. It ignores the global dimensions and implications of the ecological crisis. It is utopian in ignoring the political realities of a capitalistic society and, in particular, the reforms that corporate interest groups would rather see imposed. And finally, and most importantly, it ignores several ecological irrationalities of capitalist production and consumption that directly contribute to the present and future environmental crisis. Only a broader analysis that looks at the structure of production and consumption and the distribution of political and economic power can fully comprehend the crisis. Marginal changes alone will not save us from an ecological Armageddon.

ECOLOGY AND DOMESTIC CLASS INTERESTS

Of all families in the United States, the poorest fifth share less than six percent of the total family income generated by America's great productivity. In contrast, the richest fifth receive something in excess of forty percent of all family income, and the very richest families—the top five percent—receive one-sixth of the total.[6] What adds even more to the inequity is the highly unequal distribution of wealth ownership and the consequently unequal concentrations of corporate and political power.[7]

This unequal distribution of income, wealth, and political power is mirrored in the unequal incidence of social costs and benefits that flow from the production of pollution. Economic necessity forces many of the poor and near-poor to live in harmful environments, while many of the rich are economically better off as a result of the environmentally destructive practices of the business firms which they own. Blue-collar workers likewise suffer more than professional workers because they are more likely to work in and live near polluting plants and factories.

The urban poor suffer most of all since flight to the more desirable suburbs in order to avoid air and noise pollution is not a feasible option for them. This problem is especially intense when racial discrimination further restricts the availability of suburban housing. A direct result is that the urban poor are more likely to suffer from chronic medical disorders, a fact which contributes to the intergenerational cycle of poverty. It has been found, for example, that the rates of hospitalization for such diseases as asthma and eczema among children increase with the degree of pollution in the air over the census tracts in which they live and that the degree of air pollution they experience is inversely correlated with their socioeconomic status.[8] The high noise levels, traffic congestion, and general dinginess of many inner-city neighborhoods can hardly contribute to the mental health of their residents. The danger of lead poisoning is also particularly acute within urban areas. Paul and Anne Ehrlich report that

> It is now suspected that airborne lead is becoming a major source of exposure, at least for people in urban areas, although the overall exposure from food and beverages is still higher. But in Los Angeles and a few other cities, it is possible that more lead is now being absorbed through the lungs than through the digestive tract. Since 1924 the American consumption of tetraethyl lead in automobile fuel has risen from less than one million pounds per annum in 1924 to . . . 700 million in 1968. . . . The average concentration of lead in the blood of Americans in 1968 was about 0.25 parts per million, which is a little less than half the level at which removal from exposure is recommended for people who work with lead in industry.[9]

Studies show these atmospheric concentrations of lead are particularly high in urban neighborhoods adjacent to heavily-travelled expressways.[10]

Those groups with limited educational opportunity and geographic mobility may also have restricted *occupational* options. As a result, they often have to bear the social costs of pollution on the job. The Appalachian coalminers who develop "black lung," the Southern textile workers who contract "white lung,"[11] and the California migrant workers who are exposed to high dosages of pesticides all work in debilitating environments. But pollution on the job also strikes at the manufacturing work-force. Most industrial workers face daily exposure to extreme heat, toxic gases and fumes, and high levels of noise, dust, and humidity. *Steel*

Labor, the newspaper of the United Steel Workers union, reports that "more than half a million workers are disabled yearly by occupational diseases from the effects of asbestos, beryllium, carbon monoxide, coal dust, cotton dust, cancer-producing chemicals, dyes, pesticides, radiation, and other occupational diseases such as heat, noise, and vibration."[12]

Yet the higher social costs of pollution borne by working people are not limited to their jobs. The Gary, Indiana steelworker is not only subject to debilitating working conditions in the foundry, but in his own home he is more than likely forced to breathe air polluted by U.S. Steel's smokestacks. His respite at Lake Michigan beaches has also been impaired by water pollution, and thus his weekend recreation is invaded by pollution. Only during his annual vacation can he and his family escape the worst ravages of environmental deterioration.

On the other hand, the owners and top managers of U.S. Steel do not have to live near the plant itself. Rather, they can choose to live where they wish without forfeiting the economic benefits that accrue to absentee owners and managers of the giant steel corporation.

What this discussion points out is that the orthodox distinction between the "private" and "social" costs of production actually confuses several separate issues. Some of the environmental costs of pollution are borne *within* business firms and are shifted from the owners of these firms to their own workers. Unlike true social costs, which are dispersed widely among a variety of social classes and groups, the effects of in-plant pollution are concentrated within particular occupations and industries. Even those pollution costs that are shifted to groups *outside* business firms are seldom "social costs." Because of their unequal distribution among social classes, most pollution costs are "class costs" imposed on the poor and other working people.

However, even if the benefits of pollution control would accrue mainly to lower-income families, whether or not proposed environmental programs will be equitable is uncertain unless one first looks at who will bear the costs of stemming pollution. The pollution tax proposed by so many academic economists would probably collect the costs of pollution abatement in a most inequitable manner. A pollution tax, like any excise tax, would be highly regressive, falling most heavily on those least able to afford it.[13]

Most economists envision the pollution charge as a tax levied on business corporations but ultimately paid by the individual consumer in the form of higher product prices. As corporations pass on the costs of pollution control programs and also their pollution tax payments, the rich and the poor alike will face the *same* price hikes in the marketplace. Unless luxury goods happen to have higher price increases than necessities, poor families will end up paying a *larger portion* of their incomes for pollution abatement than will wealthier families. Thus, lower-income families might suffer a decrease in their living standards after the imposition of a tax aimed at protecting the environment unless they were simultaneously given income supplements and personal tax relief.

In an attempt to refine the pollution tax proposal, some economists argue that pollution charges should be based on the magnitude of damages done to others. This means that a polluting industry located in the Nevada desert would pay a much smaller tax per pound of pollution than would an industry located in the center of a densely populated city. This would be well and good if the result were equitable as well as efficient. However, if this reasoning were applied to consumers in terms of auto emissions, municipal sanitation services, and small business operations in the inner city, the result would be that those trapped in urban ghettos would be forced to pay more, not only in relative terms but possibly in absolute terms as well, than the more affluent, who could escape to the suburbs. The commuting low-income worker forced to pay for the air pollution and traffic congestion to which he contributes, the inner-city tenant forced to pay more rent so his slum landlord can convert coal furnances to natural gas burners, and the ghetto dweller forced to pay steeply increasing taxes and fees for nonpolluting sanitation and other pollution-free municipal services, could all end up worse off after the economist's solution is introduced—despite improvements in environmental quality that would, after all, be short-run as long as growth in production is sought.

Meanwhile, corporation owners and managers will share in the cleaner environment, but at little loss in profit or material standard of living. In fact, there is some evidence that in the monopolized industries pollution charges will be marked up before they are passed on to consumers so that price increases will more than offset the additional costs of production.[14] Then, not only will the wealthy enjoy a cleaner environment, they will increase their profit as well. Society as a whole may gain something from this solution, but some will gain much more than others, and many may lose.

ECOLOGY AND THE QUESTION OF INTERNATIONAL EQUITY

Being concerned about the equilibrium of environmental factors at home is not enough, however. The problem of maintaining a habitable environment is global, as are political economic implications of the problem.[15] It is likely, for example, that international trade competition will tend to dilute environmental protection efforts within individual nations. If the American government were to impose strict regulatory standards on the use of pesticides and chemical fertilizers and the discharge of industrial wastes, the domestic prices of numerous products would presumably rise. If European and Japanese enterprises were not subject to similarly stringent supervision, they would enjoy relative price advantages in international trading. Conservative members of the business community therefore have an economic issue that can be used to mobilize sentiment against measures to clean the environment: they are likely to use warnings about adverse effects on America's already precarious balance of payments to undercut domestic support for "overly strict" federal environmental standards.

This argument would be even more persuasive in Japan and those European countries that depend relatively heavily on export sales. Hans Dietrich Genscher, the West German interior minister, has outlined the issue:

> We must . . . avoid a situation in which individual countries exclude themselves from making investments for environmental protection, thereby securing competitive advantages for their own economy vis-à-vis those countries who do meet their responsibilities.[16]

The upshot is that the major trading countries will probably begin international negotiations over joint, mutually acceptable pollution control standards within the next few years.

But the balance of payments is only a minor part of the problem of the economics of global clean environment. More important is the question of the international distribution of natural resources and the utilization of these resources. The global crisis in ecological life arises, in large measure, from the fact that the American people, who comprise only six percent of the world's population, consume at least a third of the world's raw material production each year.[17] According to U.S. Department of the Interior calculations, the American economy produces or imports twenty-seven percent of the world's bauxite production, eighteen percent of the world's iron ore output, more than twenty-five percent of crude petroleum, and almost twenty-eight percent of world nickel production.[18] An important question is whether the United States and other industrial nations can continue to support their own economic expansion relatively cheaply by depleting natural resources on a global scale, or whether less developed countries will demand that they receive better compensation for their oil and minerals in order to finance their own economic development.

The recent bargaining between the Western oil cartel and the Organization of Petroleum Exporting Countries (O.P.E.C.) indicates the developing nations' growing awareness of their own environmental exploitation. In their 1971 agreement with the Western oil companies, the O.P.E.C. countries obtained price increases for their crude oil worth $10 to $30 billion over the next five years.[19] Since eighty-six percent of all petroleum reserves outside North America and the communist countries are located in the O.P.E.C. bloc, the eleven member countries of O.P.E.C. have a great deal of bargaining power.[20] Will other resource-exporting poor countries be able to unite in order to obtain better prices for their minerals? At present, the opportunities for this sort of "collective bargaining" between the rich and poor nations are somewhat limited: nearly half of all world trade in mineral commodities is currently *among* industrial countries, whereas only thirty-five percent flows from poor to rich nations.[21] In the future, however, the exhaustion of their own mineral reserves will force the wealthy countries to import raw materials increasingly from the poor nations.

Adequate compensation for their minerals and petroleum is not, however, the only environmental problem facing the populations of less developed countries. Large corporations in North America, Western Europe, and Japan may decide to sponsor a particularly chilling sort of international "solution" to the pollution problem facing the industrial nations: if the national governments of advanced capitalist countries in which these corporations are based agree among themselves to impose identical, stringent environmental standards, what may result is an acceleration of the growth of subsidiary and branch operations of multinational corporations in the developing countries, for the current governments of many Latin American, African, and Asian nations may be willing to tolerate high levels of pollution in order to attract some of the income-creating capital that multinational firms can provide.[22] If this should happen, the multinational corporations that increasingly dominate the nonsocialist economies may choose to locate a larger share of their "dirty" refining and fabricating operations in the poor countries while retaining administrative and financial control in the home country. Stephen Hymer's scenario of this development is alarming:

> The multinational corporation tends to create a world in its own image by creating a division of labor between countries that corresponds to the division of labor between various levels of the corporation hierarchy. It will tend to centralize high-level decision-making occupations in a few key cities in the advanced countries (surrounded by regional subcapitals) and confine the rest of the world to lower levels of activity and income; i.e., to the status of provincial capitals, towns, and villages within a New Imperial System. Income, status, authority, and consumption patterns will radiate out from the centers in a declining fashion and the hinterland will be denied independence and equality.[23]

Thus, even if, say, New York and London manage to control smog and water pollution, the environs of Caracas, Accra, and Teheran could become increasingly polluted because of the unrestrained foreign operations of powerful Anglo-American corporations. The disastrous consequences of capitalist consolidation in the poor countries are not inevitable, however. The prospect of economic inequalities, losses of political and cultural sovereignty, and worsening environmental pollution might provoke popular movements for national liberation and socialism in the Third World, or strengthen such popular movements where they have already formed.

ECONOMIC GROWTH AND ECOLOGICAL IRRATIONALITIES

Even if the American public agreed to foot the pollution bill through pollution taxes, the ecological crisis in America would still be unresolved. For at the root of the crisis is the high premium we have put on material growth. So long as either population *or* the material standard of living continues to grow, the total volume of pollution will eventually reach intolerable levels.[24] In the immediate future, of course, there are a number of things we can do to contol the growth of pollution. The levying of pollution taxes on toxic wastes *would* encourage firms to recycle more materials and to discharge less toxic substances, and the output and use of commodities the manufacture of which causes severe environmental damage *would* decline. Both of these adjustments would certainly reduce the pollution damages per dollar of Gross National Product (GNP). However, even relatively harmless emissions like carbon dioxide and waste heat could be dangerous if discharged in sufficiently large quantities. Thus, the amount of pollution damages per dollar of GNP could not fall indefinitely unless all producers and consumers eventually recycled *all their wastes.* The economic costs of total recycling would be astronomical, indeed. Thus, if ecological disasters are to be prevented and not simply postponed, material growth must eventually be restricted.

Yet the basis for our whole economy *is* material growth. Ever since the Employment Act of 1946, and especially since the election of John Kennedy in 1960, high rates of corporate investment and rapid economic growth have received high priority as goals of social policy in America. Walter Heller reports that

> Among the interlocking shifts in liberal Democratic policy in the early 1960s was the increased emphasis on investment relative to consumption, on tax cuts relative to expenditure increases, on cost-price stability relative

> to demand expansion, and on international relative to domestic considerations. What inference are we to draw from these changes in emphasis? . . . [It] is an escape from dogma . . . the practical management of a modern economy. . . . Emphasis on high levels of investment . . . is here to stay. It is essential to the economic growth and well-being of the nation.[25]

Rapid economic growth obviously promotes higher wage levels, hefty profit rates, and rising material living standards. Less obvious is the fact that rapid and continued economic growth is absolutely essential if a private corporate economy is to avoid mass unemployment and depression. In the advanced capitalist economies, total consumer spending is wholly inadequate to utilize fully all available plant capacity and employ all workers. As a result, capitalist systems are forced to turn to high levels of government and corporate spending as a means of averting depression.[26] But firms are willing to invest now only if they anticipate that their new capital equipment will be utilized in even higher rates of production in the future. Thus, a private market economy is caught on a treadmill: to forestall mass unemployment, ever higher levels of consumption must be stimulated and ever higher levels of investment must be forthcoming. The environmental problem is that the presently required future increases in GNP will certainly result in the more rapid depletion of exhaustible resources and will tend to result in more pollution.

The industrial structure of modern capitalist economies is also a source of ecological irrationalities. The large oligopolistic firms that dominate many industries do not normally engage in spirited price competition. Each corporation recognizes that price cutting in the pursuit of additional sales would provoke immediate retaliation by its rivals and that all firms in the industry would suffer financially as a result. These corporations, do, however, engage in various forms of nonprice competition: advertising campaigns, frequent styling and model changes, minor product improvements, and packaging changes are all calculated to increase a firm's share of the market and to expand the market itself.[27] Developing and marketing products that put a premium on durability and long service life is counterproductive from the point of view of the individual oligopolist and also contrary to the needs of a recession-prone economy.

An immediate consequence of this behavior is that the relatively high rates of production and environmental costs (*ceteris paribus*) are necessary in order to maintain and expand stocks of durable goods, at the same time that relatively large quantities of goods are junked or discarded each year. For example, suppose it were desirable to maintain an operating stock of ten million motor vehicles. If cars and trucks had an average life of five years, it would be necessary to produce two million new vehicles a year and to dispose of two million junked vehicles per year. If, on the other hand, the economic life of motor vehicles were extended to ten years, current production and disposal requirements would fall to one million cars and trucks per year. Although pollution and congestion resulting from the operation of the vehicles might remain substantially the same, resource depletion and pollution resulting from the production and disposal of motor vehicles would fall significantly.

In addition to rapid obsolescence and depreciation of commodities, other ecological irrationalities plague modern capitalism. Corporations that promote atomistic or individual, rather than social, consumption also contribute to the environmental crisis. In a famous popular account of the ways advertising agencies influence individual consumption, Vance Packard described "hidden persuaders" who spend vast amounts of time and money to popularize the taste for private consumption. In 1969, spending on advertising in the United States approached the rate of $20 billion annually.[28] The notion that each nuclear family *needs* its own single-family dwelling complete with a two-car garage (and that each family *needs* two cars) is an important cultural prop for the corporate economy.

When the government fails to provide and foster alternative social forms of consumption, an ideological norm such as individual consumption becomes an actual necessity. The most notorious example is the development of urban transport in America during the post World War II period. Massive public expenditures on expressways and arterial highways have encouraged popular dependence on private automobile transport in urban areas. This has led to a deterioration of commuter rail and bus services in most metropolitan areas, thereby compounding reliance on the private automobile.[29] In this manner, the corporate economy not only promotes a popular taste for private auto transport but also eliminates alternative social modes of urban transportation. This type of example has been repeated in the housing sector where federal mortgage subsidy programs, municipal zoning and building codes, and the scarcity of public housing funds favor suburban, single-family-dwelling construction.

An economic consequence of the emphasis on private, rather than social, consumption is that relatively large stocks of durable goods are necessary in order to provide a given stream of consumer services, or use values. There are several reasons for this heavy capitalization of consumption. First, most forms of consumer capital in advanced capitalist economies are substantially *underutilized.* Most private autos, for instance, are not in use at a particular given instant and consequently are not generating transportation services. These unutilized autos are, instead, creating severe storage problems in urban areas. Every single-family dwelling has its own complement of household appliances, which are also used only periodically. Second, the emphasis on atomistic consumption prevents the realization of substantial *economies of scale* in consumption. The continuing suburbanization of American cities, for example, makes the provision of water and sewage treatment systems extremely costly.

Clearly, therefore, the ecological destructiveness of our present society is not simply a consequence of its failure to ration the waste-assimilating capacity of the natural environment. That failure explains only the large quantity of pollutants created and discharged per unit of aggregate output. Oligopolistic rivalries and atomistic consumption compound the problem: rapid product obsolescence, underutilization of consumer durables, and the failure to realize scale economies via social consumption result in relatively high rates of current production per unit of consumption service. Even if a pollution tax were to result in more careful waste control and disposal, other structural characteristics of modern capitalism would tend to perpetuate depletion and pollution of the environment. Much more than a pollution tax is needed, but less than a pollution tax is forthcoming.

ECOLOGY AND CORPORATE REFORM

Indubitably, increased governmental attention to "environmental quality" is on the agenda of liberal reform. Individual corporations will no longer be permitted totally to disregard the ecological consequences of their business activities. The real task for the social analyst is to predict what particular reforms will be adopted by the liberal state and to explain whose interests they are designed to serve. In undertaking such an analysis, it is important to note who among social classes and groups are promoting environmental protection. Conspicuously, liberal capitalists and politicians are in the vanguard of the ecology-reform movement. A recent survey of 270 chief executives of *Fortune* magazine's list of the top 500 corporations reveals that a majority (fifty-seven percent) favors increased federal regulation of environmental standards and that a sizable majority (eighty-six percent) opposes reduction in federal regulation standards. A majority (fifty-three percent) even favors creation of a single federal agency to establish national pollution control standards.[30] According to *Fortune* magazine, "the way a large number of business leaders see it, substantial voluntary action on behalf of a single company is wasteful of corporate assets and ineffective in cleaning up the environment. They believe action on pollution must be collective."[31]

So we see that many corporate leaders recognize the need for federal action of some sort in order to manage the pace and forms of environmental decay.

Recourse by large corporations to public regulation is nothing new, "free enterprise" ideology notwithstanding. James O'Connor has observed:

> By the turn of the [twentieth] century, and especially during the New Deal, it was apparent to the vanguard corporate leaders that some form of rationalization of the economy was necessary. And as the twentieth century wore on, the owners of corporate capital generated the financial ability, learned the organizational skills, and developed the ideas necessary for their self-regulation as a class.[32]

Can we be reassured by this assessment? Corporate self-regulation does not mean, as it might seem, that the interests of all corporate owners and executives coincide perfectly at all times. On the contrary, the multiplicity of distinct interest groups within the capitalist class have aims that frequently conflict very sharply. For example, import brokers and domestic manufacturers obviously have very different attitudes about federal tariff policy. As for environmental protection, stiff pollution standards would affect the sales and profits of some industries far more severely than those of other industries. But with the legitimacy of capitalist institutions potentially at stake, it is in the interest of corporate leaders as a group to propose "reforms" in order to protect the ideology of private production and consumption. Moreover, the best way for particular interest groups to cushion themselves from the severity of federal antipollution legislation or to delay implementation of a federal regulation is to join together to write a favorable law themselves, always paying lip service to the rhetoric of clear skies and clean streams.[33]

Although many corporation executives are active in the leadership of the ecology movement, middle-class liberals provide a major portion of the mass support for proposed environmental reforms. One explanation is that the relatively affluent middle classes, not saddled with the need to worry about economic security, worry instead about growing environmental disamenities, something the poor and many blue-collar workers subordinate to other worries. This factor is not enough, however, to explain the bond the environmental reform coalition forms between corporation leaders and middle class liberals: the particular avenues of reform supported by these two groups could conceivably differ. What ensures the alliance is the *style* of reform normally proposed by liberal capitalists. The "professionalization of reform," as Daniel Patrick Moynihan has put it, marks a change from the past in terms of those who initiate change. "The War on Poverty," he argues, "was not declared at the behest of the poor" but rather at the prompting of academics and federal bureaucrats.[34] Likewise, the war on pollution has not been joined by those who are presently most maligned by environmental decay, but primarily by those who desire change without alterations in basic institutions.

There are numerous political advantages for large corporations participating in this kind of "professionalized" reform. The liberal style of reform permits the owners and leaders of industry to rationalize present modes of capitalist production and to defuse autonomous popular demands that have potentially anticapitalist implications. At the same time, liberal reform offers middle-class academics, managers, and technicians an opportunity to design and implement reform programs so long as these do not threaten the hierarchies and private profits of large corporations. Research grants, handsome salaries, access to data sources, and an opportunity to exercise professional skills await the reformer who is willing to play ball within the political boundaries stipulated by corporation capital. As a consequence, though middle-class acceptance of the urgency of the environmental issue is widespread, there is also a tendency to perceive the problem of protecting the environment in technical, rather than in political, terms.

On the other hand, despite the fact that blue-collar workers and the urban poor bear a disproportionate share of environmental disamenities, working-class support for liberal environmental reforms has been cautious. The reason is that, in the absence of compensatory programs, pollution abatement measures will harm the material welfare of many working families. The imposition of a pollution tax system or stringent pollution regulations will result in widespread layoffs in a number of industries. The resulting unemployment will mean wage losses, capital losses on residential properties, and migration and retraining costs for many workers, in the absence of remedial public measures. In addition to bearing the unemployment brought about by liberal reform, working people will also be especially hard hit by price increases that shift corporate pollution abatement costs to consumers. For example, the absence of adequate public transport systems in many cities means that workers will have to pay the regressive price increases that will follow the implementation of federal auto emission standards. One economic study has estimated that emission control devices will add $300 to the price of new autos in 1976.[35] Thus, in the absence of more equitable solutions, many corporation employees may be forced into the ironic position of defending the environmentally destructive practices of their employers.

The poor are understandably suspicious of concern for ecology because of a fear that pollution control will be a substitute for, rather than a complement to, federal antipoverty programs. When the middle class and corporations oppose heavier federal taxation but advocate public expenditures for preserving the environment, the public spending on better low-income housing, urban mass transit, public education, and medical care—the expenditures poor people hope for—will be threatened by the environmental expenditures unless *other* budgetary items can be cut back.[36] For the poor, a cleaner and healthier environment is simply not an acceptable substitute for adequate family income and public services.

The politically progressive alternative would be to offer lower-income families a program that does not ask them to bear a disproportionate share of either environmental disamenities *or* the costs of environment protection. A radical environment program necessarily entails linking together a variety of political reforms, most of which are not directly related to environmental ecology. For instance, a radical program must demand curbs on dumping of pollutants and also insist on corporate and federal financial aid for displaced workers. In addition, political agitation against the defense budget and regressive tax loopholes must continue in order to prevent a simple reallocation of federal funds away from other social services to environment programs. Increased public spending on mass transit, parks, medical services, and other forms of social consumption must be sought in order to offset potential increases in the prices of the necessities manufactured for private consumption and to eliminate the personal need for certain types of private consumption spending. Equity will not be served unless all of these reforms are adopted as a package.

Of course, the federal government is not yet ready to implement a comprehensive environment protection program of this sort. Even the pollution tax plan appears to appeal far less to federal policy makers and corporate leaders than it does to liberal scholars. Russell Train, chairman of the President's Council on Environmental Quality, has flatly stated that he "would never propose a system of effluent or emission charges as a substitute for regulatory action."[37] William Ruckelshaus, chief of the Federal Environmental Protection Agency, has affirmed that "while [user charges] may have merit, the path we have elected to travel . . . is standard-setting and enforcement."[38] The Nixon administration has already begun to exercise direct regulatory powers in its efforts to control industrial pollution. Using an executive order issued under the Refuse Act of 1899 as a precedent, the Environmental Protection Agency has established limits on the amount and types of wastes that industrial plants may discharge into inland and coastal waters. The Army Corps of Engineers is charged with issuing dumping permits, and industrial violators can be fined up to $10,000 per day.[39] Stern though this regulatory language is, the actual regulation benefiting the public often leaves a lot to be desired, for the regulatory language is often interpreted loosely when sensitive corporate nerves are exposed, and few regulations are comprehensive enough to cover all loopholes. Previous regulatory reforms have not fared well, as a number of reports on other regulatory commissions, such as the Federal Trade Commission, the Securities and Exchange Commission, the Federal Communications Commission, and food and drug acts, have documented well.[40] Regulation-by-Commission makes sense to corporate leaders and federal administrators: these bureaucratic tribunals provide arenas where lobbyists representing different corporate interest groups meet—not to have regulations imposed, but to arbitrate their economic differences. The result is that the war on pollution will, most likely, be timid and, consequently, crisis-oriented. If the history of regulation repeats itself, the polluters will end up being the regulators.

Corporate enthusiasm for environmental regulations hinges, however, not only on who controls the regulators, but on whether public subsidies are available to offset potential profit losses:

> When it comes to remedial action, a dominant sentiment is caution. The [corporate] executives [surveyed by *Fortune*] are concerned that government, in response to public pressure, will dictate the immediate spending of huge sums, which . . . will *sap the financial vigor* of their companies . . . It may come as quite a surprise that the elite of business leadership strongly desire the federal government to step in, set the standards, regulate all activities pertaining to the environment, and *help finance the job with tax incentives*.[41] [Italics added.]

To be specific, seventy-four percent of the corporation executives surveyed believe that accelerated depreciation allowances, investment tax credits, and government grants for corporate abatement projects would be the "most effective" environmental protection measures.[42] In effect, corporations would receive Treasury subsidies and IRS tax cuts in return for not debasing the environment.

Neither the individual firm nor the government in a capitalist society can afford to refrain from pursuing corporate "financial vigor." Oligopolistic competition compels the individual firm always to expand its sales in an attempt to protect its profit margin. For the state, economic growth is necessary in order to ensure social stability, given the unequal distribution of income and wealth. Liberal policymakers view accelerated growth as an instrument for preventing social class conflict. If the national income is growing rapidly, *absolute* deprivation can be ameliorated even if *relative* deprivation persists or even worsens.[43] It is thought that if material standards of living are rising rapidly people may be more tolerant of basically intolerable working conditions and of the impersonal corporate and government bureaucracies that dominate their lives. One of the most candid statements of this thesis is the assertion by Professor Eugene Rostow that, "the ideas of liberal planning [i.e., full employment and rapid growth via public policy] give capitalism every reason to expect even more spectacular progress in the future than in the past, *without disturbing the basic conditions of property ownership and control*."[44] [Italics added.]

The dilemma facing modern capitalism is that though a rapid rate of economic growth is necessary to service large corporations and contain class conflict, ultimately this leads to an increasing degree of environmental destruction. "Depletion and pollution of the environment are inevitable by-products of production and consumption."[45] Continued growth, even given spectacular advances in technology, will eventually result in greater absolute amounts of pollution of the air, land, and water. Since "matter and energy can be neither created nor destroyed," it follows that "technological means for processing or purifying one or another type of waste discharge do not destroy the residuals but only alter their forms. Thus [the recycling of] materials into productive uses or discharge into an alternative medium are the only general options for protecting a particular environmental medium. . . ."[46]

Even if better waste-recovery techniques are created, the complete recycling of wastes will be technologically impossible and economically unfeasible. The unavoidable conclusion is that without a significant slow-down in the rate of population growth and economic growth, the environment will eventually be destroyed. The "Spaceship Earth" that Kenneth Boulding describes in another part of this book will have depleted its life-support system.[47] Technological advances in recycling and reclamation will offer a respite from environmental destruction, but they will not provide an ecological panacea. It is clear that we must "invent institutions and technologies which will allow us to reach and maintain a stationary-state economy."[48] The necessary components of an economic program capable of saving the environment go far beyond the design and operation of a new excise tax or set of administrative regulations. Curbing population growth and the growth of material output, eliminating income and wealth inequalities, and making provision for communal forms of consumption are some of the elements of a real solution.

SOCIALISM AND ECOLOGY

If liberal reform cannot resolve the contradiction between environmental quality and capitalist modes of production and consumption, what is to be done? Because social costs will continue to increase in relation to private costs, the contradictions and dilemmas of our "private enterprise" economy are bound to become more intense. Increasingly the need for resolving social conflict through economic growth will run headlong into the problem of solving the environmental crisis. The solution will lie in socializing the economy, not in pollution taxes or self-regulation within the corporate sector.

Historically the argument for socialism has evolved from the periodic economic crises and the exploitation of labor under capitalist regimes. Yet behind these principles has always been Marx's recognition of the social character of production—the notion that all production in modern civilizations is necessarily social and not individual in origin.[49] Because the production and consumption of virtually all goods by any one person entail increasing or decreasing the welfare of others in society, the private control of production and consumption has become increasingly "inefficient" in an economic sense and inequitable in a social sense. The political implication is that a more productive activity must be socially owned and democratically directed. A growing part of consumption will have to take the form of public transport, communal shelter, and other social services. Leisure activities that emphasize the development of good interpersonal relations instead of the use of material commodities will be less disruptive of environmental ecologies.[50] And an equitable redistribution of income and wealth will be integral to the solution of the problem of protecting the environment. What is so ironic is that socialism—once thought to be the keystone for economic growth and development, and therefore of greatest necessity in underdeveloped countries of the Third World—is more a necessity now in the advanced countries where natural growth has been too extensive.

From whom should we learn the road to socialism? There are several good reasons to be skeptical of existing socialist models. In the Soviet bloc, for example, the high priority given to rapid industrial development has resulted in authoritarian rule and in environmental disruptions as well. According to one author, "a study of pollution in the Soviet Union suggests that abolishing private property will not necessarily mean an end to environmental disruption. In some ways, state ownership . . . may actually exacerbate . . . the situation."[51] Empirical evidence for this assertion is incomplete, to say the least. However, there are reasons for believing that individual state enterprises might impose pollution costs on households and other enterprises even though there is central planning of the Soviet economy. Soviet managers often receive production targets from central planning authorities that "have been set so high . . . that one third of all enterprises [fail] to fulfill their annual plans."[52] In addition, "the principal managerial incentive in Soviet industry is the bonus paid for overfulfillment of [production] plan targets."[53] As a result, one would expect to find Soviet managers utilizing their resource quotas without much regard for controlling waste and pollution.[54]

The Soviet model is somewhat encouraging in several respects, however. First, the absence of oligopolistic competition and massive advertising in the Soviet economy tends to reduce the rate of product obsolescence and the consequent rates of current production necessary to maintain desired stocks of durable goods. Second, the greater emphasis on communal consumption in the Soviet Union reduces the stocks of goods necessary to deliver desired flows of use values. During the three decades between 1928 and 1958, real per capita consumption in the USSR doubled, but real per capita communal services increased more than fivefold.[55] There is apparently some commitment to continuing this trend. A Communist Party USSR document has pledged that

> The share of the public consumption funds in the total real incomes of the Soviet population will increase up to fifty percent in twenty years. As Soviet society advances toward communism, the needs of the people will be satisfied to an increasing degree out of funds intended for collective use, for the "joint satisfaction of needs."[56]

Whether Soviet central planners and party leaders will be willing and able to devise a steady-state, communal-consumption society is questionable, however. The postwar ideological struggle between the United States and the Soviet Union has been waged primarily on the field of economic growth. Values such as participatory democracy, material equality, and respect for the natural environment have been sacrificed by both governments. One disturbing bit of evidence is that production of Fiat passenger cars at the new Togliatti plant on the Volga River is expected to reach 660,000 autos per year in 1972.[57] If similar modes of personal consumption are also adopted, the Soviet Revolution will culminate in a perverse amalgam of authoritarian bureaucracy and mass consumerism, hardly the vision of proletarian democracy that Marx foresaw.

Other models of socialist development are somewhat less depressing. The Israeli kibbutz and the Chinese commune embody a deep commitment to communal living and to the priority of good human relations over material growth. Melford Spiro reports that

> Although its land is owned by the nation, all other property . . . is owned collectively by the members of the [Israeli] kibbutz. Ideally, the individual owns nothing with the exception of small personal gifts . . . The houses are laid out in parallel rows on either side of the communal dining hall, which is the physical center of the kibbutz . . . The houses themselves are built in the form of ranch-house apartments with, as a rule, four individual living units in each apartment.[58]

The Maoist model of social development is similarly encouraging in its emphasis on communalism and its willingness to deemphasize material growth for its own sake:

> Maoists believe that, while a principal aim of nations should be to raise the level of material welfare of the population, this should be done only within the context of the development of human beings and of encouraging them to realize fully their manifold creative powers. And it should be done on an egalitarian basis . . . Maoists seem perfectly willing to pursue the goal of transforming man even though it is temporarily at the expense of some economic growth . . .[59]

The concrete effects of this social ethic on the Chinese environment have included "action in such areas as afforestation, water conservancy, land reclamation, and sanitation and public health."[60] Even more striking is the Maoist concept of "comprehensive use," which was introduced as an injunction to Chinese workers and peasants to recover and reuse industrial and agricultural wastes. There are some indications that Chinese scientists are focusing more of their attention on "comprehensive utilization" of wastes in order to supplement the innovations of workers and peasants.[61]

As interesting and even inspiring as these sketches are, they do not provide a socialist model for America and the other rich countries. In nations already affluent, socialism will differ greatly from the socialist experiments of the developing countries. Where material growth need not be the source of human progress, environmental protection is both acutely necessary and economically feasible. The developed countries have a serious obligation to reduce their own rates of economic and population growth, to reduce their own waste discharges, to produce more durable goods, and to promote sounder consumption styles so that the poor countries can claim their fair share of global clean environment. Bringing the whole of mankind into harmony with his natural environment will require concentrated effort. Minor reforms will not be good enough.

NOTES AND REFERENCES

1. See especially Alfred Marshall, *Principles of Economics*, New York: Macmillan, 1948, 8th ed., Book V; and A. C. Pigou, *The Economics of Welfare*, New York: Macmillan, 1932, 4th ed., ch. IX.
2. For examples of this line of reasoning, see Larry Ruff, "The Economic Common Sense of Pollution," *The Public Interest*, Spring 1970; J. H. Dales, *Pollution, Property, and Prices*, Toronto: Univ. of Toronto Press, 1968; and

Edwin Mills, "Economic Incentives in Air Pollution Control," *in* Harold Wolozin, ed., *The Economics of Air Pollution*, New York: Norton, 1966.

3. For a theoretical discussion of "externalities," see E. J. Mishan, *Welfare Economics*, New York: Random House, 1964. Examples of the external effects of economic activity include air and water pollution, higher noise levels, unhealthy and unpleasant working conditions, traffic congestion, and ugly architecture.
4. The common argument in orthodox welfare economics that particular social reforms should be undertaken if compensatory side payments *could* make everyone better off is politically ridiculous. Whether or not the compensation would, in fact, be made depends on the relative political strength of the different classes and groups involved.
5. Although conceptually simple, the *administrative* costs of calculating and enforcing an "optimal" set of pollution tax rates would be enormous. This fact has led some economists to advocate that physical discharge standards be imposed and that these ceilings be allocated among producers and consumers via competitive bidding. See William Baumol and Wallace Oates, "The Use of Standards and Prices for Protection of the Environment," *Swedish Journal of Economics*, March 1971, pp. 42–54. Herman Daly outlines a "depletion quota" system based on competitive bidding in "The Steady State Economy: Toward a Political Economy of Biophysical Equilibrium and Moral Growth," pages 149–174 of this volume.
6. U.S. Department of Commerce, *Current Population Reports: Income in 1968 of Families and Persons in the United States*, U.S. Government Printing Office, 1969, p. 22.
7. For a detailed study of the maldistribution of wealth in America, see Robert Lampman, *The Share of Top Wealthholders in National Wealth 1925–1956*, Princeton, N. J.: Princeton University, 1962.
8. A recently published study of the Buffalo, New York area has found that the rates of hospitalization per 100,000 children under age fifteen for such diseases as asthma and eczema increase with the degree of air pollution in the census tracts of their residence. These debilitating effects of air pollution are by no means borne equally across social classes. The researchers found that seventy-eight percent of the children in the lowest of four socioeconomic categories lived in high-air-pollution census tracts whereas only three percent of the children in the highest social class lived in similarly polluted neighborhoods. See Harry Sultz et al., "An Effect of Continued Exposure to Air Pollution on the Incidence of Chronic Childhood Allergic Disease," *American Journal of Public Health*, May 1970, pp. 891–900.
9. Paul and Anne Ehrlich, *Population, Resources, Environment*, San Francisco: W. H. Freeman and Co., 1970, p. 135.
10. Paul Craig and Edward Berlin, "The Air of Poverty," *Environment*, June 1971, p. 6.
11. "Black lung" is an impairment of an individual's respiratory capacity resulting from prolonged inhalation of coal dust. "White lung" is a similar condition caused by small cotton fiber particles.
12. Rod Such, "Job Hazards Plague U.S. Workers," *Guardian*, December 12, 1970.
13. For the reasoning underlying this fact, see discussions of regressive and progressive taxation in textbooks on public finance; for example: John Due, *Government Finance*, Homewood, Ill.: Richard D. Irwin, 1963.
14. In the absence of price competition, a monopoly or oligopoly will often set prices according to a "mark-up" formula. After calculating total costs and estimating effective demand for its product, a firm will set its prices some

percentage above average cost. An addition to total cost is therefore reflected in a higher price. If, for instance, pollution abatement equipment is installed to satisfy antipollution standards, some firms will raise price by an amount equal to the additional costs *plus* the standard mark-up on those costs. For a discussion of pricing behavior, see Richard Cyert and James March, *A Behavioral Theory of the Firm*, Englewood Cliffs, N. J.: Prentice-Hall, 1963.

15. For an excellent summary of what is known about global ecological interdependencies, see the report of the Study of Critical Environmental Problems entitled *Man's Impact on the Global Environment: Assessment and Recommendations for Action*, Cambridge, Mass.: M.I.T. Press, 1970.
16. Hans Dietrich Genscher, quoted in Clifford Russell and Hans Landsberg, "International Environmental Problems: A Taxonomy," *Science*, June 25, 1971, p. 1310.
17. Paul and Anne Ehrlich, *op. cit.*, p. 61.
18. U.S. Department of the Interior, *Minerals Yearbook 1969*, U.S. Government Printing Office, 1971, vol. I–II, p. 59. For other data on U.S. resource use, see Preston Cloud, "Mineral Resources in Fact and Fancy," on pages 50–75 of this volume.
19. William Smith, "Oil Replay," *The New York Times*, January 9, 1972.
20. John McLean, "Energy Users Must Unite," *The New York Times*, January 9, 1972. The eleven countries are Abu Dhabi, Algeria, Indonesia, Iran, Iraq, Kuwait, Libya, Nigeria, Qatar, Saudi Arabia, Venezuela.
21. U.S. Department of the Interior, *Minerals Yearbook 1969*, U.S. Government Printing Office, 1971, vol. IV, p. 7.
22. The military government of Brazil has already embraced this sort of national policy. According to João Paulo Velloso, the Brazilian planning minister: "Brazil can become the importer of pollution . . . We have a lot left to pollute . . . And if we don't do it, some other country will." See Joseph Novitski, "Brazil Shunning Pollution Curbs," *The New York Times*, February 13, 1972.
23. For a provocative discussion of potential developments in the global economy, see Stephen Hymer, "The Efficiency (Contradictions) of Multinational Corporations," *American Economic Review*, May, 1970; also Robert Heilbroner, "The Multinational Corporation and the Nation State," *New York Review of Books*, February 11, 1971.
24. Consider the following hypothetical example. Let P stand for the level of Gross National Product, in billions of deflated dollars, and W stand for the quantity of wastes, in billions of pounds, that is discharged into the environment. Let W/P be the amount of wastes discharged per dollar of production.

Year	P	W/P	W
1970	1,000	6	6,000
1971	1,050	6	6,300
1972	1,103	6	6,618
1973	1,158	4	4,632
1974	1,217	4	4,868
1975	1,277	4	5,108
1976	1,340	4	5,360
1977	1,407	4	5,628
1978	1,477	4	5,908
1979	1,552	4	6,208
1980	1,628	4	6,512
1981	1,710	4	6,840

With production growing continually at five percent annually, the volume of pollution also grows at five percent per year until 1973 when antipollution standards are introduced. The imposition of environmental standards does succeed in reducing the level of waste discharges for a number of years. However, with production continuing to grow rapidly, the volume of discharges surpasses its former peak by 1981—only eight years after a thirty-three percent reduction in the "propensity to pollute." There is some evidence that the volume of pollutants has actually grown *faster* than national output in recent decades, not the reverse. See Barry Commoner, Michael Corr, and Paul Stamler, "The Causes of Pollution," *Environment*, April, 1971. The figures above are for a trillion-dollar economy. The five percent growth rate, though high, is not implausible. Six pounds of pollution per dollar is a conservative estimate taken from Ralph d'Arge, "Essay on Economic Growth and Environmental Quality," *Swedish Journal of Economics*, March 1971, p. 25.

25. Walter Heller, *New Dimensions of Political Economy*, Cambridge, Mass.: Harvard University, 1966, pp. 79–81.
26. Some economists believe that this inadequacy of consumer spending results from the unequal distribution of incomes and wealth in private enterprise economies. For a discussion of the possibility of using a guaranteed annual income to stimulate consumer spending and thereby decrease the need for future economic growth, see Warren Johnson, "The Guaranteed Income as an Environmental Measure," *in* Warren Johnson and John Hardesty, eds., *Economic Growth vs. the Environment*, Belmont, Calif.: Wadsworth, 1971. Reprinted in this volume on pages 175–189.
27. Joe S. Bain, *Industrial Organization*, New York: Wiley, 1959, p. 321.
28. Richard Edwards et al., eds., *The Capitalist System*, Englewood Cliffs, N. J.: Prentice-Hall, 1972, p. 378.
29. For a discussion of the private highway lobby and its impact on public transport policy, see James O'Connor, "The Fiscal Crisis of the State," *Socialist Revolution*, vol. 1, pp. 40–43.
30. Robert Diamond, "What Business Thinks," *Fortune*, February, 1970, p. 119.
31. *Ibid.*, p. 119.
32. James O'Connor, *op. cit.*, p. 20.
33. A good example is the decision of the Federal Aviation Administration to withdraw a controversial proposal for measuring airport noise and to allow representatives of the Airport Operators Council and the Air Transport Association to help rewrite the standards. According to one observer, "airport managers around the nation had complained bitterly of the original proposal, arguing that it might make them liable to buy tens of thousands of homes near airports at a cost of several billion dollars." See Robert Lindsey, "F.A.A. to Let Jet Industry Help Rewrite Noise Rules," *The New York Times*, October 12, 1971.
34. Daniel P. Moynihan, "The Professionalization of Reform," *in* M. Gettleman and D. Mermelstein, eds., *The Great Society Reader*, New York: Vintage, 1967. pp. 462–465.
35. "Midget Car is Coming, Report Says," *Detroit Free Press*, March 14, 1972.
36. The defense budget is the most likely candidate. During the postwar period, the Defense Department has spent over one trillion dollars on "national security." See Richard Barnet, *The Economy of Death*, New York: Atheneum, 1969, for a critical inspection of the military-industrial sector.
37. Brian Bragg, "Taxes Eyed for Polluters," *Detroit Free Press*, December 6, 1970.

38. "White House May Determine Gasoline Additive Standards," *Ann Arbor News*, January 13, 1971. Effluent taxes have not been totally rejected, however. In his February, 1971, message on environmental protection to the Congress, President Nixon asserted that "our goal must be to harness the powerful mechanisms of the marketplace, with its automatic incentives and restraints, to encourage improvement in the quality of life." However, the only concrete examples of a preference for market incentives were his proposals for excises on sulphurous fuels and leaded gasoline. See "Nixon Asks Laws to Clean Up U.S.," *Detroit Free Press*, February 9, 1971.
39. "Nixon Acts to Control Pollution," *Detroit Free Press*, December 24, 1970. By July, 1971, the Environmental Protection Agency had failed to formulate industrial discharge standards under the Refuse Act, "leaving it up to regional officials to use their own judgment in writing thousands of federal permits." See "U.S. Drops Pollution Code," *Detroit Free Press*, July 21, 1971.
40. For the latest critiques of public regulation of corporations, refer to the Ralph Nader Study Group reports on business and government. Two staff reports on the Food and Drug Administration and the Interstate Commerce Commission, respectively, are James Turner et al., *The Chemical Feast* and Robert Fellmeth et al., *The Interstate Commerce Commission*, New York: Grossman, 1970.
41. Robert Diamond, *op. cit.*, pp. 118–119.
42. *Ibid.*, p. 172.
43. Herman Daly, "The Canary Has Fallen Silent," *The New York Times*, October 14, 1970.
44. Eugene Rostow, *Planning for Freedom*, New Haven, Conn.: Yale University, 1959, p. 29.
45. Herman Daly, *op. cit.*
46. *Ibid.*, and Robert Ayres and Allen Kneese, "Production, Consumption, and Externalities," *American Economic Review*, June 1969, p. 283.
47. Kenneth Boulding, "The Economics of the Coming Spaceship Earth," *in* Henry Jarrett, ed., *Environmental Quality in a Growing Economy*, Baltimore: Johns Hopkins Press, 1966. Reprinted in this volume, on pages 121–132.
48. Herman Daly, *op. cit.*
49. For a summary of Marx's position, see Paul Sweezy, *The Theory of Capitalist Development*, New York: Monthly Review Press, 1968, ch. 2.
50. Of leisure activities that cause little ecological disruption, group hiking requires little material paraphernalia, choral singing and lovemaking require none. Auto and jet tourism, by contrast, have far greater environmental impacts.
51. Marshall Goldman, "The Convergence of Environmental Disruption," *Science*, October 2, 1970, p. 37.
52. Joseph Berliner, "Managerial Incentives and Decisionmaking: A Comparison of the United States and the Soviet Union," *in* Morris Bornstein and Daniel Fusfeld, eds., *The Soviet Economy: A Book of Readings*, Homewood, Ill.: Irwin, 1970, 3rd ed., p. 175.
53. *Ibid.*, p. 165.
54. This does not imply, however, that "technology" is more important than economic organization in determining the severity of a society's environmental impact. It simply suggests that both the capitalist and Soviet economies currently lack environmentally sound social institutions.
55. Janet Chapman, "Consumption in the Soviet Union," *in* Morris Bornstein and Daniel Fusfeld, *op. cit.*, p. 325.

56. A. Aganbegian, "Living Standards of the Working People in the USSR and the USA," *in* Harry Shaffer, ed., *The Soviet Economy*, New York: Appleton-Century-Crofts, 1963, p. 282.
57. James Peipert, "Soviet Union is Plunging into Auto Age," *Ann Arbor News*, January 10, 1971.
58. Melford Spiro, *Kibbutz: Venture into Utopia*, New York: Schocken, 1963, pp. 19 and 64.
59. John Gurley, "Capitalist and Maoist Economic Development," *Bulletin of Concerned Asian Scholars*, June 1970, pp. 38–40.
60. Lee Orleans and Richard Suttmeier, "The Mao Ethic and Environmental Quality," *Science*, December 11, 1970, p. 1174.
61. *Ibid*, p. 1175.

Powerful or forgotten

10

LEVIATHAN OR OBLIVION?

William Ophuls

In his widely-acclaimed and controversial essay, the biologist Garrett Hardin argues that uncontrolled population growth and many other serious environmental problems can be analyzed in terms of "the tragedy of the commons." Men seek to maximize their gain. In the absence of controls, Hardin reasons, they are driven by rational calculations of self-interest to over-exploit or abuse the commons, whether it is a pasture shared by herdsmen or the earth's atmosphere. Thus, "freedom in a commons brings ruin to all." Because there are no technical solutions to this problem, says Hardin, we must establish stringent controls ("mutual coercion, mutually agreed upon") to escape the "remorseless working of things" that characterizes the logic of a free commons.[1]

Of course, the tragedy of the commons is hardly a new discovery. As the political scientist B. L. Crowe pointed out, it is "so common in the social sciences that it has generated some fairly sophisticated mathematical models."[2] However, by leaving it at that, Crowe seems to understate the extent to which the tragic quality of the logic of a free commons has dominated men's thinking about society and politics through the

1. Notes and references for this reading will be found on pages 229–230.

"Leviathan or Oblivion?" Published by permission of the author.

ages. Indeed, it is not too much to say that the central problem for all theorizers about politics, at least in the Western tradition, is precisely the tragedy of the commons writ large: how to protect or advance the interests of the whole when men behave or are impelled to behave in a selfish, greedy, and quarrelsome fashion. For example, Plato tried to design a ship of state in which the most skilled navigator would be spontaneously accepted as captain by the crew members, each of whom would perform the shipboard duties for which he was best qualified rather than striving to lay hands on the ship's tiller himself. The political philosophy of the *Republic*, the fountainhead of all Western thinking about politics, emerged directly from Plato's own historical experience: he lived through the tragedy of the Peloponnesian War and attributed the Athenian defeat to the sordid struggle for individual political advantage in a time of common peril. In this general sense then, the tragedy of the commons is a part of the human condition and has always preoccupied political philosophers. However, certain thinkers have made the kinds of issues Hardin raises the central feature of their analysis, and the greatest of these was the English philosopher Thomas Hobbes (1588–1679). In his classic work, *Leviathan*, which was published in 1651, Hobbes gave the tragedy of the commons the most profound treatment it has ever received and drew conclusions about how the tragedy could be averted that have not lost their cogency today.[3] For this reason, it will repay us to review Hobbes's thought in the light of the environmental crisis, noting the striking similarities between Hobbes and Hardin, and examining the specific political solution to the tragedy proposed by the great philosopher.

THE STATE OF NATURE AND THE WAR OF ALL AGAINST ALL

Hobbes starts from two premises: (1) men are basically alike in desiring gain, security, and reputation; (2) these things are in short supply. "Equality of hope" leads men to desire the same things, but since they cannot all enjoy "riches, honor [and] command," they become enemies and "endeavor to destroy or subdue one another." As if this cutthroat competition over the current stock of scarce resources were not enough, a man also wishes to gratify his desires "not . . . once only and for one instant of time, but to assure forever the way of his future desire." Because the only way to assure one's future desire is power, men inevitably incline toward "a perpetual and restless desire of power after power that ceases only in death." In other words, even if a man has his fair share of the commons today, it can be taken from him by someone stronger tomorrow; to protect himself he needs power; but offense is the best defense, and men therefore strive ceaselessly for power over others. Because this inexorable logic operates, Hobbes says that men in a "state of nature" with no security but their own strength will be in a condition of perpetual war. Actual violence may be temporarily in abeyance, but one is never secure in this "war of every one against every one." As a result, there is "no society; and, which is worst of all, continual fear and danger of violent death; and the life of man solitary, poor, nasty, brutish, and short."

The essential similarity to Hardin's analysis is clear. Hardin's herdsmen do not directly attack the flocks of their fellows, but in striving to gratify their selfish ends they accomplish the same result indirectly: once the capacity of the commons is reached, each sheep added to one man's fold is a threat to the survival of all. For both Hardin and Hobbes, men are driven by desire for gain in a situation of finite resources to behave in self-destructive ways. Freedom in a commons and freedom in a state of nature are alike in bringing mutual ruin. Hobbes carries the analysis one step further, showing how the specific struggle over scarce resources generates a wider struggle for political power, but the potential for violence is clearly implicit also in Hardin's description of the tragedy of the commons, demonstrated in the American experience by the range wars of the frontier.

THE SOVEREIGN ENFORCES SOCIAL RESPONSIBILITY

If men's passions and their reason both incline them to the war of all against all, how do we break out of the logic of the commons? Hobbes says that their passions and reason also show men the way out of the misery of the state of nature. Men desire an end to the fear of violent death and they hope for the "commodious living" which is impossible in a state of nature. Motivated by such passions, reason tells men that they ought to live in peace with one another; clearly, everybody would be better off if they obeyed this "natural law." However, this requires each person to give up some of his "natural rights" to do anything and to have anything and, instead, to "be contented with so much liberty against other men as he would allow other men against himself." In other words, men have the capacity—and even the right—to engage in mutually destructive behavior, but any reasonable man must see that mutual self-restraint would be greatly advantageous. The problem is that all men must renounce their natural rights together; if only some men lay down their arms, they put themselves at the mercy of those whose passions are not restrained by the dictates of reason. The crucial problem then is to create conditions that will make it safe to obey the laws of nature.

Examining the nature of agreements between men, Hobbes concludes that human passions make good intentions and voluntary compliance totally unreliable. Only a common power standing above the parties to a contract can make men fear the consequences of breaking their word enough to meet their obligations unfailingly. Although the laws of nature are always binding in conscience, "covenants without the sword are but words," and only enforcement by a civil government can put them into practical effect. Hobbes says that the only way to erect a common power sufficient to guarantee peace among men is for them to come together and by majority decision "confer all their power and strength upon one man, or upon one assembly of men that may reduce all their wills, by plurality of voices, unto one will." In this way, they become a "multitude united in one person" or a "commonwealth" ruled over by a "sovereign" holding all the power originally possessed by the multitude of "subjects."

Hobbes compares the commonwealth to a "great LEVIATHAN" or "*mortal god,*" so awesome is its power meant to be. He insists that the yielding up of power to the sovereign must be eternal, indivisible, and absolute. All who in this way will the peace of the commonwealth necessarily will the means the sovereign needs to enforce it, and because men are incapable of disinterested judgment in their own cases, public decisions must be left completely in the hands of the sovereign. The maintenance of spheres of private rights, the expression of dissent, or other acts in derogation of the absolute power of the sovereign cannot be tolerated, for divisions within the body politic threaten to recreate the state of nature. It is true that the subjects may suffer from the "irregular passions of him or them that have so unlimited a power in their hands," but Hobbes maintains that this is infinitely better than the war of all against all. In any event, "the state of man can never be without some incommodity or other." Nor are the arguments for giving up our natural political liberties purely negative. Hobbes feels that most men have a distorted idea of freedom derived from the classical democracies—i.e., they believe freedom to be untrammeled exercise of their "natural" rights as citizens to play a role in governing the political community. They conveniently forget the consequences such liberty had for Athens. In a commonwealth, Hobbes says, men will have given up almost all such political liberties but will obtain greater real freedom in exchange. Freedom in a state of nature is meaningless, but citizens of a well-ordered commonwealth can enrich themselves through industry, practice the arts and sciences, and generally enjoy the fruits of civilization. A sovereign securely in power would be able to devote himself (itself) to the promotion of trade, learning, and public amenities of every sort. Thus, the real freedom and welfare of the subjects would flow from the abandonment of natural political rights.

Again, the similarities to Hardin's argument are striking. Hardin says we are faced with the necessity to "legislate temperance"—i.e., limit certain natural freedoms we now have. However, we need to ensure that all individuals and groups in society are equally temperate lest the irresponsible continue to breed and pollute. Because conscience is likely to be self-eliminating where irresponsibility is unrestrained, we have to have definite social arrangements that produce responsibility, and these are necessarily coercive. In sum, we must have "mutual coercion, mutually agreed upon by the majority of the people affected." Hardin maintains that coercion need not imply "arbitrary decisions of distant and irresponsible bureaucrats." However, even if this danger exists, "an alternative to the commons need not be perfectly just to be preferable." Indeed, "injustice is preferable to total ruin." Along with Hobbes, Hardin insists that the unrestrained exercise of our liberties does not bring us real freedom: "individuals locked into the logic of the commons are free only to bring on universal ruin; once they see the necessity of mutual coercion, they become free to pursue other goals." By recognizing the necessity to abandon many natural freedoms we now believe we possess, we avoid tragedy and "preserve and nurture other and more precious freedoms."

Hobbes goes beyond Hardin in supplying an outline of the social arrangements he believes best fitted to resolve the tragedy. Although it is quite possible for an aristocratic or democratic assembly to exercise sovereign power, Hobbes favors monarchies, where sovereign power is entrusted to one man alone. In the first place, the monarch is more likely to identify his personal interests with his public interests: his "riches, power, and honor . . . arise only from the riches, strength, and reputation of his subjects." Assemblies of whatever constitution inevitably suffer from the conflict of public and private interest. Second, monarchy makes for greater stability and purpose in policy and execution; only one man's "inconstancy . . . of human nature" needs to be checked, rather than that of a multitude. Also, factional struggle too often characterizes assemblies of men. Although Hobbes recognizes the special problems connected with monarchy (e.g., succession), he maintains that most complaints against it as a form of government also apply to other types of civil government (e.g., assemblies holding sovereign power have been as ready to despoil certain classes of citizens as any king). Hobbes's answer to the tragedy of the commons then is a benevolent form of autocracy with power residing preferably in the hands of one man.

OBJECTIONS TO HOBBES'S CONCLUSIONS

Hobbes's conclusions are not at first glance very appealing. Even after the passage of several centuries they remain shocking, and we may wish to question their applicability to our current situation. For example, many criticize his use of self-preservation as the only criterion for founding the political order. However, while it is undeniable that Hobbes was excessively concerned with self-preservation, he makes clear that order in the commonwealth is not the goal, but the means. It is simply the *sine qua non* without which the fruits of civilization cannot be enjoyed: the sovereign is to procure the "safety of the people . . . but by safety here is not meant a bare preservation but also all other contentments of life which every man by lawful industry, without danger or hurt to the commonwealth, shall acquire to himself." And it is part of the task of the sovereign actively to promote these "contentments of life" among his subjects. Furthermore, Hobbes will not countenance tyranny. The sovereign must rule lawfully, give a full explanation of his acts to his subjects, and heed their legitimate desires. Through wise laws and education, the subjects will learn moral restraint. Also, the sovereign is not to be a dictator regulating every action of the citizen: he does not seek to "bind the people from all voluntary actions" but only guides them with laws which Hobbes likens to "hedges . . . set not to stop travelers, but to keep them in their way."

A second point on which critics have focused is Hobbes's harsh view of human nature. They feel that man's natural sociability, compassion, and reason are far stronger forces for social peace than Hobbes seems to allow. While valid in part, some of this criticism misses the point. Hobbes clearly states that man's reason and his compassion, which is both innate and acquired by reason, tell him that he ought not to harm his neighbor, and it is precisely the existence of these natural feelings that will allow the sovereign to be a ruler rather than a dictator. What Hobbes says is that, in an unstructured situation like the state of nature, the few who lack reason and compassion will set the terms of social interaction at the lowest possible level. Thus, Hobbes claims only that innate reason and compassion are insufficient to create order. These need the support provided by structure to be effective.

As further evidence that Hobbes has described an important part of what motivates us as social creatures, even his critics will admit that under certain circumstances the psychological dynamic of the state of nature does indeed rule men's behavior. For example, theorists have long analyzed international relations in Hobbesian terms because the state of nature depicts very aptly the situation of armed peace among competing nation-states owing obedience to no higher power. Also, when social or natural disaster leads to a breakdown in the ordered patterns of society which ordinarily restrain men, even the most libertarian governments have never hesitated to impose martial law as the only alternative to anarchy. So it appears that Hobbes's analysis is most cogent at the extreme. Self-interest moderated by self-restraint is not a poor means of social control. On the contrary, it is by many standards the most desirable and the easiest to administer—but it may not be workable when extreme conditions prevail. If the issue is nuclear devastation (not merely war) or destruction of the biosphere (not merely loss of amenity), the extremity of Hobbes's analysis may well accord with the extremity of the situation.

IS SCARCITY DEAD?

Although Hobbes deeply influenced all later thinkers about politics, even those most directly in his debt rejected much of his analysis and most of his gloomy conclusions. There are many reasons—some of them enumerated above—why men like John Locke (whose life overlaps Hobbes's, 1632–1704) and Adam Smith (who followed both Hobbes and Locke, 1723–1790) could not share all of Hobbes's views, which were, like the views of any man, the result of particular personal experiences in a certain historical setting, but the question of scarcity seems to have been crucial. Locke and Smith agreed with Hobbes about man's nature: men are selfish hedonists rationally seeking gain. However, the goods men desire are not so scarce that they must inevitably fight over them. Men could instead enrich themselves by founding a business or working new lands in the colonies—in other words, by applying their intelligence and labor to an unexploited part of the commons, where the carrying capacity has not yet been reached. In fact, this being possible, only a fool would try to despoil his neighbor, for it is so much easier and safer simply to create your own wealth. Of course, some things are still in short supply: many men can obtain "honor" (if only because of their "riches"), but "command" can never be universal. Locke, however, though not denying the role of vainglory in producing political strife, believes this becomes a minor problem once economic scarcity is relaxed. When power over others is not necessary to ensure survival and men can safely relax into private enjoyment of the good things of life, only a few will compete seriously for political position, and the intensity of the struggle will be greatly reduced. Thus, Locke and Smith find that by removing Hobbes's zero-sum-game assumptions they can relax his political conclusions. Competition is not dangerous as long as the stakes are not total and every man can take away some sort of prize. In fact, through the working of what Smith called the "invisible hand" of the political and economic marketplace, the greatest good for the society as a whole is produced. Government is required only to keep participants in the game honest. As a mere referee, it needs only modest powers and minimal institutional machinery. Thus, the assumption that the carrying capacity of the commons has not been reached is crucial. Given this assumption, one can permit a wide sphere of private rights without seriously compromising stability and other public goods.

The dependence of this philosophical stance on a particular set of historical conditions has been carefully documented by the American historian Walter Prescott Webb. Webb notes that before the discovery of the New World, Europe was "closed" with "very little freedom." Then the Great Frontier, "an enormous body of wealth without proprietors" became available in the New World, and the "by-product of this wealth was freedom and our peculiar modern institutions and values" such as individualism and democracy. However, the Great Frontier is no more: the New World has been filled up, the wealth has been appropriated, and our basic institutions need reexamination. In particular, says Webb, "we must admit that the individual, this cherished darling of modern history, attained his glory in an abnormal period when there was enough room to give him freedom and enough wealth to give him independence."[4] Thus, the Lockean conception of politics had a specific historical setting for which it was in most respects entirely realistic and even morally appropriate.

As is well known, it is principally the Lockean conception of politics that has molded our own institutions.[5] It is therefore hardly surprising that B. L. Crowe would find our political machinery unequipped to provide answers to the tragedy of the commons. Although Crowe shows cogently how it fails in several key areas, the issues he raises are for the most part derivative. The real problem is that our system was quite deliberately set up along the lines propounded by John Locke and Adam Smith to allow—nay, to encourage—the ruthless, competitive exploitation of the commons. The logic of the commons is thus enshrined in our political institutions and mores. The government's role as referee has grown over the years as the number of players has risen and the complexity of the game has increased, but the fundamental nature of the game has changed not a whit. Our problem is not so much that our institutions no longer work the way they should—they work only too well even now in permitting the continued ruthless exploitation of the environment—but that the assumptions about the carrying capacity of the commons which supported these institutions are no longer true. We now have a large and still-growing population which is increasing its demands on the environment exponentially; and far from having an abundance of virgin resources to exploit, we confront emerging shortages of resources of nearly every kind. The more alarmist fears that we will decline into classical poverty are probably wrong, but the most sober and careful analysis shows that our resource problems are indeed quite serious.[6] We are also approaching limits on the way we use resources to create wealth. The world is too crowded now for us not to control pollution, and, after a certain point, the cost of control grows faster than revenue, making continued expansion pointless.[7] In fact, the overall "abnormality" of the era of growth has long been recognized.[8] For these kinds of reasons, more and more natural and social scientists (including many who can scarcely be dismissed as having an antiscientific or antitechnological bias) are telling us that we may have to move toward a "steady-state" or "stationary-state" society.[9] Although the concept is still being refined, a steady-state society is essentially one which has achieved a basic long-term balance between the demands of a population and the environment that supplies its wants. Implicit in this definition is the preservation of a healthy biosphere, the careful husbanding of resources, and a general attitude of trusteeship toward future generations. The exact nature of the balance at any time is dependent on technological capacities and social choice, and as choices and capacities change, organic growth can occur. For this reason, the steady-state is by no means a state of stagnation, but is instead a dynamic equilibrium affording ample scope for continued artistic, intellectual, scientific, and spiritual growth.

We are obliged to achieve the steady state now because, in Hardin's terms, we are reaching the carrying capacity of the commons. Suddenly, many of those best things in life we always thought were free, such as clean water and pure air, have become increasingly scarce and valuable goods that must be allocated by political decision-making. One useful way of viewing the problem is with Boulding's conception of a "spaceman economy": if we must cease living on our capital and begin living on our income while at the same time tailoring our numbers to our income, which is what a steady-state exploitation of the commons implies, we are like men on a spaceship which has no mines or sewers; our welfare depends not upon rapid consumption or more and more consumers—this is fatal—but on the extent to which we can wring the maximum richness and amenity for a reasonable population from minimum resources; a good, perhaps even affluent, life is possible, but "it will have to be combined with a curious parsimony":

> Far from scarcity disappearing, it will be the most dominant aspect of the society. Every grain of sand will have to be treasured, and the waste and

> profligacy of our own day will seem so horrible that our descendants will hardly be able to bear to think about us . . .[10]

LEVIATHAN OR OBLIVION?

If scarcity is not dead, if it is in fact with us in a seemingly much more intense form than ever before in human history, how can we avoid reaching the conclusion that Leviathan is inevitable? Given current levels of population and technology, I do not believe that we can. Hobbes shows why a spaceship earth must have a captain. Otherwise, the collective selfishness and irresponsibility produced by the tragedy of the commons will destroy the spaceship, and any sacrifice of freedom by the crew members is clearly the lesser of evils. Excepting very small and tightly-knit social groups, education or the inculcation of rigid social norms is not proof against the logic of the commons. Some people say that, once they are aware of the gravity of the situation, men will naturally moderate their desires for children and other demands on the environment. However, a recent study of members of Zero Population Growth (ZPG), a radically antinatalist pressure group, produced this melancholy conclusion:

> In short, knowing that one child is necessary for immediate population stability . . . has no bearing on personal intentions for less than two versus two natural children, and a majority of those recognizing the necessity of the one-child family intended to have two children—even when they believe the United States is already past its optimum population size.[11]

If the individuals who are among the most knowledgeable and concerned about population growth will not restrain themselves, how much less can we expect of the common man? As Hardin notes, hypocrisy is rampant: "It is fair to say that most people who anguish over the population problem are trying to find a way to avoid the evils of overpopulation without relinquishing any of the privileges they now enjoy." Perhaps this harsh judgment is merited in some cases, but I believe that these ZPG members are neither hypocritical nor irrational. They are simply caught in the Hobbesian dilemma and recognize, consciously or unconsciously, that their sacrifice of a desired good, in this case the second natural child, avails nothing unless everybody else goes along too. A second example also illustrates that mere awareness of the gravity of the problem is not a sufficient force for environmental protection. A panel of scientists selected by the Environmental Protection Agency to study the advisability of a ban on DDT admitted that DDT was an "imminent threat to human welfare" but stated that an outright ban on its use would be unwarranted, because the "world burden of DDT is so high compared to the current annual use in the U.S."[12] But it is precisely the essence of the tragedy of the commons that one's own contribution to the problem seems infinitesimally small, while the disadvantages of self-denial loom very large. Whenever one's real interests are engaged, self-restraint appears to be both unprofitable and ultimately futile unless one can be certain of universal compliance.

Others look for a solution not so much to individual conscience but instead to the development of a collective conscience in the form of a world view or religion that would see man as the partner of nature rather than its antagonist.[13] While this will undoubtedly be an essential development for our survival in the long term, the geographer Y.-F. Tuan points out that the treatment of the environment in China in ideal and in actuality differed considerably. Despite a philosophy that was profoundly respectful of nature, the Chinese people have damaged their environment in many ways throughout their long history. Their ideals were not proof against the urgency of human desires. Ironically, a reversal of this trend is now taking place under a Communist government whose philosophy is the very antithesis of the traditional values embodied in Taoism and Buddhism.[14] Some social observers, like Charles Reich,[15] say that our age is different and that a new consciousness is emerging. This view cannot be brushed aside, for substantial value changes are clearly occurring in some segments of American society. However, the belief that these new values will become universal in the future would appear to be essentially a matter of faith at this point. Since past hopes for the emergence of a "new man" have been rudely treated by history, I find it difficult to be optimistic. Also, serious questions can be raised about the appropriateness of many so-called counter culture values, which often seem to be mere inversions of those held by the majority culture. In any event, it would seem unwise, to say the least, to base public policy on what must regretfully be regarded as prophecy.

It appears therefore that individual conscience and the right kind of cultural attitudes are not by themselves sufficient to overcome the short-term calculations of utility that lead men to cause environmental degradation. Real altruism and genuine concern for posterity may not be entirely absent, but they are not present in sufficient quantities to avoid tragedy. Only a Hobbesian sovereign can deal with this situation effectively, and we are left then with the problem of determining the concrete shape of Leviathan. What political structure will guarantee survival (for surely the worst fate would be to get *both* Leviathan *and* oblivion) while giving us a life worth living? And how do we achieve it without creating as many problems as we solve or causing abysmal human suffering? I have no ready answers to these questions. Nor does anyone else. We have only just begun to think seriously in these terms. Perhaps the most fundamental task of our era is to construct a new political philosophy, which will show us what we must do to survive with dignity and will incorporate as many as possible of the values and institutions we now rightly cherish. What seems clear is that to allow people to attack the very structure of life—the spaceship on which we all ride—on the grounds that to restrain them is to infringe on their personal and political rights is to make the old French saying *après nous le déluge* the watchword of society and to enshrine selfishness as the dominant political value. People must be restrained, and the only question is how to go about achieving the necessary ends with the least odious and most effective means.

One possible avenue of development, often thought to be the most likely, is Aldous Huxley's "Brave New World," which is ecologically sound in its general outlines and fulfills all of Hobbes's requirements quite nicely. Future men, totally conditioned by behavioral techniques foreshadowed in current writings,[16] will have become virtual insects, but they will be "happy" (all except for a rare accidental deviant and those unfortunate rulers who have to keep this world going). It is possible to doubt that we will ever possess the capability of running such a world—disease, poverty, and other evils we have sworn to eradicate are still remarkably common—but it is not in principle unworkable. Those who recoil from such a prospect suggest that we must reduce the scale of material civilization and decentralize our societies. By simplifying our lives, we can stop pressing on the capacity of the commons. Crowe favors this kind of "tribal" solution: "as we stand 'on the eve of destruction,' it may well be that the return to the face-to-face life in the small community . . . is a very functional response in terms of perpetuation of the species." This school of political thought has long and honorable antecedents, associated primarily with the name of Rousseau. In assessing the desirability of such a response, it is worth recalling that a turn to Rousseau, whose spirit pervades the political philosophy of our own Thomas Jefferson, would actually be a return to the roots of American democracy. I myself favor a solution along these lines. On ecological and other grounds, I believe that a strong case could be made for the revival, in a suitably modified form and on an entirely new technological base, of the classic city-state, but now as a constituent part of a planetary government. The virtues of this organic form of political and social community have inspired countless historians and philosophers, and in the era of the steady state it could become once again the most appropriate vehicle of man's search for the good life. Nevertheless, whatever the merits of the Rousseauian response to our modern problems, it provides no escape from our political dilemma: reforming a "corrupt people" is a Herculean task, and only a sovereign (a "Legislator" in Rousseau's language) would be strong enough to exact the sacrifices needed to return to the simple life. Also, once men have returned to it, what, if not the sovereign, will make sure they do not become corrupted again?

That we must give some man or body of men absolute powers over many of our actions is a profoundly distasteful thought for most Americans. We tend to see political systems which do not have our kind of political and economic liberties as "totalitarian," a word that evokes all the evil features of past dictatorships. However, as pointed out above, Hobbes, no matter how firm his convictions on the necessity of absolutism, certainly did not have Stalinesque tyranny in mind, and many different styles of rule and of life are compatible with his basic analysis. Provided an essential network of laws controlling war, population growth, destruction of the environment, etc., was enforced, one could have a large degree of decentralization and great social diversity. Rigid hierarchical structures (to say nothing of monarchy in our era) and lock-step discipline are neither inevitable nor workable in the long run. If we act before we reach extremity, we can design macro-autocracy to give us a maximum of micro-democracy. We should begin to think about what style of rule we would prefer, especially how to preserve as many of our traditional liberties as possible. Indeed, we can no longer avoid thinking about it, for final destruction of the commons in a "crisis of crises" threatens.[17] For example, in another part of this book Jørgen Randers and Donella Meadows explain the results found by their research group, which devised a computer model of world systems in order to determine the ecological consequences of current trends. Admittedly only crude first efforts, these computer simulations of the global ecosystem nevertheless provide a graphic picture of the way in which exponential growth is rapidly thrusting us up against natural limits; they seem to show that only quite radical changes in policy will allow us to avoid catastrophic situations in the inevitable transition from growth to equilibrium.[18] Even though most of our problems have theoretically straightforward solutions, it will be extremely difficult to put these solutions into effect. As Buckminster Fuller, the physicist John Platt, and numerous other diagnosticians of our many ills have said, our only choice now lies between utopia and oblivion; and the erection of Leviathan appears to be the first indispensable step toward the establishment of that minimum degree of utopia which will preserve the peace and guarantee human posterity.

At first glance, the necessity for Leviathan may seem shocking, but it is not the environmental crisis alone which pushes us in this direction.

Spengler has noted the Hobbesian implications of the "revolution of rising expectations,"[19] and Leon Kass, in the article reprinted in the first part of this book, explores the challenge to our accustomed political views posed by the "new biology."[20] Also, ever since Hiroshima, analysts have agreed that the only certain solution to the problem of nuclear war is a world government capable of coercing individual nation-states. Despite this, we do not yet have a world government. Not only are the practical difficulties enormous given the strong ideological commitment to the nation-state, but also heads of individual states have calculated, rightly or wrongly, that the disadvantages of yielding up sovereignty outweigh the relatively small risk of nuclear annihilation. We have assumed that the hair suspending the nuclear Sword of Damocles above our heads may continue to hold, and we put the danger out of awareness and try to go about our daily business as if it did not exist. The threat of environmental breakdown is of an entirely different character. The Sword has broken free and we cannot avoid being struck. The only question is how best to parry the blow. Thus, we will not be able to avoid thinking about it. The pressure will increase constantly, and we shall sooner or later be forced to choose Leviathan over oblivion. Because of the tragedy of the commons, environmental problems cannot be solved by cooperation between individual sovereign states in a world of scarcity, and the rationale for world government with major coercive powers is overwhelming, raising the most fundamental of all political questions: Who should rule, and how?

THE TRAGIC PERSPECTIVE

Hobbes was the first philospher to make the individual rather than the group the basis of political theorizing, yet ironically he also showed that the free exercise of individual rights in practice produced tragedy—the tragedy of the commons or the war of all against all in the state of nature. Those who followed Hobbes exalted individualism and individual rights in reaction to the political and religious absolutism of the Middle Ages. Abnormal historical conditions which are not likely to be repeated allowed individual freedom to flourish. Now we have rediscovered that the logic of individualism creates conditions that require the reimposition of some kind of absolutism in order to avoid ruin. The effects on our society will be profound. Up to now, we in the United States have been able to escape the hard realities of classical politics. The commons was assumed to be large enough for all, and American politics could therefore be a more or less amicable discussion over the division of the growing spoils. We have never had to make the hard decision about who should get what out of a constant stock of scarce goods, and, just as importantly, why they should get it. Now we confront this kind of painful choice and find that we will be required to submit ourselves to a higher power as the means of solution. However much we may realize upon reflection that nothing in nature is without limit or free from the constraints imposed by natural design, our habit of mind is to equate freedom with liberty, and we find it hard to see how our real freedom could be greater once we gave up many things we now think of as rights.

Thinking about politics in such pessimistic terms is unpalatable, but it is clearly time to discredit the Enlightenment myth that all things are possible for the society of man. The commons is not infinite, and men must accept less than they want. In fact, they may have to accept very much less than they want at a time when worldwide expectations are rising. Thus, even more than a better understanding of the nature of politics, we need deeper insight into the human condition. As Hobbes phrased it, the "condition of man in this life shall never be without inconvenience." There may be, as the Greeks believed, a remorseless working of things beyond the power of man to control or avert. For the Greeks, what has been called the moral impotence of reason was the essence of tragedy: the protagonist knew the good but was unable to act on that knowledge. Hobbes himself was not optimistic that men would follow his advice. Nor are we assured that utopia—even in the most limited sense described above—is attainable. Without abandoning hope or ceasing to promote solutions to our problems, we might be advised to readopt the tragic perspective. Because even if we avoid the tragedy of the commons, it will only be by recourse to the tragic necessity of Leviathan.

NOTES AND REFERENCES

1. G. Hardin, "The Tragedy of the Commons," *Science*, vol. 162, p. 1243 (1968). Reprinted in this volume on pages 133–148. In Hardin's example, each herdsman will continue to add sheep to his fold, even when a finite common pasture land—a metaphor for the planetary life support system humanity shares in common—can no longer tolerate any additional grazing without damage, because he gets all the benefit from the additional sheep while damage to the

commons is parcelled out among all users. But, of course, every other herdsman adds sheep for the same reason, and competitive over-exploitation brings ruin to all.

2. B. L. Crowe, *Science*, vol. 166, p. 1103 (1969).
3. *Leviathan, or the Matter, Form and Power of a Commonwealth, ecclesiastical and civil* (London, 1651). The following summary of Hobbes's thought draws on chapters 11, 13–15, 17–21, 24, and 29–31. Many modern editions are available; the quotations are from that edited by H. W. Schneider, New York: Bobbs-Merrill, 1958.
4. W. P. Webb, *in* G. R. Taylor, ed., *The Turner Thesis*, Boston: Heath, 1956, p. 86. The long quote is from p. 94.
5. L. Hartz, *The Liberal Tradition in America*, New York: Harcourt, Brace, 1955.
6. Committee on Resources and Man, National Academy of Sciences–National Research Council, *Resources and Man*, San Francisco: W. H. Freeman and Co., 1969.
7. S. F. Singer, paper presented to symposium "Is There an Optimum Level of Population," 136th annual meeting of American Association for the Advancement of Science, Boston, December 29, 1969.
8. H. Brown, *The Challenge of Man's Future*, New York: Viking, 1954; C. Darwin, *The Problem of World Population*, New York: Cambridge Univ. Press, 1958; J. Platt, *Science*, vol. 149, p. 607 (1965); D. de S. Price, *Science Since Babylon*, New Haven: Yale University Press, 1961.
9. R. Dubos, *Science*, vol. 166, p. 823 (1969); H. E. Daly, *The New York Times*, October 14, 1970, p. 47; P. Medawar, *Encounter*, vol. 37, December 1970, p. 90; and G. T. Seaborg, *Saturday Review*, 6 March 1971, p. 53.
10. K. E. Boulding, *Public Interest*, vol. 5, p. 36 (1966).
11. L. D. Barnett, *BioScience*, vol. 21, p. 764 (1971). Because of our "young" population, *immediate* population stability can only be achieved if many couples elect not to replace themselves with two children. Otherwise, the American population will continue to grow well into the next century.
12. R. Gillette, *Science*, vol. 174, p. 1109 (1971).
13. L. White, *Science*, vol. 155, p. 1205 (1967).
14. Y.-F. Tuan, *American Scientist*, vol. 58, p. 244 (1970).
15. C. A. Reich, *The Greening of America*, New York: Random House, 1971.
16. B. F. Skinner, *Beyond Freedom and Dignity*, New York: Knopf, 1971. Some believe that the rapid development and application of these techniques provides us with the answer to the problem of conscience discussed above. In effect, behavioral conditioning will render the whole question of conscience moot. However, this provides no escape from the political dilemma, for who, if not some kind of sovereign (as is made explicit in Huxley's work), will decree the nature of the conditioning and control the techniques?
17. J. Platt, *Science*, vol. 166, p. 1115 (1969). See also J. W. Forrester, *World Dynamics*, Cambridge, Mass.: Wright-Allen, 1971, as well as reports of the follow-up work done under the auspices of the Club of Rome by Dennis L. Meadows and colleagues at MIT, reported in *The New York Times*, February 27, 1972.
18. Thanks to a high level symposium held to explain the findings of the Meadows group (and reported by *The New York Times*, March 3, 1972), this work has already had a measure of political impact.
19. J. J. Spengler, *South Atlantic Quarterly*, vol. 68, p. 443 (1969).
20. L. R. Kass, "The New Biology: What Price Relieving Man's Estate?" *Science*, vol. 174, p. 779 (1971). Reprinted in this volume on pages 90–113.

11

BUDDHIST ECONOMICS

E. F. Schumacher

'Right Livelihood' is one of the requirements of the Buddha's Noble Eightfold Path. It is clear, therefore, that there must be such a thing as Buddhist Economics.

Buddhist countries, at the same time, have often stated that they wish to remain faithful to their heritage. So Burma: "The New Burma sees no conflict between religious values and economic progress. Spiritual health and material well-being are not enemies: they are natural allies."[1] Or: "We can blend successfully the religious and spiritual values of our heritage with the benefits of modern technology."[2] Or: "We Burmans have a sacred duty to conform both our dreams and our acts to our faith. This we shall ever do."[3]

All the same, such countries invariably assume that they can model their economic development plans in accordance with modern economics, and they call upon modern economists from so-called advanced countries to advise them, to formulate the policies to be pursued, and to

1. References for this reading will be found on pages 238–239.

"Buddhist Economics." From *Resurgence*, Vol. 1, No. 11, January–February 1968. Reprinted by permission of the author and publisher.

construct the grand design for development, the Five-Year Plan or whatever it may be called. No one seems to think that a Buddhist way of life would call for Buddhist economics, just as the modern materialist way of life has brought forth modern economics.

Economists themselves, like most specialists, normally suffer from a kind of metaphysical blindness, assuming that theirs is a science of absolute and invariable truths, without any presuppositions. Some go as far as to claim that economic laws are as free from "metaphysics" or "values" as the law of gravitation. We need not, however, get involved in arguments of methodology. Instead, let us take some fundamentals and see what they look like when viewed by a modern economist and a Buddhist economist.

There is universal agreement that the fundamental source of wealth is human labour. Now, the modern economist has been brought up to consider labour or work as little more than a necessary evil. From the point of view of the employer, it is in any case simply an item of cost, to be reduced to a minimum if it cannot be eliminated altogether, say, by automation. From the point of view of the workman, it is a "disutility": to work is to make a sacrifice of one's leisure and comfort, and wages are a kind of compensation for the sacrifice. Hence the ideal from the point of view of the employer is to have output without employees, and the ideal from the point of view of the employee is to have income without employment.

The consequences of these attitudes both in theory and in practice are, of course, extremely far-reaching. If the ideal with regard to work is to get rid of it, every method that "reduces the work load" is a good thing. The most potent method, short of automation, is the so-called division of labor and the classical example is the pin factory eulogized in Adam Smith's *Wealth of Nations*. Here it is not a matter of ordinary specialization, which mankind has practised from time immemorial, but of dividing up every complete process of production into minute parts, so that the final product can be produced at great speed without anyone having had to contribute more than a totally insignificant and, in most cases, unskilled movement of his limbs.

WORK

The Buddhist point of view takes the function of work to be at least threefold: to give a man a chance to utilize and develop his faculties; to enable him to overcome his ego-centredness by joining with other people in a common task; and to bring forth the goods and services needed for a becoming existence. Again, the consequences that flow from this view are endless. To organize work in such a manner that it becomes meaningless, boring, stultifying, or nerve-racking for the worker would be little short of criminal; it would indicate a greater concern with goods than with people, an evil lack of compassion and a soul-destroying degree of attachment to the most primitive side of this worldly existence. Equally, to strive for leisure as an alternative to work would be considered a complete misunderstanding of one of the basic truths of human existence, namely, that work and leisure are complementary parts of the same living process and cannot be separated without destroying the joy of work and the bliss of leisure.

From the Buddhist point of view, there are therefore two types of mechanization which must be clearly distinguished: one that enhances a man's skill and power and one that turns the work of man over to a mechanical slave, leaving man in a position of having to serve the slave. How to tell the one from the other? "The craftsman himself," says Ananda Coomaraswamy, a man equally competent to talk about the Modern West as the Ancient East, "the craftsman himself can always, if allowed to, draw the delicate distinction between the machine and the tool. The carpet loom is a tool, a contrivance for holding warp threads at a stretch for the pile to be woven round them by the craftsman's fingers; but the power loom is a machine, and its significance as a destroyer of culture lies in the fact that it does the essentially human part of the work."[4] It is clear, therefore, that Buddhist economics must be very different from the economics of modern materialism, since the Buddhist sees the essence of civilization not in a multiplication of wants but in the purification of human character. Character, at the same time, is formed primarily by a man's work. And work, properly conducted in conditions of human dignity and freedom, blesses those who do it and equally their products. The Indian philosopher and economist J. C. Kumarappa sums the matter up as follows:

> If the nature of the work is properly appreciated and applied, it will stand in the same relation to the higher faculties as food is to the physical body. It nourishes and enlivens the higher man and urges him to produce the best he is capable of. It directs his freewill along the proper course and disciplines the animal in him into progressive channels. It furnishes an excellent background for man to display his scale of values and develop his personality.[5]

If a man has no chance of obtaining work he is in a desperate position, not simply because he lacks an income but because he lacks this nourishing and enlivening factor of disciplined work which nothing can replace. A modern economist may engage in highly sophisticated calculations on whether full employment "pays" or whether it might be more "economic" to run an economy at less than full employment so as to ensure a greater mobility of labour, a better stability of wages, and so forth. His fundamental criterion of success is simply the total quantity of goods produced during a given period of time. "If the marginal urgency of goods is low," says Professor Galbraith in *The Affluent Society*, "then so is the urgency of employing the last man or the last million men in the labor force." And again: "If . . . we can afford some unemployment in the interest of stability—a proposition, incidentally, of impeccably conservative antecedents—then we can afford to give those who are unemployed the goods that enable them to sustain their accustomed standard of living."[6]

From a Buddhist point of view, this is standing the truth on its head by considering goods as more important than people and consumption as more important than creative activity. It means shifting the emphasis from the worker to the product of work, that is, from the human to the subhuman, a surrender to the forces of evil. The very start of Buddhist economic planning would be a planning for full employment, and the primary purpose of this would in fact be employment for everyone who needs an "outside" job: it would not be the maximization of employment nor the maximization of production. Women, on the whole, do not need an outside job, and the large-scale employment of women in offices or factories would be considered a sign of serious economic failure. In particular, to let mothers of young children work in factories while the children run wild would be as uneconomic in the eyes of a Buddhist economist as the employment of a skilled worker as a soldier in the eyes of a modern economist.

While the materialist is mainly interested in goods, the Buddhist is mainly interested in liberation. But Buddhism is 'The Middle Way' and therefore in no way antagonistic to physical well-being. It is not wealth that stands in the way of liberation but the attachment to wealth; not the enjoyment of pleasurable things but the craving for them. The keynote of Buddhist economics, therefore, is simplicity and nonviolence. From an economist's point of view, the marvel of the Buddhist way of life is the utter rationality of its pattern—amazingly small means leading to extraordinarily satisfactory results.

THE STANDARD OF LIVING

For the modern economist this is very difficult to understand. He is used to measuring the standard of living by the amount of annual consumption, assuming all the time that a man who consumes more is "better off" than a man who consumes less. A Buddhist economist would consider this approach excessively irrational: since consumption is merely a means to human well-being, the aim should be to obtain the maximum of well-being with the minimum of consumption. Thus, if the purpose of clothing is a certain amount of temperature comfort and an attractive appearance, the task is to attain this purpose with the smallest possible effort, that is, with the smallest annual destruction of cloth and with the help of designs that involve the smallest possible input of toil. The less toil there is, the more time and strength is left for artistic creativity. It would be highly uneconomic, for instance, to go in for complicated tailoring, like the modern West, when a much more beautiful effect can be achieved by the skillful draping of uncut material. It would be the height of folly to make material so that it should wear out quickly and the height of barbarity to make anything ugly, shabby or mean. What has just been said about clothing applies equally to all other human requirements. The ownership and the consumption of goods is a means to an end, and Buddhist economics is the systematic study of how to attain given ends with the minimum means.

Modern economics, on the other hand, considers consumption to be the sole end and purpose of all economic activity, taking the factors of production—land, labour, and capital—as the means. The former, in short, tries to maximize human satisfactions by the optimal pattern of consumption, while the latter tries to maximize consumption by the optimal pattern of productive effort. It is easy to see that the effort needed to sustain a way of life which seeks to attain the optimal pattern of consumption is likely to be much smaller than the effort needed to sustain a drive for maximum consumption. We need not be surprised, therefore, that the pressure and strain of living is very much less in, say, Burma than it is in the United States, in spite of the fact that the amount of labour-saving machinery used in the former country is only a minute fraction of the amount used in the latter.

THE PATTERN OF CONSUMPTION

Simplicity and nonviolence are obviously closely related. The optimal pattern of consumption, producing a high degree of human satisfaction by means of a relatively low rate of consumption, allows people to live without great pressure and strain and to fulfill the primary injunction of Buddhist teaching: "Cease to do evil; try to do good." As physical resources are everywhere limited, people satisfying their needs by means of a modest use of resources are obviously less likely to be at each other's throats than people depending upon a high rate of use. Equally, people who live in highly self-sufficient local communities are less likely to get involved in large-scale violence than people whose existence depends on worldwide systems of trade.

From the point of view of Buddhist economics, therefore, production from local resources for local needs is the most rational way of economic life, while dependence on imports from afar and the consequent need to produce for export to unknown and distant peoples is highly uneconomic and justifiable only in exceptional cases and on a small scale. Just as the modern economist would admit that a high rate of consumption of transport services between a man's home and his place of work signifies a misfortune and not a high standard of life, so the Buddhist economist would hold that to satisfy human wants from far-away sources rather than from sources nearby signifies failure rather than success. The former might take statistics showing an increase in the number of ton/miles per head of the population carried by a country's transport system as proof of economic progress, while to the latter—the Buddhist economist—the same statistics would indicate a highly undesirable deterioration in the *pattern* of consumption.

NATURAL RESOURCES

Another striking difference between modern economics and Buddhist economics arises over the use of natural resources. Bertrand de Jouvenel, the eminent French political philospher, has characterized "Western man" in words which may be taken as a fair description of the modern economist:

> He tends to count nothing as an expenditure, other than human effort; he does not seem to mind how much mineral matter he wastes and, far worse, how much living matter he destroys. He does not seem to realise at all that human life is a dependent part of an ecosystem of many different forms of life. As the world is ruled from towns where men are cut off from any form of life other than human, the feeling of belonging to an ecosystem is not revived. This results in a harsh and improvident treatment of things upon which we ultimately depend, such as water and trees.[7]

The teaching of the Buddha, on the other hand, enjoins a reverent and nonviolent attitude not only to all sentient beings but also, with great emphasis, to trees. Every follower of the Buddha ought to plant a tree every few years and look after it until it is safely established, and the Buddhist economist can demonstrate without difficulty that the universal observance of this rule would result in a high rate of genuine economic development independent of any foreign aid. Much of the economic decay of Southeast Asia (as of many other parts of the world) is undoubtedly due to a heedless and shameful neglect of trees.

Modern economics does not distinguish between renewable and nonrenewable materials, as its very method is to equalize and quantify everything by means of a money price. Thus, taking various alternative fuels, like coal, oil, wood or water power: the only difference between them recognized by modern economics is relative cost per equivalent unit. The cheapest is automatically the one to be preferred, as to do otherwise would be irrational and "uneconomic." From a Buddhist point of view, of course, this will not do; the essential difference between nonrenewable fuels like coal and oil on the one hand and renewable fuels like wood and waterpower on the other cannot be simply overlooked. Nonrenewable goods must be used only if they are indispensable, and then only with the greatest care and the most meticulous concern for conservation. To use them heedlessly or extravagantly is an act of violence, and while complete nonviolence may not be attainable on this earth, there is nonetheless an ineluctable duty on man to aim at the ideal of nonviolence in all he does.

Just as a modern European economist would not consider it a great economic achievement if all European art treasures were sold to America at attractive prices, so the Buddhist economist would insist that a population basing its economic life on nonrenewable fuels is living parasitically, on capital instead of income. Such a way of life could have no permanence and could therefore be justified only as a purely temporary expedient. As the world's resources of nonrenewable fuels—coal, oil and natural gas—are exceedingly unevenly distributed over the globe and undoubtedly limited in quantity, it is clear that their exploitation at an ever increasing rate is an act of violence against nature which must almost inevitably lead to violence between men.

THE MIDDLE WAY

This fact alone might give food for thought even to those people in Buddhist countries who care nothing for the religious and spiritual values of their heritage and ardently desire to embrace the materialism of modern economics at the fastest possible speed. Before they dismiss Buddhist economics as nothing better than a nostalgic dream, they might wish to consider whether the path of economic development outlined by modern economics is likely to lead them to places where they really want to be. Towards the end of his courageous book *The Challenge of Man's Future*, Professor Harrison Brown of the California Institute of Technology gives the following appraisal:

> Thus we see that, just as industrial society is fundamentally unstable and subject to reversion to agrarian existence, so within it the conditions which offer individual freedom are unstable in their ability to avoid the conditions which impose rigid organization and totalitarian control. Indeed, when we examine all of the foreseeable difficulties which threaten the survival of industrial civilization, it is difficult to see how the achievement of stability and the maintenance of individual liberty can be made compatible.[8]

Even if this were dismissed as a long-term view—and in the long term, as Keynes said, we are all dead—there is the immediate question of whether modernization, as currently practised without regard to religious and spiritual values, is actually producing agreeable results. As far as the masses are concerned, the results appear to be disastrous—a collapse of the rural economy, a rising tide of unemployment in town and country, and the growth of a city proletariat without nourishment for either body or soul.

It is in the light of both immediate experience and long-term prospects that the study of Buddhist economics could be recommended even to those who believe that economic growth is more important than any spiritual or religious values. For it is not a question of choosing between "modern growth" and "traditional stagnation." It is a question of finding the right path of development, 'The Middle Way' between materialist heedlessness and traditionalist immobility, in short, of finding 'Right Livelihood.'

That this can be done is not in doubt. But it requires much more than blind imitation of the materialist way of life of the so-called advanced countries.[9] It requires above all, the conscious and systematic development of a "Middle Way in technology," as I have called it.[10] A technology more productive and powerful than the decayed technology of the ancient East, but at the same time nonviolent and immensely cheaper and simpler than the labour-saving technology of the modern West.

REFERENCES

1. *Pyidawtha, The New Burma.* (Economic and Social Board, Government of the Union of Burma, 1954, p. 10.)
2. *Ibid.*, p. 8.
3. *Ibid.*, p. 128.

4. Ananda K. Coomaraswamy. *Art and Swadeshi.* (Ganesh and Co., Madras, p. 30.)
5. J. C. Kumarappa. *Economy of Permanence.* (Sarva-Seva-Sangh-Publication, Rajghat, Kashi, 4th ed., 1958, p. 117.)
6. J. K. Galbraith. *The Affluent Society.* (Penguin, 1962, pp. 272–273.)
7. Richard B. Gregg. *A Philosophy of Indian Economic Development.* (Navajivan Publishing House, Ahmedabad, 1958, pp. 140–141.)
8. Harrison Brown. *The Challenge of Man's Future.* (The Viking Press, New York, 1954, p. 255.)
9. E. F. Schumacher, "Rural Industries" in *India at Midpassage.* (Overseas Development Institute, London, 1964.)
10. E. F. Schumacher. "Industralisation through Intermediate Technology" in *Minerals and Industries.* Vol. 1, no. 4. (Calcutta, 1964.) Vijay Chebbi and George McRobie. *Dynamics of District Development.* (SIET Institute, Hyderabad, 1964.)

12

ECONOMIC GROWTH VERSUS EXISTENTIAL BALANCE

Walter A. Weisskopf

This paper is concerned with a reexamination of the concept of economic growth not as a short-run goal of economic policy but as a basic orientation and a mode of life.[1] Such reexamination may put in doubt some of the values which underlie our scientific, technological, and business activities and institutions. Such an inquiry will have to transgress the traditional limits of economic thought. It will require criticism of economic values from the point of view of psychology and philosophy. The main guidepost for this inquiry is the effect which economic concepts, values, and activities have on the individual and how they affect his existence. I would like to advance the hypothesis, for discussion among social scientists, that there is a conflict between the idea of continuous economic growth on the one hand and certain prerequisities of human existence on the other.

There is hardly any disagreement among economists, businessmen, and

1. References for this reading will be found on pages 250–251.

"Economic Growth versus Existential Balance." From *Ethics*, Vol. 75, No. 2, January 1965. University of Chicago Press. Reprinted by permission of the author and publisher.

politicians about the desirability of aggregate growth of the economy defined as an ever increasing national income or product. There are differences about the details of national-income-accounting and serious differences about the means of accomplishing economic growth. The desirability of overall growth for the individual and for society is hardly questioned. A Gross National Product (GNP) growing, if possible, at an increasing rate has become a dogma of economic reasoning and an object of economic worship. There is an obsessive preoccupation with the growth and the rate of growth of the GNP which one could call *GNP fetishism.* GNP figures, conjectural and tentative at best, are watched by businessmen and politicians alike. Their decline, or allegedly insufficient growth, is considered a national calamity. The comparison of growth rates of Eastern and Western nations has become a part of the cold war and a matter of international competition.

As far as economic thought is concerned, the present almost exclusive concern with growth is somewhat puzzling because economic thought has centered on two ideas: the idea of continuous economic expansion and growth on the one hand, and the idea of equilibrium on the other. Historically, the emphasis on growth preceded the concept of equilibrium. The classical school considered economic growth on the individual and social level as the goal of economic activity. Adam Smith stated that "every individual is continually exerting himself to find the most advantageous employment for whatever capital he can command."[2] His theory of harmony of interests is based on the assumption that, individually and socially, the striving for more and more production and wealth is a desirable activity. The individual is supposed to increase his own wealth and thereby also increase the national produce, thus promoting the common welfare.

The labor theory of value is also related to this emphasis on growth, expansion, and acquisition. According to this theory greater effort, measured in terms of labor time, is supposed to receive a higher reward.[3] That implies that an increase in labor, work, and output, that is, economic growth, is a desirable goal which should be rewarded. Thus, the classical ideal of welfare is identical with the concept of economic growth for the individual and for society.

This approach was modified in economic thought toward the third quarter of the nineteenth century when utility became the foundation of economic value. In marginalism and in neoclassical thought the concept of equilibrium became the focal idea. The individual is assumed to maximize utility by equalizing satisfactions at the margin. The economy was assumed to maximize aggregate satisfactions through optimum allocation of resources.[4] Both situations were and are interpreted as states of equilibrium.

These two concepts used in economic thought are more than theoretical constructs and models. They reflect basic existential propensities as well as the value attitudes of their times. The concept of growth reflects the value-attitude system of early capitalism before and during the Industrial Revolution. The terms "acquisitive society" (Tawney) or the "*civilisation de toujours plus*" (the civilization of more and more [Bertrand de Jouvenel])[5] characterize this attitude. Max Weber has called it the "spirit of capitalism" and described it as a value system which elevates the acquisition of riches pursued systematically through hard work, frugality, and thrift to the dignity of a way of life and of an ultimate goal.[6] In distinction from previous societies where the pursuit of wealth and hard work were considered as inferior activities and as a curse, left to slaves, women, and inferior social groups, industrial society made the acquisition of wealth morally acceptable and considered it as a moral obligation. Economic thought justified this attitude by assuming that acquisitiveness and the propensity to truck, barter, and exchange in order to increase one's wealth is a basic human propensity.[7] Here, a unique historical phenomenon, the acquisitive attitude, was interpreted as a universal human inclination. Thus it made acceptable an ideal which ran counter to the traditional Christian ethics.[8] For the individual, economic growth is identical with acquisition of wealth; but already in the *Wealth of Nations* the idea of harmony of interests brought about by the symbolic "invisible hand" tied together the pursuit of individual and social wealth. Thus the ideas of economic growth on the individual and on the social levels are conceptualizations of the ethics of acquisition. In present discussions this origin has been forgotten because growth and acquisition have become accepted values. Growth is discussed not from the ethical psychological but from the functional point of view. The pursuit of economic growth has been rationalized by arguments that it is necessary for full employment, for defense, for the increase in population, for the maintenance of the current economic institutions; whether it should be accepted as a basic economic value is hardly ever questioned.

This acquisitive attitude was appropriate in the early stages of capitalism where the main problem consisted in the expansion of productive capacity through increased production, saving, reinvestment, and capital accumulation in the financial and the real sense. The trend of the period before and during the Industrial Revolution was expansionary. Population increased and the demand for higher standards of living made an increase in economic capacity necessary. People in the West came to believe that they can enjoy ever increasing material benefits of labor and production in the here and now. This required, above all, capital accumulation and increasing productive capacity. Thus the desire for more and more wealth was mutually interdependent with the economic conditions and the psychological climate of early capitalism. Economic growth and expansion were the predominant aspirations; continuous acquisitive striving was the appropriate attitude. Under these conditions the question of equilibrium and the problem of the balance of higher and lower needs did not arise as yet.

However, this question arose in the last quarter of the nineteenth century and was reflected in the doctrines of the marginalists and of the neoclassical schools. The idea of declining marginal utility presupposes that need satisfaction can reach a point of satiation and saturation, that people can have enough and even too much of a good thing (negative marginal utility). This idea arose and became the center of economic thought at a time when productive capacity had become relatively ample in Western economies and when the basic problem of the economy changed from one of expansion of productive capacity and increase in production to one of selling and distribution and thus to the psychology of the consumer. Consumers' wants and satisfaction became important; therefore Marshall first among authors of *Principles of Economics* included in his work a part on "Wants and Their Satisfaction," using the concept of equilibrium. There are two kinds of equilibrium in Marshall's system: one based on the natural sciences, especially on mechanics and physiology, and another one based on ethical insight and psychological principles. These two approaches are more than the subjective ideas of Marshall; they reflect conflicting but basic trends of the times and of industrial society.

Marshall's idea of equilibrium, as applied to the consumer, contains elements borrowed from physics. He thinks about equilibrium as "balancing opposing forces . . ." and compares it to "the mechanical equilibrium of a stone hanging by an elastic string, or to a number of balls resting against one another in a basin."[9] The emphasis shifts to biological and psychological factors when Marshall talks about the "boy who picks blackberries for his own eating. . . . Equilibrium is reached when at last his eagerness to play and his disinclination for the work of picking counterbalances the desire for eating."[10] Here physiological and psychological forces lead to an equilibrium situation. This analysis is based on the idea of declining marginal utility, which also implies physiological and psychological satiation.

This equilibrium of the consumer and the worker is a physiological one and, as such, is a temporary stage of saturation. It is modeled according to the pattern of physiological needs and their satisfaction. There is the "pain" of tension which is relieved by the "pleasure" of need satisfaction. There is a general trend in economics as well as in psychology to interpret all needs according to this pattern. "The needs that are taken as the starting point for motivation theory are the so-called physiological drives."[11] The physiological needs are appetites caused by an actual physical need or lack in the body; the drives "aim" at procuring what is lacking and thereby move toward a state of saturation, equilibrium, and homeostasis.[12] Such states of equilibrium are temporary; tension arises again and again in the life of the individual organism to be eliminated by need satisfaction leading to homeostatic equilibrium.

Economic growth and acquisition can lead only to such a temporary, homeostatic equilibrium. No lasting satisfaction or equilibrium can be reached on the physiological level. The "pleasure" of such need satisfaction presupposes a state of tension which is relieved by satisfaction. Without the emergence of tension no pleasure can be received from physiological need satisfaction. Without hunger the intake of food is not pleasurable.

This statement is so trite that one hestiates to make it. However, this obvious truth is overlooked when it comes to an evaluation of economic acquisition and growth. The principle of declining marginal utility applies not only to specific kinds of needs and their satisfaction but also the entire field of acquisition of goods and services which are produced by our economy. The industrial economy has immensely enlarged the field of need satisfaction and raised the standards of living to a peak never reached before. We have come such a long way that many social scientists and philosophers talk about an imminent state of affairs in which men will be freed of economic necessity altogether.[13] They predict that, in the foreseeable future, man in the advanced industrial economy may be able to take the "leap from the realm of necessity into the realm of freedom." However that may be, even at the present time the advanced Western economies have reached a level of production which has reduced immensely the marginal utility of additional goods and services. This is not a situation of which people are conscious. The ideology of "more and more" is still so strong that people are not aware of the fact that they are forced into more work and more acquisition by the socioeconomic system rather than by their free inclination.[14] However, the intensive advertising and the pervasive fact of artificial obsolescence are clear and present symptoms of this unconscious situation. Artificial obsolescence is the man-made correlate to physiological needs. *Nolens volens*, people get hungry several times a day. Planned obsolesence replaced the emergence of physiological tension where no automatic tension arises. What firms and advertisers are doing is to create a hunger where nature has not provided for it. By changing styles of such articles as cars and clothes and by exploiting the desire for conformity and for avoidance of being different from the "other," they "force" people to develop a "need" for change. The same purpose is accomplished by the continuous development of new products. Once the new product is marketed, the pressure of conformity creates a need for it.

Therefore, a relatively permanent balance and equilibrium is impossible as long as all needs are experienced and interpreted as physiological ones. On this level pleasure requires preceding pain and tension. In order to have pleasure, pain and tension have to be artificially created. This was age-old wisdom of mankind until Western civilization buried it under its empirical, naturalistic approach. That sensual satisfaction requires ever more excitation, titillation, tension, and pain was known not only to the Hindus and Buddhists but also the Greek philosophers. It was of course known to Christian thought from the fathers of the church to the Middle Ages. Only modern civilization has elevated physiological satisfaction to the dignity of an ultimate goal. Economic growth as an individual and social ideal is a reflection of this attitude which has pulled modern man into a vortex of continuous change and expansion without peace and without end.

In modern Western civilization the center of life has moved toward the control and manipulation of nature and of the external world for the purpose of physiological need satisfaction. The entire scale of values inherited from Greek and Roman antiquity and from the Hebrew-Christian tradition has been reversed. Hannah Arendt has traced this development from the time of the Greek polis to the present day.[15] In modern society the hierarchy of values of the Greek polis—political action as the highest pursuit of the free citizen, with laboring for necessities as the lowest occupation done by slaves and women—was reversed. Laboring for the necessities of life became the most important goal of individuals and societies. The present emphasis on economic growth as the goal is the end product of this development; it implies that the procurement of the means of need satisfaction is the highest and ultimate concern.

This overemphasis on the economic dimension of existence was accompanied by the disintegration of faith in the reality and existence of ideas and ideals which are considered derivatives of socioeconomic conditions not only by Marx but also in most Western social thought. The economic dimension was equated with the biological one; life in its biological and economic sense became its own source of meaning because there was no belief in a realm of ideas and ideals as an objective reality apart from economic and biological life. The philosophy of life as formulated by Nietzsche, Bergson, and others reflects the situation of the individual in industrial civilization who strives for economic success and growth in order to affirm the power of his being. Heidegger calls this attitude nihilism because neither life nor economic activity equated with life can be its own source of meaning. A dimension of existence can receive its meaning only from another dimension that is experienced as a higher one. The dimension of ideas and ideals has been destroyed in industrial civilization and has become a derivative of the economic and the biological. Therefore, life and economic activity, including the striving for continuous economic growth, exposed industrial man to the despair of meaninglessness which is so prevalent in our time.

Implicitly, Marshall was aware of this situation. His concept of equilibrium is not only patterned after the model of physiological saturation, his *Principles* also contain the idea of a balance between lower and higher needs. The opening chapters of the *Principles* present the picture of an inner struggle. Marshall feels compelled to start his monumental work with a defense of economics against the frequent accusation that it is concerned merely with materialistic, selfish competition and neglects the higher goals in life.[16] In chapter I he emphasizes the influence of business activity on character formation. He rejects competition as the main characteristic of industrial life. His own ideal is "a certain independence and habit of choosing one's own course for oneself, a self-reliance; a deliberation and yet promptness of choice and judgment, and a habit of forecasting the future and of shaping one's course with reference to distant aims. . . . It is deliberateness, not selfishness, which is the characteristic of the modern age."[17] Deliberate rational conduct combined with independence and self-reliance is Marshall's ideal. One could call it the ideal of rational freedom. He proposes to use the term "economic freedom" for the combination of self-reliant habits, forethought, and deliberate and free choice, which he considers characteristic of modern business and industry.[18] The acquisition of wealth is, for him, an instrument of character formation. He is against poverty not because it causes suffering but because it is degrading. Competition is necessary not because of its utilitarian function for more acquisition but because "it is essential to the maintenance of energy and spontaneity," and he maintains that "constructive competition is less beneficent than ideal altruistic cooperation." What he is really interested in is "to understand the influences exerted on the quality and tone of man's life by the manner in which he earns his livelihood and by the character of this livelihood."[19]

Basically, Marshall is a moralist, and it was "only through ethics that he first reached economics."[20] In the second chapter of his *Principles* Marshall emphasizes that the use of money as a measurement of action does not mean that only materialistic selfish motives are relevant and that the "various affections belonging to man's higher nature" are excluded. He wants "to know whether the desires which prevail are such as will help to build up a strong and righteous character."[21] He repeatedly rejects the idea that "money . . . or command over material wealth is the centre around which economic science clusters," and he approves "of the splendid teachings of Carlyle and Ruskin as to the right aims of human endeavour and the right uses of wealth." He stresses as important qualities in business conduct, honesty, faith, the absence of meanness, pride in acquitting oneself well, the exercise of men's faculties, the desire to earn approval and to avoid the contempt of those around one, family affections, etc.[22]

In all his discussion of individual conduct Marshall implies a balance and an equilibrium of opposite forces, not merely as a theoretical construct but as ethical maxims in line with the Protestant ethic combined with Victorian prudence. His logico-mathematical treatment of wants and demand is interspersed with many wise remarks on how an intelligent person should allocate his time, energy, and income. The housewife who equalizes at the margin when allocating wool for vests and socks and the young married couple whom he admonishes not to spend impulsively a great deal of money on furniture and to "subordinate the desire for transient luxury to the attainment of solid and lasting resources" are examples of wisdom applied to real life situations.[23] These and other similar passages containing Victorian moral casuistry are based on the ideas of balance and equilibrium.

All this leads to the conclusion that Marshallian thought reflects an ideal quite different from the one of indiscriminate continuous economic growth in whatever direction. Marshall's ideal is a combination of free deliberate action with forethought and life-planning directed at the establishment of an equilibrium or balance based on wisdom and insight into the moral essence of human existence.

All this is quite in line with some findings of modern psychology. A. H. Maslow[24] suggested that there is a hierarchy of needs. Proceeding from the lower and progressing to the higher needs he classifies them as follows: physiological needs, such as hunger; safety needs, such as the need for physical *and mental* security, including the need for a comprehensive "philosophy that organizes the universe and the men in it into a sort of satisfactorily coherent meaningful whole"; the needs for belongingness and love; the need for esteem; and the need for self-actualization. What matters is not whether this classification is correct and exhaustive, but that there is a hierarchy of needs. "It is quite true that man lives by bread alone—when there is no bread. But what happens to man's desires when there *is* plenty of bread and when his belly is chronically filled? At once, other (and higher) needs emerge." Various needs related to different dimensions of existence have to be brought into balance although certain physiological and quasi-physiological needs are prevalent if they are not satisfied. "Basic human needs are organized into a hierarchy of relative prepotency."[25] Consequently, *need satisfaction which continuously increases the supply of means along one level and neglects needs on a different level is contrary to human well-being.* What is required is a *balanced system of need satisfaction* on various levels.

Marshall's ethical ideals and the psychological analysis of the hierarchy of needs suggest the concept of a *balance of existence* in the widest sense of the word. Such a balance requires an equilibrium of forces which are opposed to each other and form an antimony in such a way that they are merely the opposite sides of the same entity, like the two poles of the earth. This situation is present in Marshall's distinction between higher and lower needs; they are both different aspects of the entity man. If one branch of this antimony is neglected and another one is overemphasized, human existence is disequilibrated. This, then, is the consequence of the one-sided emphasis on economic growth because it neglects entirely the existential necessity for such an equilibrium. It over-emphasizes some dimensions of human existence and completely neglects others.

The dimensions that are neglected in industrial society are those which transcend the dimension of physiological and creature comforts because all goals of life are reduced to a quasi-physiological level. Neglected are thus all the "higher needs" in Maslow's terms, the needs for mental safety in the form of a unifying world philosophy, the needs for love and belongingness, the need for self-actualization in work. In Hannah Arendt's hierarchy of values the neglected dimensions are the field of creative work where a durable whole is created that forms a part of our stable environment; the opportunity for meaningful political action by individuals; and the dimension of contemplation in the broadest sense: where man opens his mind and soul receptively to truth, beauty, justice, and the good (the Platonic *agathon*).

Our overemphasis on economic growth and on acquisition leads to a disturbance of the balance of our existence. Too much time and energy used for the procurement of goods and services for the market must, by necessity, lead to a neglect of all those faculties and modes of life for which not enough time and energy is left. Our excessively economic orientation develops only those faculties which are necessary for economic growth. We are sacrificing those alternative faculties and attitudes which cannot contribute to an increase in wealth. Too much economic growth tends to destroy the balance between activistic effort and receptivity, doing and being, grasping and receiving, between conscious intentional effort and passive inner experience, between intellect and feeling. This destructive effect is wrought by excessive individual striving for acquisition as well as by the exclusive emphasis on national economic growth. Unless an increase in the national income is counterbalanced by some gains in these neglected dimensions, such an increase may actually cause a decline in human wellbeing.

Economists usually assume that wants are unlimited and that, therefore, there is no upper limit to consumption. This assumption runs counter to the wisdom of all ages before the Industrial Revolution. In antiquity and in the Middle Ages the expansion of needs was considered as unhealthy and bad. The principle of balance requires the conception of an optimal supply of goods and services. This idea seems to have been abandoned today. Introspection and observation indicates that people may be surfeited with goods. Man's limited time and energy may be inadequate to adjust to an ever increasing amount and variety of goods. Less than fifty years ago a person could reach the economic goals of his life when he married, bought and furnished a house, educated his children, and accumulated some savings for his old age. Today he is lured further and further from rest and satisfaction by more and more new goods and gadgets; they keep him tied to the leash of work and acquisition until he is buried without ever having reached a moment of peace where he could look back on his work and say: It is good. If ours is an "achieving society" it must give to people at least once in a while the feeling of having achieved their goal. An economy bent on continuous individual and social growth and expansion makes the experience of achieving a goal difficult, if not impossible, and leads to an unbalanced existence. The neuroses of the "status seekers" and of the "pyramid climbers" are symptoms of this disequilibrium. People may get tired of a way of life which prevents them from ever reaching an economic goal. In order to restore a balance they may refuse to absorb additional wealth and turn to other pursuits. The "Buddenbrook dynamics" and the "drive beyond consumption" which W. W. Rostow predicted may already have appeared on the horizon.

The necessity of such a balance between the satisfaction of needs on various levels also requires a certain degree of stability and security of life; this is what Maslow means when he talks about the safety needs. The modern economy does not provide for these needs. It has been compared to a gale of creative destruction. An increasingly faster rate of change is a characteristic of our present economy. Although much attention is paid to the difficulties of adjustment to a fast-changing economy, there is hardly any discussion of an optimal rate of change.[26] Is there a limit beyond which economic change, even if desirable in terms of more output, becomes intolerable for individuals and detrimental to their well-being? It is, of course, difficult to give an answer to this question in quantitative terms; but it should be established that change is not always a gain but can inflict discomfort and suffering.

Modern society and modern economy are pervaded by a general tendency to change everything that is stable, secure, and traditional, not only in the fields of consumption and habitat but also in the field of ideas and cultural pursuits. We are changing our ideas and ideals and our modes of thought as we do our cars, clothes, and roads. Thus, in our own lifetime, traditional education was replaced by progressive education only to be replaced today again by more rigorous methods. The nature of academic disciplines changes several times during the life of an academician. Tastes in art, dance, and music change from year to year; and so do the philosophical systems which take hold of the minds of the people. These developments in the fields of ideas and cultural pursuits are reflections of what happens in the economy. Philosophical and psychological insight leads to the conclusion that there can be too much change and too fast a rate of change. An existential balance requires more of an equilibrium between change and stability than modern economy and modern society provide.

In order to remedy this situation we will have to reexamine our basic value attitudes. Economists will have to abandon their purely short-run thinking about economic policies and will have to become aware of the unconscious value assumptions which underlie their reasoning. Blind GNP fetishism will have to be discarded in favor of more balanced goals of long-run economic and social policies that should lead to a more balanced way of life.

REFERENCES

1. This paper was first read at the annual meeting of the Midwest Economic Association, Chicago, April 17, 1964.

2. Adam Smith, *Wealth of Nations* (New York: Modern Library edition, 1937), p. 421.
3. W. A. Weisskopf, *The Psychology of Economics* (Chicago and London, 1955), pp. 22 ff.
4. Hla Myint, *Theories of Welfare Economics* (Cambridge, Mass., 1948), p. 89.
5. Bertrand de Jouvenel, "Organisation du travail et l'aménagement de l'existence," *Free University Quarterly*, VII (August, 1959), pp. 6 ff.
6. Max Weber, *The Protestant Ethic and the Spirit of Capitalism* (New York, 1958).

7. Smith, *op. cit.*, p. 13.
8. Weisskopf, *op. cit.*, p. 14.
9. Alfred Marshall, *Principles of Economics* (8th ed.; London), p. 323.
10. *Ibid.*, p. 331.
11. A. H. Maslow, *Motivation and Personality* (New York, 1954), p. 80.
12. *Ibid.*, pp. 80 ff., 123 ff.
13. J. K. Galbraith, *The Affluent Society* (Boston, 1958); R. Theobald, *Free Men and Free Markets* (New York, 1963); H. Marcuse, *Eros and Civilization* (Boston, 1955); D. N. Michael, "Cybernation: The Silent Conquest" (Santa Barbara, Calif.: Center for the Study of Democratic Institutions, 1962).
14. H. Marcuse, *One-Dimensional Man* (Boston, 1964).
15. H. Arendt, *The Human Condition* (Chicago, 1958).
16. Marshall, *op. cit.*, chap. I; Weisskopf, *op. cit.*, pp. 163 ff.
17. Marshall, *op. cit.*, chap. I.
18. Marshall, *op. cit.*, p. 10; Weisskopf, *op. cit.*, pp. 164 ff.
19. Marshall, *op. cit.*, pp. 8, 9, 13.
20. J. M. Keynes, in *Essays in Biography*, pp. 150 ff.
21. Marshall, *op. cit.*, p. 17.
22. *Ibid.*, pp. 23, 24.
23. *Ibid.*, pp. 66, 117, 119.
24. *Ibid.*, pp. 80, 83, 88.
25. Maslow, *op. cit.*, p. 83.
26. G. Vickers, *The Undirected Society* (Toronto, 1959), pp. 73, 114.

13

ELECTRIC POWER, EMPLOYMENT, AND ECONOMIC GROWTH: A CASE STUDY IN GROWTHMANIA

Herman E. Daly

Every living thing is a sort of imperialist, seeking to transform as much as possible of the environment into itself and its seed.
Bertrand Russell

INTRODUCTION

The salient fact about electric power production is that it is growing at seven percent annually, doubling every ten years. Even ardent supporters of energy growth recognize the absurdity of projecting such a rate very far into the future, lest the entire environment be transformed into electric power and electric power generators. For example, John W. Simpson, president of Westinghouse Power Systems Company, says:

> At some point in time, well before plants crowd us into the ocean or we change the climate of the earth through the rejection of heat into the atmos-

"Electric Power, Employment, and Economic Growth: A Case Study in Growthmania." Presented at the 1971 AAAS Convention "Symposium on the Energy Crisis," and previously published in the Congressional Record, February 8, 1972, at the request of Senator Hart.

> phere, we will reach an energy plateau, a level at which our technology will have placed us through the super-efficient utilization of power. In other words we will have learned to do so much more with so much less power that more power plants as we know them today probably would be superfluous.[1]

How many more years before we reach this "energy plateau"? Simpson says only that "well before that hypothetical 200 years from now, we will have seen a leveling off in the rate of increase of power consumption."[2] A "leveling off in the rate of increase" within 200 years? Presumably this means a zero rate of increase rather than some constant positive rate. But he leaves a date for the achievement of the important concept of an energy plateau vague, arguing that for the "forseeable future" (thirty to fifty years?) more power plants as we now know them will be necessary. Congressman Chet Holifield, of the Joint Committee on Atomic Energy, puts a minimum figure of thirty years on the forseeable future in stating that ". . . the doubling factor every decade for the next thirty years is basic to our standard of living, now and in the future."[3] According to this point of view, one can make the loose inference that at the minimum, eight times our present electric power output might be enough—then we can begin to talk seriously about an energy plateau, not before. But certainly we could not abruptly decelerate from seven percent to zero growth immediately at the end of thirty years. Indeed, it would most probably be necessary to double electric power output at least once more over a longer period in order to overcome the inertia of growth without shaking up the economy too badly. Thus the "energy plateau" appears to be at least sixteen times the present output! Furthermore we are to grow as rapidly as we can (at least at seven percent) for the next thirty years, which is to say, for the next generation, or sufficiently far into the future not to affect the capitalized market values of electric utility "growth" stocks. After us, the energy plateau—or is it perhaps, after us, the deluge?

For the regulated electric utilities, growth and profitability are closely related. The regulated "fair rate of return on capital" has been interpreted by the courts to be based on three criteria. The rate of return must be (1) commensurate with returns on investments in other enterprises having commensurate risks, (2) sufficient to insure the financial integrity of the enterprise, (3) able to maintain the credit of the enterprise and attract capital. For those of us who study growth the criterion most relevant is the last. In order to attract the capital needed to finance the rapid expansion of capacity, the rate of return must be *higher* than in other investments of equal risk. The need for rapid growth, if established to the satisfaction of regulatory agencies, leads to requests for a higher allowable rate of return, and it is notable that higher rates have already been

1. Notes for this reading will be found on pages, 276–277.

granted to some utilities and that many petitions for other rate increases are now pending. Furthermore, even if the regulated rate of return is held constant, the utilities have abundant incentive to expand productive capacity in order to increase the base to which the regulated rate is applied, and thus to increase total profits. If the rate of return must be raised to attract capital, so much the better. But in order to expand and to raise the rate, utilities must convince the regulatory commission of the need for expansion. To do this, the utilities must be able to point to a "shortage," which they can by showing that demand is increasing faster than supply. To increase demand it is necessary to advertise and to give lower rates for use in large quantities. Perhaps this explains the curious fact that the electric utilities, a public monopoly, spend eight dollars on advertising for every one dollar spent on research and development.[4] Another incentive to growth beyond the optimum is that a large part of the cost of increased electric power is the social cost of environmental deterioration, which is paid by society in general, rather than by the parties directly responsible for the costs. Although one is not accustomed to thinking of electric utilities as a "growth stock," Standard and Poor now inform the investor that "electric power is not only the backbone of the American economy [!], it is also a vigorous growth industry."[5]

Electric power is now used to illuminate advertising signs during daylight hours, to run electric toothbrushes, and to convey shoppers through parking lots on movable sidewalks. With so many trivial uses of electricity in present vogue, one wonders just what we will possibly do with twice as much electricity in 1980, four times as much in 1990, etc. It is not my intention to belittle the tremendous importance of electrical energy or of production in general. The French economist de Jouvenel has put the issue very well:

> But if I do not at all object to the much enhanced status of production, I may point out that production has come to embrace so much that it would be foolish to grant any and every productive activity the moral benefit of an earnestness not to be found in so-called "nonproductive activities." When popular newspapers propose to bring out their comic strips in color, I find it hard to regard such "progress in production" as something more earnest than planting flowering shrubs along the highways. I am quite willing to regard poetry as a frivolous occupation as against the tilling of the soil but not as against the composing of advertisements.
>
> When organizers of production have to relieve a situation of hunger, efficiency is the one and only virtue. But when this virtue has been thoroughly developed and comes to be applied to less and less vital objects, the question surely arises of the right choice of objects.[6]

The importance of this declining intensity of needs for increased production to satisfy is recognized also by advocates of growth, but as an *obstacle to be overcome* in order to increase the flow of output and employment. For example, economist Joseph N. Froomkin explains:

> The big challenge to the U.S. and other Western economies is to bring out cheaply, through automation or otherwise, new products that will tempt the consumer's jaded tastes. These new products in turn will stimulate investment.[7]

Again, if the "big challenge" presently is to tempt the consumer's "jaded tastes," what are we going to do with sixteen times as much electricity? Population growth will absorb only a small and declining part of it. The big increase will be, and has been recently, in per capita consumption. Perhaps we must all learn to imitate President Nixon's idiosyncracy of turning the air conditioner on full blast so that he can enjoy warming himself by the fireplace in midsummer![8] The President's idea is rather logical: central heating in the winter warms the White House too much to make a hearth fire—something man has loved from earliest times—enjoyable, but in the summer air conditioning chills the air too much, and thus makes it possible to enjoy a fire. Such self-cancelling uses are capable of absorbing great amounts of electric power, and perhaps of jading consumer's tastes to the very limit. But is such "production" more earnest than weeding a flower garden? The question of electric power for the poor—whose tastes have not had the opportunity to become jaded—is considered later.

What we've considered so far raises doubts that advocates of increased power growth take the impossibility of growing forever at seven percent seriously; perhaps they mention the notion of an "energy plateau" just in passing in order to fend off an easy *reductio ad absurdum* by opponents. At least they do not develop the concept. As one reads four main arguments most often used as reasons defending the growth position in the media and in congressional hearings, the doubts increase. The *Congressional Record* contains fuller statements of these arguments, which are summarized below.[9] Examining them critically, we find them to be grossly deficient both in their logic and premises.

The growth advocates state that we must have continued rapid growth in energy:

A. To increase the standard of living (level of consumption) of the present population and to extend that rising standard of living to some 70–100 million more Americans by the year 2000.

B. To clean up the pollution and recycle the waste which has resulted from past production and consumption, and which will accumulate with current and increased production and consumption.

C. To maintain an acceptable level of employment, because (1) labor is used directly in the production of electric power, and more importantly because (2) power indirectly affects employment, being an input in most production processes which also use labor and being necessary in order to operate many consumer goods produced through employment of people.

D. To produce the devices that give us the capacity for military defense and deterrence "upon which world peace depends."

Our attention will mainly be directed to reasons A and C, but it is important by way of introduction to realize that the four reasons are part of a whole point of view and are not independent of one another. The tacit, unifying point of view, the unarticulated preconception, is that of open ended growth, which, though sometimes obscured by refusing to project the growth of the energy sector beyond one generation, remains an implicit assumption of each of the four arguments for the "temporary" necessity of continued rapid growth. Reason A postulates the goal of an increasing level of consumption without reference to a "consumption plateau." Even the growth-oriented President's Council of Economic Advisers has told us that "growth of GNP has its costs, and beyond some point they are not worth paying."[10] Is some such point evident to those who cite reason A in defense of growth in energy production? No. Although many suspect that we in the United States may have already passed the critical point, defenses of the type illustrated by reason A fail to recognize even the existence of such a point.

Total output continues to grow and grow, and so does total waste and pollution. Reason B—that more energy is needed to clean up—is thus guaranteed by reason A, as well as by a backlog of accumulated pollution. Since matter and energy can be neither created nor destroyed but only transformed, the more we "consume," the more waste we must clean up. Thus the first round of matter-energy degradation (production) requires a second round to clean up after the first, and in turn the second round of matter-energy degradation requires a third round to clean up after it, etc. There are infinite rounds of clean-up uses of energy. Granted the residue of each round, like the dirt remaining after each sweep into the dust pan, probably diminishes rapidly, nevertheless there is something of a vicious circle in using resources to power industry, and then having to use more resources to produce the energy to power the industry called for to remove the soot or repair the effects of chemical corrosion brought about by the increased industrial production. What is ultimately scarce in the physical world is not energy but low entropy. The more energy we use, even for the purpose of cleaning up, the more rapidly we use up the stock of low entropy—i.e., the more rapidly we degrade the total environment. Thus, reason B derives from reason A and also reinforces reason A by falsely suggesting that cleaning up *cancels* the environmental cost of production growth. Cleaning up is *part* of the environmental cost of production, necessary but certainly not an activity to be pursued beyond some limits. At some point the degradation cost of energy needed for cleaning up will be greater than the cost of the pollution it cleans up.

Reason C argues for more energy in order to provide more employment. But the labor done by energy is a *substitute* for human labor as well as a complement to it. Given a total output, an increasing supply of nonhuman energy will surely be used to substitute for human labor (what else could it be used for?) and will result in higher productivity per worker, but *less* employment. The reduced hours of employment would probably result in the employment of fewer men, although it could result in the same number of men working fewer hours. But since power-growth advocates seldom mention reducing the hours worked per man, a plan that could increase the number of men employed independently of changes in the uses of energy, it is clear that reason C assumes that total output is growing faster than the rate at which energy is becoming a substitute for human labor. In other words we are back to reason A and unlimited growth in the total product.

Reason D says energy growth is needed for national defense or deterrence of enemies. But military deterrence has become a self-escalating process of open-ended growth, by which military strength remains balanced, but only if each side achieves the defensive might available to the other. Both sides grow continually in tandem, and reason D seems to have less pertinence to actual warfare than to the growthmania assumption of reason A, with which it meshes perfectly. The more the military depletes the civilian economy of resources and technical personnel, the lower will be growth of output per input that is the important measure of the productivity of the civilian economy. The slower the growth in civilian productivity the greater must be the growth in raw material and energy inputs to maintain a given rate of increase in total product. And so the depletion of the civilian economy by burgeoning military needs has reduced possibilities of the one kind of growth we all welcome, growth in productivity—less input per output. The "energy plateau" becomes much harder to attain.

The counter-arguments above leave the strong impression that merely to mention limits or plateaus in the growth of energy needs is nothing more than a digression, a debating parry, and that the paradigm underlying the four principal arguments advanced by advocates of growth in the energy utilities remains one of "growthmania." In addition to recognizing the absurdities of projecting high growth rates of electric power into the future, we must recognize the absurdity also of projecting high rates of growth of total output, now that we have taken the four arguments at their logical face value. To paraphrase Westinghouse's President Simpson, it seems that at some time in the future, well before power plants crowd us into the ocean, we will have already been driven into the ocean by our commodities, the pollution they have caused, and their corpses. Our economy, as Bertrand Russell describes "every living thing," is succeeding too well in its imperialist drive to "transform as much as possible of the environment into itself"—i.e. into commodities and people. The electric power industry has simply been more successful in doing what all other industries are striving to do—namely, to grow, and when possible, to avoid paying the full social cost of the increased production. This points to serious irrationalities at the overall systems level of our economy, some radical implications of which will be treated in the last section of this reading.

But now, further attention must be given, in the next section, to reason C—that increased energy production is necessary to maintain employment—since in a period of unemployment it is both particularly influential and particularly fallacious. The key argument, however, is A, open-ended growth in consumption. If A falls the other arguments fall with it, so it will merit our special attention in the last section.

ENERGY AND EMPLOYMENT

Bernard de Mandeville, in his "Fable of the Bees," argued in favor of the most extravagant luxury consumption by the upper class on the grounds that it provided employment for the poor. Frédéric Bastiat, in his "Petition of the Candlemakers . . ." proposed blocking sunlight from all houses and buildings in order to increase employment among candlemakers, who in turn, through their increased expenditures, would stimulate employment in whaling, match making, wick production—in effect, in all industries—to the immense benefit of all the classes of the realm. These two writers were of course telling tongue-in-cheek tales with the object of analogizing, through satire, proposals their contemporaries had made in sincere attempts at special pleading. Whether special pleading is at the heart of the employment rationale put forth by today's electric power interests I will leave for the reader to judge, presuming only to list a number of considerations that might be relevant in making such a judgment.

The Confusion, through Crude Empiricism, of Substitutes and Complements for Labor

Physical labor is, at the margin, a negative factor in the enjoyment of life and leisure is, at the margin, a positive factor. Thousands of years ago man domesticated animals to relieve his toil, substituting the labor of animals for that of humans as the source of energy for production. Later, man harnessed inanimate energy and made a further substitution of it for human labor, deriving leisure previously unavailable when human labor was needed for production. It might appear that historically such substitutions dominate the relation of human energy to nonhuman energy: the more of one, the less of the other—a negative correlation. Yet what we find is a positive correlation—throughout history the number of men employed has increased as use of nonhuman energy has increased—and one is therefore tempted to argue that more employment necessitates more use of inanimate energy. But expose this crude empiricism to simple rational analysis and it will not stand up. The increase of nonhuman energy along with human employment means instead that energy use and employment both correlate to some other factors that have been increasing historically, namely total output and total population. The positive indirect correlations via the growth of these other factors has outweighed the negative direct correlation of energy and employment. For constant output and population we know that the correlation between energy and employment is bound to be negative, for as we asked in the previous section, what conceivable use does nonhuman energy have other than as a substitute for human labor in producing the same or a smaller quantity of goods, or as a complement to human labor in producing a greater quantity of goods? If we rule out the second use we are left with the first. If we insist on more employment and more nonhuman energy we must also insist on more output. The real world uses nonhuman energy as both a substitute and a complement simultaneously. Only if total product growth creates more jobs for humans than are eliminated by the growth of nonhuman energy will employment increase. This is self evident.

Congressman Chet Holifield, a supporter of energy growth, came dangerously close to defeating the logic of his own argument recently while extolling the importance of energy:

> Our standard of living is the highest of any nation in the world because we use the highest ratio of mechanical power versus manpower. . . . One man can do the work of 350 men.[11]

This is a clear recognition of the overwhelming importance of increasing substitution as the major factor in increasing the standard of living. Furthermore, for one man to do the work of 350 men means that 349 men are doing something else. If they are employed doing something else, total product will increase. If total product does not increase they must remain unemployed. Clearly what is responsible for increasing total employment is the increase in total product, not the increase in inanimate power consumption which in fact, taken by itself, must *decrease* employment.

The Least Energy-Intensive Sector Accounts for Nearly All New Employment

As nonhuman energy replaced human energy in agriculture it was not possible to increase employment in this sector even with vast increases in total agricultural product. Instead, employment was provided by growth in a new sector, industry. As nonhuman energy now replaces men in industry, even with large increases in the total output of the industrial sector the major source of new employment has been another new sector, service, rather than industry. The total employment within the service sector has grown from approximately forty percent in 1929 to over fifty-five percent in 1967. Of the total net increment of fourteen million jobs between 1947 and 1965, the service sector accounted for an increase of thirteen million, industry accounted for an increase of four million, but agriculture accounted for a decrease of three million.[12] Services, using less energy than the other two sectors, have provided nearly the entire net increase in employment since 1947. Service institutions, such as banks, hospitals, retail stores, schools, insurance companies, and others, now provide the new employment, and they require energy for lighting, space heating and cooling, and office machines—needs perhaps no more energy intensive than are found, on a per capita basis, in the average household. The most energy-intensive sectors are also the most highly capitalized and automated sectors, and consequently do not provide significant increases in new employment. Thus, to allege that large increases in energy input are needed to provide new jobs seems to presuppose that the average new worker will work in a steel or aluminum plant, a counterfactual presupposition, inasmuch as it is likely he will work in a service institution.

What is the reason for the drastic shift of employment toward the service sector? Victor Fuchs's authoritative study, *The Service Economy*, considers three hypotheses: (1) a more rapid growth of final demand for services, (2) a relative increase in the intermediate demand for services, and (3) a relatively slow increase in output per man in services. Hypothesis 1 could not be very important since the percentage of total output accounted for by the service sector was the same in 1965 as it was in 1929, measured in constant dollars. Measured in current dollars it increased only from forty-seven percent of fifty percent. Hypothesis 2 was examined statistically by Fuchs and found to account for less than ten percent of the total change. The major explanation is hypothesis 3, that output per man grew much more slowly in the service sector than in the other sectors. This means that the amount of labor required for a given output fell more rapidly in agriculture and industry than in the service sector. In other words, services employ relatively more people because agriculture and industry need relatively less labor year after year.

But *why* has productivity per man risen more slowly in the services than in industry? Are services inherently less subject to technological improvement than manufacturing? Fuchs suggests perhaps this is so, but there is another reason that should not be overlooked. The industrial sector of the economy is characterized by much greater monopoly power than is the services sector. This power tends to be countervailing, the oligopolistic managements of the industrial sector being offset by the monopolistic labor unions. Although more than half the persons employed in industry are union members, only about ten percent of service sector employees are unionized.[13] Unionized labor succeeds in temporarily pushing wages above MRP_L, the marginal revenue product of labor. Management reacts by seeking to reestablish the equality in order to keep short run profits at a maximum.[14] Thus higher wages lead to a higher marginal revenue product of labor, and consequently, to a higher average revenue product of labor. Since the latter is the statistical measure of labor productivity it is clear that union-induced wage increases tend to increase measured labor productivity in the short run. In the long run, management reacts to union power by seeking to substitute capital for labor, thus further increasing the productivity of labor and reducing the number of laborers needed. By contrast with industry, in the service sector we witness neither much unionization nor much monopoly power, since entry into services is not blocked by the high initial capital outlays found in industry. Such cartelization as does exist in services (as, for example, among physicians and lawyers) involves no conflict between labor and management and results in no upward pressure on productivity per man. It seems, therefore, that at least a part of the difference in productivity and employment between industry and services has its origin in different market power rather than in different susceptibility to technological progress.

One third of service sector employment is in nonprofit institutions, where the profit-maximizing, employment-limiting rule of wage equal to MRP_L loses its rationale from the very beginning. The service sector also has a much higher rate of self-employment, where the rule of wage equal to MRP_L applies with less force and where a decline in employment often takes the form of work sharing, with fewer hours worked by the same number of people. Many small entrepreneurs in services are also, however unintentionally, "nonprofit institutions," and are providing temporary employment while in the process of slowly going out of business. Retail gasoline stations are a case in point. Finally, for many services, output is so hard to measure that it is estimated for national income purposes by the value of input (e.g., government services), with the result that productivity loses all meaning. Often productivity in services, even when it can be roughly measured, depends as much on the consumer as on the producer. For example, a physician's productivity is influenced by the patient's ability to supply an accurate medical history, and the teacher's productivity varies according to the interest and intelligence of the student. In sum, the whole notion of productivity in the service sector is often very vague, or completely meaningless (as when we estimate the value of output by the value of input), or of little consequence in determining employment (as in both intentionally and unintentionally nonprofit institutions). The upshot is that service sector employment is much less strictly limited by productivity considerations than is industrial employment.

On the demand side ever rising standards of minimum consumption for certain services (in education, medical care, legal counsel, insurance, and government welfare services) have helped demand to keep up with supply and to make growing employment possible in these areas. But there is a limit to the amount of services people will voluntarily consume. Much service consumption is already involuntary—e.g., compulsory schooling, quasi-compulsory college attendance in order to get a job, compulsory insurance and retirement services and related medical exams, compulsory psychiatric care for the mentally ill, etc. How far such forced consumption is justifiable is now becoming a hotly debated issue. Books are written on "deschooling society" and on "how to avoid probate" and associated legal fees. The notion of legal insanity and forced consumption of psychiatric services is also under attack.

It has long been argued that in underdeveloped countries the service sector, particularly the government itself, acts as a sponge to absorb the unemployed, a policy that serves distribution more than it serves production. Might not the same apply to the United States?

Little Employment Is Created Directly by Energy Transformation

One must recognize, of course, that men are employed directly in energy extraction, in refining, pipeline transportation, and energy utilities. This employment amounted to 2.6 percent of total employment in 1947, 2.3 percent in 1955, and 1.8 percent in 1965. The energy industry accounted for a much larger percentage of total investment: 16.1 percent in 1947, 22.0 percent in 1955, and 19.4 percent in 1965. The percentage of GNP originating in the energy industry was 4.5 percent in 1947, 4.7 percent in 1955, and 3.8 percent in 1965. Note that the percentage of energy industry investment is very high relative to its percentage of total product. Note also that energy's percentage of employment is low relative to its percentage of the total product. Thus a relatively large investment in energy produces a relatively small amount of employment.[15] Energy transformation is probably the most capital-intensive, labor-saving part of the economy, and direct employment from its growth will be very small.

Indirect Employment and Special Pleading

Indirect employment is another matter, and in the previous section we mentioned that advocates of growth in energy output believe such growth will indirectly create employment. We may consider two kinds of indirect employment effects: those arising from the interdependence of supplies, of which energy is one, and those arising from demand. Undeniably, energy is a necessary input to the supplies of nearly all sectors. But it does not necessarily follow that increasing the production of energy will increase the number of jobs in these sectors. In fact, to the extent that an increased supply of it lowers the price of energy, the result is more likely to be a reduction in employment as cheaper energy replaces human labor. Nor does it always follow that other sectors cannot expand employment without an increase in energy input (though increased energy is needed to increase employment when coefficients of production are fixed). In general, increasing the input of energy to the supply side of the economy is neither a necessary nor a sufficient condition for increasing employment. The same would apply to many other inputs, not just energy. Minerals are necessary inputs to most production; to that extent, the jobs of all people in all sectors are influenced by the supply of minerals. Water is a necessary input; to that extent, jobs are influenced by water. For some production processes a ¾ inch no. 8 countersunk chromium-plated-brass wood screw is a necessary input. And though the jobs of all people in all sectors may depend on the availability of this type of screw, or of minerals, or of water, a surplus of countersunk chromium-plated-brass wood screws or minerals or water does not usually send a personnel manager to his job-applicant file.

On the demand side, indirect employment effects do result from new investment in energy production. As we have seen, energy accounts for some twenty percent of new investment, a significant amount. This high percentage of investment results from rapid growth and the high capital-intensity of energy production. These investments generate a chain of respending, or multiplier effects, throughout the economy, stimulating output and employment (and inflation). But once again, this Keynesian argument is perfectly general and can be applied to new investment in any industry. Indeed, it can be applied to increased expenditure of any kind (increased welfare payments, unemployment compensation, or military spending), not just to investment. Arguments claiming indirect employment effects, either by way of supply or demand, are therefore obvious cases of special pleading of a condition that applies to all industries, not just energy. Such arguments, relying on the need for investment, are also premised on open-ended growth in total product—reason A on the list advanced by its advocates as evidence for the need of energy growth.

Power for the Poor

An occasional variant of the argument that energy growth increases employment is what might be called the "power for the poor" argument. To quote John Simpson again, "If we were to freeze our rate of power generation and consumption, we would effectively deny those millions who are below the average any chance to improve their lot in the future."[16] The statement is a non sequitur. Improving the lot of those below the average does not depend on electric power alone, and even if it did their lot could still be improved by cutting down the consumption of those who are above average—evidently a thought too horrible to contemplate! But the claim that in effect the increment in power would go largely to the poor has never been supported by evidence. Indeed, there is reason to expect, on the basis of evidence, that just the reverse would happen.

Consider the "power for the poor" argument expressed in the "Energy Marketing" section of a recent issue of *Electrical World*.[17] An article entitled "Zero Growth Power Advocates Ignore Effect on the Poor" argues that zero growth in power is a policy "which, by a sort of grandfather clause, would seek to prevent those of lower income and darker skin from sharing in the not-inconsiderable comforts and conveniences afforded by modern electric appliances . . ." As "evidence" the article presents us with Table 1, which shows that a much larger percentage of wealthy and white people own major electric appliances than do low-income and nonwhite people. The "conclusion" that the reader is encouraged to draw from these statistics is that "future growth will consist of gradual accumulation by lower income families of the more modern appliances first accumulated by their wealthier cousins." But if gradual accumulation by the poor comes about it will be because of general economic growth and the resulting growth in employment, not from growth in electric power, by itself something likely to have the opposite effect, as we have already seen. More importantly, the conclusion following from the fact that the rich own more appliances than the poor is that the rich use more electricity than the poor. How can the poor use much

TABLE 1
Appliance ownership by income and race in New York City (by percent)

Ownership	Air conditioner	Dish washer	Vacuum cleaner
Income			
$ 0–3,000	12	1	40
3–5,000	11	2	46
5–10,000	28	5	69
10–15,000	48	15	89
15,000 and over	58	36	95
Race			
White	40	12	81
Nonwhite	8	3	41

Source: Electrical World, *March 15, 1971, p. 148.*

more electricity without buying air conditioners, dish washers, vacuum cleaners, frost-free refrigerators, washers, dryers, color TVs, etc.? And how can they buy these applicances if they are poor? If the increment in electric power were truly directed to the poor, one would expect to find the energy-marketing people striving to promote mainly simple, low-priced appliances with low operating and maintenance costs, designed to be advantageous for the poor. One would expect to see research and development receive eight times as much as advertising instead of one-eighth as much, as is now the case, and one would also expect to see rate discrimination in favor of the small rather than the large users.

That the energy marketeers prefer to concentrate on production for those who can pay high prices is obvious from other articles appearing in the "Energy Marketing" section of *Electrical World.* Consider two other articles in this section of the very issue I just cited. One extols the virtues of a moving sidewalk projected for Boston, the object of which is to convey consumers from a parking area to an adjacent shopping area more quickly. Since conveyor belts have speeded up production, bringing the commodity to the market more rapidly, apparently we must speed up consumption also by putting the consumer on conveyor belts. Does *Electrical World* really think moving sidewalks will be a boon to the inner-city ghettos? A second new dimension in energy marketing is described in another article, about a Gold Medallion home, all electric (so as to avoid pollution!), with central vacuum cleaning systems and electronic security systems, the latter no doubt to safeguard the considerable wealth represented by all the other electric appliances, appliances available to everyone, rich and poor alike, provided he has the money! Sandwiched as it is between these two articles on the latest technological advance toward trivial energy consumption for the jaded tastes of the affluent, the article defending the poor against the selfishness of the zero growth advocates raises the suspicion of trumpery. Needless to add, none of the articles warns readers that production of power causes pollution, and that though the benefits of power production go mainly to the rich, the external costs fall mainly on the poor. For example, consider the giant Four Corners power complex in the desert of northeastern Arizona. The electricity generated there is used mainly in Southern California and other distant places more affluent than the Four Corners area. The nearby Navajo hogans do not have air conditioners and other major electrical appliances. The Indians and other local residents are subjected to the air pollution and the strip mining that accompany electricity production, and the benefits of "clean" electricity go to affluent suburban Americans.

Increasing Costs and Decreasing Benefits per Kilowatt

It should be clear that growth in efficiency is not being questioned. If we can get more service from the same physical fund, that is all to the good. But increasing the physical fund is clearly a limited process. No one objects to getting more satisfaction per kilowatt or more kilowatts per BTU of primary fuel. But if kilowatts keep on growing we will witness a decline in the ratio of satisfaction per kilowatt. Although a trend in the ratio of energy to GNP fell until 1966, since 1966 the ratio has risen sharply, and in 1970 the actual ratio was thirteen percent greater than it would have been had the pre-1966 trend continued. (See Figure 1.) Thus a dollar's worth of satisfaction now costs more kilowatts than in 1966, and the new trend seems to be rising. Furthermore, new products and quality improvements notwithstanding, the amount of satisfaction represented by a dollar's worth of GNP is itself probably falling. We satisfy our most pressing wants first, and each extra dollar of income is dedicated to the satisfaction of a less important want. Furthermore, GNP increases currently overstate welfare increases since more and more of what is counted in GNP is the cost of defending ourselves from the unwanted side effects of production. Therefore the fact that GNP per capita has been growing means that the incremental dollars represent less satisfaction. With decreases in both satisfaction per dollar and in dollars per kilowatt, it is very clear that satisfaction per kilowatt must also have fallen. This does not square very well with Mr. Simpson's prediction that "we will have learned to do so much more with so much less power. . . ."

It seems instead we are learning to use more power to do less, at

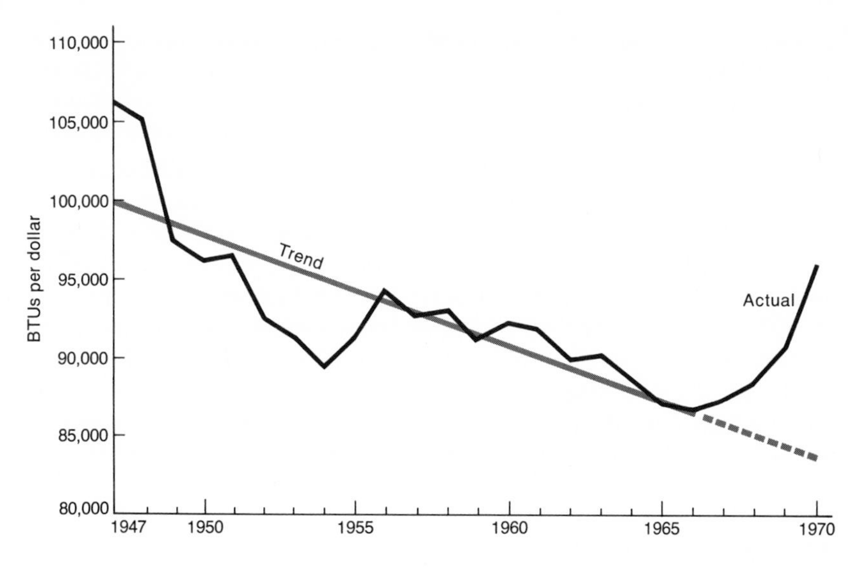

FIGURE 1.
The ratio of energy to Gross National Product, 1947–1970. [Source: National Economic Research Associates, "Energy Consumption and Gross National Product in the United States," March 1971. Also Earl Cook, "The Flow of Energy in an Industrial Society," *Scientific American*, September 1971, p. 140.]

least in terms of the significance of what is done. This by itself does not mean that we have overshot the optimum. Falling marginal benefits of kilowatts may still be greater than rising marginal costs. We do know that the marginal cost of a kilowatt, in terms of alternative satisfactions sacrificed, is bound to rise. There is a thermodynamic limit to the efficiency of converting energy, so improvement in kilowatts per BTU of primary fuel is limited. Continued increases will require more primary fuel, and more rivers and lakes to supply coolants, which implies the sacrifice of increasingly more important alternative satisfactions that could be derived from aquatic resources. We are now learning that the ecological value of the land and water that would be used for more kilowatt production is "invisible," and that the environmental services provided by the resource *in natura* are often far greater than the services they render within the economy of pecuniary calculation. Externalities have become so important relative to internalities that monetary price calculations have now become, if not blind, at least one-eyed guides, deficient in depth perception and less to be trusted than the common sense reasoning we have been using, reasoning that cannot prove, but does suggest, that one or two or three more doublings of electric power output will probably push marginal cost well above marginal benefits. In any case, those who are proposing electric power increase need to undertake the burden of proving that such increases will not overshoot the optimum. The power growth arguments offered and analyzed earlier fall far short of establishing their presumption that the benefits of sixteen times as much electric power will outweigh the costs. Ironically, continued growth of electric output when marginal cost exceeds marginal benefit might well stimulate employment. Since we would, in view of this, in effect be getting poorer by producing more, power growth lobbies would likely combat our reduced well-being in the traditional way, proposing to increase production and employment even more, which would make us still worse off, and so forth. Indeed, this is painfully similar to reason B, the argument that we must grow more so that we will be rich enough to afford the cost of cleaning up. That neatly begs the question whether growth is not already making us poorer instead of richer!

ECONOMIC GROWTH

As noted in the introduction and demonstrated repeatedly in the previous section on energy and employment, arguments that employment will result from power growth (reason C) must, if they are to make any sense at all, presuppose continuing growth in total product (reason A). Reason A is in fact the linchpin of the whole case for continued power growth at current rates. But it is a linchpin that is rapidly wearing thin. The goal of increased employment itself raises a number of fundamental questions. After all, labor is a cost, and like all costs it is pushed to a minimum by the long run logic of technical and economic progress. Such long run behavior poses difficulties in the total economy, but since energy production has no reason for existence other than to function in the total economy, its attitude toward growth or nongrowth cannot be analyzed apart from the total context. Furthermore, the electric power industry is causing problems not because it is aberrant, but because it has succeeded so well in doing what all other industries are trying to do, namely, increase profits and growth.

Why, since labor is a cost of production, do we not rejoice instead of fret whenever jobs are eliminated, whenever one man can do the work of 350 men? Why, in the face of idle capacity do we insist on increased investment to create still more productive capacity? The answers to these questions, of course, have little to do with production but have everything to do with distribution. In a profit-maximizing capitalistic economy in which most people own no productive assets save those embodied in their own person, employment, or income through jobs, is the major institution for distribution. The possibility of a conflict between the

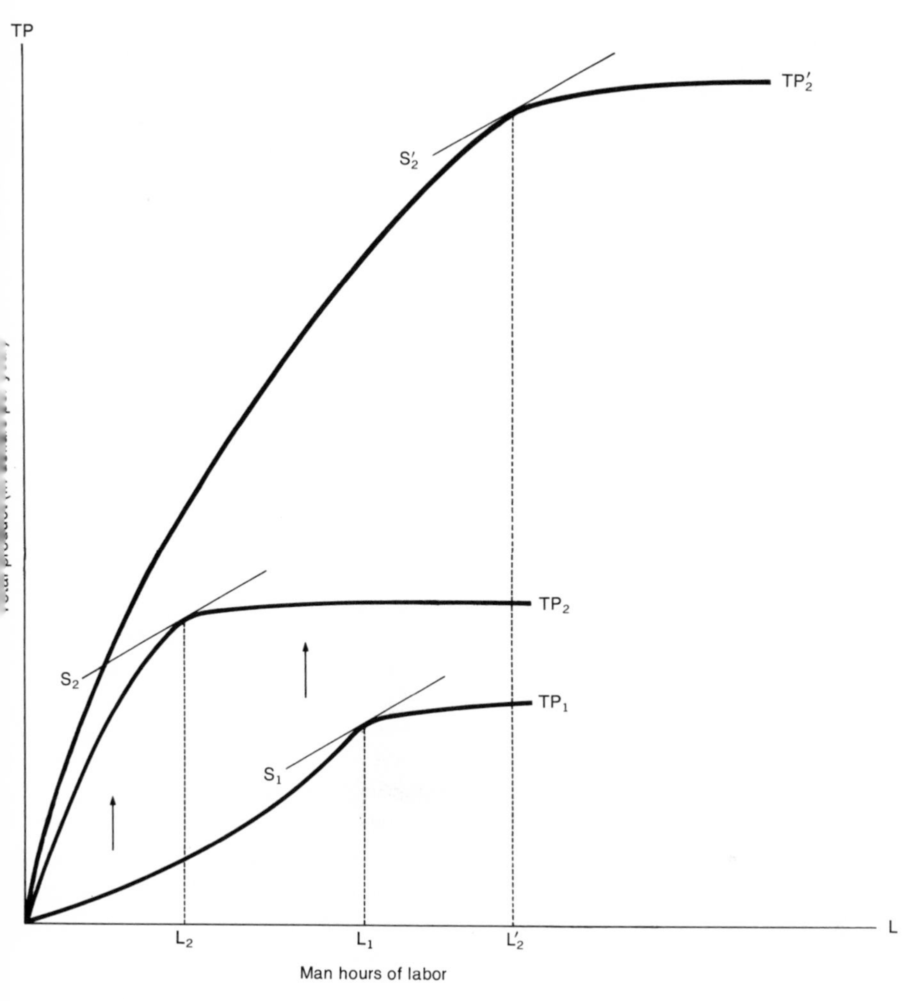

FIGURE 2.
Employment and total product in a low-energy, low-automation economy (TP_1) and a high-energy, high-automation economy (TP_2 and TP_2').

efficiency of production and the equity of distribution is a familiar theme in the history of economic thought. The goal of productive efficiency in a high-energy, automated economy conflicts very sharply with the goal of distributive efficiency and equity, given our present economic institutions. To see this conflict more clearly consider Figure 2.

Let TP_1 represent the total product of labor for an economy before it has access to high energy and automation (it rises and then levels off to reflect eventually diminishing returns to labor). TP_2 is the total product curve after that economy has shifted to high-energy, automated kinds of production—a much higher total product is attained with a much smaller number of laborers, but again, beyond a certain limited number of laborers, further employment does not increase the total product. The slope of the total product curve at any point represents the productivity of labor at "the margin" where additional hours of labor are added. The corresponding quantity of labor employed is measured along L. Marginal productivity falls to zero more rapidly in the automated, high-energy economy, represented by the curve of TP_2, than on TP_1. In capitalistic profit-maximizing economies, the wages labor earns tend to be equal to the marginal product of labor. But wages—unlike interest, rent, and profit—cannot be zero. There is a positive limit to the basic wage, a minimum acceptable wage, or "subsistence." Let "subsistence" be the (equal) slopes of line S_1 and line S_2. The maximum number of jobs under the kind of production corresponding to TP_1 is L_1, and that corresponding to TP_2 is L_2. Assuming that L_1 represented full employment in an economy with little automation, then the distance L_2L_1 represents technological unemployment. The TP_2 kind of production supports fewer workers, even though total output is vastly greater. A smaller proportion of total output goes to wages, a larger proportion to interest, rent, and profit. Distribution of income becomes more concentrated, with a corresponding increase in luxury production.

How realistic is this "scenario"? If we apply it only to the transformation the agricultural sector has made from human labor to automation over the past fifty years, it is highly realistic. If we apply it to the current similar changes in industry, it also seems realistic. But if we apply it to the service sector the graph is unrealistic, a crucial fact since, as noted in the previous section, the service sector now accounts for over fifty-five percent of total employment and almost all net new employment. The ability of the service sector to absorb this quantity of employment indicates that so far the service sector has not experienced the kind of technical change that has occurred in agriculture and industry, and that employment is not so strictly limited by the rule that wage is equal to marginal revenue-product, for reasons discussed earlier. What this means is that we have maintained employment by bending the rule that wage is equal to marginal product in the service sector. We have also bent the income-through-jobs principle with an increase in the "grants economy" and in government transfer payments. Behaving the way it does, the service sector compensates for the mass unemployment that would otherwise be caused by the introduction of energy-using, labor-saving techniques in agriculture and industry. But what about the future? If one advocates the use of ever more energy, then one should, it appears, seek to reduce the very necessity of employment itself by advocating alternative distributive institutions, rather than by trying to make the case that more energy means more employment. (Or we can hope that the service sector will continue to expand to provide jobs.) For automated sectors (those with total product curves shaped like TP_2) there is really only one way to increase employment, and that is through rapid growth in total product, represented in the diagram not by moving along the curve (TP_2) but by shifting the entire curve upward (to TP_2'). The shift cannot be only vertical, as this would reflect a marginal product of labor (slope of TP_2) unchanged at every L, and employment which has not increased with total product. The total product must not only shift upward, but must extend also to the right so that the marginal product will fall to subsistence only after achievement of greater employment (L_2'). In other words the employment-creating effect of further growth in total product must not be cancelled out by further advances in labor-saving technology. Therefore, we see that economic growth (growth in TP) does not by itself guarantee an increase in employment, though for future argument we will grant that one can always increase employment by increasing total product fast enough, for this assumption is, at basis, the proposition on which the power growth advocates rest their case. How realistic and how reasonable is it?

We already know that physical growth is a limited process, and long-run dependence on it is unrealistic. But there are shorter run dilemmas as well, such as those noted by Evesy Domar in his classic article on growth and employment:

> In a private capitalist society where the [marginal propensity to consume] cannot be readily changed, a higher level of income and employment at any given time can be achieved only through increased investment. But investment as an employment creating instrument is a mixed blessing because of its effect [in increasing productive capacity]. The economy finds itself in a serious dilemma: if sufficient investment is not forthcoming today, unemployment will be here today. But if enough is invested today, still more will be needed tomorrow. . . . So far as unemployment is concerned, investment is at the same time a cure for the disease and the cause of even greater ills in the future.[18]

The conventional way to employ unused capacity is to build still more capacity—to grow! But how to induce businessmen and corporations to invest more when they already have idle capacity? By giving all sorts of "bribes" such as lower interest rates and faster depreciation write-offs. But an alternative would be to encourage consumption by those at the bottom of the income pyramid rather than investment expenditures at the top. If, by way of tax reductions and negative income taxes, new expenditure is fed in from below, it will "trickle up" as the poor spend it without being bribed. Businessmen will then expand output and employment as they produce more of the things lower income people buy. This is indeed consumer sovereignty, subsidizing the consumer, not the producer. In this way we escape the infinite regress of the ever increasing productive capacity needed to maintain full employment, at the same time we move the distribution of income toward equality. The remaining gap between private saving and private investment could be filled by public investment in social goods and services, and by government purchase and stockpiling of goods. The stockpile of goods could be saved for use in disaster, or until such time as we have discovered better institutions of distribution. The real counterpart to private monetary saving would then not be unused productive capacity, but a stockpile of unused commodities. Unused commodities can be used in the future, whereas unused productive capacity is irrevocably lost, since time cannot be accumulated. Selling from the commodity stockpile could be an effective form of antiinflation policy, something already done with some strategic materials. Under such a policy productive capacity would be increased only after all existing capacity had been used, and only in response to actual demand of the low income groups in the society. This truly would be growth for the poor, and those who are so anxious to sell more electric power to the poor should welcome such a plan.

But a continually growing economy offers further anomalies. To examine some of these, let us start from the premise that the legitimate goal of economic activity is the satisfaction of human wants. The satisfaction of wants is a nonmaterial service, a flow of psychic income that is rendered or yielded by the stock of all physical wealth. All goods and all people who perform services constitute the stock of wealth, i.e., physical capital. Maintenance of this nonphysical flow of services requires the maintenance of the physical stock of wealth, and maintenance of the physical stock of wealth requires a physical flow of production to offset the physical depreciation of the stock resulting from wear and tear, from the mere passage of time. Now we are in an area that will be somewhat familiar to those who have read the Introduction to this volume and Kenneth Boulding's "The Economics of the Coming Spaceship Earth." Let us think of the physical stock as being maintained in a steady state by a "maintenance throughput," i.e., by matching an outflow of high-entropy matter-energy with an equal inflow of low-entropy matter-energy (primary resources). That this maintenance throughput is a cost is clearly seen by looking at each end of the pipeline. Inputs necessitate depletion, outputs necessitate pollution. Furthermore the maintenance of the stock requires human labor, the sacrifice of leisure to production. Inasmuch as depletion, pollution, and labor are all costs, the flow of maintenance throughput (production) is also a cost; then production in the sense that it is a physical maintenance throughput is *not* something to be maximized.

In the steady-state economy any technological advance that allows more service to be yielded by the same physical stock is always to be welcomed. Psychic income is nonmaterial, and its increase may be unlimited. Likewise, any technological advance that allows the same stock to be maintained by a smaller flow of throughput is also always to be welcomed. Limits to minimal throughput are imposed by the second law of thermodynamics. But to increase the throughput for its own sake makes no sense, and to increase it for the sake of building up and maintaining a larger stock is a limited process. It is limited physically by ecological interdependence and by spatial finitude, and it is limited economically by the laws of diminishing marginal utility and increasing marginal costs.

In the light of the above observations GNP becomes a largely irrelevant number. For the goods component of GNP we may interpret the number as an index of the annual flow of quantity of goods produced (something to be minimized for a given stock, not maximized). The services component presents problems. To be consistent logically we should not even try to count services but to count instead the new production of the physical things that yield the service, skilled people—just as we count durable consumer goods. But there is no market for buying and selling skilled people, only for renting them; therefore we do not know the price of, say, a physician, although we could use the present value of expected future earnings. The problem is that even though "service" in the sense of "psychic income" is nonphysical, service defined in the sense of the national income accountant measures something physical, a stock at one's disposal for a certain duration of time. Because of the physically accountable dimension of most services, we cannot say that because the "services" component is *wholly* nonphysical GNP could grow forever. A physician cannot sell a thirty minute consultation and then just leave his disembodied medical knowledge in his office, there to dispense medical advice to another patient while the physician's body is out playing golf. The doctor's services require the participation of his entire physical self. An increase in measured medical service for the GNP requires more physical bodies functioning as physicians, more hospitals, more X-ray machines, and on and on. Thus we do not escape physical limits on GNP by saying it is simply a matter of enlarging the service component.

Why is this flow-fetishism—this emphasis on the throughput, which eclipses the stock dimension from view—at present so important in economics? In a society in which the stock of wealth is very unequally distributed (see Table 2) demands for social justice are more conservatively dealt with by focusing on the flow of income, seeking to direct more of it to the poor without directing less of it to the rich, something possible only if the flow is growing. Since a stock is measured at some given point in time it must always be seen as a constant at the moment

TABLE 2

Wealth compared to income (1962)

Characteristic of population	Distribution through population	Extent of wealth (dollars), and distribution (percent)											
		Negative	Zero	$1–999	1,000–4,999	5,000–9,999	10,000–24,999	25,000–49,999	50,000–99,999	100,000–199,999	200,000–499,999	500,000–999,999	1,000,000 and over
Total	100 percent	2	8	16	19	16	23	11	4	1	1		
Income	$0–2,999	1	23	19	18	15	17	7	1				
	3,000–4,999	3	8	29	20	11	17	8	2	1			
	5,000–7,499	2	1	15	25	21	22	8	5				
	7,500–9,999	2		7	18	18	36	14	3	1	1		
	10,000–14,999	1		2	13	16	35	20	10	3	1		
	15,000–24,999				3	10	21	29	24	7	5	1	
	25,000–49,999						5	8	22	27	27	7	4
	50,000–99,999							1	9	7	45	20	17
	100,000 and over									1	5	56	38
Age	Under 35	5	9	36	26	14	8	2					
	35–44	2	7	14	20	21	25	8	4	1			
	45–54	1	7	10	20	10	31	14	5	1	1		
	55–64	1	8	7	12	16	28	16	8	3	2		
	65 and over		11	8	13	18	25	15	5	1	2	1	

Source: Dorothy S. Projector and Gertrude S. Weiss, Survey of Financial Characteristics of Consumers, *Board of Governors, Federal Reserve, 1966.*

Note: Some rows do not add to exactly 100 percent due to rounding. Blank entries signify values of less than 1/2 unit.

it is measured, and more of the stock to the poor must also mean less to the rich. Better to think, say those most influential in deciding economic policy, in terms of the flow, the additions to the stock, and to channel a bit more of the flow to the poor through our tax system (or at least let's pretend that is what we are doing). Once it seemed a good idea to make sure that the flow would grow year after year, so that even with the same proportional division of wealth, the poor would get absolutely more. Furthermore, welfare economics teaches us that a policy represents an unambiguous increase in social welfare only if it makes some people better off without making anyone worse off. Otherwise we are forced to make interpersonal comparisons of utility, and that is an ethical matter with which science cannot deal. Once again the policy of increasing A's income without diminishing B's income requires growth in total income.

We are used to hearing that we do not have enough, and that an even distribution of income would make all evenly poor, a view that has always been morally questionable since if there is really not enough for all, then it is all the more objectionable that the few should receive so much more than the average while the many receive much less. However, with current United States per capita disposable income in excess of $3,000, even this argument is no longer possible.[19] The average before-tax income for a family of four in 1971 was close to $16,000—not exactly poverty. Of course this is a very unrepresentative mean, since the distribution of income is so badly skewed. In 1968 the twenty million Americans in the top ten percent of income recipients got around twenty-seven percent of the total national income, and the twenty million in the lowest ten percent received about one percent of the total income. (See Table 3.) Contrary to the assumptions of growthmania, distribution is, at the margin, a more pressing issue than production. Nevertheless, there are strong vested interests in growth throughout our society. The growth aspirations of any one industry, such as electric power, cannot be properly understood apart from the context of the overall functioning of the economic system. Although an annual growth goal of seven percent is high compared to other industries, the case of electric power is important not because it is an exception, but because it so clearly illustrates the general rule of growthmania.

Our arguments against power growth have assumed continued use of a reasonably safe technology. Yet present commitments are to the development of fast breeder reactors, which represent a technology that is quite unsafe. Even if the considerable technical problems of nuclear power-generation are eventually solved, there will remain the nontechnical problems of safeguarding ever increasing stocks of plutonium and fissile isotopes. Once again it is growthmania that causes intemperate haste in commercializing an extremely dangerous technology—one which

TABLE 3
Percentage distribution of income in the United States through five-percentile divisions (1960–1968)

5-percent quantiles	1960	1961	1962	1963	1964	1965	1966	1967	1968
1 and 2 (lowest)	0.64	0.67	0.71	0.77	0.77	0.85	0.94	0.94	1.03
3	1.04	1.02	1.08	1.06	1.08	1.10	1.12	1.14	1.20
4	1.50	1.45	1.53	1.51	1.52	1.54	1.56	1.58	1.64
5	1.95	1.89	1.97	1.95	1.95	1.97	1.99	2.00	2.07
6	2.40	2.32	2.40	2.39	2.38	2.40	2.42	2.43	2.49
7	2.84	2.75	2.82	2.83	2.82	2.83	2.85	2.84	2.91
8	3.27	3.18	3.24	3.27	3.25	3.26	3.28	3.26	3.33
9	3.70	3.61	3.66	3.70	3.68	3.68	3.71	3.67	3.74
10	4.13	4.04	4.08	4.14	4.12	4.12	4.14	4.09	4.16
11	4.57	4.48	4.32	4.58	4.56	4.55	4.58	4.52	4.58
12	5.00	4.92	4.97	5.03	5.01	5.00	5.01	4.96	5.00
13	5.44	5.37	5.45	5.49	5.46	5.45	5.45	5.41	5.44
14	5.89	5.83	5.95	5.95	5.93	5.92	5.90	5.88	5.89
15	6.35	6.30	6.48	6.42	6.40	6.40	6.35	6.37	6.49
16	7.04	7.00	7.05	7.14	7.12	7.07	7.09	7.00	6.94
17	7.67	7.76	7.81	7.76	7.81	7.74	7.71	7.64	7.54
18	8.61	8.73	8.73	8.66	8.71	8.65	8.61	8.56	8.44
19	10.29	10.47	10.34	10.26	10.31	10.26	10.21	10.22	10.06
20	17.66	18.18	17.21	17.09	17.13	17.19	17.08	17.50	17.05
Top 1 percent	6.08	6.33	5.77	5.73	5.74	5.00	5.76	6.01	5.81

Source: Edward C. Budd, "Postwar Changes in the Size Distribution of Income in the U.S." American Economic Review, *Papers and Proceedings, May 1970, p. 253.*

is certain to increase vastly our vulnerability to sabotage, terrorism, and disasterous accidents.[20]

The alternative to growthmania is the steady-state economy, and the big task for physical and social scientists is to work out the technologies and institutions that will allow us to attain such a steady state. The even bigger task is for all citizens to find the moral resources necessary to overcome the vested interests and hag-ridden compulsions of growthmania.

NOTES AND REFERENCES

1. U.S. Congress, *Congressional Record*, March 8, 1971, p. E1566.
2. *Ibid.*
3. U.S. Congress, *Congressional Record*, June 4, 1971, p. H4722.
4. Neil Fabricant and Robert Hallman, *Toward a Rational Power Policy: Energy, Politics, Pollution*, New York, Braziller, 1971, p. 7.
5. Standard and Poor's Industry Surveys, *Utilities—Electric*, *Current Analysis*, May 27, 1971.
6. Bertrand de Jouvenel, "Efficiency and Amenity," reprinted in *Microeconomics*, Edwin Mansfield, ed. New York: W. W. Norton, 1971. p. 428.
7. Joseph N. Froomkin, "Automation," *International Encyclopedia of the Social Sciences*, Vol. I, p. 488.
8. Interview with Tricia Nixon, reported as national news.
9. See "Electric Power—More or Less?" speech delivered by John W. Simpson, printed in *Congressional Record*, March 8, 1971, p. E1564. Also, "Electrical Energy and Pollution," speech delivered by Representative Chet Holifield, printed in *Congressional Record*, June 4, 1971, p. H4722.
10. *Economic Report of the President*, Washington, D.C.: U.S. Government Printing Office, 1971, p. 88.
11. U.S. Congress, *Congressional Record*, June 4, 1971, p. H4725.
12. See Victor R. Fuchs, *The Service Economy*, New York: National Bureau of Economic Research–Columbia University Press, 1968, p. 2.
13. Victor Fuchs, *op. cit.*, p. 8.
14. As long as the wage is less than the marginal revenue product of labor the firm can increase profit by hiring more laborers. If the wage is greater than the marginal revenue product of labor, profits can be increased, and equality reestablished, if fewer laborers are hired (i.e., the last laborers hired cost more than they are worth to the firm). When wage equals the marginal revenue product of labor it is impossible to increase profit either by hiring more labor *or* less labor—in other words, profit is at a maximum.
15. See Resources for the Future Staff, *U. S. Energy Policies: An Agenda for Research*, Baltimore: Johns Hopkins Press, 1968, p. 22.
16. U.S. Congress, *Congressional Record*, March 8, 1971, p. E1565.
17. "Zero Power Growth Advocates Ignore Effect on Poor," *Electrical World*, March 15, 1971, p. 147.
18. Evesy Domar, "Expansion and Employment," *American Economic Review*, March 1947.
19. For income figures, see *Statistical Abstract of the U. S.*, Washington, D.C.: U.S. Government Printing Office, 1969, p. 13.
20. See Allen Hammond, "Fission: The Pro's and Con's of Nuclear Power," *Science*, October 13, 1972, pp. 147–149.

III

VALUES AND THE STEADY STATE

INTRODUCTION

Man, craving for the infinite, has been corrupted by the temptation to satisfy an insatiable hunger in the material realm. Turn these stones into bread, urges Satan, and modern man sets to it, even to the extent of devising energy-intensive schemes for grinding up ordinary rock for minerals—to eat the spaceship itself! But Jesus' answer to the same temptation was more balanced: man does not live by bread alone. The proper object of economic activity is to have *enough* bread, not infinite bread, not a world turned into bread, not even vast storehouses full of bread. The infinite hunger of man, his moral and spiritual hunger, is not to be satisfied, is indeed exacerbated, by the current demonic madness of producing more and more things for more and more people. Afflicted with an infinite itch, modern man is scratching in the wrong place, and his frenetic clawing is drawing blood from the life-sustaining circulatory systems of his spaceship, the biosphere.

It is important to be very clear on the paramount importance of the moral issue. We could opt to scratch ourselves to death, destroying the spaceship in an orgy of procreation and consumption. The *only* arguments against doing this are religious and ethical: the obligation of stewardship for God's creation, the extension of brotherhood to future generations, and of some lesser degree of brotherhood to the subhuman world.

The issue of extending brotherhood to future generations is central to the article by Jørgen Randers and Donella Meadows. The major ethical problem, they argue, is to decide on the length of the time period over which one tries to trace out, sum up, and compare the costs and benefits of current actions.

Theologian John Cobb considers the extension of brotherhood to the subhuman world and develops the thesis that our ethics should be based on feeling, and on a perception of the hierarchy of feeling in the biotic pyramid. Nonhuman feeling, Cobb contends, must be considered valuable, though its value is not on an equal footing with human feeling. Man may be the apex of the biotic pyramid from which he evolved, but an apex with no pyramid underneath is a dimensionless point.

The reader may be forgiven the cynical question that since brotherhood has not yet been extended to all men existing at the same time in the same society, is it not premature to speak of extending it to the future, and to animals and rocks? Does not true brotherhood require more growth for the sake of the poor, not less?

Certainly the first extension of brotherhood must be to presently existing people. This is agreed by all. But it does not follow that this extension requires more rather than less growth. Past economic growth has not eliminated poverty, since distribution has remained very unequal, and since population has grown rapidly, especially the poorer populations of the world. Distribution is a moral problem, as is population control, and what we lack are the moral resources to solve these problems, because our limited energies have been overwhelmingly devoted to material growth. We thought we could grow our way out of poverty and injustice, but we were wrong. There is just not room for that much growth. Brotherhood means sharing what one has *now*, not the exponentially swollen sum one hopes to have in the future.

The final essay by C. S. Lewis, the late British theologian, historian, and writer of science fiction, was first published in 1947, long before the wave of environmental concern had swelled. When, as in Lewis's article, the relevance of the article increases with time, it is a good indication the author has based his arguments upon something very solid. Controlling nature, as Lewis shows, becomes after some point a very dangerous undertaking, and if carried to the limit, the whole enterprise blows up in our face—"Man's conquest of Nature turns out, in the moment of its consummation, to be Nature's conquest of Man."

14

THE CARRYING CAPACITY OF OUR GLOBAL ENVIRONMENT: A LOOK AT THE ETHICAL ALTERNATIVES

Jorgen Randers and Donella Meadows

For which of you, intending to build a tower, sitteth not down first, and counteth the cost, whether he have sufficient to finish it?
Luke 14:28

The main thesis of this reading is very simple: because our environment—the earth—is finite, growth of human population and industrialization cannot continue indefinitely. The consequences of this simple and obvious fact pose an unprecedented challenge to mankind, for in a limited world we cannot maximize everything for everyone. In the near future we will have to decide just what ethical basis we should use for making the trade-offs which will be necessary in a world with finite limits.

THE ENVIRONMENT IS FINITE

It should be quite unnecessary to point out that the global environment is finite. However, most considerations of the world's future tend to lose sight of this finitude. Because it is not generally recognized how very close we are to the physical limitations which define the carrying capacity of our globe, it will be worthwhile to spend some time discussing these limitations.

Agricultural Land

The quantity most obviously limited on our earth is arable land. There are about 3.2 billion hectares of land suitable for agriculture. Approximately half of this land is under cultivation today. Immense investments of capital will be required to settle, clear, irrigate, or fertilize the remaining half before it can produce food. The capital costs are so high that the United Nations Food and Agriculture Organization, which is seeking desperately to stimulate greater food production, has concluded that in order to expand food output it must rely on more intensive use of currently cultivated land, not on new land development.

If we were to decide to incur the costs necessary to cultivate all possible arable land and to produce as much food as possible, how many people could we expect to feed? A graph indicating the increasing need for agricultural land caused by the growing world population is shown in Figure 1. The lower curve in Figure 1 shows the amount of land *needed* to feed the growing world population, assuming that the present world average of 0.4 hectares per person is sufficient. (If we wanted to feed everyone at U.S. standards, we would require 0.9 hectares per person.) From 1650 to 1970 world population grew from .5 billion to 3.6 billion; the land that has been needed to feed these people at the present world standard is depicted with a heavy line. The lighter line indicates future need for land, assuming that the population continues to grow at the projected 2.1 percent per year after 1970. The upper curve indicates the actual amount of arable land *available*. This line slopes downward because each additional person requires a certain amount of land (0.08 hectares assumed here) for housing, roads, waste disposal, power lines, and other uses which essentially "pave" land and make it unusable for farming. The graph in Figure 1 tells us that, even with the optimistic assumption that we can utilize all possible land, we will still face a serious land shortage before the year 2000 if the population continues to grow at 2.1 percent per year.

Figure 1 also illustrates two other very important facts about exponential growth within a limited space. First, it shows how the condition

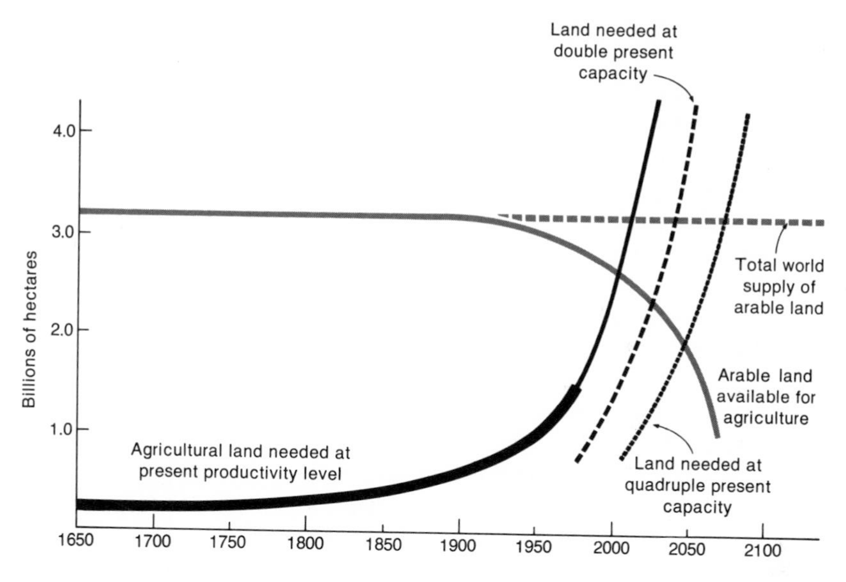

FIGURE 1.
Total world supply of arable land is about 3.2 billion hectares. About 0.4 hectares per person of arable land are needed at present productivity. The curve of land needed thus reflects the population growth curve. The light line after 1970 shows the projected need for land, assuming that world population continues to grow at its present rate. Arable land available decreases because arable land is removed for urban-industrial use as population grows. The dotted curves show land needed if present productivity is doubled or quadrupled.

of mankind can change within a few years from great abundance to great scarcity. The human race has had an overwhelming excess of arable land for all of its history, and now, within thirty years, or one population-doubling period, mankind will be forced to deal with a sudden and serious shortage. A second lesson to be learned from Figure 1 is that the exact numerical assumptions made about the limits of the earth are essentially unimportant when one faces the inexorable progress of exponential growth. For example, one might assume that *no* arable land is taken for cities, roads, or other nonagricultural uses. Then the amount of available land would be constant, as the horizontal dashed line shows, and the point at which the two curves cross can be delayed, but by only about ten years. Or one can suppose that the productivity of the land will be doubled or even quadrupled through advances in agricultural technology, the effect of which is shown by the dotted lines in Figure 1. Each doubling of productivity gains us just one population-doubling period, or about thirty years.

Some people look to the sea to provide the extra food we will need as our population grows. But the total world fish catch in 1969 represented only a few percent of the world's caloric requirements, and the total catch decreased in 1970. The 1970 catch was the first decreased total since World War II, and it occurred in spite of increasing investment and technological developments in the fishing industry. Most experts agree that the world's fish banks have been overexploited and that future prospects for output from the sea indicate further decline, not increase. The seas thus cannot make up for the constraints limited land imposes on growth.

Heat Release

Man faces further obvious constraints on natural resources, such as fresh water, metals, and fuels. Indications are that resources such as these will be in short supply even at higher prices within the next forty years, if present growth continues. However, it is frequently argued that by mining low grade ores and desalting sea water we can alleviate resource shortages, which may indeed be so, assuming we can satisfy the enormous demands for energy such operations would present. Whether or not these arguments are based on reasonable assumptions is one of the topics Preston Cloud discusses in "Mineral Resources in Fact and Fancy," on pages 50–75.

A consideration of the energy that will be necessary to meet man's growing needs leads to a more subtle but much more fundamental physical limitation imposed by our environment. Even if one assumes that we find the means to *generate* the needed energy—for instance, through controlled fusion—we still face the fundamental thermodynamic fact that virtually all energy unleashed finally ends up as heat in the environment. An everyday example is the energy originally stored in the gas of a car. A significant part of this energy is immediately released as heat through the engine and the radiator, because the engine is necessarily inefficient in converting the potential energy in the gas to the useful mechanical motion of the wheels. But the point is that even the energy resulting in *useful* mechanical motion finally generates heat, in the brakes as they slow the wheels, in the tires as they turn on the road, in the road, and ultimately in the air surrounding the road and the auto. The dissipation of energy into heat is characteristic of all energy-using processes. On a scale larger than autos, there is the vast heat release created by the process of condensation of water vapor to form distilled water in a desalination plant—another example of energy usage adding heat to the environment.

The final fate of energy expended is easily confused with what is commonly called "thermal pollution," namely the waste heat produced locally at power plants, for example, in the generation of electricity, but energy dissipation and thermal pollution are not the same. Waste heat is given off by generating processes, which, in obedience to physical laws, cannot be completely efficient, and the consequent "thermal pollution" heats the environment, of course. But once again, the point is that even the *useful* energy output from the power plant finally ends up as heat, regardless of whether the energy was generated by burning coal or oil, or by nuclear reactions, and regardless of what the energy is being used for. It is theoretically impossible to avoid heat release if one wants to consume energy. No technical gadgetry or scientific breakthrough will circumvent it.

The heat released from all of mankind's energy-using activities will begin to have worldwide climatic effects when the released amount reaches some appreciable fraction of the energy normally absorbed from the sun. Experts disagree on exactly what the fraction is. They do agree, however, that if man wants to avoid major unpredictable changes in the climate he must recognize the fundamental limit to the amount of energy that can be consumed on the surface of the earth.

If worldwide energy consumption increases at four percent per year for another 130 years, man will then be releasing heat amounting to one percent of the incoming solar radiation—enough to increase the temperature of the atmosphere by an estimated ¾ degree centigrade. That may sound like an unimpressive figure, but on a worldwide basis it may lead to climatic upheavals, such as increased melting of the polar ice caps. Local weather perturbations may come much sooner. In just thirty years it is estimated that in the Los Angeles Basin heat released through energy consumption will be eighteen percent of the normal incident solar energy of that area.

Pollution Absorption

A third limitation to population and industrial growth is the earth's finite capacity for absorbing pollution. As we've noted, until quite recently the environment was considered essentially infinite: it seemed impossible that the use of soap for one's laundry or pesticides for one's roses could affect the workings of the world ecosystem. But clearly man's activities *do* affect the world ecosystem. Lake Erie, one of the world's largest fresh-water lakes, has been brought to the verge of ecologic death, CO_2 has increased in the atmosphere all around the world, and the sale of swordfish in the U.S. has been prohibited because of its mercury content. It is becoming abundantly clear that our environment is able to absorb and degrade only a limited amount of emissions and wastes every year. When we exceed this absorptive capacity, we not only cause pollutants to accumulate in nature faster than they can become degraded, but we also run the risk of destroying the natural degradation processes themselves, thus decreasing the future absorptive capacity. This general principle can be described with very real examples. Discharging a small amount of waste into a pond will only slightly lower the water quality, because the pond's microorganisms manage to degrade the pollution as it occurs. A constant higher discharge rate will result in a constant water quality that is lower. The absorptive capacity of the pond is exceeded, however, if one increases the discharge rate to the point where the absorbing microorganisms die because of oxygen depletion or accumulation of toxic wastes. When that happens, continued constant discharge to the pond will simply build up, continually reducing the water quality. This, essentially, is what has nearly "killed" Lake Erie, by no means a small pond.

Thus man is beginning to realize that absorptive capacity—far from being a good in unlimited supply—is an extremely valuable, scarce resource, which in fact limits the total possible pollution arising from human activity.

THE PRESENT GLOBAL TREND: GROWTH

Growth in a Finite World

Having acknowledged the existence of purely physical limitations of our earth (and we have described here only a few of the biological and physical limits that exist), we may now ask whether mankind's present behavior takes into account their existence.

On a global scale man is presently experiencing an exponential growth in population and in what we will call capital—buildings, roads, cars, power plants, machinery, and ships. Some inevitable consequences of this growth are the exponentially increasing demands for food and energy and also the exponentially increasing additions of pollution to the environment.

Because we know that there are upper limits to the supply of food and energy the earth can provide and limits also to the amount of pollution that can be absorbed by the environment, it seems obvious that the material growth that brings us toward these limits cannot continue indefinitely. In fact, matters are most urgent, since indications are that we will surpass several of these constraints within the next few generations if current growth continues. The growth must stop.

How? Are there mechanisms in the world system as it is currently organized that will bring about smoothly the necessary shift from present physical growth trends to other trends consistent with the world's finite capabilities? Or will the transition be sudden and stressful?

These are the questions the Systems Dynamics Group of the A. P. Sloan School of Management at the Massachusetts Institute of Technology set out to illuminate when, in the fall of 1970, it embarked on an effort to devise a model for mathematical simulation of population and capital growth in the world system.

The World Model

The world model is a set of assumptions relating world population, industry, pollution, agriculture, and natural resources. Explicitly, the model represents the growth of population and industry as a function of the biological, political, economic, physical, and social factors that influence this growth. The model also recognizes that population and industrial growth in turn provide feedback to adjust each of those biological, political, economic, physical, or social factors.[1]

The exponential growth of population and capital is inextricably linked with most global problems—unemployment, starvation, disease, pollution, the threat of warfare, and resource shortages. All are influenced importantly by the dynamic interaction of population and capital. No attempt to understand man's long-term options can succeed unless it is firmly based on an understanding of the relationships between these two forces and the ultimate limits to their growth. We can briefly outline some of these relationships as they are reflected in the assumptions on which the world model is based.

Population and births are represented in our model by a positive feedback loop. If there are more people, there will be more births each year, and more births result in more people (as Figure 2 shows). Wherever there is a dominant positive feedback loop of this form, exponential growth will be observed. Capital and investment constitute another positive feedback loop, also shown in Figure 2. Capital produces output of goods and services. If all else is equal, greater output results in a larger investment and thus in more capital. The interactions among population and capital determine the rate at which each grows. These interactions take many forms, as are shown in Figure 3.

Let us examine material output. As output is diverted from investment, the growth of capital decreases. Output may be diverted to services, to agricultural capital such as fertilizer, tractors, or irrigation ditches, and to consumption. As output is diverted to services, these increase: health and education improve, average lifetime becomes greater,

1. Notes and references for this reading will be found on page 306.

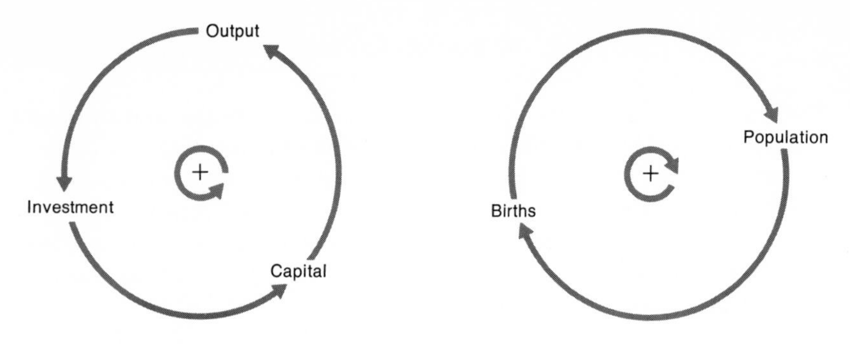

FIGURE 2.
The positive feedback loops governing the growth in population and capital.

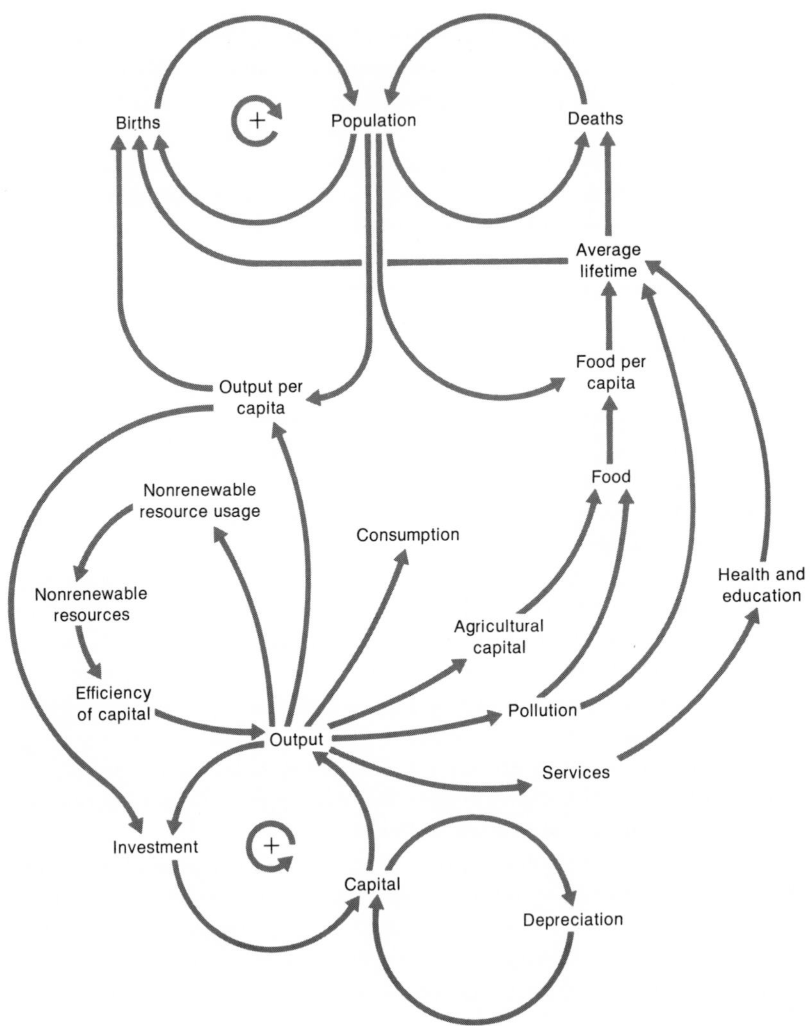

FIGURE 3.
Basic interactions between population growth and capital accumulation.

deaths decrease, and population grows. Similarly, output diverted into agricultural capital results ultimately in more food and a higher average lifetime. Primarily what determines how much output is reinvested and how much is diverted is per capita output. Where output per capita is low, most of it must be diverted to consumption, services, and food, allocations which reduce the rate of accumulation of the capital base and, at the same time, stimulate the growth of population. Population can increase much more easily than capital in societies that have maintained traditional technologies. Hence, output per capita remains low in these countries and they find it very difficult to achieve economic growth.

When output is diverted to consumption it subtracts capital from the system and does not generate future growth directly. Production of material goods consumes resources, and output diverted to consumption through industrial manufacture leads to the depletion of natural resources. As natural resources decline, lower-grade ores must be mined and raw materials must be transported longer distances. Since more capital must be allocated to obtaining resources, the overall production efficiency of capital decreases, and more capital is needed to produce a given amount of output.

Output per capita is the single force with a potential for slowing the population explosion in the model. As output per capita increases, the family size thought to be most desirable declines and birth control efficiency increases. The birth rate then goes down and the population growth rate decreases. That this is a typical trend can be seen in Figure 4, where birth rate is plotted against per capita product. The influence of this trend is accelerated somewhat by the fact that as death rates decline there is a further decrease in desired family size, for a large number of the world's parents bear children primarily as a source of support during old age. If there is a high mortality rate, parents must bear three or four sons to insure that one will live. Thus, as the perceived death rate decreases, so too does the birth rate decline. Material output has one additional impact: it leads to the generation of pollution. Pollution may decrease food production and also decrease the average lifetime.

The simple set of interactions shown in the feedback loops of Figure 3 contain the roots of most important global problems. But though these constitute the essential structure of the world model, a much more accurate description of the assumptions is needed before the model can be used for formal analysis of the consequences of the world assumptions. Figure 5 shows a diagram of the degree of detail included in the final world model. Four main advantages result from collecting assumptions about the world into a formal computer model of this sort. First, the assumed interrelations are listed explicitly, and they are readily available for criticism and improvement by those with knowledge in any

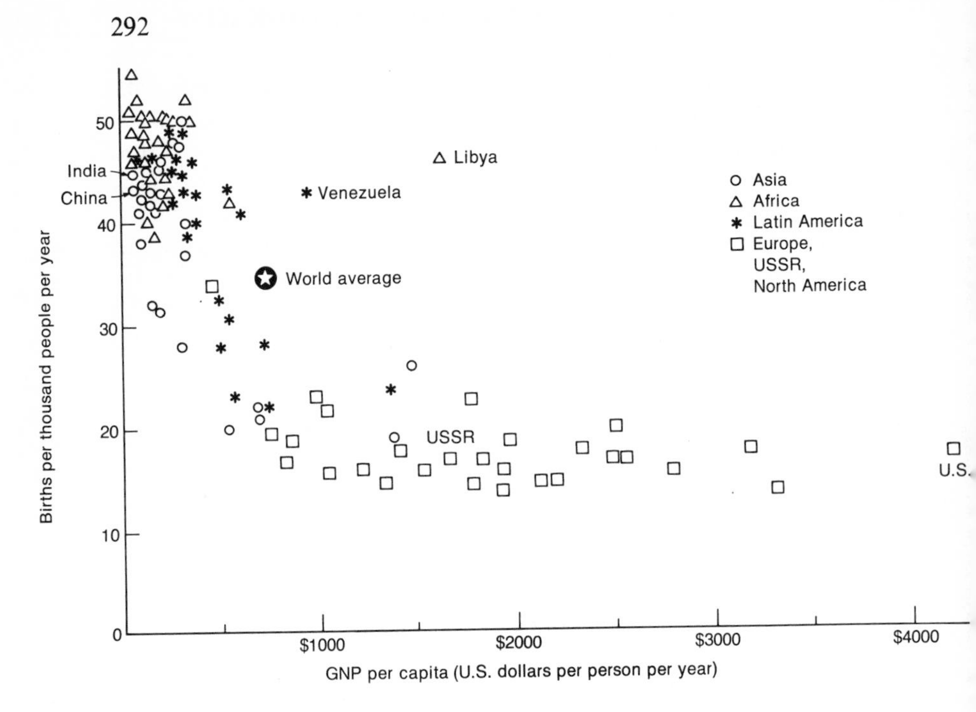

FIGURE 4.
Birth rates in the world's nations show a regular downward trend as GNP per capita increases. More than one-half of the world's people are represented in the upper left-hand corner of the graph, where GNP per capita is less than $500 per person per year and birth rates range from forty to fifty per thousand persons per year. The two major exceptions to the trend, Venezuela and Libya, are oil-exporting nations, where the rise in income is quite recent and income distribution is highly unequal. [Source: U.S. Agency for International Development, *Population Program Assistance* (Washington, D.C.: Government Printing Office, 1970).]

specific problem area. Second, it is possible, with the aid of a computer, to follow the way a set of assumptions about the world system will behave as a function of time. Third, it is possible through such simulation to test the effect of some change in the basic assumptions on which the model rests, and hence, one may investigate which interrelations are critical to the behavior of the system (and thus deserve close study) and which are not. And fourth, the model permits one to study the effects of policies introduced to improve the behavior of the system. Use of the computer speeds up the calculations necessary to consider all the interconnections between variables, mathematical work which would otherwise be very tedious and time consuming.

Given the assumptions about the behavior of the world system outlined above and statistics about world limits and realities, the computer produces diagrams such as those in Figures 6, 7, and 8, showing differing effects of different policies with respect to natural resource usage, pollution control, and allocation of capital investment.

The computer plots the change in eight quantities over time: population (the total number of people), industrial output per capita (measured as the dollar equivalent of output per person per year), food per capita (measured as kilogram-grain equivalent of food per person per year), pollution (measured in relation to the 1970 amount), and nonrenewable resources (measured in relation to the reserves that existed in 1900). The crude birth rate (births per 1000 persons per year) is plotted as B, the crude death rate (deaths per 1000 persons per year) as D, and services per capita (dollar equivalent of services per person per year) is plotted as S.

Each of these variables is plotted on a different vertical scale. The vertical scales have deliberately been omitted and though the horizontal time scale runs through a two hundred year period from 1900 to 2100, these dates have also been made somewhat symbolic in order to emphasize the general behavior modes of the computer results instead of numerical values, which are not precisely but only approximately known. The scales are, however, exactly equal in all the computer runs presented here, so results of different runs may be easily compared. The computer results show only the consequences of the assumptions made in constructing the model. Because the simulation runs are not exact numerical predictions of the future, providing instead qualitative projections of possible future trends, the precise timing of events is less significant than the changes in behavior among simulations, and the years shown at the bottom of each figure are given only as approximate reference points. As mentioned earlier, when we attempt to study the consequences of exponential growth toward the limits of the earth, precise numerical values have relatively little effect in altering the time over which such growth can take place.

Continued Growth Leads to Collapse

The computer simulations show that only if physical growth halts will the earth be able to support comfortable human life. But they show something else too: the transition from growth to nongrowth must be made smoothly. The transition will have to be engineered by man—not by nature. Furthermore, there are no currently existent social mechanisms that will bring physical growth to a smooth and orderly end when the maximum growth that can be supported by the finite global environment is reached. Continued societal emphasis on physical growth will overshoot environmental limitations. A basic redirection of society's

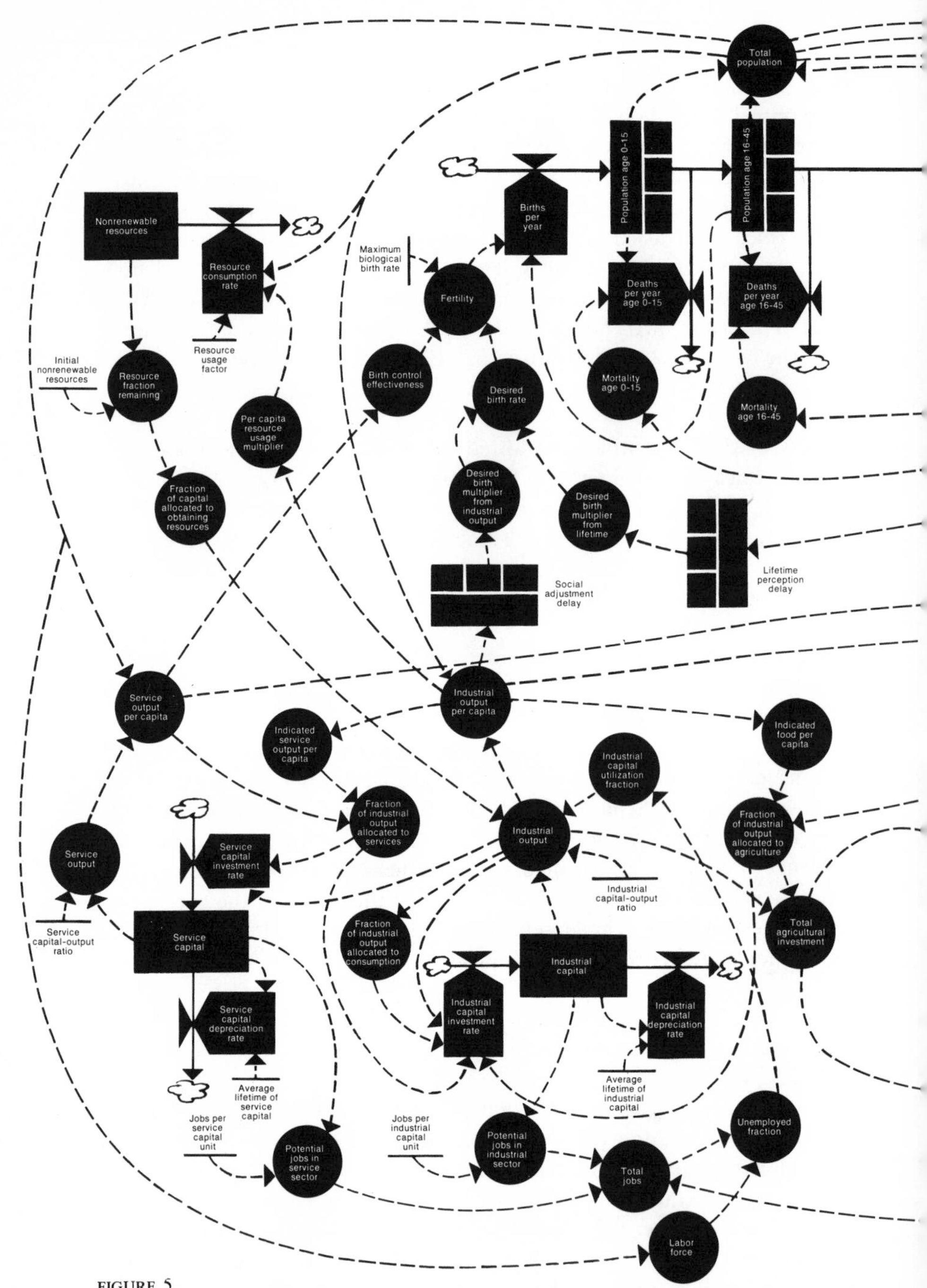

FIGURE 5.
The entire world model is represented here by a flow diagram, in formal system dynamics notation. Levels, or physical quantities that can be measured directly, are indicated by rectangles ▬ , rates that influence those levels by valves ▬⧓ , and

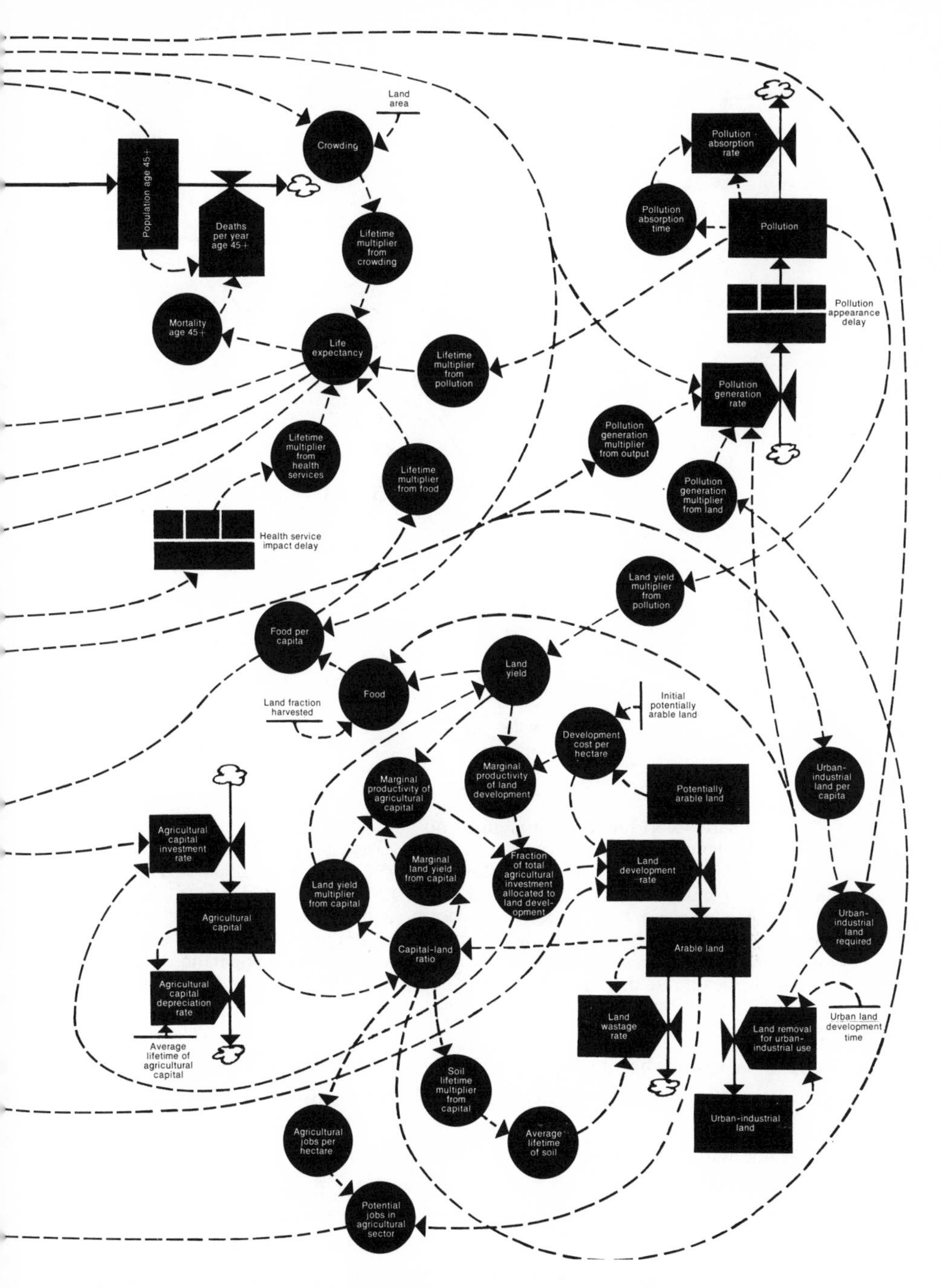

auxiliary variables that influence the rate equations by circles ●. Time delays are indicated by sections within rectangles. Real flows of people, goods, money, etc. are shown by solid arrows ⟶ and causal relationships by broken arrows - - -➔. Clouds represent sources or sinks that are not important to the model behavior.

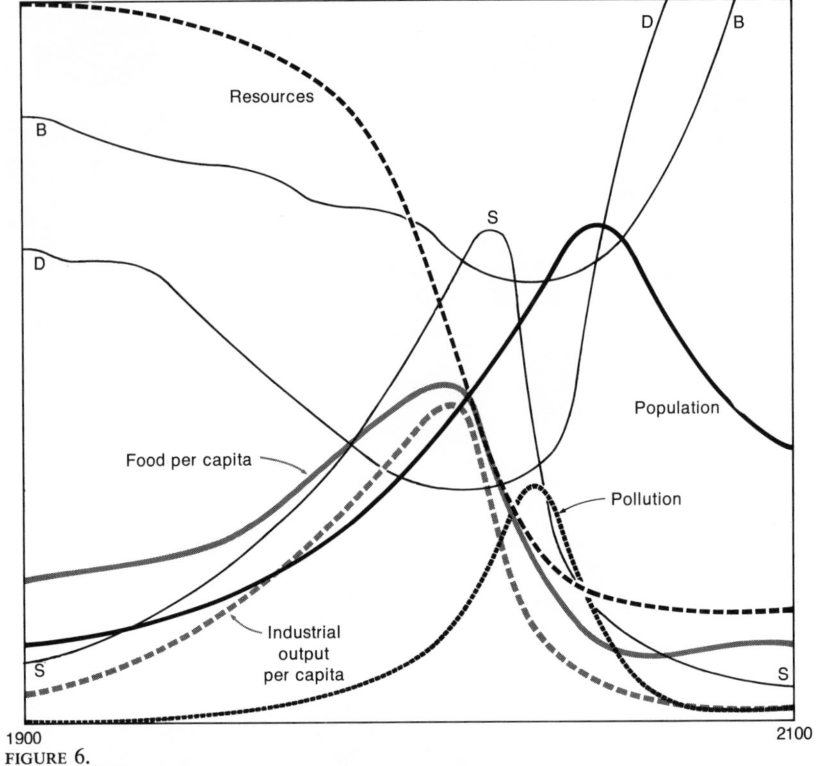

FIGURE 6.
The "standard" world model run assumes no major change in the physical, economic, or social relationships that have historically governed the development of the world system. All variables plotted here follow historical values from 1900 to 1970. Food availability, industrial output, and population grow exponentially until the rapidly diminishing resource base forces a slowdown in industrial growth. But because of natural delays in the system, both population and pollution continue to increase for some time after the peak of industrialization. What finally halts population growth is a rise in the death rate due to decreased food availability and decreased medical services.

goals—a value change away from the current ideal of maximizing material growth—seems to be needed to achieve a smooth end to the current growth.

What will happen in the absence of societal value changes? The physical growth will stop, of course, even without a change through values oriented toward reduced growth. But in that event society will not experience an orderly transition to some feasible final state. Rather the human population will most likely overshoot the physical limitations of the earth, and then be forced into a traumatic decline back to some level of population and industrialization that can be supported by the physical environment—an environment which by then will be sorely de-

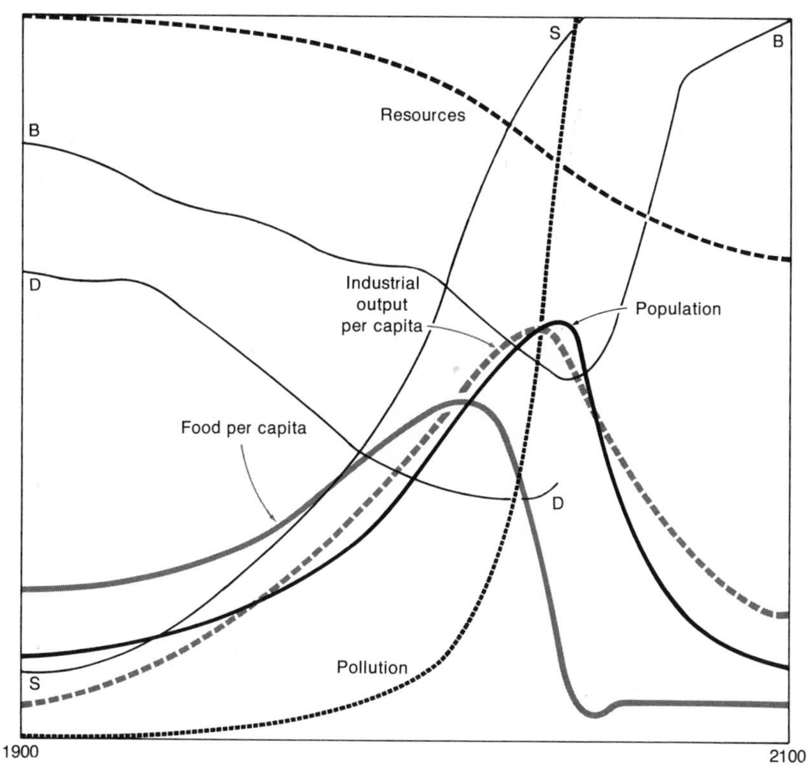

FIGURE 7.
As means of avoiding the resource depletion depicted in Figure 6, resource depletion in the world model system is eliminated by two assumptions: first, that "unlimited" nuclear power will double the resource reserves that can be exploited and, second, that nuclear energy will make extensive programs of recycling and substitution possible. If these changes are the *only* ones introduced in the system, growth is still stopped, by rising pollution.

pleted. For once we exceed any natural constraint, tremendous natural pressures will develop to halt growth. If it happens that the pollution we create exceeds the environmental absorptive capacity, the pressures will take the form of increases in death rates due to impurities in food, water, and air, decreases in crops and fish catches due to reductions in plant and animal life, and a significant reduction in the effectiveness of investment, due to the high costs of controlling the extreme pollution which will then exist in all input factors. These involuntary pressures will mount until population and industrialization finally start to decline, and the pressures will cease only when the world returns to levels of population and industrialization which are consistent with the supporting capacity of the physical environment.

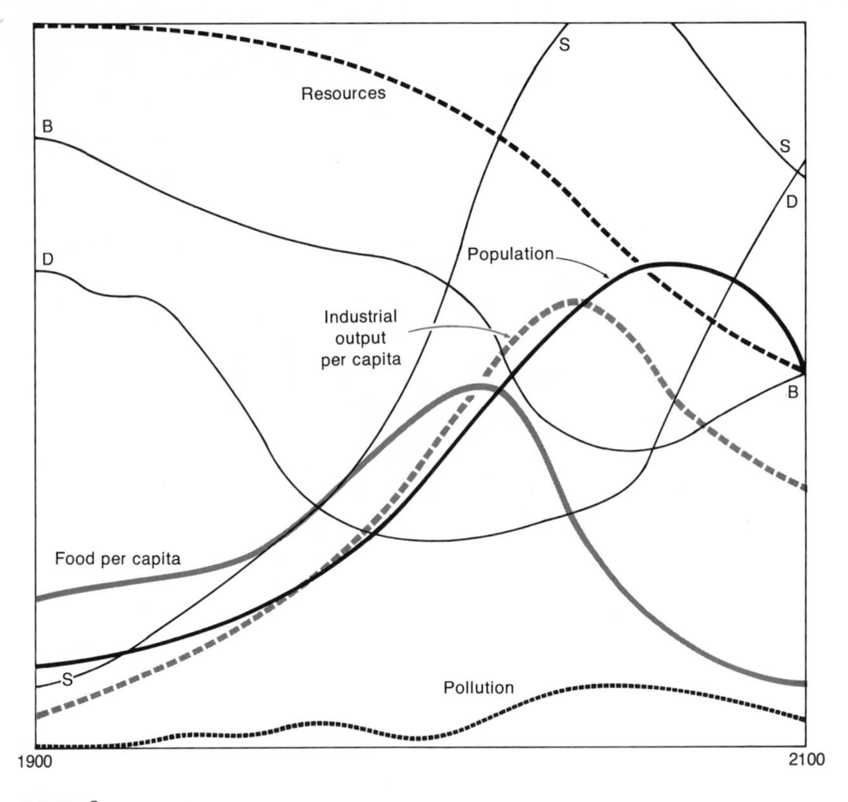

FIGURE 8.
A further technological improvement is added to the world model to avoid the resource depletion and pollution problems of previous model runs. Here we assume that in 1975 pollution generation per unit of industrial and agricultural output can be reduced to one-fourth of its 1970 value. Resource policies are the same as those in Figure 7. The changes allow population and industry to grow until the limit of arable land is reached. Then food per capita declines, and industrial growth is also slowed as capital is diverted to food production.

If man attempts to continue growth by removing one kind of pressure—for instance, by increasing food output with fertilizers and high-yield grains—he alleviates the situation only until he encounters the next constraint. If he manages to remove that constraint, he will soon reach another one. World limitations are analogous to a room with infinitely many ceilings in which man is forever growing taller: one does not *solve* the problem by removing the first ceiling upon contact, nor by removing the second, third, etc. The only solution to growth in a finite space is to halt the growth.

THE ETHICAL BASIS FOR ACTION

The Short-Term Objective Function

We face the fact that continuation of current material growth-practices will inevitably lead to some sort of collapse, with a subsequent decrease in the cultural and economic options of the human race. Inasmuch as this is clearly undesirable, one is naturally led to ask: What shall we do?

It is important to realize that an answer to this question is completely dependent on a choice of criteria for what is "good." If we do not know what we want to obtain, if we don't know our "objective function," it is meaningless to try to decide what to do in a given situation. If one's objective is to maximize the benefits of the people alive today, one's actions will be quite different from what they will be if the goal is to maximize the benefits of all people who are going to live on our planet over the next 200 years.

At least in principle (and it is clear that this is far from being realized) present human behavior is guided by the general idea that all people alive *today* are equally important and that man's objective function is to maximize today's total benefits for all of these people. People have decided in the Western democracies that this objective is best served by letting each individual be free to pursue his own interest. It is assumed, very simply, that if every citizen and institution in the society acts to maximize his own position in the short term, society as a whole will benefit.

This acceptance of the "invisible hand" of classical economic theory has, however, introduced a strong emphasis on short-term benefits in present societies and a disregard for the future. When an action will bring both benefits and costs over time, it is considered acceptable business practice to appraise the net *present* value and to discount the *future* implications in determining whether an action is profitable—and hence whether it should be taken. The result of this procedure is that essentially zero value is assigned to anything happening more than twenty years from now. In other words, plans are acted on even though their cost to society twenty years hence will be enormous—just because the benefits are larger than the costs in the short run (for example, over the next decade).

If we continue to adhere strictly to the objective of maximizing the short-term rewards for the present generation, then we disregard long-term environmental trade-offs. We simply continue what we have practiced in the past, maximizing the current benefits and neglecting any possible future costs. The question about use or nonuse of DDT, for example, is easily resolved for the present generation. The fact that 1.3 billion people today can live in safety from malaria thanks to DDT outweighs the costs—for instance, in the form of inedible fish—inflicted upon future generations through continued use of the chemical, if the short-term objective is man's only concern.

What about the value of human life in the short term? The short-term objective function supports the currently accepted belief that the value of each additional human being is infinite. The severe restrictions each additional human will impose on the choices and perhaps even on the lives of future generations by virtue of his consumption of nonrenewable natural resources and his contribution to the destruction of the life support system of the earth—this is completely neglected when the short-term objective function is used to judge the value of another human being.

Thus we see that adherence to the short-term objective function avoids very simply all trade-offs of current benefits for future costs. Of course, man is left with the more usual trade-offs that affect people alive today—for instance, the choice between denying the firm upstream freedom to dump waste in the river and denying those who live downstream pure drinking water. But conflicts within the short term are not our concern here, because we *do* have mechanisms in our society to resolve conflicts between people alive today.

We do *not* have, however, mechanisms or even moral guidelines for resolving conflicts between the population of the present and the people of the future. This at the same time the world model indicates that the present preoccupation with what seems pleasant and profitable in the short run fuels the growth which will ultimately cause the world's human population to overshoot some physical constraint, forcing us—but especially our descendants—into a period of abrupt and traumatic change.

The Long-Term Objective Function

It is, however, possible to change the objective function, in the same way that, for Western man, the Judeo-Christian religious tradition turned the objectives of man away from selfish gratification and toward consideration of the welfare of all people living at the same point in time. We could, for example, adopt as our cardinal philosophy the rule that no man or institution in our society may take any action that decreases the economic and social options of those who will live on the planet over the next 100 years. Perhaps only organized religion has the moral force to bring about acceptance of such a rule, but perhaps it could result also from an enlightened, widespread program of public education.

So basically there is only one ethical question in the impending global crisis. Should we continue to let our actions be guided by the short-term objective function, or should we adopt a long-term perspective? In other words, what time horizon should we use when comparing the costs and benefits of current actions?

The moral and ethical leaders of the world's societies should, we believe, adopt the goal of increasing the time horizon that forms the context within which all the activities of mankind are set—that is, they should urge acceptance of the long-term objective function that maximizes the benefits for those living today, subject, of course, to the constraint that it should in no way decrease the economic and social options of those who will inherit this globe, our children and grandchildren. This goal is of course not completely foreign to contemporary society. People in general feel responsibility for the lives of all offspring entering the world within their lifespan, and the long-term objective function seems to be the value implicit in the actions of environmental conservationists. However, ultimately it must be present in *all* of our activities—as it is said to have been for the native tribes of Sierra Leone, where nothing could be done to the jungle which would leave it unfit for the use of *any* future generation.

GLOBAL EQUILIBRIUM: A DESIRABLE POSSIBILITY

A Lasting Solution

Assuming that we accept the long-term objective function as the guideline for our actions, what can we do about the approaching collision between our growing societies and the physical limits of the earth? As soon as we are committed to the creation of a long-term, viable world system, our most important task will be to avoid the trauma caused if we actually exceed any of the earth's physical limitations—food production capability, pollution absorption capacity, or resource supply. This can only be done through a deliberate decision to stop physical growth. We must engineer a smooth transition to nongrowth—a "global equilibrium" or steady state in accord with the earth's physical limits. Our generation must halt the growth by developing and utilizing legal, economic, or religious pressures, social substitutes for those pressures that would otherwise be exerted by nature to halt physical growth.

By starting now we may still be able to *choose* the set of pressures we prefer to employ in stopping population and capital growth. We cannot avoid pressures. As we continue growing, nature will supply counterforces—forces that *will* pressure us until growth stops. However, a deliberate choice to live with those counter-forces which are least objectionable is likely to leave many more of our fundamental, long-term objectives intact than will a refusal to recognize the limits nature can enforce through the blind and random action of such natural forces as starvation or social breakdown.

The first requirement for a viable steady state is a constant level of population and capital—that is, the number of people and physical objects must remain constant. A second requirement is equally important. Since we want to create a system capable of existing for a long time, the state of global equilibrium must be characterized by minimal consumption of nonrenewable materials and by minimal production of nondegradable waste. In this way we can maximize the time before resources are depleted and avoid a critical load on the environment.

A computer simulation of the achievement of equilibrium is depicted in Figure 9. Many different possible paths to global equilibrium exist, however, and the choice depends on society's objectives. For instance: should the world support many people at a low material standard of living or a few people at a higher standard? Should the societal objective be exotic, fancy foods or just the basic daily ration of calories, protein, and vitamins?

In an equilibrium phase of human civilization, science and technology will be busy developing ways of constructing products which last very long, do not emit pollution, and can be easily recycled. Competition among individual firms may very well continue, the main difference being that as the total market for material goods will no longer expand, emphasis will shift to repair and maintenance and away from new production.

Although global equilibrium implies nongrowth of all *physical* activities, this need not be the case for cultural activities. Freed from preoccupation with material goods, people may throw their energy into development of the arts and sciences, into the enjoyment of unspoiled nature, and into meaningful interactions with their fellow man, a goal that can be achieved if the production of services flourishes.

The Distribution of Wealth and Responsibility

Stopping the population explosion is becoming more readily accepted as an important task to be accomplished as fast as possible, but what about stopping physical growth? Can the world's wealthy nations really suggest a deliberate restriction of material production, leaving the poor of the world in their present miserable situation?

Striving towards global equilibrium does *not* imply "freezing" the

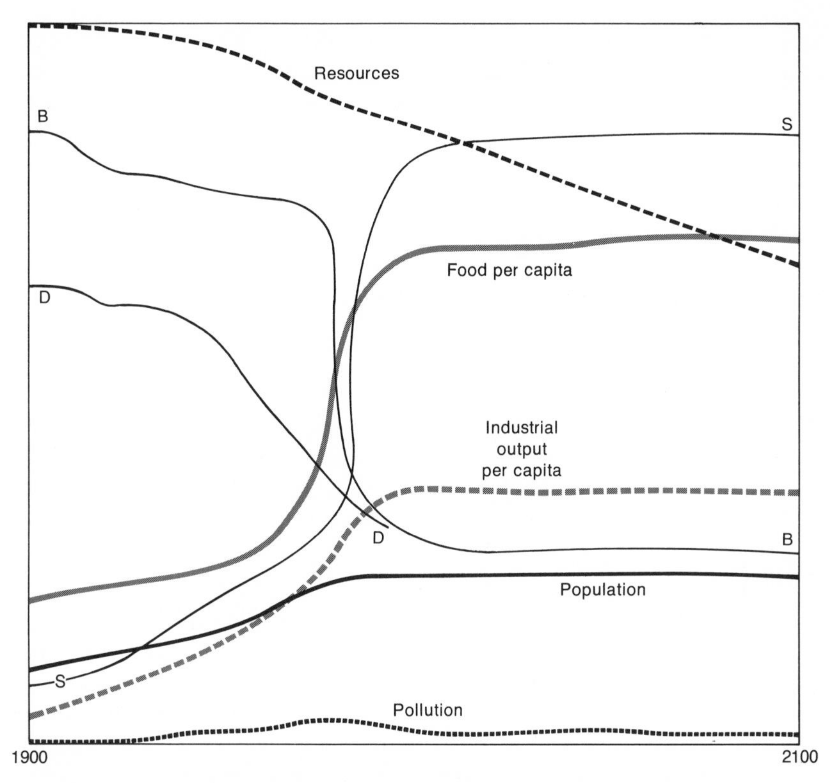

FIGURE 9.
An equilibrium state has been achieved that is sustainable far into the future. Technological policies include resource recycling, pollution control devices, increased lifetime of all forms of capital, and methods to restore eroded and infertile soil. Value changes include increased emphasis on food and services rather than on industrial production. Births are set equal to deaths and industrial capital investment equal to capital depreciation. Equilibrium value of industrial output per capita is three times the 1970 world average.

present configuration of the world's rich and poor nations and peoples. What must finally stop is *overall* material growth, but that does not preclude redistribution of the world's existing material wealth. One possibility is for the developed nations deliberately to stop their growth, possibly even to let themselves "shrink" somewhat, while the developing world is allowed (and maybe helped) to grow materially to an acceptable, but not unbounded state. Thus initially it will be the developed world which has to take the lead in the path toward equilibrium; however, the developing world will have serious responsibilities in attempting to stop its rapidly growing populations.

Many people believe that the goal of maximizing economic growth must be clung to simply because we are still so *very* far from having attained the utopia where everything is plentiful for everyone. However, we must remember the conclusion that a continued reliance on short-term objectives and continued physical growth only makes it certain that there will be no acceptable future—for *any* country. In other words: such a utopia does not exist, and striving toward it is futile.

Also it should be made quite clear that material growth as we have experienced it over the last century in *no* way has resulted in increased equality among the world's people. To the contrary, growth in its present form simply widens the gap between the rich and poor, as indicated by the data in Figure 10.

An end to overall physical growth, however, might very well ultimately lead to a more equitable distribution of wealth throughout the world—because no one would accept material inequalities in the present under the (false) pretense that they would be removed through future growth. Of course the state of global equilibrium will also have its problems, mainly political and ethical. As Herman Daly notes in the introduction to this volume:

> For several reasons the important issue of the steady state will be distribution, not production. The problem of relative shares can no longer be avoided by appeals to growth. The argument that everyone should be happy as long as his absolute share of the wealth increases, regardless of his relative share, will no longer be available. . . . The steady state would make fewer demands on our environmental resources, but much greater demands on our moral resources.[2]

But these political problems have solutions, and society is certainly more likely to find those solutions in an equilibrium state than in a collapsing one.

Stopping the overall physical growth on our planet should not be construed as an attempt by the rich countries to divert attention from economic development to the protection of "their" environment. Rather, global equilibrium is a necessity if mankind wants to have an equitable future on what is altogether a small, fragile planet.

The Golden Age

The presence of global equilibrium could permit the development of an unprecedented golden age for humanity. Freedom from the pressures of providing for ever-increasing numbers of people would make it possible to put substantial effort into the self-realization and development of the individual. Instead of struggling merely to keep people alive, we could

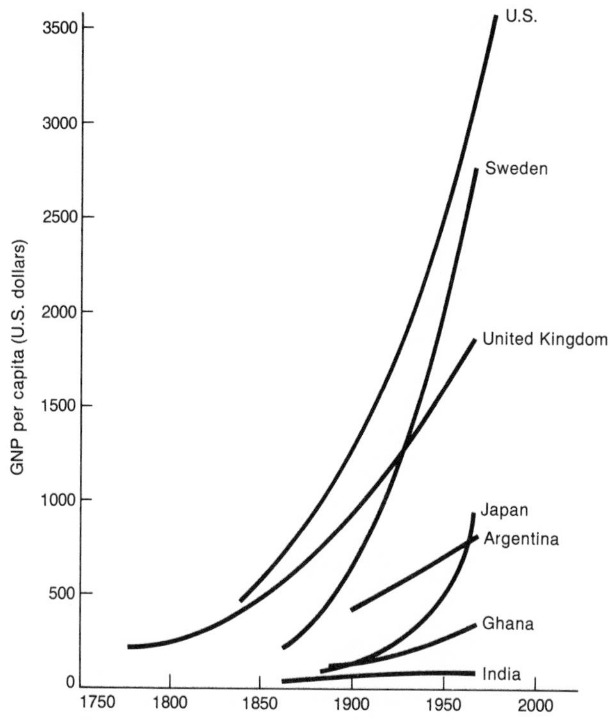

FIGURE 10.
The economic growth of individual nations indicates that differences in exponential growth rates are widening the economic gap between rich and poor countries. [Source: Simon Kuznets, *Economic Growth of Nations*, Cambridge, Mass.: Harvard University Press, 1971.]

employ more of our energy in developing human culture, in increasing the quality of life for the individual far above the present subsistence. The few periods of equilibrium in the past—for example, the 300 years of Japan's classical period—often witnessed a profound flowering of the arts.

The freedom from ever-increasing capital—i.e., from more concrete, cars, dams, and skyscrapers—would make it possible even for our great-grandchildren to enjoy solitude and silence. The desirable aspects of the steady state were first realized more than a century ago. John Stuart Mill wrote in 1857:

> It is scarcely necessary to remark that a stationary condition of capital and population implies no stationary state of human improvement. There would be as much scope as ever for all kinds of mental culture, and moral and social progress; as much room for improving the Art of Living and much

> more likelihood of its being improved, when minds cease to be engrossed by the art of getting on. Even the industrial arts might be as earnestly and as successfully cultivated, with this sole difference, that instead of serving no purpose but the increase of wealth, industrial improvements would produce their legitimate effect, that of abridging labor.[3]

This, then, is the state of global equilibrium, which seems to be the logical consequence of the adoption of the long-term objective function. The changes needed during the transition from growth to global equilibrium are tremendous, and the time is very short. But the results seem worth striving for, and the first step must be to increase our time horizon—to accept the long-term objective function.

NOTES AND REFERENCES

1. More information about the modeling project can be found *in* Meadows, D. H., Meadows, D. L., Randers, J., and Behrens, W. W., *The Limits to Growth*, New York: Universe Books, 1972. This is a popular description of the effort and its conclusions. A formal description of the original world model is contained *in* Forrester, J. W., *World Dynamics*, Cambridge, Mass.: Wright-Allen Press, 1971.
2. This volume, page 19. Originally published in *The Patient Earth*, John Harte and Robert Socolow, eds., New York: Holt, Rinehart and Winston, 1971.
3. J. S. Mill, *Principles of Political Economy*, Vol. II, London: John W. Parker and Son, 1857.

15

ECOLOGY, ETHICS, AND THEOLOGY

John Cobb

Western ethics, like Western thought generally, has been radically anthropocentric. But the disruptions of ecological systems which have brought the world to crisis have called our attention to the need for adopting different patterns of behavior with respect to our environment. Ecological crisis opens the question of whether the moral necessity of behavioral changes follows from the same anthropocentric principles we have had in the past or whether our ethical principles themselves are partly at fault and need alteration. If the latter, on what ground can such alteration be effected? Surely ultimate ethical principles cannot be altered only because we do not like their results.

There are two basic elements in almost any ethical theory, although one or the other is often more implicit than explicit. We require some judgment as to what is good or desirable, and we require some principles of right action. Those who concentrate on the first of these elements, developing a theory of value, often assume that when their work is done the answer to the question of how we ought to act is self-evident. That is, having determined good or desirable values, they suppose that we

"Ecology, Ethics, and Theology." Published by permission of the author.

ought to maximize those values. But this ignores the complex question of exactly what our obligation is if maximization presents conflicts. Should we maximize values in general or our own values? Should we maximize present values or be equally concerned about future values? Are there any acts that we should not perform regardless of the value of their consequences? Is the relation of our present action to past commitments a relevant factor in deciding how we ought now to act? Answering these questions is not a further development of a theory of value but a treatment of the formal questions that belong to ethics proper.

VALUE THEORY

In a value theory it is customary to distinguish types of values. One important distinction is between intrinsic value and instrumental value. An automobile is of instrumental value to me in that it enables me to get places and thereby to have experiences that I would otherwise be denied. Perhaps it may also be instrumentally valuable to me as an object of aesthetic contemplation or as contributory to my feeling of power. So long as its value is only instrumental it must be measured by its potential for contributing to the intrinsic value of my feeling of beauty and power, and by that alone. Hence intrinsic value is our primary consideration.

Although the distinction between instrumental and intrinsic values is important, it should not be exaggerated or misunderstood. There may be some things whose *only* value is instrumental, but there is nothing whose only value is intrinsic. That is, everything or every event has consequences for other things or events. These consequences can be evaluated as relatively favorable or unfavorable. Hence, though not everything can be evaluated in terms of its intrinsic value, everything does have its instrumental value.

It is my contention that whereas everything has instrumental value, only feeling is the locus of intrinsic value. The existence or nonexistence of something that has no feeling seems to me a matter of indifference unless it somehow contributes to the feeling belonging to something else, either actually or potentially. That is to say, what has no feeling has no intrinsic value and its instrumental value is a function of its contribution to something that does feel. Feeling, on the other hand, is intrinsically valuable, while it also has instrumental value in its relation to other feelings.

This doctrine is not far removed from common sense or from traditional theories of value. Utilitarianism proposed to regard only pleasure (and pain) as valuable (and disvaluable). Pleasure is of course a matter of feeling. Critics of utilitarianism have rightly complained that either the notion of pleasure must be taken very broadly or else it must be recognized that men find other feelings beside pleasure valuable. But in general they agree that the locus of intrinsic value is in the sphere of feeling.

However, it is noteworthy that despite a passing reference to the value of feelings of other sentient beings by John Stuart Mill in Chapter II of *Utilitarianism*, utilitarians limited the feeling that is valuable to the feeling humans have, a restriction most value theorists have tended to leave unquestioned. To be concerned about the feelings of other animals has appeared sentimental, and philosophers are even more eager than most men not to appear sentimental.

The most famous opposition to this restriction came from G. E. Moore. It is striking that in order to oppose it he thought he had to give up the locus of value in feeling. In place of "feeling," Moore argues that "good," a nonnatural property, is an objective ingredient in states of affairs. When we contemplate alternative states of affairs, he argues, we recognize one as better than the other, but our judgment is not based on the amount of pleasure present in these alternative states of affairs.

Moore proposes, in Section 50 of his *Principia Ethica*, that we consider two "worlds" in the following way.

> Let us imagine one world exceedingly beautiful. Imagine it as beautiful as you can; put into it whatever on this earth you most admire—mountains, rivers, the sea; trees, and sunsets, stars and moon. Imagine all these combined in the most exquisite proportions, so that no one thing jars against another, but each contributes to increase the beauty of the whole. And then imagine the ugliest world you can possibly conceive. Imagine it simply one heap of filth, containing everything that is most disgusting to us, for whatever reason, and the whole, as far as may be, without one redeeming feature.

In order to separate out the question of the value of these worlds in themselves from their value for a human observer, Moore asks that we suppose that no human being can ever *see* either world. Do we not, he then asks, still believe that it is better for the beautiful world to exist rather than the ugly one?

Moore, however, has not been very convincing. At least he has not convinced me. The beauty and ugliness of which he speaks are relational qualities, that is, they do not exist apart from the way certain formal patterns are apprehended by the human observer. Even though he asks us to imagine them as existing apart from observation or the possibility of observation, we are still visualizing them. But we are asked to suppose they have no effect, actual or potential, on any visualizing activity at all. In that case it simply has no meaning to say that one is beautiful and the other ugly.

My view of value can be sharply juxtaposed to Moore's by introducing into the ugly world something from the filth heap that has not been previously included: a number of worms and insects that men agree are utterly repulsive. Let us suppose that we had purposely excluded such life from the beautiful world. And let us assume further that the ugly world constitutes a suitable environment for our insects and worms, that these are able to secure adequate food and are free from excessive pain. In that case I would contend the ugly world had more value than the beautiful one. For in the ugly world there exist feelings of a level excluded from the beautiful world, namely, the feelings of the worms and insects. Since men are excluded in principle from both worlds, the fact that men would prefer to see and live in the beautiful world is irrelevant. If, on the other hand, we characteristically fill the beautiful world with birds and animals, and restrict residence in the ugly one to insects and worms, I would affirm much greater value to the beautiful world, not because it would appear beautiful to men, which of course it would, but because the feelings of birds and animals are more valuable than those of insects and worms. This I believe is more realistic because there is in fact considerable correlation between what *we* find beautiful and the sort of environment hospitable to higher forms of life.

Thus, whereas I reject Moore's position, I wish strongly to affirm with him, against the anthropocentric tendencies of most value theory, that values do exist apart from man's knowledge of them. If I contemplate two situations which I suppose no man to be cognizant of or affected by, one in which a dog is thoroughly enjoying life and the other in which it is suffering agony from a broken leg, I have no difficulty in judging between them. Enjoyment is an intrinsic good, and agony is an intrinsic evil, whether or not men know about it.

How far does intrinsic value extend beyond man? The question requires us to consider how far feeling extends beyond human feeling. To suppose that only men have feelings is surely arbitrary and contrary to the clear implications of our evolutionary connection with other forms of animal life. The reasonable issue is only how far to extend the category "feeling" or "experience." Do unicellular organisms feel? What about the individual cells in multicellular organisms? Can a sharp line be drawn between cells and subcellular entities? My own view is that no line at all can be drawn, that wherever one deals with actual unitary entities one is dealing with feelings. But of course much that is most important in human feeling depends on such a high evolutionary product as consciousness, and I doubt that there is consciousness where there is no central nervous system. Hence, the feeling we can attribute to lower forms of life, and *a fortiori* to so-called "inanimate" entities like molecules and submolecular forms, is very different from human feeling.

Utilitarianism affirmed that each human being should count for as much as every other. This is a laudably democratic principle, but it has highly questionable features even when applied to humans. It is not really evident that the advantage of a mongoloid idiot or human vegetable should count equally with that of a healthy child. Also there is no objective way of determining the point in development at which a fertilized ovum should count equally with an adult. And the principle cannot function at all when we recognize that there are subhuman intrinsic values as well. It would be quite arbitrary to count a dog's pleasure or pain as equally important with that of a human being. If we extended such a principle to microorganisms the absurdity would become still more apparent. Hence the extension of intrinsic value beyond man to the subhuman world forces consideration of criteria for appraising values.

Utilitarianism did, of course, have criteria. Pleasure is good and pain is bad. What it assumed was that the state of feeling of any person could be plotted somewhere along the continuum between optimal pleasure and maximal pain. It ignored the fact that among persons there may be significant differences in the degree of feeling present. For example, there may be a very intense experience in which the factors of extreme pleasure and extreme pain are so nearly balanced that the utilitarian calculus would yield a negligible value either way. There may be another experience at very low ebb of feeling in which such minimal feeling as is present is purely pleasurable. This would be assigned a top plus score on the utilitarian calculus. The distortion thus introduced would be immeasurably magnified when the subjects compared were a man and a unicellular organism.

For a satisfactory theory of intrinsic value we require initially a quite different measure than pain and pleasure. It must be a quantitative measure of the experience as such rather than of its pleasurableness. A man enjoys *more* experience than do paramecia. How can this "more" be interpreted? One measure is intensity of feeling. We can distinguish between experiences according to their intensity, and other things being equal, we can meaningfully assert that more is happening in the more intense experience than in the less intense experience. But intensity may be gained at the expense of breadth and inclusiveness: how much is included in an experience and how different factors harmonize within it are also meaningful in comparing experiences. Of two experiences one may be more intense and the other more inclusive. Between these a judgment of which is "more" of an experience would be difficult to come by. However, we can judge that an experience in which inclusiveness *and* intensity are combined involves more feeling than would an experience consisting of either in isolation. Thus intensity and inclusiveness and their ideal combination can function as norms for ranking the experiences of men in relation to subhuman forms of life as well as in relation to each other.

There is a high degree of correlation between the amount of pleasure present in an experience and the amount of inclusiveness and intensity. The more broadly we conceive pleasure the more closely we can correlate it with inclusiveness and intensity. Yet the correlation of pleasure with harmony and intensity of experience is not perfect; as for pain the lack of correlation is much too great to be overlooked. Pain, therefore, must be introduced as a distinct factor in the value appraisal. Physical pain or spiritual anguish may be so intense that the annihilation of one experience and even of the possibility for future experiences may be preferable to the continuation of a relatively intense painful experience.

Suffice it to say that a fully developed value theory would have to relate the negative value of pain and suffering to the positive values of inclusiveness and intensity in some coherent way. For purposes of this paper the problem is only indicated.

ETHICS PROPER

With this sketchy indication of the locus of value and the criteria of evaluation, we come to the question of ethics proper. Are we obligated to act so as to maximize value? If so, whose value? Are there other considerations that weigh upon ethical choices?

One major question is whether there is any meaning at all in sentences that state obligations, but let us simply assume here that statements of ethical obligation do have meaning. Our task is to decide which general statement, from among several alternatives is correct. Consider the following:

1. So act as to maximize value for yourself in the present.
2. So act as to maximize value for yourself for the rest of your life.
3. So act as to maximize value for all men for the indefinite future.
4. So act as to maximize value in general.

Of these the first would hardly be viewed as an ethical principle. There are those who suppose that in fact this describes human behavior and that the ethical call to consider a wider sphere is useless. But this is an exceedingly doubtful judgment. Most would recognize that we act with some regard to some future consequences of our actions at least to ourselves.

The second principle is the maxim of prudence. This is recognizably ethical in character. Against the tendency to consider only short-run consequences it calls for full consideration of long-term consequences. Yet it, too, is highly questionable. First, it cannot be defended as describing actual human behavior. There is no clear evidence that men do consider the consequences of their actions for themselves in the distant future more seriously than they consider more immediate consequences to their friends and children. If they do not maximize value for themselves for the rest of their lives, on what grounds can we say they *should*? The argument is sometimes made that consideration of long-term consequences is the one *rational* basis for making decisions. But such a view entails many questionable assumptions. It assumes absolute self-identity through time and absolute separation between one self and all other selves. I believe this is psychologically and metaphysically false, and hence I cannot see how the ethics based upon it can be regarded as uniquely rational.

The third principle is the familiar utilitarian one. An ethical action is one that seeks the greatest good for the greatest number of men. This is profoundly plausible and attractive to all who have been shaped by the Judeo-Christian tradition. Indeed it is a restatement of the fundamental teaching that we should love our neighbors as ourselves.

The basic utilitarian assumption is that it is right to increase value, a principle I accept. That does not mean that people do in fact act in the way such a principle requires. But it means that the sense of rightness points toward this kind of action. I may disregard my neighbor's good and seek only my own, but insofar as I realize that my neighbor's good is in fact, objectively, just as important as my own, I recognize a disproportion between my action and what would be objectively appropriate. I see my action as irrational and hence morally wrong.

My present point, however, is not to defend this view of morality in detail but to point out its instability. If the reason I should seek the greatest good of the greatest number of persons is that it is right to increase value, then limiting this action to human value is arbitrary. It could be justified only if subhuman entities had no intrinsic value. Since the denial of intrinsic value to subhuman entities is false, excluding subhuman entities from the influence of the third principle is without justification. Therefore, only the fourth principle is sufficiently encompassing to be stable and acceptable.

The calculation of pleasure and pain and the multiplication by the number of persons affected, called for by utilitarianism, has never been practicable in detail. Although it has provided a rough and useful guide for making decisions, the extension of such calculations to the subhuman world would be impossibly complex. To be at all functional, we require an image of that state of affairs in which some optimum of value obtains.

We are helped toward an image for this state of affairs by the idea of the biotic pyramid, a concept that describes the movement of life from the soil and the microorganisms therein through vegetation, through the herbivores, and to the carnivores and primates. The total amount of value in a pyramid is roughly correlative with the richness of the base, the number of levels, the diversity of forms and total numbers at each level, and the complexity of living forms at the top. These measures correlate closely with each other.

The more valuable biotic pyramids would clearly place man at the top. Hence the biotic pyramid does not provide an antihuman view of value. Nevertheless, up to a considerable, not yet determined point, man, unlike any other species, can increase his numbers at the top of the pyramid by reducing the number of levels in the pyramid and the diversity of life at each level. For the rich biotic community of the American prairie, man substituted the wheat field and thereby fed a much larger human population. Hence there is a tension between the comprehensive biotic model that is inclusive of man and specialized biotic models in which man's needs alone are better satisfied.

We are warned today that the highly specialized biotic communities produced by man are more precarious than we had previously supposed and that for man's own survival it is important he modify them. However, that is not now the issue before us. *Without* such specializations the total human population would have to be much smaller than it can be *with* such specializations. There is therefore also a tension between what is optimal for man alone and what is optimal when viewed in terms of the biotic pyramid. The problem we face is how to balance these optimalities. If we count only human values, the levels and diversity in the biotic pyramid will be relevant only insofar as they support economic and aesthetic values in human experience, that is, they will be relevant *only* instrumentally. Unless we deny altogether the hierarchical ranking of values, a ranking reflected in the pyramid itself, we cannot discount the great increase of value a larger human population gives so long as population size does not impair the quality of human life. But if we take seriously the fact that all forms of life have value, we cannot ignore the loss of value entailed by man's simplification of the pyramid.

This discussion points to the need for moderating, without renouncing, man's structuring of the world around his own needs. He must of course develop a more realistic view of his actual long-term needs and seek to practice the utilitarian ethic more wisely. When he does so, the value of the biotic pyramid will be more adequately conserved than it is now. But the force of the present argument is that ethical action will require still further moderation of man's actions so as to give greater scope to the biotic pyramid. He must learn to balance his values against the others rather than to judge the others as only instrumental to his. Practically, this points, for example, to the moral obligation to preserve wilderness even beyond the values accruing to man from it.

Thus far the ethical principles considered have been oriented entirely to consequences. There is another tradition in philosophical ethics that is sharply critical of exclusive attention to the consequences of actions, a tradition which interests itself instead in the intrinsic rightness of actions. The most famous spokesman of this tradition is Kant.

Kant's position is extreme. He seems to say, incorrectly, I believe, that the advantages accruing from actions are irrelevant to ethical judgment. However, analysis of his thought indicates that there are two important considerations introduced by his approach which are neglected in the utilitarian approach followed above.

First, Kant points out that an ethical action must be in some way generalizable. It is not enough to calculate that the probable consequences of one's acting in a certain way will increase value. One must also ask what the consequences would be if people in general acted in that way. For example, I might calculate that there would be more increase in value by picking and taking home some wildflowers than by leaving them in the woods. But that would not make this action ethically right unless I could also decide that value would be increased in general by others who picked wildflowers and took them home under similar circumstances. What Garrett Hardin pointed out in "The Tragedy of the Commons" graphically illustrates this principle in relation to the ecological crisis. Since the reader can follow Hardin's logic in another part of this volume, I will not develop it here.

Second, Kant shows that the judgment of the rightness of an action must include consideration of its relationship to the past as well as to the future. If I have made a serious promise, I should not simply ignore that fact when I later face a decision impinging on it. Kant is so convinced of this that he makes extreme—and I think false—judgments about the absolute moral necessity of living up to promises. Most of us could agree that there are many circumstances under which I ought not fulfill a promise no matter how solemnly I made it. But that is not to say that the fact of my having made the promise should have no weight in deciding what to do. If that were the case, as Kant notes, the very notion of a promise would be destroyed.

I have selected the notion of promise as an example. Kant stresses truth-telling. The very nature of society presupposes some kind of mutual commitment to truthfulness except when there are overriding reasons against it. Society presupposes other commitments as well. The acceptance of a job entails implicit as well as explicit commitments. The legal enforcement of contracts is intended to support their moral weight. Marriage is based on mutual vows. Bringing children into the world is understood to entail obligations to them.

My point is that in general what happened at some time before making a decision sets a context for reflection on what one should do on the decision. This is complicated by the fact that what others have done for us may be as important as what we have ourselves done. For me to ignore the great generosity previously extended me by another man when I make a present decision that affects him would be morally wrong. However, what one's debts *really* are cannot be determined by examining's one's *feelings* of gratitude.

There is no simple objective way of determining what commitments one makes in his life, what debts one incurs, and how all of these are to be balanced against each other. Much of the anguish of the ethically sensitive person comes from his realization of the impossibility of living up to all his commitments and repaying all his debts. Further, giving too much consideration to the way in which present action should relate to these "givens" from the past can block fresh and creative action in the present that is oriented to the production of new and greater values in the future.

THEOLOGY

At this point I find myself forced across the threshold from ethics proper to theology. How can a man deal with the inescapable experience of guilt that is engendered by ethical sensitivity? Should he desensitize himself? Or can he persuade himself that he is in fact not guilty? Or can he satisfy himself by balancing the scales and then tipping them toward the side of virtue? Or must he constantly defend himself from the self-accusation of guilt that he projects into every criticism directed toward him by others, however gentle? Or can he experience both the reality and the forgiveness of guilt?

These are all important questions, but they are not the ones that can be appropriately treated here. For our present purposes other functions of theology are more pertinent.

First, since there are no objective bases for determining exactly what commitments one has made and how his indebtedness is to be evaluated, how one defines his basic perspective on life and his fundamental self-understanding become crucial. One man may see himself as self-made, owing little or nothing to society and family. Another man may see society chiefly as a corrupt institution and a corrupting force, and he may locate any power that works for good in the virtue of individual men. A third man may see all that is most valuable in his own life as given to him through society and he may deplore his own tendencies toward ingratitude and violation of the rules of society. Evaluation of these several judgments, so important for the functioning of the ethical principles we discussed earlier, belongs to theology.

The most important theological question for our discussion is whether men have any commitments or debts beyond the limits of human society. Now the theological diversity becomes still clearer. Certainly Kant had no perception of such a relation of ethics to the natural environment. And in this respect his position is typical of that of Western ethics in general. But there are exceptions.

It is possible to see one's life neither as self-made nor as the product of human society alone but as a gift of the total evolutionary process. If I view myself primarily in this way, then it is appropriate for my response to be one of gratitude. The fitting ethical action then is service of that to which I find myself so comprehensively indebted. To serve the evolutionary process can be understood to mean furthering its inclusive work. One would then strive in general to contribute to the progress or growth of life in all its diversity of forms, beginning with human life but by no means limiting oneself to it.

This religious objective is thus far stated very vaguely. Its clarification is a theological task. What is the "total evolutionary process"? And how should we understand it? It would, of course, be possible to understand evolution in such a way that commitment to it would have quite opposite effects from those I have listed. For example, if one's vision of evolution is dominated by the notion of "survival of the fittest" then he might rejoice in man's continuing success in stamping out all competitive forms of life. He might also encourage ruthless competition among human individuals and societies so as to accelerate the evolutionary process if evolution were understood in this way.

I suggest that far more basic to the evolutionary process than survival of the fittest is the urge for survival itself. In living things there is an urge for life, for continued life, for more and better life. Theories of evolution describe the results of this pervasive urge, which certainly produces competition as well as cooperation. But theories of evolution presuppose the urge, apart from which there would be nothing to compete for. But I think this urge itself, rather than the formulae which describe aspects of its consequences, is what one may reasonably feel indebted to for his existence.

If this urge works toward more and better life, one must have some criteria for understanding what that means. Here we can return generally to the theory of value with which we began. More and better life is that in which there is enhancement of feeling. Feeling is enhanced when it can be more inclusive and intense and when pain is not excessive. Consciousness marks and enriches higher levels of feeling. A man may reasonably understand the very rich potentiality of feeling that is his as the product of millions of years of evolutionary development in which the urge for more and better life has been at work. One's sense of what is ethically appropriate can be deeply affected by this vision.

Even here, however, the implications can be ambiguous. Since the values of human experience represent the consummate achievement of the evolutionary process, one might still deduce that evolution's lesser achievements are of trivial importance for the furtherance of the evolutionary process. One might suppose that it is appropriate for ethics to be instrumental in furthering the development, through the human species, of superhuman forms of life. The question here is how to appraise the rich variety of the products of the evolutionary process. Is there value in the variety as such, apart from the relatively minor value that most evolutionary products have for human contemplation, exploitation, and study. Does the evolutionary process in some way prize its own products?

The importance of this question can be seen if we consider again the kind of intrinsic value that variety can have. We have seen that inclusiveness enriches the value of experience. Reducing what is available for inclusion thus reduces the potential value of subsequent experience. Thus reduction of the number of species of living things on the earth would mean some reduction also of potential for future value. Yet the great variety of species now existing has but trivial relevance for most human experience, and if the value of variety is based on consideration of relevance alone, it would count but little.

When we say we feel variety has great value, we tend to think of this variety in terms of an inclusive perspective. We conceive of the biota of the planet earth not as life viewed by man but as life viewed by a larger, more inclusive perspective. When we do so, we attribute a value to the whole that is greatly enriched by all the complex contrasts and interrelations of the parts, man being one of those parts.

Is the perspective from which this rich value can be contemplated a real perspective? The *idea* of an inclusive perspective is a real idea, but if it is only an idea in the minds of men, the values a *real* perspective would generate do, in fact, not obtain, and the prizing of variety of life is then mostly sentimental.

If, however, reality is such that there *is* an inclusive perspective in addition to the limited ones which are human, the value of the variety of life is real. And our callous disregard of the values of the whole for the sake of values of parts is a violation and desecration that has great ethical importance. To believe this is to believe, implicitly if not explicitly, in God.

Theology has yet another importance to an ecological ethics, and in this connection theology and ecological ethics relate to each other much the way theology relates to purely humanistic ethics, but it is worthwhile to consider this additional relation in the context of ecological ethics: ethical theory focuses attention on clearly conscious decision-making, telling us how we should balance the factors on which we reflect when making such decisions. Conscious decision-making depends on calculations of probable consequences of alternative actions and on the relation of action to behavior shaped by past commitments and obligations.

I do not want to disparage ethical behavior. In comparison with the widespread tendency to thoughtless selfishness, mere conventionalism, and compulsiveness, ethical behavior is of utmost desirability. Yet ethical living or ethical behavior also has its problems and limitations. We can take time to note only two.

First, life is a constant series of subtle decisions, many of them unconscious, and it is therefore easy to exaggerate the importance of what are really rather rare instances calling for reflective decision-making. To extend reflective decision-making as a norm too far toward trivial decisions would be to make wholesome living impossible.

Second, ethical reflection necessarily operates with the knowledge that is presently available. The decision must be made in terms of the expectation of consequences established by this limited knowledge. This is inevitable. That part of his knowledge which can be easily and articulately expressed also takes precedence over less easily expressible sensitivities and implicit understandings. The subtle lure of as yet unimagined values has little opportunity to play its role. Ethical action is almost always conservative.

The problem can be seen in human history. It can be illustrated in the characteristic tensions between art and morality. Moral principles tend to formulate and enforce practices supportive of fully apprehended goods, i.e., those values recognized and established in the community. The artist is often exploring the fringes of his sensibility in ways that cannot be but destructive of the established order of values.

If we place these considerations in the still wider context of the whole evolutionary process they become still more important. The urge toward continued, increased, and enhanced life has pushed and pulled living things through hundreds of millions of years toward new and unforeseeable forms. Unforeseeable ends cannot come into the calculation of the utilitarian ethicist. Hence, to serve the evolutionary process cannot be simply identical with making ethical decisions calculated to further it. We need to work with the process rather than only to manipulate it.

What then is the alternative? The alternative, I think, would be sensitivity to the urge toward life as it operates both within oneself and in the entire world. The alternative would be attunement of the self to that creative process. And this can lead to a spontaneity that is informed by rational ethics but at the same time transcends rational ethics.

16

THE ABOLITION OF MAN

C. S. Lewis

It came burning hot into my mind, whatever he said and however he flattered, when he got me to his house, he would sell me for a slave.
John Bunyan

"Man's conquest of Nature" is an expression often used to describe the progress of applied science. "Man has Nature whacked" said someone to a friend of mine not long ago. In their context the words had a certain tragic beauty, for the speaker was dying of tuberculosis. "No matter," he said, "I know I'm one of the casualties. Of course there are casualties on the winning as well as on the losing side. But that doesn't alter the fact that it is winning." I have chosen this story as my point of departure in order to make it clear that I do not wish to disparage all that is really beneficial in the process described as "Man's conquest," much less all the real devotion and self-sacrifice that has gone to make it possible. But having done so I must proceed to analyse this conception a little more closely. In what sense is Man the possessor of increasing power over Nature?

Let us consider three typical examples: the aeroplane, the wireless, and the contraceptive. In a civilized community, in peacetime, anyone

---

"The Abolition of Man." From *The Abolition of Man*, by C. S. Lewis. The Macmillan Company. 1947. Reprinted by permission of the publisher.

who can pay for them may use these things. But it cannot strictly be said that when he does so he is exercising his own proper or individual power over Nature. If I pay you to carry me, I am not therefore myself a strong man. Any or all of the three things I have mentioned can be withheld from some men by other men—by those who sell, or those who allow the sale, or those who own the sources of production, or those who make the goods. What we call Man's power is, in reality, a power possessed by some men which they may, or may not, allow other men to profit by. Again, as regards the powers manifested in the aeroplane or the wireless, Man is as much the patient or subject as the possessor, since he is the target both for bombs and for propaganda. And as regards contraceptives, there is a paradoxical, negative sense in which all possible future generations are the patients or subjects of a power wielded by those already alive. By contraception simply, they are denied existence; by contraception used as a means of selective breeding, they are, without their concurring voice, made to be what one generation, for its own reasons, may choose to prefer. From this point of view, what we call Man's power over Nature turns out to be a power exercised by some men over other men with Nature as its instrument.

It is, of course, a commonplace to complain that men have hitherto used badly, and against their fellows, the powers that science has given them. But that is not the point I am trying to make. I am not speaking of particular corruption and abuses which an increase of moral virtue would cure. I am considering what the thing called "Man's power over Nature" must always and essentially be. No doubt, the picture could be modified by public ownership of raw materials and factories and public control of scientific research. But unless we have a world state this will still mean the power of one nation over others. And even within the world state or the nation it will mean (in principle) the power of majorities over minorities, and (in the concrete) of a government over the people. And all long-term exercises of power, especially in breeding, must mean the power of earlier generations over later ones.

The latter point is not always sufficiently emphasized, because those who write on social matters have not yet learned to imitate the physicists by always including Time among the dimensions. In order to understand fully what Man's power over Nature, and therefore the power of some men over other men, really means, we must picture the race extended in time from the date of its emergence to that of its extinction. Each generation exercises power over its successors: and each, insofar as it modifies the environment bequeathed to it and rebels against tradition, resists and limits the power of its predecessors. This modifies the picture which is sometimes painted of a progressive emancipation from tradition and a progressive control of natural processes resulting in a continual increase of human power. In reality, of course, if any one age really attains, by eugenics and scientific education, the power to make its descendants what it pleases, all men who live after it are the patients of that power. They are weaker, not stronger: for though we may have put wonderful machines in their hands we have preordained how they are to use them. And if, as is almost certain, the age which had thus attained maximum power over posterity were also the age most emancipated from tradition, it would be engaged in reducing the power of its predecessors almost as drastically as that of its successors. And we must also remember that, quite apart from this, the later a generation comes—the nearer it lives to that date at which the species becomes extinct—the less power it will have in the forward direction, because its subjects will be so few. There is therefore no question of a power vested in the race as a whole steadily growing as long as the race survives. The last men, far from being the heirs of power, will be of all men most subject to the dead hand of the great planners and conditioners and will themselves exercise least power upon the future. The real picture is that of one dominant age—let us suppose the hundredth century A.D.—which resists all previous ages most successfully and dominates all subsequent ages most irresistibly, and thus is the real master of the human species. But even within this master generation (itself an infinitesimal minority of the species) the power will be exercised by a minority smaller still. Man's conquest of Nature, if the dreams of some scientific planners are realized, means the rule of a few hundreds of men over billions upon billions of men. There neither is nor can be any simple increase of power on Man's side. Each new power won *by* man is a power *over* man as well. Each advance leaves him weaker as well as stronger. In every victory, besides being the general who triumphs, he is also the prisoner who follows the triumphal car.

I am not yet considering whether the total result of such ambivalent victories is a good thing or a bad. I am only making clear what Man's conquest of Nature really means and especially that final stage in the conquest, which, perhaps, is not far off. The final stage is come when Man by eugenics, by prenatal conditioning, and by an education and propaganda based on a perfect applied psychology, has obtained full control over himself. *Human* nature will be the last part of Nature to surrender to Man. The battle will then be won. We shall have "taken the thread of life out of the hand of Clotho" and be henceforth free to make our species whatever we wish it to be. The battle will indeed be won. But who, precisely, will have won it?

For the power of Man to make himself what he pleases means, as we have seen, the power of some men to make other men what *they* please. In all ages, no doubt, nurture and instruction have, in some sense, attempted to exercise this power. But the situation to which we must look forward will be novel in two respects. In the first place, the power will be enormously increased. Hitherto the plans of educationalists have achieved very little of what they attempted and indeed, when we read them—how Plato would have every infant "a bastard nursed in a bureau," and Elyot would have the boy see no men before the age of seven and, after that, no women,[1] and how Locke wants children to have leaky shoes and no turn for poetry[2]—we may well thank the beneficent obstinacy of real mothers, real nurses, and (above all) real children for preserving the human race in such sanity as it still possesses. But the man-moulders of the new age will be armed with the powers of an omnicompetent state and an irresistible scientific technique: we shall get at last a race of conditioners who really can cut out all posterity in what shape they please. The second difference is even more important. In older systems both the kind of man the teachers wished to produce and their motives for producing him were prescribed by the *Tao*—a norm to which the teachers themselves were subject and from which they claimed no liberty to depart.[3] They did not cut men to some pattern they had chosen. They handed on what they had received: they initiated the young neophyte into the mystery of humanity which over-arched him and them alike. It was but old birds teaching young birds to fly. This will be changed. Values are now mere natural phenomena. Judgments of value are to be produced in the pupil as part of the conditioning. Whatever *Tao* there is will be the product, not the motive, of education. The conditioners have been emancipated from all that. It is one more part of Nature which they have conquered. The ultimate springs of human action are no longer, for them, something given. They have surrendered —like electricity: it is the function of the Conditioners to control, not to obey them. They know how to *produce* conscience and decide what kind of conscience they will produce. They themselves are outside, above. For we are assuming the last stage of Man's struggle with Nature. The final victory has been won. Human nature has been conquered—and, of course, has conquered, in whatever sense those words may now bear.

The Conditioners, then, are to choose what kind of artificial *Tao* they will, for their own good reasons, produce in the Human race. They are the motivators, the creators of motives. But how are they going to be motivated themselves? For a time, perhaps, by survivals, within their own minds, of the old "natural" *Tao*. Thus at first they may look upon themselves as servants and guardians of humanity and conceive that they have a "duty" to do it "good." But it is only by confusion that they can remain in this state. They recognize the concept of duty as the result

1. Notes and references for this reading will be found on page 332.

of certain processes which they can now control. Their victory has consisted precisely in emerging from the state in which they were acted upon by those processes to the state in which they now use them as tools. One of the things they now have to decide is whether they will, or will not, so condition the rest of us that we can go on having the old idea of duty and the old reactions to it. How can duty help them to decide that? Duty itself is up for trial: it cannot be also the judge. And "good" fares no better. They know quite well how to produce a dozen different conceptions of good in us. The question is which, if any, they should produce. No conception of good can help them to decide. It is absurd to fix on one of the things they are comparing and make it the standard of comparison.

To some it will appear that I am inventing a factitious difficulty for my Conditioners. Other, more simpleminded, critics may ask "Why should you suppose they will be such bad men?" But I am not supposing them to be bad men. They are, rather, not men (in the old sense) at all. They are, if you like, men who have sacrificed their own share in traditional humanity in order to devote themselves to the task of deciding what "Humanity" shall henceforth mean. "Good" and "bad," applied to them, are words without content: for it is from them that the content of these words is henceforward to be derived. Nor is their difficulty factitious. We might suppose that it was possible to say "After all, most of us want more or less the same things—food and drink and sexual intercourse, amusement, art, science, and the longest possible life for individuals and for the species. Let them simply say, This is what we happen to like, and go on to condition men in the way most likely to produce it. Where's the trouble?" But this will not answer. In the first place, it is false that we all really like the same things. But even if we did, what motive is to impel the Conditioners to scorn delights and live laborious days in order that we, and posterity, may have what we like? Their duty? But that is only the *Tao*, which they may decide to impose on us, but which cannot be valid for them. If they accept it, then they are no longer the makers of conscience but still its subjects, and their final conquest over Nature has not really happened. The preservation of the species? But why should the species be preserved? One of the questions before them is whether this feeling for posterity (they know well how it is produced) shall be continued or not. However far they go back, or down, they can find no ground to stand on. Every motive they try to act on becomes at once a *petitio*. It is not that they are bad men. They are not men at all. Stepping outside the *Tao*, they have stepped into the void. Nor are their subjects necessarily unhappy men. They are not men at all: they are artifacts. Man's final conquest has proved to be the abolition of Man.

Yet the Conditioners will act. When I said just now that all motives fail them, I should have said all motives except one. All motives that claim any validity other than that of their felt emotional weight at a given moment have failed them. Everything except the *sic volo, sic jubeo* has been explained away. But what never claimed objectivity cannot be destroyed by subjectivism. The impulse to scratch when I itch or to pull to pieces when I am inquisitive is immune from the solvent which is fatal to my justice, or honour, or care for posterity. When all that says "it is good" has been debunked, what says "I want" remains. It cannot be exploded or "seen through" because it never had any pretensions. The Conditioners, therefore, must come to be motivated simply by their own pleasure. I am not here speaking of the corrupting influence of power nor expressing the fear that under it our Conditioners will degenerate. The very words *corrupt* and *degenerate* imply a doctrine of value and are therefore meaningless in this context. My point is that those who stand outside all judgments of value cannot have any ground for preferring one of their own impulses to another except the emotional strength of that impulse. We may legitimately hope that among the impulses which arise in minds thus emptied of all "rational" or "spiritual" motives, some will be benevolent. I am very doubtful myself whether the benevolent impulses, stripped of that preference and encouragement which the *Tao* teaches us to give them and left to their merely natural strength and frequency as psychological events, will have much influence. I am very doubtful whether history shows us one example of a man who, having stepped outside traditional morality and attained power, has used that power benevolently. I am inclined to think that the Conditioners will hate the conditioned. Though regarding as an illusion the artificial conscience which they produce in us their subjects, they will yet perceive that it creates in us an illusion of meaning for our lives which compares favourably with the futility of their own: and they will envy us as eunuchs envy men. But I do not insist on this, for it is mere conjecture. What is not conjecture is that our hope even of a "conditioned" happiness rests on what is ordinarily called "chance"—the chance that benevolent impulses may on the whole predominate in our Conditioners. For without the judgment "Benevolence is good"—that is, without reentering the *Tao*—they can have no ground for promoting or stabilizing their benevolent impulses rather than any others. By the logic of their position they must just take their impulses as they come, from chance. And Chance here means Nature. It is from heredity, digestion, the weather, and the association of ideas, that the motives of the Conditioners will spring. Their extreme rationalism, by "seeing through" all "rational" motives, leaves them creatures of wholly irrational behavior. If you will not obey the *Tao*, or else commit suicide, obedience to impulse (and therefore, in the long run, to mere "nature") is the only course left open.

At the moment, then, of Man's victory over Nature, we find the whole human race subjected to some individual men, and those individuals subjected to that in themselves which is purely "natural"—to their irrational impulses. Nature, untrammelled by values, rules the Conditioners and, through them, all humanity. Man's conquest of Nature turns out, in the moment of its consummation, to be Nature's conquest of Man. Every victory we seemed to win has led us, step by step, to this conclusion. All Nature's apparent reverses have been but tactical withdrawals. We thought we were beating her back when she was luring us on. What looked to us like hands held up in surrender was really the opening of arms to enfold us forever. If the fully planned and conditioned world (with its *Tao* a mere product of the planning) comes into existence, Nature will be troubled no more by the restive species that rose in revolt against her so many millions of years ago, will be vexed no longer by its chatter of truth and mercy and beauty and happiness. *Ferum victorem cepit:* and if the eugenics are efficient enough there will be no second revolt, but all snug beneath the Conditoners, and the Conditioners beneath her, till the moon falls or the sun grows cold.

My point may be clearer to some if it is put in a different form. Nature is a word of varying meanings, which can best be understood if we consider its various opposites. The Natural is the opposite of the Artificial, the Civil, the Human, the Spiritual, and the Supernatural. The Artificial does not now concern us. If we take the rest of the list of opposites, however, I think we can get a rough idea of what men have meant by Nature and what it is they oppose to her. Nature seems to be the spatial and temporal, as distinct from what is less fully so or not so at all. She seems to be the world of quantity, as against the world of quality: of objects as against consciousness: of the bound, as against the wholly or partially autonomous: of that which knows no values as against that which both has and perceives value: of efficient causes (or, in some modern systems, of no causality at all) as against final causes. Now I take it that when we understand a thing analytically and then dominate and use it for our own convenience we reduce it to the level of "Nature" in the sense that we suspend our judgments of value about it, ignore its final cause (if any), and treat it in terms of quantity. This repression of elements in what would otherwise be our total reaction to it is sometimes very noticeable and even painful: something has to be overcome before we can cut up a dead man or a live animal in a dissecting room. These objects *resist* the movement of the mind whereby we thrust them into the world of mere Nature. But in other instances too, a similar price is exacted for our analytical knowledge and manipulative power, even if we have ceased to count it. We do not look at trees either as Dryads or as beautiful objects while we cut them into beams: the first man who did so may have felt the price keenly, and the bleeding trees in Virgil and Spenser may be far-off echoes of that primeval sense of impiety. The stars lost their divinity as astronomy developed, and the Dying God has no place in chemical agriculture. To many, no doubt, this process is simply the gradual discovery that the real world is different from what we expected and the old opposition to Galileo or to "body-snatchers" is simply obscurantism. But that is not the whole story. It is not the greatest of modern scientists who feel most sure that the object, stripped of its qualitative properties and reduced to mere quantity, is wholly real. Little scientists, and little unscientific followers of science, may think so. The great minds know very well that the object, so treated, is an artificial abstraction, that something of its reality has been lost.

From this point of view the conquest of Nature appears in a new light. We reduce things to mere Nature *in order that* we may "conquer" them. We are always conquering Nature, because "Nature" is the name for what we have, to some extent, conquered. The price of conquest is to treat a thing as mere Nature. Every conquest over Nature increases her domain. The stars do not become Nature till we can weigh and measure them: the soul does not become Nature till we can psychoanalyse her. The wresting of powers *from* Nature is also the surrendering of things *to* Nature. As long as this process stops short of the final stage we may well hold that the gain outweighs the loss. But as soon as we take the final step of reducing our own species to the level of mere Nature, the whole process is stultified, for this time the being who stood to gain and the being who has been sacrificed are one and the same. This is one of the many instances where to carry a principle to what seems its logical conclusion produces absurdity. It is like the famous Irishman who found that a certain kind of stove reduced his fuel bill by half and thence concluded that two stoves of the same kind would enable him to warm his house with no fuel at all. It is the magician's bargain: give up our soul, get power in return. But once our souls, that is, ourselves, have been given up, the power thus conferred will not belong to us. We shall in fact be the slaves and puppets of that to which we have given our souls. It is in Man's power to treat himself as a mere "natural object" and his own judgments of value as raw material for scientific manipulation to alter at will. The objection to his doing so does not lie in the fact that his point of view (like one's first day in a dissecting room) is painful and shocking till we grow used to it. The pain and the shock are at most a warning and a symptom. The real objection is that if man chooses to treat himself as raw material, raw material he will be; not raw material to be manipulated, as he fondly imagined, by himself, but by mere appetite, that is, mere Nature, in the person of his dehumanized Conditioners.

We have been trying, like Lear, to have it both ways: to lay down our human prerogative and yet at the same time to retain it. It is impossible. Either we are rational spirit obliged forever to obey the absolute values of the *Tao*, or else we are mere nature to be kneaded and cut into new shapes for the pleasures of masters who must, by hypothesis, have no motive but their own "natural" impulses. Only the *Tao* provides a common human law of action which can overarch rulers and ruled alike. A dogmatic belief in objective value is necessary to the very idea of a rule which is not tyranny or an obedience which is not slavery.

I am not here thinking solely, perhaps not even chiefly, of those who are our public enemies at the moment. The process which, if not checked, will abolish Man, goes on apace among Communists and Democrats no less than among Fascists. The methods may (at first) differ in brutality. But many a mild-eyed scientist in pince-nez, many a popular dramatist, many an amateur philosopher in our midst, means in the long run just the same as the Nazi rulers of Germany. Traditional values are to be "debunked" and mankind to be cut out into some fresh shape at the will (which must, by hypothesis, be an arbitrary will) of some few lucky people in one lucky generation which has learned how to do it. The belief that we can invent "ideologies" at pleasure, and the consequent treatment of mankind as mere υλη, specimens, preparations, begins to affect our very language. Once we killed bad men: how we liquidate unsocial elements. Virtue has become *integration* and diligence *dynamism*, and boys likely to be worthy of a commission "potential officer material." Most wonderful of all, the virtues of thrift and temperance, and even of ordinary intelligence, are *sales resistance*.

The true significance of what is going on has been concealed by the use of the abstraction Man. Not that the word Man is necessarily a pure abstraction. In the *Tao* itself, as long as we remain within it, we find the concrete reality in which to participate is to be truly human: the real common will and common reason of humanity, alive, and growing like a tree, and branching out, as the situation varies, into ever new beauties and dignities of application. While we speak from within the *Tao* we can speak of Man having power over himself in a sense truly analogous to an individual's self-control. But the moment we step outside and regard the *Tao* as a mere subjective product, this possibility has disappeared. What is now common to all men is a mere abstract universal, an H.C.F., and Man's conquest of himself means simply the rule of the Conditioners over the conditioned human material, the world of post-humanity which, some knowingly and some unknowingly, nearly all men in all nations are at present labouring to produce.

Nothing I can say will prevent some people from describing this lecture as an attack on science. I deny the charge, of course: and real Natural Philosophers (there are some now alive) will perceive that in defending value I defend *inter alia* the value of knowledge, which must die like every other when its roots in the *Tao* are cut. But I can go further than that. I even suggest that from Science herself the cure might come. I have described as a "magician's bargain" that process whereby man surrenders object after object, and finally himself, to Nature in return for power. And I meant what I said. The fact that the scientist has succeeded where the magician failed has put such a wide contrast between them in popular thought that the real story of the birth of Science is misunderstood. You will even find people who write about the sixteenth century as if Magic were a medieval survival and Science the new thing that came to sweep it away. Those who have studied the period know better. There was very little magic in the Middle Ages: the sixteenth and seventeenth centuries are the high noon of magic. The serious magical endeavour and the serious scientific endeavour are twins: one was sickly and died, the other strong and throve. But they were twins. They were born of the same impulse. I allow that some (certainly not all) of the early scientists were actuated by a pure love of knowledge. But if we consider the temper of that age as a whole we can discern the impulse of which I speak. There is something which unites magic and applied science while separating both from the "wisdom" of earlier ages. For the wise men of old the cardinal problem had been how to conform the soul to reality, and the solution had been knowledge, self-discipline, and virtue. For magic and applied science alike the problem is how to subdue reality to the wishes of men: the solution is a technique; and both, in the practice of this technique, are ready to do things hitherto regarded as disgusting and impious—such as digging up and mutilating the dead. If we compare the chief trumpeter of the new era (Bacon) with Marlowe's Faustus, the similarity is striking. You will read in some critics that Faustus has a thirst for knowledge. In reality, he hardly mentions it. It is not truth he wants from his devils, but gold and guns and girls. "All things that move between the quiet poles shall be at his command" and "a sound magician is a mighty god."[4] In the same spirit Bacon condemns those who value knowledge as an end in itself: this, for him, is to use as a mistress for pleasure what ought to be a spouse for fruit.[5] The true object is to extend Man's power to the performance of all things possible. He rejects magic because it does not work,[6] but his goal is that of the magician. In Paracelsus the characters of magician and scientist are combined. No doubt those who really founded modern science were usually those whose love of truth exceeded their love of power; in every mixed movement the efficacy comes from the good elements not from the bad. But the presence of the bad elements is not irrelevant to the direction the efficacy takes. It might be going too far to say that the modern scientific movement was tainted from its birth: but I think it would be true to say that it was born in an unhealthy neighbourhood and at an inauspicious hour. Its triumphs may have been too rapid and purchased at too high a price; reconsideration, and something like repentance, may be required.

Is it, then, possible to imagine a new Natural Philosophy, continually conscious that the "natural object" produced by analysis and abstraction is not reality but only a view, and always correcting the abstraction? I hardly know what I am asking for. I heard rumours that Goethe's approach to nature deserves fuller consideration—that even Dr. Steiner may have seen something that orthodox researchers have missed. The regenerate science which I have in mind would not do even to minerals and vegetables what modern science threatens to do to man himself. When it explained it would not explain away. When it spoke of the parts it would remember the whole. While studying the *It* it would not lose what Martin Buber calls the *Thou*-situation. The analogy between the *Tao* of Man and the instincts of an animal species would mean for it new light cast on the unknown thing. Instinct, by the only known reality of conscience and not a reduction of conscience to the category of Instinct. Its followers would not be free with the words *only* and *merely*. In a word, it would conquer Nature without being at the same time conquered by her and buy knowledge at a lower cost than that of life.

Perhaps I am asking impossibilities. Perhaps, in the nature of things, analytical understanding must always be a basilisk which kills what it sees and only sees by killing. But if the scientists themselves cannot arrest this process before it reaches the common Reason and kills that too, then someone else must arrest it. What I most fear is the reply that I am "only one more" obscurantist, that this barrier, like all previous barriers set up against the advance of science, can be safely passed. Such a reply springs from the fatal serialism of the modern imagination—the image of infinite unilinear progression which so haunts our minds. Because we have to use numbers so much we tend to think of every process as if it must be like the numeral series, where every step, to all eternity, is the same kind of step as the one before. I implore you to remember the Irishman and his two stoves. There are progressions in which the last step is *sui generis*—incommensurable with the others—and in which to go the whole way is to undo all the labour of your previous journey. To reduce the *Tao* to a mere natural product is a step of that kind. Up to that point, the kind of explanation which explains things away may give us something, though at a heavy cost.

But you cannot go on "explaining away" forever: you will find that you have explained explanation itself away. You cannot go on "seeing through" things forever. The whole point of seeing through something is to see something through it. It is good that the window should be transparent, because the street or garden beyond it is opaque. How if you saw through the garden too? It is no use trying to "see through" first principles. If you see through everything, then everything is transparent. But a wholly transparent world is an invisible world. To "see through" all things is the same as not to see.

NOTES AND REFERENCES

1. Sir Thomas Elyot, *The Boke Named the Governour* (1531), I. iv: "Al men except physitions only shulde be excluded and kepte out of the norisery." I. vi: "After that a childe is come to seuen yeres of age . . . the most sure counsaile is to withdrawe him from all company of women."
2. John Locke, *Some Thoughts concerning Education* (1693), § 7: "I will also advise his *Feet to be wash'd* every Day in cold Water, and to have his Shoes so thin that they might leak and *let in Water*, whenever he comes near it." § 174: "If he have a poetick vein, 'tis to me the strangest thing in the World that the Father should desire or suffer it to be cherished or improved. Methinks the Parents should labour to have it stifled and suppressed as much as may be." Yet Locke is one of our most sensible writers on education.
3. [*Tao* means 'The Way,' the path of virtuous conduct in Confucianism, the ultimate principle of the universe in Taoism. As close synonyms for his usage of *Tao*, Lewis elsewhere suggests "natural law or traditional morality or the first principles of practical reason."—*Ed.*]
4. Christopher Marlowe, *Dr. Faustus* (1588), 77–90.
5. Francis Bacon, *Advancement of Learning* (1605), Bk. I (p. 60 in Ellis and Spedding, 1905; p. 35 in Everyman Edn.).
6. Francis Bacon, *Filum Labyrinthi* (1653), i.